IN SEARCH OF GOOD ENERGY POLICY

Drawing on political science, economics, philosophy, theology, social anthropology, history, management studies, law, and other subject areas, *In Search of Good Energy Policy* brings together leading academics from across the social sciences and humanities to offer an innovative look at why science and technology, and the type of quantification they champion, cannot alone meet the needs of energy policy making in the future. Featuring world-class researchers from the University of Cambridge and other leading universities around the world, this innovative book presents an interdisciplinary dialogue in which scientists and practitioners reach across institutional divides to offer their perspectives on the relevance of multi-disciplinary research for 'real world' application. This work should be read by anyone interested in understanding how multidisciplinary research and collaboration is essential to crafting good energy policy.

Marc Ozawa is an associated researcher of the Energy Policy Research Group (EPRG) at the University of Cambridge. His current research examines the role of trust in international relations, NATO-Russian relations and Russian, East European and Eurasian affairs.

Jonathan Chaplin is a specialist in political theology and a member of the 'In Search of "Good" Energy' Project. He was Director of the Kirby Laing Institute for Christian Ethics, based in Cambridge, from 2006 to 2017. Currently an independent scholar, he is a member of the Divinity Faculty of Cambridge University, a Senior Fellow of the Canadian think-tank Cardus and a consultant researcher for the London-based religion and society think-tank Theos.

Michael Pollitt is Professor of Business Economics at the Cambridge Judge Business School in the University of Cambridge and a Fellow of Sidney Sussex College, Cambridge. He is chair of the 'In Search of 'Good' Energy Policy' Grand Challenge initiative of Energy@Cambridge and an Assistant Director of the Energy Policy Research Group (EPRG).

David Reiner is Senior Lecturer at the Cambridge Judge Business School and Assistant Director of the Energy Policy Research Group at Cambridge University. His research focuses on energy and climate change politics, policy, economics, regulation and public attitudes, with a particular focus on social license to operate.

Paul Warde is a Reader in Environmental History at the University of Cambridge, previously having been Professor of Environmental History at the University of East Anglia. His previous publications include *The Invention of Sustainability: Nature and destiny, 1500–1870* (2018); *The Environment: A History of the Idea* (2018); and *Power to the People: Energy in Europe Over the Last Five Centuries* (2013).

In Search of Good Energy Policy

Edited by

MARC OZAWA
Cambridge University Energy Policy Research Group

JONATHAN CHAPLIN
Cambridge University Faculty of Divinity

MICHAEL POLLITT
Cambridge University Judge Business School

DAVID REINER
Cambridge University Judge Business School

PAUL WARDE
Cambridge University Faculty of History

CAMBRIDGE
UNIVERSITY PRESS

University Printing House, Cambridge CB2 8BS, United Kingdom

One Liberty Plaza, 20th Floor, New York, NY 10006, USA

477 Williamstown Road, Port Melbourne, VIC 3207, Australia

314–321, 3rd Floor, Plot 3, Splendor Forum, Jasola District Centre, New Delhi – 110025, India

79 Anson Road, #06–04/06, Singapore 079906

Cambridge University Press is part of the University of Cambridge.

It furthers the University's mission by disseminating knowledge in the pursuit of education, learning, and research at the highest international levels of excellence.

www.cambridge.org
Information on this title: www.cambridge.org/9781108481168
DOI: 10.1017/9781108639439

First published 2019

Printed in the United Kingdom by TJ International Ltd. Padstow Cornwall

A catalogue record for this publication is available from the British Library.

ISBN 978-1-108-48116-8 Hardback
ISBN 978-1-108-45546-6 Paperback

Contents

Figures

Tables

Contributors

Atif Ansar, a fellow of the University of Oxford (Keble College) and Programme Director of the MSc in Major Programme Management at Oxford Saïd Business School, is a British-Pakistani academic of an international reputation. His research on $1B+ big capital projects – such as large infrastructure; investments in oil and gas, downstream energy, or extractive industry investment programmes; and construction innovations – is widely cited and frequently featured in the media. Outside his scholarly work, he advises CFOs and finance teams on capital allocation decisions. He has worked with HM Treasury in the UK, the World Bank and Fortune 500 companies, and is an external, partner-level advisor to McKinsey & Company. He has been on the forefront of helping governments and corporates use 'reference class forecasting' to improve cost, time and benefit outcomes of large capital investments and megaprojects. His commercial advice is based on peer-reviewed and rigorous research bringing a fresh perspective to boards, entrepreneurs and top management teams.

Behnam Taebi is Associate Professor in Ethics of Technology at Delft University of Technology, and Associate with the Harvard Kennedy School's Belfer Center for Science and International Affairs. His research interests are in energy ethics, nuclear ethics, responsible research and innovation (RRI) and engineering ethics. He studied material science and engineering (2006) and received his PhD in philosophy of technology (2010). Taebi is currently working on a project on ethics and governance of multinational nuclear waste repositories (with a personal Veni-grant) and a joint RRI project on understanding controversies in energy technologies (both projects awarded by the Netherlands Organisation for Scientific Research). He is the coordinating editor of a volume on *The Ethics of Nuclear Energy* (Cambridge University Press, 2015) and five special issues on 'Socio-Technical Challenges of Nuclear Power Production' (*Journal of Risk Research* –

2015), 'Sustainability and Ethics; Reflections on Sustainable Development Goals' (*Sustainability* – 2018), 'Ethics in Modern Universities of Technology' (*Science and Engineering Ethics* – 2018), 'Risk Governance: New Perspectives' (*Journal of Risk Research* – 2019) and 'Multilateral Governance of Nuclear Risks' (*Risk, Hazard, Crisis and Public Policy* – 2018). Taebi is currently writing a monograph on ethics and engineering (under contract with Cambridge University Press). He is a member of the Young Academy of the Royal Netherlands Academy of Arts and Sciences.

Jonathan Chaplin is a specialist in political theology and a member of the 'In Search of "Good" Energy' Project. He received his PhD in political theory from London School of Economics and Political Science and has taught at institutions in the UK, Canada and the Netherlands. He was Director of the Kirby Laing Institute for Christian Ethics, based in Cambridge, from 2006 to 2017. Currently an independent scholar, he is a member of the Divinity Faculty of Cambridge University, a senior fellow of the Canadian think tank Cardus and a consultant researcher for the London-based religion and society think tank Theos. He is author of *Herman Dooyeweerd: Christian Philosopher of State and Civil Society* (2011) and editor or co-editor of seven volumes, including *God and the EU: Faith in the European Project* (2016); *Living Lightly, Living Faithfully: Religious Faiths and the Future of Sustainability* (2013) and *God and Global Order: The Power of Religion in American Foreign Policy* (2010). He has written two reports for Theos and is author of many articles and essays in political theology, including 'The Global Greening of Religion' (2016) and a forthcoming book chapter, 'Responding to Earth's Lament: Public Justice and the Ecological Crisis – Framing a Research Agenda'.

Chi Kong Chyong is Director of the Energy Policy Forum and Research Associate of the Energy Policy Research Group at the Cambridge Judge Business School, University of Cambridge. Kong holds a PhD in energy economics and policy from Cambridge Judge Business School and an MPhil in technology policy from Cambridge. Before coming to Cambridge, he worked as a researcher at the National Academy of Sciences in Ukraine. Since completing his PhD, Kong has been a research associate at EPRG working mostly on natural gas market modelling and Eurasian gas trade relations as well as on energy infrastructure investment.

Seth Collins is Co-Founder of Metronome Energy Ltd. Prior to Metronome, Seth worked as an associate at the Climate Investment Funds at the World Bank Group focused on the Scaling Up Renewable Energy Program (SREP) fund. Seth has also worked in several policy roles in Washington D.C. relating to environmental and energy issues. He was a Pershing Square Scholar at the University of Oxford, completing both an MBA and MSc in environmental change and management.

John Deutch, Emeritus Institute Professor at the Massachusetts Institute of Technology, served as Director of Energy Research and Undersecretary of the US Department of Energy in the Carter Administration. He was a member and Chair of the Secretary of Energy Advisory Board during the Obama Administration.

Søren Djørup is an assistant professor in energy planning at Aalborg University. He has a background in economics and political economy and a PhD in energy planning. He has done research into the markets, regulation and policies in the energy sector and its coherence with the aim of transitioning to a renewable energy system. He applies an interdisciplinary approach where economics and social science are combined with a technical understanding of energy systems.

Leslie-Anne Duvic-Paoli is a lecturer at The Dickson Poon School of Law, King's College London. She teaches and researches in different areas of public international law, with a focus on international environmental law and climate and energy law. Before joining King's College London in August 2017, she was a Philomathia Post-doctoral Research Associate in the Department of Land Economy at the University of Cambridge. Leslie-Anne is the author of *The Prevention Principle in International Environmental Law* (Cambridge University Press, 2018). She is a fellow of the Cambridge Centre for Environment, Energy and Natural Resource Governance and the Project Leader of the Platform on International Energy Governance, a network of excellence that fosters the conduct of research in unexplored areas of international energy law. Leslie-Anne holds master's degrees from Sciences Po Paris and the University of Panthéon-Sorbonne, as well as a PhD from the Graduate Institute in Geneva.

Christian Growitsch has served as Deputy Director at the Fraunhofer Institute for Microstructure of Materials and Systems IMWS since January 2018, where he has also been Director of the Center for Economics of Materials (CEM) since July 2017. He taught economics at the Martin-Luther-University Halle-Wittenberg and University of Hamburg, and from September 2014 to September 2015 he was Managing Director of the Hamburg Institute for International Economics. Earlier, he served as Director of Applied Research and Member of the Management Board of the Institute of Energy Economics at the University of Cologne, where he taught as Associate Professor (*Privatdozent*) of Economics. Christian studied business administration, economics and social sciences in Hamburg and Lüneburg and pursued post-graduate studies in economics at the Universities of Lüneburg and Cambridge, where he was a visiting scholar in 2004. In May 2010 he qualified as a professor at the University of Halle-Wittenberg. From 2007 to 2010 he headed the Department of Energy Markets and Energy Regulation at the Scientific Institute for Infrastructure and Communication

Services (WIK). The focus of his economic research and politico-economic consultation presently lies is in the field of applied microeconomics.

Yang Han received his MSc degree in computer science with distinction from the University of Hong Kong (HKU) in 2014. He obtained his bachelor's degree from the Department of Information Systems, Beihang University, Beijing, China, in 2013. He is a PhD student in the Department of Electrical & Electronic Engineering at the University of Hong Kong. His recent work focusses on the spatio-temporal data analysis and its applications in environmental pollution and policy studies in China. He has published in environmental science and policy.

Felix Höffler has published widely in the field of industrial organisation and energy economics. He was Director of the Institute for Energy Economics (EWI) and the Institute for Economic Policy (iwp), both at the University of Cologne. His research interests included regulatory economics, industrial economics, competition policy, energy economics, and law and economics.

Caroline Humphrey is a social anthropologist who has worked in the USSR/Russia, Mongolia, Inner Mongolia, Nepal and India. Her research interests include socialist and post-socialist society, moral economy, the relation between history and anthropology, and the aesthetics of daily life. Until 2010 she was Sigrid Rausing Professor of Anthropology at the University of Cambridge and she is currently a research director at the university's Mongolia and Inner Asia Studies Unit. Her major publications include: *Karl Marx Collective: Economy, Society and Religion in a Siberian Collective Farm* (Cambridge University Press, 1983); *The Archetypal Actions of Ritual*, illustrated by the Jain rite of worship with James Laidlaw (1994); *Shamans and Elders: Experience, Knowledge and Power among the Daur Mongols with Urgunge Onon* (1996); *The Unmaking of Soviet Life: Everyday Economies After Socialism* (2002); *A Monastery in Time: the Making of Mongolian Buddhism*, with H. Ujeed (2013); *Frontier Encounters: Knowledge and Practice at the Russian, Chinese and Mongolian Border*, ed. with Franck Billé and Gregory Delaplace (2012); and *Trust and Mistrust in the Economies of the China-Russia Borderlands* (2018).

Frede Hvelplund is a professor in energy planning at Aalborg University, and has a background in economics and social anthropology. He has a Dr. Tech. degree in social engineering and has written many books and articles on the interrelationship between social science, politics and technological change.

Charlotte Johnson is an anthropologist who studies urban energy transitions. She uses anthropological theory and methods to examine the interaction between social and technical systems, focusing particularly on decentralised energy infrastructure and smart systems in the home. Charlotte works at University College London's Energy Institute collaborating on interdisciplinary research projects that investigate energy demand. Her work often takes a participatory approach, and she held a public engagement fellowship to run a community energy project in London. She has been interviewed by national print and broadcast media about public participation in urban energy transitions. She has also participated in government and NGO knowledge transfer programmes, providing expertise on resident involvement with District Heating in the UK. Her research has been published in anthropological and interdisciplinary journals.

Tae Hoon Kim is a postdoctoral researcher at the Division of the History of Science, Technology and Environment at the Royal Institute of Technology (KTH) in Stockholm, Sweden. He received his PhD at the Faculty of History at the University of Cambridge. His doctoral project, which was funded in part by the Committee of the History of Electricity at EDF, examined the politics behind the decision-making process on British fuel and power generation policy from 1957 to 1989. His current research analyses the nuclear energy policies of France and the UK, with a special emphasis on the economic, environmental and social viability of nuclear energy in the green energy transition policies of both countries. Tae Hoon has previously worked as a military intelligence officer in the Republic of Korea Army, where he worked on energy and military technology issues and has also worked as a research assistant at the International Institute for Integration Studies(IIIS) at Trinity College Dublin.

Vladimir Kmec is a research associate at the Von Hügel Institute and the European Centre, and an associate member of St Edmund's College at the University of Cambridge.

Jacqueline C. K. Lam is the Associate Professor in the Department of Electrical and Electronic Engineering at the University of Hong Kong and Co-Director of the HKU-Cambridge Clean Energy and Environment Research Platform. She was the Hughes Hall Visiting Fellow and the Visiting Senior Research Fellow and Associate Researcher in Energy Policy Research Group at Judge Business School, the University of Cambridge. Her research studies clean energy and the environment using interdisciplinary approaches with a special focus on China and the UK. Her recent research focuses on the use of big data and machine learning techniques to study personalised air pollution monitoring and health management. Her work is published in *IEEE, Applied Energy, Environmental Science and Policy*, and *Energy Policy*. In her capacity as PI or co-PI, Jacqueline received three research grants from the Research Grants Council, HKSAR Government from 2011 to 2017, totalling GBP 5.5 M. Her recent research study on PM2.5 pollution and environmental inequality in Hong Kong, undertaken in joint collaboration with Yang Han and Victor OK Li, has been published in *Environmental Science and Policy* and widely covered by more than thirty local and overseas newspapers and television stations.

Tim Lewens is Professor of Philosophy of Science at the University of Cambridge, where he is also a fellow of Clare College. His recent books include *The Meaning of Science, Biological Foundations of Bioethics* and *Cultural Evolution: Conceptual Challenges*, all published in 2015. From 2009 to 2015 he was a member of the Nuffield Council on Bioethics.

Victor O.K. Li received SB, SM, EE and ScD degrees in electrical engineering and computer science from MIT. Victor is Chair of Information Engineering, Cheng Yu-Tung Professor in Sustainable Development, and Head of the Department of Electrical & Electronic Engineering at the University of Hong Kong. He is the Director of the HKU-Cambridge Clean Energy and Environment Research Platform, an interdisciplinary collaboration with Cambridge. He was the Associate Dean (Research) of Engineering and Managing Director of Versitech Ltd. He serves on the board of Sunevision Holdings Ltd., listed on the Hong Kong Stock Exchange and co-founded Fano Labs Ltd., an artificial intelligence (AI) company with his PhD student. Previously, he was Professor of Electrical Engineering at the University of Southern California (USC) in Los Angeles and Director of the USC Communication Sciences Institute. His research interests include big data, AI, optimisation techniques and interdisciplinary clean energy and environment studies. In January 2018 he was awarded a USD 6.3 M RGC Theme-based Research Project to develop deep learning techniques for personalised and smart air pollution monitoring and health management in HK. Sought by government, industry and academic organisations, he has extensively lectured and consulted internationally. He has received numerous awards, including the PRC Ministry of Education Changjiang Chair Professorship at Tsinghua University, the UK Royal Academy of Engineering Senior Visiting Fellowship in Communications, the Croucher Foundation Senior Research Fellowship, and the Order of the Bronze Bauhinia Star, Government of the HKSAR. He is a fellow of the Hong Kong Academy of Engineering Sciences, the IEEE, the IAE and the HKIE.

Kun-Chin Lin is a university lecturer in politics and Director of the Centre for Rising Powers at the University of Cambridge. He graduated magna cum laude from Harvard College and obtained his PhD in political science from the University of California at Berkeley. Kun-Chin was a Leverhulme Postdoctoral Fellow at the University of Oxford and taught at King's College London and the National University of Singapore. His research focuses on the politics of market reform in developing countries. His current projects include federalism and regulatory issues in transport infrastructure and electricity grid expansion in China, industrial policy and privatisation of Chinese state-owned enterprises, and the economic and security nexus in maritime governance in Asia and the Arctic. He is a member of Energy@Cambridge; Cambridge Centre for the Environment, Energy and Natural Resource Governance; and Centre for Science & Policy of the University of Cambridge, and is a collaborating partner of the Global Biopolitics Research Group based at King's College London. Kun-Chin is an editorial board member of *Business & Politics* and an advisory board member of Routledge Research on the Politics and Sociology of China Series and Palgrave Macmillan Studies in the Political Economy of Public Policy Series. He is an associate fellow of the Asia Programme of the Chatham House.

Magnus Lindmark is Professor in Economic History at Umeå University, Sweden. He has studied various aspects of long-term relationships between economic development and environmental impact and energy use and has published articles in economic history, business history and environmental economics.

Dan Madrigal is the Head of Acquisitions, Europe – Data Center Strategy for Facebook. Prior to Facebook, he held senior-level development and acquisition positions at Equinix and Devonshire Investors in London, the private equity arm of Fidelity Investments and was also the Chief Real Estate Officer for Amgen and for Clorox. Dan is an alumnus of the University of Chicago's Booth School of Business and Oxford University's Said Business School.

Dr Tibisay Morgandi is Lecturer in International Energy and Natural Resources Law at Queen Mary University of London. She is a public international lawyer focusing on international energy law, international environmental law and international economic law. Before joining Queen Mary, Dr Morgandi held a Swiss National Science Foundation Postdoctoral Fellowship at the Centre for Environment, Energy and Natural Resource Governance (C-EENRG) at the University of Cambridge, during which time she published a database on state bilateral energy agreements www.energybilaterals.org.

David Newbery, CBE, FBA, is the Director of the Cambridge Energy Policy Research Group and Emeritus Professor of Applied Economics at the University of Cambridge. He is a fellow of the British Academy and of the Econometric Society. He was President of the European Economic Association in 1996 and President of the International Association for Energy Economics in 2013. Educated at Cambridge with degrees in mathematics and economics, he has managed research projects on utility privatisation and regulation, road pricing, transition from state socialism to the market economy in central Europe, electricity restructuring and market design, and transmission access pricing and has active research on market integration, transmission planning and finance, climate change policies, and the design of energy policy and energy taxation. He has been an occasional economic advisor to Ofgem, Ofwat and ORR and has served as Member of the Competition Commission, Chairman of the Dutch Electricity Market Surveillance Committee and Member of the Panel of Technical Experts offering quality assurance to DECC on the delivery of the UK's Electricity Market Reform. He is currently an independent member of the Single Electricity Market

Committee of the island of Ireland and a panel member of Ofgem's Network Innovation Competition. His books include *Privatization, Restructuring and Regulation of Network Utilities* (2000) and with Joe Stiglitz, *The Theory of Commodity Price Stabilization: A Study in the Economics of Risk* (1981).

Michael Northcott is Professor Emeritus of Ethics at the University of Edinburgh and has been Visiting Professor at Claremont School of Theology, Duke University, Flinders University, Heidelberg University, the Indonesian Consortium of Religious Studies and the University of Malaya. His principal research has been on the religious roots, and ethical implications, of environmental concern and climate change. He has conducted fieldwork in, and published many papers on, the relationship between religion and environmental concern in the UK, the United States and Southeast Asia. His PhD was published as *The Church and Secularisation: Urban Industrial Mission in Northeast England* (1991), and his first major research monograph was *The Environment and Christian Ethics* (Cambridge University Press, 1996). Other monographs include *Life After Debt: Christianity and Global Justice* (1999); *An Angel Directs the Storm: Apocalyptic Religion and American Empire* (2005); *A Moral Climate: The Ethics of Global Warming* (2007); *A Political Theology of Climate Change* (2013) and *Place, Ecology and the Sacred* (2015). His co-edited books include *Diversity and Dominion: Dialogues in Ecology, Ethics, and Theology* (2009), *Theology After Darwin* (2009) and *Systematic Theology and Climate Change* (2016).

Lord Ronald Oxburgh taught geology and geophysics at Oxford, Cambridge, Stanford and Caltech. He was Head of the Department of Earth Sciences in Cambridge and served for seven years as President of Queens' College. He served as Chief Scientific Adviser to the UK Ministry of Defence (1987–1993) and chaired the inquiry into the safety of UK nuclear weapons. He subsequently became Rector of Imperial College. Ron advises the Government of Singapore in matters of environment, water and higher education. He is Chairman of Green Energy Options and 2OC, is the former Honorary President of the Carbon Capture and Storage Association and former Chairman of Shell Transport and Trading. He is a fellow of the Royal Society and of the Royal Academy of Engineering, and a foreign member of the US Academy of Sciences. He has served as President of the European Union of Geosciences, and of the British Association for the Advancement of Science. He has chaired the Trustees of the Natural History Museum. Ron was created a life Peer in 1999 and for four years chaired the Science and Technology Committee of the House of Lords.

Marc Ozawa is an associated researcher of the Energy Policy Research Group at the Judge Business School, University of Cambridge. He began his career analysing the first joint oil and gas ventures in Russia and Central Asia following the collapse of the Soviet Union. More recently, he worked as a research associate for Energy@Cambridge and was the Associate Director of the Energy Policy Forum, University of Cambridge. He held previous research and editorial positions at IHS CERA, Harvard Business School and the *Yale Journal of International Affairs*. His current research examines the role of trust in international relations, NATO-Russian relations and Russian, East European and Eurasian affairs. Marc has an interdisciplinary background that includes politics, economics and area studies. He is a graduate of the University of Alaska (BA), Yale University (MA) and the University of Cambridge (MSt, PhD).

Michael James Platts is Senior Teaching Associate at the Institute for Manufacturing, University of Cambridge. Jim spent twenty-three years in industry. With a civil/structural engineering background, he was a partner in the consulting engineering practice Gifford and Partners and Managing Director of Composite Technology Ltd in the 1980s, where he created the designs, the manufacturing processes, the team and the company that manufactured all the large wind turbine blades in the UK, now the global blade technology centre for the wind turbine company Vestas. For the last twenty-nine years he has been based in the Institute for Manufacturing in the University of Cambridge, where he was Course Director for the Manufacturing Engineering Tripos and Leading Examiner and Tutor for the Manufacturing Leaders' Programme and supervised well over 300 technical development projects in companies. He was also a director of studies for the executive-level Cambridge Interdisciplinary Design for the Built Environment (IDBE) Course, a tutor and examiner for the Engineering for Sustainable Development (ESD) Course and an associate researcher of the Energy Policy Research Group (EPRG). He initiated and led Summer Academies for European Students of Industrial Engineering and Management (ESTIEM) on 'Deep Entrepreneurship' and initiated and headed the European Professors of Industrial Engineering and Management (EPIEM) network. He is involved in leadership training, innovative manufacturing and development projects across many industries worldwide. He has been involved with technology transfer to, and design and manufacturing development of, wind energy technology in China. He served on the Malaysian Palm Oil Board Programme Advisory Committee and coordinated the development of its forward strategy recommendations in 2010, and served on FELDA's R&D Advisory Panel. He brings valuable experience in design and manufacturing, particularly skill-based manufacturing, to projects. His academic interests include ethical leadership, development of skill and competence in design and manufacturing and optimisation of manufacturing processes. He is a Quaker and holds an MA from the University of Cambridge, is a Chartered Engineer and a member of the Institution of Civil Engineers, a member of the Institute of Materials, Minerals and Mining and a fellow of the Royal Society of Arts, Manufacture and Commerce. He is a member of the Cambridgeshire Ecumenical Council.

Michael Pollitt is Professor of Business Economics at the Cambridge Judge Business School in the University of Cambridge and a fellow of Sidney Sussex College, Cambridge. He is Chair of the 'In Search of "Good" Energy Policy' Grand Challenge initiative of Energy@Cambridge and an assistant director of the Energy Policy Research Group (EPRG). His energy research focuses on future electricity market design and regulation for high shares of renewables. Michael has advised Ofgem, BEIS/DECC, the European Commission and the World Bank, among others, on energy policy. He is the author of more than eighty articles and ten books on energy policy and business ethics. He holds an MA in economics from the University of Cambridge and an M.Phil. and D.Phil. in economics from the University of Oxford.

Tim Reilly is a PhD candidate at the Scott Polar Research Institute, University of Cambridge, and a graduate research fellow at the Centre for Rising Powers in the international affairs department at Cambridge. He is the Founder of Arctic Advisory Group, an Arctic risk management and research consultancy. Previous appointments include Government Affairs Adviser to Shell Gas & Power in the Caspian region, as well as work in the Caucasus, Central Asia, Russia and Ukraine for companies such as Chevron and JKX Oil & Gas. His first experience of the (Norwegian) Arctic was as a young paratrooper officer in the 1980s, trained in Arctic warfare. Tim is a Russian speaker and was educated at Cambridge, Durham and the Moscow State Institute of International Relations. He worked in the CIS in commercial security/intelligence in the 1990s (Kroll/DSL). He is also a senior associate fellow at the Institute for Statecraft in London, where he is their resident Arctic expert. Tim was called as an expert witness to both the House of Commons Environmental Audit Committee on the Arctic, and more recently, the House of Lords Select Committee on the Arctic. In addition, he was invited to author a UK Arctic defence paper for the House of Commons Defence Committee.

David Reiner is University Senior Lecturer at the Cambridge Judge Business School. He is a political scientist and is an assistant director of the Energy Policy Research Group at Cambridge University. His research focuses on energy and climate change politics, policy, economics, regulation and public attitudes, with a particular focus on social license to operate. Specific topics include retail markets, smart meters, subsidy reform, low-carbon technologies, industrial decarbonisation and dynamics of demonstration. Methods include large- and small-scale public and stakeholder surveys, public communications and engagement exercises; and economic, policy and historical analysis.

Sabine Roeser is Professor of Ethics (Distinguished Antoni van Leeuwenhoek Chair) and Head of the Ethics and Philosophy of Technology Section at TU

Delft, Netherlands. Her research covers theoretical, foundational topics concerning the nature of moral knowledge, intuitions, emotions and evaluative aspects of risk, but also urgent and hotly debated public issues on which her theoretical research can shed new light, such as nuclear energy, climate change and public health issues. Roeser argues that moral emotions and intuitions can highlight important ethical issues concerning risky technologies and provide insights for responsible innovation. She has led various research projects on these topics for which she received highly competitive grants from the Netherlands Organization for Scientific Research (NWO), as well as an H2020-FET Open project, BrainHack, on BNCI-related art and its ethical implications. She has given more than 230 presentations at conferences and seminars, and more than 100 interviews for popular media. Sabine served on various Dutch governmental advisory boards concerning risky technologies and their responsible innovation, such as those concerning genetic modification and nuclear waste. She has published ten books, five special issues, numerous peer-reviewed articles and book chapters with leading international publishers and journals, as well as numerous articles in other outlets. In 2018 she published her second monograph, entitled *Risk, Technology, and Moral Emotions*.

Emily Shuckburgh is a climate scientist and mathematician based at the British Antarctic Survey (BAS). She leads the national research programme on the Southern Ocean and its role in climate (ORCHESTRA), serves as Deputy Head of the Polar Oceans Team and leads the Data Science Group at BAS. She holds a number of positions at the University of Cambridge (Fellow of Darwin College, Fellow of the Cambridge Institute for Sustainability Leadership and Associate Fellow of the Centre for Science and Policy). In the past she has worked at Ecole Normal Superieure in Paris and at MIT. She is a fellow of the Royal Meteorological Society and Co-Chair of their Climate Science Communications Group. She has also acted as an advisor to the UK government on behalf of the Natural Environment Research Council. In 2016 she was awarded an OBE for services to science and the public communication of science. She is co-author, with HRH The Prince of Wales and Tony Juniper, of *Climate Change* (2017).

Sandy Skelton is an environmental economist with a particular interest in the motivations and trade-offs associated with greater material efficiency and demand reduction. She holds the Charles and Katherine Darwin Research Fellowship at Darwin College and was awarded a wholeSEM bilateral fellowship to collaborate with the GEM-E3 macroeconomic model. Sandy's PhD focused on the incentives for greater material efficiency in the use of steel. The work was funded by the WellMet2050 project under the supervision of Prof Julian Allwood, University of Cambridge. Sandy has an undergraduate degree in economics from the University of Cambridge and an MSc in metals and energy finance from the

Imperial College Business School. Between degrees, Sandy worked for the policy research consultancy Brook Lyndhurst, advising the public sector on pro-environmental behaviour change policy. During the three years she spent there, she worked on a variety of environmental issues, first as a researcher and later as a project manager.

Karl Sperling is an associate professor in energy planning at Aalborg University. He has a background in environmental management and a PhD in integrated energy planning. He has undertaken research on strategic energy planning at the city and municipality level, as well as on the past, present and future of community energy and grassroots innovations in the energy sector. He addresses these fields with an interdisciplinary approach, taking as a point of departure his technical understanding of energy systems and a focus on public regulation and economic and social analyses.

Jorge E. Viñuales is the Harold Samuel Professor of Law and Environmental Policy at the University of Cambridge, where he founded the Cambridge Centre for Environment, Energy and Natural Resource Governance (C-EENRG). He is also the Chairperson of the Compliance Committee of the UNECE/WHO-Europe Protocol on Water and Health. He has published extensively in international law, environmental law and sustainability transitions, and has wide experience as a practitioner in these areas.

Shanshan Wang received comprehensive multidisciplinary training during her study. She received her master of philosophy in environmental policy from the University of Cambridge in 2017 after completing her bachelor degree in civil engineering and business (first honour) at the Hong Kong University of Science and Technology. She is currently a practicing civil engineer in Hong Kong.

Paul Warde is a reader in environmental history at the University of Cambridge. He was Professor of Environmental History at the University of East Anglia. His publications include *The Invention of Sustainability: Nature and Destiny, c. 1500–1870* (Cambridge University Press, 2018); with Libby Robin and Sverker Sörlin, *The Environment: A History of the Idea* (2018); and with Astrid Kander and Paolo Malanima, *Power to the People: Energy in Europe over the Last Five Centuries* (2013).

Corine Wood-Donnelly is an interdisciplinary researcher in international relations and political geography, with research interests in issues and models of maritime governance, comparative policy, performances of sovereignty and materiality. Currently based at the Institute of Russian and Eurasian Studies at Uppsala University, she is affiliated with the Scott Polar Research Institute and the Centre for Rising Powers at the University of Cambridge and is a Bye-Fellow in Geography at Downing College. She specialises in studies of the Arctic, making connections between territorial and sovereignty issues, conducting empirical research on maritime search and rescue, materiality of energy/resource development and theoretical research on evolutions in normative frameworks including vertical sovereignty, justice and environmental stewardship. Recent work includes publications comparing different periods of energy development in the Arctic, effective occupation in policy practices and the performances of sovereignty over territory by Arctic states.

Acknowledgments

The editors owe many debts of gratitude for the writing of this volume.

This book is an output of the Energy@Cambridge Interdisciplinary Research Centre, which adopted In Search of 'Good' Energy Policy as a grand challenge activity in 2015. Energy@Cambridge brings together over 250 academics from thirty faculties across the university with interests in energy. We particularly wish to thank the team there: Isabelle de Wouters, Shafiq Ahmed and Raheela Rehman, who have given us continuing assistance in securing financial support and have offered practical help and encouragement. We thank the University of Cambridge for its HEIF contribution and support for our activities via the ESRC and EPSRC Impact Acceleration Accounts.

The book arose directly from our regular In Search of 'Good' Energy Policy seminar series hosted at CRASSH, the Centre for Research in the Arts, Social Sciences and Humanities, which began in autumn 2015. CRASSH has provided us with the perfect interdisciplinary venue for our regular meetings and many of the chapters in the book were first presented during the 2015–16 seminar series. Our particular thanks there go to Professor Tim Lewens, Deputy Director of CRASSH, and an early supporter of this project.

We have received much encouragement from our outside stakeholders. We would particularly wish to thank officials at the then Department of Energy and Climate Change (DECC), the GB energy regulator Ofgem and the British Embassy in Beijing for, respectively, generously contributing ideas for our research, jointly sponsoring some of our CRASSH seminars and supporting our work in China.

We have received much practical help and financial support from the research centres at Cambridge to which we belong. David Reiner and Michael Pollitt would like to thank the Energy Policy Research Group (EPRG) for its support. We would also like to thank Professor Jorge Viñuales at EPRG's sister research group C-EENRG (Cambridge Centre for Environment, Energy and Natural Resource Governance).

Jorge Viñuales also gave us essential encouragement and support in putting forward this volume to Cambridge University Press. We very are grateful to all of those who have assisted us in the Press's publication process and have turned our various writings and discussions into this completed volume.

We would like to acknowledge the continuing inspiration of the late Professor Sir David MacKay, inaugural Regius Professor of Engineering, former Chief Scientist at the Department of Energy and Climate Change and early enthusiast for this project – who combined being an academic of the highest order with deep concern for real-world energy policy. We would like to think David would have been pleased to see the contents of this book arising from the work of his colleagues at Cambridge.

We would also like to express our gratitude to one of the authors, Professor Felix Höffler, who tragically passed away before the publication of this book. We are honoured to have been able to include his chapter and wish to express our condolences to his family and colleagues.

Finally, we wish to express our thanks to the many contributors to this book who generously responded to our request and gave their time and expertise to bring this project to fruition.

Marc Ozawa
Jonathan Chaplin
Michael Pollitt
David Reiner
Paul Warde

1

Introduction

Marc Ozawa, Jonathan Chaplin, Michael Pollitt, David Reiner, and Paul Warde

I recently read two books, one by a physicist, and one by an economist . . . How could these two smart people come to such different conclusions?[1]

OVERVIEW

A common complaint from policymakers and scientists is voiced when a policy is implemented but yields unexpected results. The argument asserts that the technology is sound and the policy is rational. Yet the policy is often met with unexpected public reactions based on 'irrational' responses. When energy policy is confronted with real-world social and institutional forces, the importance of multidisciplinary analysis becomes all the more important. As the late David MacKay put it in his quest to understand why substantive and effective energy policy is so elusive, 'We are inundated with a flood of crazy innumerate codswallop.'[2]

The approach of scientists and technologists to energy policy tends to be characterised by the promotion of preferred technologies with desirable theoretical properties, and an oft-stated exasperation at the speed at which political systems put in place policies to adopt such technologies. Thus scientists and technologists frequently promote particular combinations of nuclear power, renewables, carbon capture and storage and smart demand-side management to solve future energy problems. They justify their positions with reference to quantitative models of energy and climate systems. 'Good' energy policy is, for them, about getting the technology right. Considering the promise of reduced carbon emissions, economic growth and greater efficiency of industries, there is good reason for technology to play a role at the start of the policymaking process. But the start of that process is actually about society and what society wants. There are several excellent books, including those by authors from some of our technology and science colleagues at the University of Cambridge, such

[1] David J. C. MacKay, *Sustainable Energy – Without the Hot Air*, 1st edition (Cambridge: UIT Cambridge Ltd., 2008), 2.
[2] MacKay.

as David MacKay's *Sustainable Energy – Without the Hot Air* and Allwood and Cullen's *Sustainable Materials Without the Hot Air*, that exemplify a technology-focused approach.[3] Among academics, it appears that there is a hierarchy of disciplines as to how climate change is framed. As O'Neill et al. point out, 'an epistemological hierarchy exists in the framing of climate change whereby the geosciences disproportionately influence the representation of climate change as primarily an environmental issue'.[4] Government agencies also often follow this pattern. When doing a search for publications from their website, the first page of publications from the UK's Department for Business, Energy and Industrial Strategy (BEIS) provides a glimpse of what factors the department emphasises with 'energy' as the selected category. In the most recent list of publications ranging from 25 January to 12 February 2018, out of forty-one publications based on titles and abstracts, only three indirectly reference non-economic social constraints.[5] A cursory search of publications from the independent UK Committee on Climate Change and the Directorate General for Energy of the European Commission illustrates a similar-patterned focus on technology. Policy questions of implementation are often relegated to solely market mechanisms.[6] Even the work of the Intergovernmental Panel on Climate Change (IPCC) 'has been characterized as "unidisciplinary", as it is based on a clear separation between the natural sciences and social sciences, and an understanding that social sciences are based on natural sciences'.[7] These examples share an implicit assumption about policy goals, and thus limit the strength of their supporting arguments. Specifically, the limitation is that the policy goal is defined as 'reasonable' or 'rational' according to technical parameters, and any barrier to implementation is seen as a type of 'politics' that is by definition less 'reasonable' or 'rational'.

This pattern is, of course, part of a wider problem of considering social sciences and humanities under the umbrella of scientific advice. Although in the UK, science advice nominally includes the social sciences, the House of Commons Science and Technology Committee, which oversees government policy, expressed concern that the then-Chief Scientific Adviser's 'advocacy of social science has been lower profile than his contributions in areas of natural and physical science'.[8]

3 Julian M. Allwood and Jonathan M. Cullen, *Sustainable Materials Without the Hot Air: Making Buildings, Vehicles and Products Efficiently and with Less New Material*, 2nd edition (Cambridge: UIT Cambridge Ltd., 2015); MacKay, Sustainable Energy – Without the Hot Air.

4 Saffron J. O'Neill et al., 'Disciplines, Geography, and Gender in the Framing of Climate Change', Bulletin of the American Meteorological Society 91, no. 8 (16 March 2010): 997–1002.

5 'Publications – GOV.UK', accessed 13 February 2018, https://www.gov.uk/government/publications.

6 'Publications', *Committee on Climate Change* (blog), accessed 13 February 2018, www.theccc.org.uk/publications/.

7 Eleftheria Vasileiadou, Gaston Heimeriks, and Arthur C. Petersen, 'Exploring the Impact of the IPCC Assessment Reports on Science', *Environmental Science & Policy* 14, no. 8 (1 December 2011): 1052–61, https://doi.org/10.1016/j.envsci.2011.07.002.

8 'Scientific Advice, Risk and Evidence Based Policy Making', House of Commons Science and Technology Committee, Seventh Report of Session 2005–06 (London: House of Commons, 26 October 2006), 15, https://publications.parliament.uk/pa/cm200506/cmselect/cmsctech/900/900-i.pdf.

As Cooper notes, 'Science advice is normally seen in the context of physical science advice.'[9] The House of Lords Science and Technology Committee even issued several reports calling for a Chief Social Scientist, but such a position was never adopted.[10]

Our book, on the other hand, is written as an antidote to a technocentric view of energy policy. As demonstrated by the cases comprising this book, we argue for a genuinely multidisciplinary approach – drawing on political science, economics, philosophy, theology, social anthropology, history, management studies and law inter alia – which takes social sciences and humanities thinking seriously in energy policy, thereby leading to a much richer set of insights into what makes for 'good' energy policy. Science and technology, and the type of quantification they champion, remain important, but they need to be combined with other disciplinary approaches. This is because many people are, quite rightly, not fully convinced by scientific arguments in the way that scientists assume they can be or should be. In fact, multidisciplinary approaches are better prepared to handle the complexity of the social policy environment in which policies are implemented. Purely technical approaches cannot account for the multilayered nature of social forces. Moreover, science is highly disputed, but scientists often oversimplify when it comes to policy. And this can undermine their own credibility by visibly dumbing down their arguments for a general audience. Instead, many of our authors would start from the premise that 'good' energy policy is much more multilayered, nuanced and non-obvious than it might appear, especially when we focus in on specific energy policy problems.

As is illustrated in the following chapters, what is clear is that policymaking is a complex and multidimensional process. The process of policymaking has been extensively studied by a large number of disciplines. It involves many different actors who often maintain irreconcilable goals and perspectives, and therefore a governance approach that listens to these groups and makes allowances for them becomes all the more important. Hence energy policy is not exclusively, or indeed, primarily, about energy, it is as much about policy itself.

As starting points for developing a multidisciplinary approach to 'good' energy policy, we draw on the cumulative lessons learned from a three-year-long seminar series titled 'In Search of "Good" Energy Policy', hosted at the Centre for Research in the Arts, Social Sciences and Humanities (CRASSH) at the University of Cambridge. The 2015–2016 series, where many of the following chapters were first presented, brought together some twenty academics from a dozen departments in the University of Cambridge, as well as academics and practitioners from around the

9 Adam CG Cooper, 'Exploring the Scope of Science Advice: Social Sciences in the UK Government', Palgrave Communications 2 (5 July 2016): 16044.

10 'The Role and Functions of Departmental Chief Scientific Advisers – Science and Technology Committee', Science and Technology Committee (House of Lords, 14 February 2012), https://publications.parliament.uk/pa/ld201012/ldselect/ldsctech/264/26402.htm.

world, to approach energy policy from a multidisciplinary perspective. What became clear, early on, from our discussions is that the quest for 'good' energy policy requires a deep understanding of local, regional and national preconditions, of history and of social, political and cultural institutions, indeed the very understanding exhibited in the chapters of this book.

A number of lessons stood out. First, if it is to be at all manageable even in a multidisciplinary project, the term 'good' needs to be defined in the context of policy. Second, starting points matter, and legacy investments by companies and consumers cannot be lightly written off in favour of new technologies. Starting points immediately suggest the importance of timing and place, in other words context, for what makes for 'good' policy. Third, 'bad' policies can and do persist for decades after both their problems and their solutions have been identified. Fourth, predictions about the future have a poor track record, but asserting claims about the future lie at the centre of a technology-based approach. And finally, 'good' policy processes involve consultation and the taking into account of various interests and views; this necessarily gives rise to the modification of original plans. These starting points are common to many disciplines, and they offer an antidote to the assumption that there are technologically 'obvious' answers in energy policy.

This is not to say that there are no clear answers in the study of energy policy or that there is no basis for ranking alternatives according to defined sets of criteria. Neither the editors, nor any of the contributing authors of this book, set out to argue that. For example, some policies will very clearly raise the level of energy security by diversifying energy supply sources. Others will clearly contribute to social welfare by targeting support to vulnerable segments of society, the recent discussion about energy poverty in the UK being a case in point.[11] Other examples in the cases comprising the bulk of this book will focus more on the environment. The UK's momentous Clean Air Act or Germany's Energy Transformation (*Energiewende*) are cases in point. In these examples, society sets a goal and the policy may be evaluated by how clearly and effectively it contributes to meeting the goal.

1.1 WHY DO WE NEED A MULTIDISCIPLINARY SOCIAL SCIENCE- AND HUMANITIES-BASED APPROACH TO ENERGY POLICY?

As we have suggested, there is a tendency for debates about energy policy to start with the science and technology (with generic statements such as 'because of climate science we need more nuclear/solar/wind energy') and then proceed to policy

[11] 'Energy Prices, Profits and Poverty', House of Commons Energy and Climate Change Committee (UK Parliament), accessed 13 February 2018, www.parliament.uk/business/committees/committees-a-z/commons-select/energy-and-climate-change-committee/inquiries/parliament-2010/energy-prices-profits-and-poverty.

solutions, with far less attention to the social and political aspects of policy implementation. In the words of one foundational IPCC report:

> The effectiveness of measures to mitigate or adapt to climate change depends to a great extent on technological innovation and the diffusion of technologies. The transfer and/or diffusion of [technologies] across and within countries is now considered a major element of global strategies to achieve climate stabilization and support sustainable development.[12]

One renowned technologist who did recognise the role of social constraints and who began this project with us before his untimely death was David MacKay, our colleague at the University of Cambridge in the Department of Engineering. MacKay was not only a talented physicist, he drew from his experiences of practical policymaking from his time as a civil servant in the Department of Energy and Climate Change (DECC), since 2016 part of the Department for Business, Energy and Industrial Strategy (BEIS). Energy policy is fundamentally about policymaking. Thus, one would think that law, politics, economics and history are actually the obvious places to start rather than beginning with questions of technology. Nonetheless, we do not challenge the ordering of the traditional policymaking process, beginning with science and technology as the starting point. Nor do we advocate that moving immediately to formulating policy options is the problem. Rather, what becomes clear in the analysis of real-world cases in this book is the need to insert other disciplinary perspectives early on into the policy formulation stage before moving too hastily without taking these perspectives into consideration. There will, of course, be cases where urgency precludes time to pause for reflection, but in general, most of the problems raised by the cases in this book, not to mention the most common energy policy goals of modern societies, represent multiyear and even multidecade processes. Without stating the obvious, the consequences of reckless policy making are dire, economically and politically. Some important examples over the past half-century range from energy's role in the access to Middle East supplies, the oil embargo resulting from the Yom Kippur War to, more recently, the stand-off between Ukraine and Russia over natural gas, which played a central role in the Ukraine Crisis.[13] Energy policy is important because of the economic significance of energy within individual economies and in international relations. Expenditures on energy can be around 10 per cent of GDP, in the UK for example, and are subject to significant volatility due to changes in

12 'Working Group 3 Third Assessment Report (TAR)', Intergovernmental Panel on Climate Change (IPCC), accessed 6 March 2018, www.ipcc.ch/ipccreports/tar/wg3/index.php?idp=421.

13 Daniel Yergin, *The Prize: The Epic Quest for Oil, Money, and Power* (New York: Simon & Schuster, 1991); Michael L. Ross, 'How the 1973 Oil Embargo Saved the Planet', Foreign Affairs, 15 October 2013, www.foreignaffairs.com/articles/north-america/2013-10-15/how-1973-oil-embargo-saved-planet; Chi Kong Chyong, 'The Role of Natural Gas in Ukraine's Economy and Politics' (26 May 2014), http://www.eprg.group.cam.ac.uk/wp-content/uploads/2015/02/Chyong_presentation-EE-26-May-2014.pdf.

international commodity prices. For energy-exporting countries, energy can be a significant share of GDP, tax revenue and exports, making these countries particularly vulnerable to the state of the global energy market.

One would think that the sheer ubiquity of energy policies would lead to the emergence of a clear and shared understanding of what makes for 'good' energy policy. However, that is not the case. Countries (and indeed regions within them) differ sharply on their approach to energy as evidenced by different levels of tolerance for energy insecurity, wildly differing final energy prices and different attitudes to the environmental aspects of energy production and use. And this is not unique to energy policy. The same can be said for other policy areas such as education and healthcare.

In almost every country, energy policy is politically controversial and the subject of vigorous debate. In fact, many of the cases in this book point to the fact that this is a 'normal' state of affairs in democratic societies these days. This is because energy takes different forms and policy needs to address energy use in electricity, heating and transport and to reconcile the interests of households, commercial businesses and industry. Policies that are good for one sector or group of users may not work so well for others. Energy-intensive industry, such as steel producers, driven by their exposure to international trade, may simply want the cheapest possible energy and may be unwilling to support policies aiming to clean up the environmental aspects of energy production. Households may express contradictory views on energy, simultaneously wanting cleaner energy, while not being willing to pay more for it or to have renewable sources of energy – such as wind turbines – located near to their property. This represents a tension between behaviour as a citizen-voter and likewise as an energy consumer or producer.[14] At the heart of these contradictions is the idea that there is a trade-off between what are widely regarded as the three central objectives of energy policy, namely reliability of supply, low energy prices and the environmental impact: security, affordability, sustainability. This assumes that improving the outcomes of two of the energy policy goals can only be done at the expense of the third. Therein lies the contentious area of government policy, which is often described as requiring the reconciliation of affordable, clean and secure provision of electricity, heating and transport fuel.[15] Unpacking each term of the 'energy trilemma' can be fraught: promoting energy investment may be in tension with lower residential prices; reducing greenhouse gas emissions does not necessarily imply lower local and regional adverse impacts; and more reliable supplies may not necessarily be indigenous supplies.[16]

14 Elcin Akcura et al., 'From Citizen to Consumer: Energy Policy and Public Attitudes in the UK', in *The Future of Electricity Demand: Customers, Citizens and Loads*, ed. Tooraj Jamasb and Michael G. Pollitt (Cambridge: Cambridge University Press, 2011), 231–48.

15 Michael Pollitt, 'In Search of "Good" Energy Policy: The Social Limits to Technological Solutions to Energy and Climate Problems', Working Paper Series (Energy Policy Research Group, November 2015).

16 'The Energy "Trilemma": How Did We Get Here? | The Big Energy Debate | The Guardian', accessed 18 April 2016, www.theguardian.com/big-energy-debate/energy-trilemma-how-did-we-get-here.

Many developing countries appear to have disastrous energy policies that manage to worsen energy security, result in high delivered prices and are associated with high negative environmental impact. The willingness of developing countries, such as Malaysia, China or the UK of the past, to tolerate such a mix of policies can be difficult to comprehend in developed countries. Remarkably, countries that have objectively worse energy policies from a social welfare and environmental perspective can be perceived internally to have good energy policies. According to a recent Edelman global survey, the publics of China and Russia have a much higher degree of trust in their governments concerning the energy sector than businesses.[17] The comparison of measurements for China is 76 per cent trust in government versus 67 per cent for businesses. In Russia, the level of trust is lower than China but still higher for the government at 44 per cent compared to 39 per cent for businesses. The reverse is true in the UK and US (and other liberal democracies such as Canada, France and Australia) with a higher degree of the public's trust placed in businesses compared to government. This occurs in the energy sector because bad policymaking is not unique to energy *and* because of different valuations of some aspects of energy supply. Thus energy consumers in developing countries may be more willing to tolerate poor air quality (or less willing and able to pay the costs of cleaning it up) or they may be more willing to get some energy very cheaply, even though underpayment directly leads to very poor continuity of supply. Historians have recently pointed out that in phases of rapid economic development it may be that improving environmental quality may be seen to conflict with energy comfort whether it be cooking demand in Rome 2,000 years ago or mining silver in Peru during the sixteenth century.[18]

In developed countries, energy policy is not so obviously problematic as supplies are often reliable and the local environmental impact is much less, partly because prices are significantly higher and there is more commitment to the adequate financing of companies involved in energy supply. Instead what we often observe are a large number of individual energy policies, many of which may appear to be sensible on their own, but which in aggregate result in a 'mess' of policies, in the spirit of Rhodes.[19]

1.2 MULTIDISCIPLINARY APPROACHES TO ENERGY POLICY

We would expect the contents of this book to appeal to a broad audience owing to its multidisciplinary theme and relevance to both current events and historical

17 Edelman, '2016 Edelman Trust Barometer – Energy Results', 12:59:29 UTC, www.slideshare.net/EdelmanInsights/2016-edelman-trust-barometer-energy-results?ref=http://www.edelman.com/insights/intellectual-property/2016-edelman-trust-barometer/turbulent-times-call-for-new-strategies-in-building-trust/.

18 Jim Morrison, 'Air Pollution Goes Back Way Further Than You Think', Smithsonian, 2016, www.smithsonianmag.com/science-nature/air-pollution-goes-back-way-further-you-think-180957716/.

19 See Lave (1984), who notes the tendency in the United States (and everywhere else) to regulate one externality at a time, rather than jointly optimise regulations.

developments in energy policy studies. The disciplines highlighted in this book aim for a balanced representation and include, in no particular order of emphasis, economics, politics, law, history, anthropology, management and policy studies, theology and philosophy. We recognise we are not being fully comprehensive, as space and time have limited our inclusion of other relevant disciplines such as behavioural science and psychology. Likewise, considering its energy and policy focus, this book would also be useful for all stakeholder groups involved in energy policy including industry, policymakers and technologists.

Moreover, the book follows in a line of previous studies that incorporate different disciplines in the analysis of policy, making a contribution in the specific field of energy policy studies. Our emphasis on multidisciplinary approaches, one that draws from several social science disciplines, puts us in the company of a rather small group of academic centres of energy policy. Other examples of multidisciplinary research groups where energy policy plays a leading role include the Steyer-Taylor Center for Energy Policy and Finance at Stanford University, the Energy Research Group at the University of California at Berkeley, the Sussex Energy Group within the Science Policy Research Unit at the University of Sussex and the Department of Engineering and Public Policy at Carnegie Mellon University, not to mention an entire faculty of Technology, Policy and Management at TU Delft. Between universities, a notable interdisciplinary project is SHAPE Energy, an EU-funded, Horizon 2020 platform. More recently, all of these groups have advanced the policy debate through multidisciplinary research and are to be commended as the pioneers in this field. With respect to energy and resource policy think tanks, a recent ranking of the top ten shows that the overwhelming majority are monodisciplinary and primarily economics based.[20] Although there may be several academic groups that focus on multidisciplinary energy policy-related activities, books that draw on the multidisciplinary collaborative experience are still lacking.

In this research environment, it is not surprising that there has yet to be a single volume that synthesises multidisciplinary work on energy policy in the way presented in this book. No work has yet appeared that ties together the multidisciplinary efforts of a full series of cases and geographic contexts. This book is also unique insofar as it is explicit about disciplinary perspectives rather than attempting to seamlessly integrate them. While we present case studies from different individual disciplines in the second part, the third part attempts to go further by offering examples of cases where several disciplines have collaborated in the quest for genuine multidisciplinarity.

Not surprisingly, much of the scholarship on energy policy research is presented from the perspective of one discipline. When academics have examined energy policy through multiple disciplines, they have typically focused on one dimension,

[20] 'TTCSP Global Go To Think Tank Index Reports | Think Tanks and Civil Societies Program (TTCSP) | University of Pennsylvania', accessed 7 March 2018, https://repository.upenn.edu/think_tanks/.

such as nuclear energy or renewables. Scholars from the social sciences have sometimes collaborated to produce multidisciplinary books, but these tend to be geographically specific, such as EU energy policy, energy policy in the United States or energy policy in China.[21] While the merits of drawing from multiple disciplines to address a single geographic region is a step forward, a multidisciplinary book with a global view that addresses the complexities of the whole energy system, including normative questions of fairness and justice, was still lacking.

1.3 EXAMPLES OF DIFFERENT DISCIPLINARY APPROACHES IN SOCIAL SCIENCES AND HUMANITIES

The simultaneous reconciliation of multiple competing objectives in energy policy is not new, in our culture or our history. The Jesus of the Bible, speaking two millennia ago, even told a story in which ten young women faced a trade-off between energy security and cost![22]

Our aim here is to identify the areas in which the social sciences and humanities may contribute to our understanding of 'good' energy policies, and to build a framework for future multidisciplinary approaches. 'Good' energy policy attempts to simultaneously deliver on the multiple objectives of energy policy – which, inter alia, include clean, secure and affordable energy – with minimal negative social consequences. By way of illustration, we will highlight the potential contributions that the disciplines of political science, economics, philosophy, theology, history, social anthropology and law offer to the study of energy and climate policies.

Political science can analyse the opinions of members of society, key stakeholders and the limitations of political processes to deliver change. Economics can help frame the incentive design aspects of institutions and what markets and incentive regulation might be able to deliver if appropriately calibrated to the particular situation at hand. Philosophy explores fundamental questions about the ethics of energy production and end use in addition to normative obligations (and aspirations) of current generations to future generations including the fairness of distribution along existing consumption patterns. Theology raises wider issues about humanity's relationship to and responsibility for nature. It poses questions about the cultural and moral driving forces that may be sustaining environmentally and socially damaging energy practices, as well as what role religious leaders may have to play in promoting sustainable living and the role of community versus state in both

21 Energy policy books examining geographic regions are vast. A few notable and recent examples of these regions include: P. Andrews-Speed, *The Governance of Energy in China: Transition to a Low-Carbon Economy* (Basingstoke, UK: Palgrave Macmillan UK, 2012); Peter Z. Grossman, *US Energy Policy and the Pursuit of Failure* (Cambridge: Cambridge University Press, 2013); Jale Tosun, Sophie Biesenbender, and Kai Schulze, eds., *Energy Policy Making in the EU: Building the Agenda* (London: Springer-Verlag, 2015).

22 Hendrickson Publishers, *The Holy Bible: King James Version*, Gospel of Matthew, 25: 1–13 (Peabody, MA: Hendrickson Publishers, 2004).

secular and religious communities. Social anthropology pays attention to the cultural understanding of communities towards energy production and locally specific end use, which may limit or facilitate energy transitions. History has much to teach about the successes and failures of past policies, in particular how policies that we now think of as very successful often required several decades to have their full effect. Management and business studies, much like economics, is a common discipline in the study of energy policy, but it is also inherently a 'bridging discipline' with subfields spanning a range of social sciences.[23] Law may assist with the governance context, shedding light on how formal rule changes may or may not contribute to society's goals in local, national and international contexts. Meanwhile the physics and engineering of the energy system remain important. Therefore, they will continue to set the technical constraints, and likewise, starting points for sensible policy.

It is also important to note that because social constraints are geographically and culturally contextual, regional studies scholars, by virtue of their inherent interdisciplinary nature, may be ideally suited for energy policy analysis. The disciplinary list is certainly not exhaustive, and the next part's chapters will further develop the preceding points on disciplinary contributions to energy policy discussions.

1.4 BOOK STRUCTURE

This book explores a number of research themes that are common to a significant number of disciplines in social sciences and humanities. These include:

1. the differing perceptions of problems being addressed by policy
2. the role of quantification and the use of quantification in establishing a scientific argument
3. the basis of well-being assessments for those affected by energy policies
4. how to build public trust in policies, and to respond to public concerns
5. the complementary roles of the state, different layers of government and nonstate actors
6. the competence of the parties involved and the role of hubris in delivery
7. parallels between energy policy and other policy areas, such as healthcare

What emerges is a not a set of answers but at least a set of questions and possible ways forward much more nuanced and sophisticated than might initially be thought possible within a singular disciplinary line of inquiry, drawing widely on experiences of policymaking across energy technologies, other sectors and jurisdictions around the world. From multiple perspectives, the following parts will also explore the central question of establishing what might be considered a 'good' energy policy. Does 'good' necessarily imply 'desirable outcomes' where ends are more important

[23] Dawn Youngblood, 'Multidisciplinarity, Interdisciplinarity, and Bridging Disciplines: A Matter of Process', Journal of Research Practice 3, no. 2 (5 December 2007): 18.

than means? Or is the proper conception of 'good' one of 'fairness' as assessed by philosophers, 'conducive to human flourishing' as assessed by theologians, 'efficient' as assessed by economists, 'better environmental outcomes' as assessed by scientists, even if these neglect other dimensions? Perhaps 'good' suggests rather a reframing of the 'trilemma' by calling for a balanced integration of economic, social and environmental objectives. And in practical terms, what if an analyst thinks one policy is better while the public broadly supports another policy because it is outwardly more salient? The book also clearly illustrates that a further obstacle to defining what a 'good' policy may be is the fact that academic disciplines, and even subdisciplines, will differ sharply over what is meant by a 'good' policy.

The book is organised around a set of case studies in energy policy, drawing on the cumulative experience of a large number of writers. The first part lays the groundwork for the case studies by offering a number of disciplinary perspectives on energy policy. The second provides examples of diverse disciplinary perspectives illustrated in several case studies. For each of the chapters, the authors describe what makes the case interesting from their disciplinary perspective. Each of the case chapters also includes a short response from another specific disciplinary perspective. Comments from the respondents are aimed at identifying bridging concepts and points that both disciplines, in the context of the specific case, have in common. We have attempted to include a balance of respondents that represent the disciplines included in this book. For example, the first case study on the ethics of nuclear power presented from a philosophical perspective, by Sabine Roeser and Behnam Taebi, receives a response from an economist, Sandy Skelton.

Next, the third part of the book takes the disciplinary bridging to the next level by expanding into multidisciplinary inquiry. These two cases, which examine clean air policies and Eurasian pipelines respectively, incorporate at least three social science disciplines in the design and analysis of specific policies. They are intended to demonstrate in a practical way different approaches to multidisciplinary analysis. The editors introduce the part with a chapter that overviews the current scientific thinking of multidisciplinary research.

In the final part, we include some short commentaries from authors who offer technological and industrial perspectives on energy policymaking. We respond to their comments by highlighting what some of our earlier chapters say about their suggestions. This final engagement sets the tone for measuring the efficacy and practical application of multidisciplinary studies, such as those included in this book.

The editors continued revising this book up to August, 2018.

1.5 HIGHLIGHTS AND KEY LESSONS

One might expect that a starting point for studying energy policy would be political science itself. Accordingly, this is where Part II begins. David Reiner in Chapter 2 shows, however, that energy has not become the theme of a distinct subfield of the discipline of political science. Rather, energy has featured as a factor in investigations of both domestic politics and geopolitics, often in relation to shocks such as the 1970s oil crisis. More broadly, Reiner sets out how political scientists tend to work out of distinct philosophical frameworks through which problems are viewed, the most significant of which are 'realists' who focus on states as self-interested rational actors, and 'liberals' who grant more importance to nonstate actors and other institutions. By contrast, constructivists stress identity and the wider social determinants of actions, while Marxists argue for the centrality of the link between political actions and relations of production. These framings can lead to very divergent outcomes; what they share in common is the expectation of a philosophical frame.

Over time, debates about energy have become more integrated into the field of environmental politics, a process that has accelerated since the Rio summit of 1992 and the emergence of climate change as a leading international issue. This has put a transition away from fossil fuels at the heart of the political agenda, and in turn shaped work in political science. Arguably, the field has thus hitherto been rather reactive to events, and the positions adopted by political theorists often reflect entrenched philosophical dispositions.

In Chapter 3, the economist David Newbery addresses the implications of supposed market failure for good energy policy. He challenges the popular assertion that economists are market fundamentalists, that their goal is to get governments out of markets, and that they are indifferent to the social and distributional impacts of markets. Economic theory has demonstrated the specific conditions under which markets produce competitive efficiency. Economic theory has equally demonstrated that where such conditions for competitive efficiency are not present, government intervention is necessary. Intervention in markets is appropriate where there is indeed market failure. Such intervention may not be best placed to address problems of distributional justice (such as poverty). That should be, and often is, the task of public finance and public policy, such as through targeted public expenditure (on health, for example) or regulation of natural monopolies. Here goals such as fairness and equity properly apply and are balanced against efficiency considerations.

The chapter illustrates these features of markets in relation to energy policy. The limitations of markets, such as failure to supply non-excludable public goods like energy security or not pricing 'externalities' or environmental quality, justify government intervention through both market correction and regulation. Climate change mitigation is cited as a central example of how governments can correct for market failure through carbon pricing.

In Chapter 4, Tim Lewens provides a philosopher's perspective on energy policy, distinguishing between good outcomes and good processes. He argues that it is in considering the latter that philosophy may offer a greater contribution. In terms of good outcomes, the key dimensions he examines are: (i) energy justice, which explores concepts such as equal treatment and the trade-offs resulting from differential impacts on affected groups; (ii) future generations, since those making energy policy decisions will struggle to take account of those not yet alive; (iii) 'non-identity', since current decisions can also affect which future people will actually exist, completely changing the way we can interpret harm; and (iv) as the final challenge, the dizzying array of dimensions along which energy policies might be assessed including emissions, biodiversity, food availability and ways of life, particularly when there may be positive impacts along some dimensions, and negative impacts along others.

The chapter then turns to 'good processes', since philosophers have argued that 'answers to complex questions like these are those that derive from good processes of deliberation'. One process consideration is the proper balance to be struck between technical elites and politicians who will be influenced by the public and other stakeholders. Any expert judgment will inevitably be value laden, so the question then is how to move beyond simple yes/no answers and find ways of introducing probabilities and uncertainties into the decision-making process. More generally, participation requires both disciplinary and ideological diversity among policy advisors as well as finding ways to incorporate the relevant knowledge possessed by laypeople. Finally, Lewens argues that precaution requires tolerating 'significant uncertainties while making decisions about risk reduction' and, as such, there is a need for a precautionary approach to govern how society regulates risks, rather than seeking out some all-encompassing simplifying 'principle'.

In Chapter 5, Jonathan Chaplin describes how public theology would seek a 'grounded' energy policy rooted in a clear understanding of what makes for a 'good' or 'virtuous' human life, which includes both our relations with the non-human world and the wider pursuit of a 'good' society. Drawing on the statements issued by the major religions in the run-up to the Paris Accord in December 2015, Chaplin identifies five stances that are broadly convergent across the different religions and supported by public theology more broadly: (i) nature as a '"divine" ordering of a universe marked by integration, equilibrium, balance and harmony' rather than as infinitely exploitable; (ii) a call for human 'stewardship' or 'trusteeship' of nature; (iii) a shared acceptance of climate science and an urgent need to shift away from fossil fuels; (iv) questioning the potential for unlimited economic growth and finally, (v) situating energy and environmental questions within a broader commitment to a just social order.

According to many public theologians, not only is consumerism damaging our environment, economy and politics, but it is also 'a debilitating spiritual and moral poverty which further enfeebles the human capacity to make the behavioural changes needed to combat environmental problems generally'. This perspective leads to critiques of the concentrations of power including large corporations in the energy sector as well as scepticism on the wider impact of carbon markets. Public theology seeks to introduce concepts of social justice and challenge definitions of economic growth or consumerism, which might prevent a deeper flourishing of both humans and the environment, while recognising at the same time the wider context and need for 'historical patience' in seeking out solutions to the problems identified.

Then in Chapter 6, Charlotte Johnson opens up the realm of possible examinations of energy policy by explaining how approaches used in anthropology have the potential to explore new aspects of energy policy and to do so in new ways. She gives an overview of the burgeoning field of the study of energy in anthropology, or 'energopolitics' as it is sometimes called in anthropological studies. She points out that the exploration of energy policy 'offers fertile ground for anthropological investigation, impacting on some of the discipline's core theoretical concerns: power, value, identity, symbolism and myth'. Johnson then situates energy policy within four developed debates in which anthropologists are engaged, including: anthropology of the state, economic anthropology, material culture of the home and consumption, and digital and design anthropology.

Johnson then explains the approaches that anthropologists have used to explore energy policy including traditional ethnography, multi-sited ethnography that may follow infrastructure from place to place such as pipelines, and new approaches such as sensory ethnography and design anthropology, which transitions the anthropologist from 'observer into a position of active interventions' in experimental research designs. With respect to traditional ethnography, 'An anthropological approach suits the study of energy policy because it can examine in detail ways that people's livelihoods, their lifestyles, their sense of self and their ethics can be impacted or directly targeted by energy policy'.

Paul Warde offers a challenging perspective on what historians bring to the study of energy policy in Chapter 7. He distinguishes between history in the sense of the use of historical information to inform current policy and History – with a capital H – in the sense of the study of historical phenomena by Historians. Historians, according to Warde, bring a particular set of perspectives and methodologies – such as archival research – to the study of the past, which can help with the study of current policy. Indeed, he is critical of history – with a small h – which is often built on doubtful historical data. However, as he points out, historians are not primarily concerned about current policy and the assumption that anything can be learned from the past for current policy is not to be taken for granted.

However, historians do bring important perspectives to the study of the past: these include the idea that the success or failure of past policies are likely to be complex – though not necessarily complicated – and will likely involve the interaction of many different factors playing out on different timescales. Warde uses the history of failed energy predictions to illustrate what he means by the perspective of historians. Thus what historians might want to know about past predictions is not primarily why the predictions were wrong, but what process led to them being framed in the way they were, what determined how they were used in past policymaking and why voices that were subsequently shown to be correctly predicting the future were supressed at the time.

In Chapter 8, Jim Platts, an engineer with many years of project management experience in the wind industry, offers a fascinating perspective on the management of large energy engineering projects. Such projects often go wrong and end up being delivered late and over budget. Using an example from Hong Kong, he points out that many large engineering projects are unique one-off feats of management, which rely on the successful collaboration of a large number of specialists and highly skilled individuals. When things start to go wrong it is very easy for projects to descend into a blame game, where no one individual, company or group takes responsibility for the project's failure to be delivered on time. Good management is required to lead such a complex team.

Platts goes on to point out that management is not just about 'giving orders' but about collaboration and listening. He proceeds to apply this principle of good management to the global wind industry, which has developed incredibly since its humble beginnings in the early 1980s. He points out that the culture of sharing learning, between engineers, and the long-term commitment of companies and individuals within the industry to building something that will last has been key to its success. This has led to sustained innovation which has enabled the scaling up of individual turbines and overall production and resulted in massive increases in installed capacity and falling unit costs.

In the final chapter of the first part, Chapter 9, Tibisay Morgandi and Jorge Viñuales show why, since 'law is the language through which energy policies are formulated and enacted', an assessment of a transition towards 'good' energy policy must reckon with both the capacities and limitations of 'legal form'. They note that the basic design of an energy policy already involves a range of legally complex choices. Carbon pricing, for example, could be pursued variously via: a tax; an emissions trading system; a regulation imposing a ceiling on certain types of emissions or the use of certain technologies promoted through a wider set of policies such as removing fossil fuel subsidies; setting renewable energy targets or supporting renewable energy. But there are further choices to be made in determining the precise legal form of such a policy: a tax law will differ according to what is taxed, how it is taxed and why it is taxed; it must rest on a proper legal basis, which in turn depends on questions of devolution of powers and proper implementation; and it must be consistent with broader legal norms. Such complexity is, however, frequently bypassed in technological and economic approaches.

The complexity of legal form is illustrated through three case studies. The extraction of shale gas in the European Union shows the importance of the question of whether an EU recommendation would be more successful if it were binding or nonbinding. The challenges of pursuing low-carbon policies in the United States demonstrate that highly specific choices of legal wording bear substantial consequences for the political options pursued at both domestic and international levels. The Indian government's policy of supporting the production of renewable energy equipment by imposing local content requirements (LCRs) shows that, even though such a policy is vulnerable to long-term legal challenge by virtue of its breaching WTO trade rules, it may turn out to achieve short-term success in supporting indigenous producers. They conclude that energy policies are more likely to overcome political constraints and to be effective in securing stakeholder buy-in if they are expressed in a legal form that is 'adaptive to existing political conditions' and 'resilient to future legal challenges or amendments'.

After a review of how the different disciplines interpret 'good energy policy', Part II then presents a number of specific case studies that are developed by scholars from the different disciplines across a range of topics within the broad domain of energy policy.

In Chapter 10 on the ethics of nuclear energy, philosophers Behnam Taebi and Sabine Roeser show that while the Fukushima-Daiichi nuclear disaster led to major changes in nuclear energy policy in Japan and some European states, the demand for nuclear power facilities will continue to grow over the next decades given rapidly rising global demands for electricity, especially in Asia. Problems of nuclear waste disposal and of nuclear energy governance will continue to pose difficult challenges. The ethics of nuclear energy, then, will demand attention for a long time to come. Against the background of ethical debates about nuclear arms proliferation, the chapter begins by reviewing the course of debates about the ethics of nuclear safety (unintentional harm) and security (intentional harm) since the 1970s, noting that substantial technological advances in safety do not remove all risk or pre-empt difficult ethical choices where not all desirable criteria – affordability, fuel efficiency, minimisation of waste, reduced possibility of nuclear proliferation – can be simultaneously met.

Questions of intergenerational justice arise both because uranium is non-renewable while only current generations benefit from it and because the problem of waste will last for decades, forcing difficult and costly choices between 'open' and 'closed' fuel cycles. Management of waste from decommissioned, existing and new nuclear facilities, where multinational cooperation is increasingly favoured for security reasons, also creates major risks of both intra- and inter-generational injustice and of international injustice. Nuclear energy and waste in turn create the need for new and better instruments of global governance which, however, must work to overcome a continuing jealous defence of national sovereignty. The power of intense public emotions in the face of the risks of nuclear power will continue to present ongoing political challenges. Yet both 'technocratic' and 'populist' responses to such emotions fall short by assuming only quantitative measures of risk are relevant while they are inevitably value laden, ducking the ethical issues at stake and wrongly assuming that such 'irrational' emotions can shed no light on ethical dilemmas such as such as justice, fairness and autonomy. These considerations do not suggest a rejection of nuclear energy but rather that, to achieve better nuclear energy decision making, ethical reflection must be central to the process.

Next in Chapter 11, Christian Growitsch and Felix Höffler, both economists, provide an explanation for what really happened to the direction of Germany's national energy transition policy, or *Energiewende*. By examining relevant data over a decade and a half, they show that the impact of Fukushima on German energy policy was minimal. The most important change was a slight acceleration to the phasing out of nuclear energy by the decommissioning of older plants. However, this was a process that had already begun in 2005. They also give a historical context to the *Energiewende* which explains, for those new to the subject, why the German public has long been uneasy with nuclear power relative to its neighbours, which is what makes Germany unique in Europe from an energy policy perspective.

Despite the media hype within Germany about the policy changes in response to Fukushima, as Chancellor Merkel explained to the Bundestag parliament, the *Energiewende* was already well underway with its policy roots formed nearly a decade before the Fukushima disaster of 2011. The authors also offer an insightful, almost anthropological explanation of social tendencies in Germany. They propose that, as an export-driven manufacturing economy, German society is predisposed to accepting technological solutions to wide-scale challenges such as climate change. Therefore, any policy that can demonstrate a new or transformative type of technology will be advantaged in its implementation.

The historical background to the adoption of high-carbon taxes in Sweden, as described in Chapter 12, by the historian Magnus Lindmark, is the tale of a first mover. Sweden has currently the highest effective carbon price – averaged price across all GHG emissions – in the world. Lindmark discusses the imposition of carbon taxes at around this level in 1991, significantly ahead of the EU ETS (2005) and almost every other country, save a handful of near neighbours.

The chapter makes three important points about Sweden's leading role. First, Sweden's starting point was extreme. It was the second most oil import-dependent country in the OECD before the first oil shock. Second, the imposition of such high taxes was not motivated by environmentalism per se, but by the need to reform the tax system in a more fiscally sustainable way. This involved taxation of what had become – after large reductions in oil use before 1990 – a relatively stable carbon tax base. And finally, while environmentalism did not cause the tax regime to be reformed in this way, it did motivate the form of the tax reform and advanced a political case for Pigovian environmental taxation.

Continuing with a Scandinavian theme in Chapter 13, Frede Hvelplund, Søren Djørup and Karl Sperling draw on multiple disciplines including social anthropology, politics and history to address a complex question drawing from the Danish experience. The question deals with overcoming path dependency in order to move economies to an 'integrated energy system', which is, they argue, what is needed for any modern economy to transition away from fossil-fuel dominant energy systems.

The authors note how Denmark transitioned to a decentralised heating model and the implications of this transition to that of an integrated energy system, one that they argue would apply to countries worldwide. The key to understanding how to move from a centralised to decentralised system is illustrated at three levels: the normative, regulative and cognitive. In order to overcome the path dependency of centralised systems, they argue that policymakers may devise policies that transfer more responsibilities to ever more local stakeholders.

In Chapter 14 David Reiner, a political scientist, explores the example of carbon capture and storage (CCS) to show that it is not possible to explain how or why a specific energy technology is adopted in terms of technological feasibility alone but that grasping the broader social and political forces shaping support for it is essential. CCS has existed for decades and has many recognised advantages – for example, it is much less disruptive of existing energy technologies and business models than renewable technology and it can assist towards making rapid progress on climate targets. It is now seen as a vital element in any mitigation programme aimed at moving towards net-zero emissions. Yet, apart from a period of global political enthusiasm in the mid-2000s, it has struggled to secure a critical mass of advocates due to opposition, indifference or ambivalence from diverse stakeholder interests. Initial government support has waned and CCS has been disconnected from industrial policy; the technology struggles to demonstrate its potential profitability; energy utilities lack the resources even to assess opportunities; the shale gas surge undermined demand for coal generation and damaged coal industry profits; and the response of environmental NGOs has been divided and sceptical. The obstacles presented by these disparate interests have meant that, notwithstanding the promise of CCS to reduce energy costs substantially, this has not translated into the sustained, widespread support necessary to convince stakeholders that the initial high costs of large-scale projects will be worthwhile. CCS has rightly been described as an 'orphan' technology with 'numerous well-meaning aunts and uncles but no parents'.

Chapter 15, by Atif Ansar, Dan Madrigal and Seth Collins, offers an examination of an emerging type of energy megaproject, data centres. Unbeknownst to many, the sector has grown over one thousand times from 2002 to 2018. As such, the demand for electricity that data centres put on existing power grids is a growing challenge for electricity providers. Drawing from business and management studies, the authors introduce the factors that are driving the growth of this sector. They note that although industry appears to have an insatiable thirst for electricity that will continue to present new challenges for providers, the efficiency of data centres is higher when compared to power demand from distributed computing. The authors point out that the key constraint in the growth of data centres is low-carbon energy; they then explore cases of high-profile data centres such as Facebook, Google and IBM. By identifying the factors that drive the selection of sites and the drivers of innovation in this field, they argue that co-locating data centres alongside onsite energy facilities offers the most promising options for overcoming the low-carbon energy constraint.

In Chapter 16, Leslie-Anne Duvic-Paoli, a legal scholar, explores the neglected role in discussions of energy governance of the Convention on Access to Information, Public Participation in Decision-Making and Access to Justice in Environmental Matters (the 'Aarhus Convention'). The Aarhus Convention, established pursuant to the concept of 'environmental democracy' affirmed in the 1992 Rio Declaration, is widely seen as an example of a best practice upon which to model 'better' global environmental policies, and energy activities are accorded a central place in its remit. The Convention is shown to be a novel instrument of global energy governance, challenging the traditional assumption that energy policy is a '*domaine réservé*' of the state and thus moving beyond mere energy multilateralism. It also enhances concern with the public interest in policymaking and encourages the decentralisation of energy systems in the transition to a low-carbon economy.

The chapter assesses the central role of the Convention's compliance committee. In two cases – the Hinkley Point nuclear power station and renewable energy policy in Scotland – the UK government was found to be non-compliant with the Convention. These and other cases disclose the committee's potential as an instrument of environmental democracy while also revealing its limitations as a non-judicial body: its rulings are nonbinding, it possesses competence only over process and not substance, and it can only recommend future compliance not enforce redress of previous breaches. While questions remain over whether the motivations of citizen claimants are self-interested or oriented to the public good, Aarhus illustrates how international law can give citizens a forum that protects their right to democratic decision-making processes. It shows that energy governance is becoming more democratic, global and focused on sustainability, and shows that public participation as a principle of 'good' energy governance can lend energy decisions greater legitimacy and increase their social acceptance.

Chapter 17 considers one of the starkest examples of the damage that can be done by energy policy. Theologian Michael Northcott tells about the case of biofuels derived from palm oil plantations in Malaysia and the implications for the vulnerable in society, global justice and the impact on traditional ways of life. The impact in Borneo on wildlife is substantial (such as the decimation of the rainforest and that of the orangutan population, which have both been fairly well documented), but he focuses not just on environmental devastation and climate impacts, but also on the livelihoods of native groups. He traces how policy decisions made on the other side of the world in the European Union first encouraged this environmental devastation and then, after alarms were raised (and even then only after years had elapsed), stricter guidelines were enshrined, which helped discourage further exploitation.

Northcott highlights how the environmental disaster has been driven by 'systemic political corruption, extensive criminal activity, and destruction of the habitats of native peoples and wildlife'. He also explores the role played by science as 'an ambiguous handmaiden' in the biofuels story. He highlights how the regional government (whose corruption has been exposed by investigative journalists) assumed the role of 'trustee' of the forests because it could claim the ability to take a modern approach in both managing and exploiting the island's resources, thus eliminating the need to trust the more primitive aboriginal groups to act as guardians of the forests.

The final chapter in Part II, Chapter 18, continues with a theological theme. In his chapter on *Ladauto Si'* – the far-reaching (and groundbreaking) papal encyclical on the environment issued by Pope Francis on the eve of the Paris climate negotiations in 2015 – political theologian Jonathan Chaplin provides a critical assessment of the substance of the document and the challenge of following through with action. He acknowledges some concrete manifestations growing out of the encyclical, such as the 'Laudato Si' Pledge' to mobilise Catholics on climate action and its inspiring of others to create a 'Laudato Si' Startup Challenge'.

Nevertheless, Chaplin highlights how there is still much more to be done to translate 'the inspiring content of *Laudato Si* into more specific strategic environmental and energy policy guidelines'. He describes the balance struck by Francis of highlighting the enormity of the problems and challenging the standard anthropocentric view while avoiding a bleak disempowering 'catastrophist' view. In this telling, Francis does well at the macro- and micro-levels to make the problems concrete but falls short at the 'meso level' by failing to offer solutions in terms of technology, states and markets.

The last part of the book, Part III, offers two intentionally multidisciplinary and international case studies. They were completed by two multidisciplinary teams examining clean air policies and a Eurasian pipeline policy with its ripple effects in the region. The editors, Michael Pollitt and Marc Ozawa who were contributing authors to these chapters, introduce the cases in Chapter 19. They offer an introduction to the topics, examine the distinction between multidisciplinary and interdisciplinary approaches and provide a practical reflection on the two different approaches used by the teams in the following two chapters.

In Chapter 20, Jacqueline Lam, Yang Han, Shan-Shan Wang, Victor OK Li, Michael Pollitt and Paul Warde offer a multidisciplinary chapter comparing energy policy in historical London with contemporary Beijing. The chapter brings together history, political science, economics and engineering approaches to urban air pollution arising from the burning of fossil fuels. Lam et al. begin by discussing London. Historical London was famous throughout the world for its 'fog', which was in reality black smoke or a form of particulate emissions from the burning of coal. In 1952 London experienced its 'Great Smog' over a four-day period which resulted in thousands of excess deaths. The reaction to this event resulted in the enactment of the UK Clean Air Act (CAA) of 1956, which for the first time gave local authorities the authority and resources to reduce air pollution. Subsequent to this there was a significant improvement in air quality in London as restrictions were placed on domestic and industrial coal burning. Lam et al. document this improvement and discuss why the policies the CAA promoted were effective.

The average annual concentration of black smoke or PM10 dropped from two hundred micrograms per meter cubed in 1950 to around fifty by 1966 in London. Lam et al. show that in 2000 air quality in Beijing was roughly the same as in 1950s London, however, by contrast its air quality did not improve significantly in the sixteen years to 2016. While the two cities bear striking similarities in their starting points both in terms of income per head and the level of air pollution, their situations are somewhat different. The sources of air pollution are different in the two cases: London's was coal for heating and power, while Beijing's recent air pollution is increasingly from vehicles and roughly one quarter of it is from industry in neighbouring provinces. Beijing has continued to grow rapidly in terms of population and GDP per capita, while London's population was very stable between 1950 and 1966, and GDP per capita growth was much lower. However, the persistence of Beijing's air pollution problem and the ineffectiveness of the many policies aimed at reducing it, are in striking contrast to the undoubted success of the CAA. Public outcry in London following the 'Great Smog' was important in the lead up to the CAA, whereas public pressure has been more muted in the case of Beijing. Effective enforcement of policies to reduce the local consequences of fossil fuel burning was possible in London and had a visible and material impact.

In the next multidisciplinary case study, Chapter 21, a group of six social scientists representing five disciplines, including Politics, Economics, Geography, Area Studies and Social Anthropology, examine natural gas pipelines as an energy policy. Marc Ozawa, Chi Kong Chyong, Caroline Humphrey, Kun-Chin Lin, Tim Reilly and Corine Wood-Donnelly begin by posing the question of whether natural gas pipelines as a policy are good for Russia. The case focuses on one of Russia's newest pipelines, the Power of Siberia, designed to deliver natural gas from newly developed in Siberia to the Chinese market, connecting the two countries by pipeline. The pipeline project has been in negotiations between the two countries for over a decade, but Russia's economic 'pivot to the East', which was in part a reaction to Western sanctions after the Ukraine crisis of 2014, brought a new level of importance to the project.

One distinctive advantage of multidisciplinary studies is the breadth and depth of the authors' ability to examine a policy from multiple perspectives and dimensions. This chapter takes full advantage of the authors' areas of expertise by investigating the commercial value of the project, which is perhaps the easiest aspect to characterise monetarily, the geopolitical implications, the project's impact on Russia's relations with its neighbours in the East particularly China, the pipeline's impact on local communities, and the environmental and legal-institutional constraints of building such megaprojects under a more authoritarian government. Given the multiple perspectives represented in this sort of collaboration, another advantage is that it allows for the testing of disciplinary concepts and assumptions.

The authors drew from their respective disciplines to create benchmarks for measuring positive aspects of the pipeline. These range from welfare effects and regional political power to political and community stability as well as environmental impacts. Considering these dimensions, the authors conclude that the Power of Siberia project, although in its infancy, appears to have a mixed track record. On the one hand, it provides both Russia and China with important market and supply diversification. And although this contributes to greater energy security, the economic advantages look to be more one-sided, benefitting Russia in the short term but raising questions about the long-term viability of the project. The pipeline evades the scrutiny of international norms and legal frameworks, on which both countries seem to place less emphasis compared to similar pipelines connecting Russia to Europe. Related to this, the construction of the pipeline has not met the same international environmental standards of westbound pipelines, and this is adversely affecting indigenous communities in the Russian Far East. On a more global scale, however, the authors also raise the prospect of greater geopolitical instability in the region. As the Power of Siberia raises the energy supply independence of the region, there will be less of a need for the United States and other suppliers to maintain a presence in the region.

As we have provided the highlights of the book and our main conclusions drawn from the cases in this introductory chapter, Chapter 22 is devoted to responses by policy practitioners who have dealt with the realities of constructing and implementing policies. They include John Deutch, currently Institute Professor at the Massachusetts Institute of Technology and former Deputy Secretary of Energy in the United States, Emily Shuckburgh, OBE, deputy head of the Polar Oceans Team at the British Antarctic Survey and a former advisor to the UK Department of Energy and Climate Change and Lord Ronald Oxburgh, who is a British parliamentarian, member of the House of Lords, a former chairman of Shell and himself a geologist and geophysicist. These three 'technologists' provide three essays as perspectives on the topic of 'good energy policy'. The last word, however, is reserved for us, the editors, who will respond to their comments and offer suggestions for future directions of multidisciplinary research in energy policy.

PART I

Multidisciplinary Perspectives

2

Political Science and Energy

David M. Reiner

2.1 INTRODUCTION

What does political science have to say about energy? In general, very little. Unlike economics or law, where energy economics and energy law have developed into separate, well-defined and largely coherent subdisciplines with their own journals and professional associations, the treatment of energy in political science is much more intermittent, erratic and disconnected. Despite the ubiquitous nature of energy in the global economy, energy has only emerged as a subject for prolonged study in a handful of cases. Nevertheless, there are some insights that political science might be able to offer because of its focus on dimensions often neglected by economists or legal scholars working on energy.

Goodin (2011) describes political science as the study of 'the constrained use of social power', by focusing on the actors and institutions exerting power as well as those that constrain it. In that context, the role of energy can be valuable both in enabling the exertion of that power and in contributing to the constraints. Thus, American military, economic and geopolitical power are facilitated by rising domestic production of shale gas and oil, but equally, foreign intervention and influence in the Middle East are constrained by significant oil and gas production in many Arab states (Victor et al., 2006).

Insofar as energy has been the subject of attention for political scientists, it has been as a key factor in domestic politics (particularly in resource-rich states) and/or international relations, a source of instability (such as perceived insecurity from relying on foreign sources of energy) or as a major transformative event (notably the oil crises of 1973–79). In large part, the absence of a separate field of energy politics is due to the fact that there is no distinguishable 'politics' associated with energy, in the sense that politics describes a particular configuration and specific sets of interactions of actors and institutions.

There are, for example, local politics associated with siting infrastructure but in that context, wind farms are not perceptibly different from mobile phone masts or landfills. The politics of nationalising and privatising firms to advance the national interest afflicts energy, but no more and no less than water, railways or telecommunications, at least in advanced economies. The politics of regulatory reform or consumer policy is relevant for food and drug prices just as it is for energy prices, and the politics of energy security in the form of keeping open shipping lines or building liquefied natural gas (LNG) terminals is but one element in wider considerations of national and international security. Apart from nuclear power, which has been intricately tied to the emergence of nuclear-weapons states and so has wider geopolitical ramifications (Kennan, 1982), there have been remarkably few studies on specific energy technologies or energy markets in general.

2.2 ENERGY AND THE POLITICAL SCIENCE LITERATURE

It is instructive to consider how energy is treated in leading journals.[1] Energy is a frequent topic in the more 'policy-' or practitioner-oriented journals such as *Foreign Affairs*, which regularly has published articles on the topic, whether by leading figures such as Ernest Moniz, Amory Lovins or Daniel Yergin, or by past or current energy policy fellows at the Council on Foreign Relations such as Michael Levi, Varun Sivaram and David Victor. There have been notable peaks and troughs in the attention being paid to energy in policy (as opposed to political science) circles, as seen by the number of articles in *Foreign Affairs*. There were four articles on the subject between 1951 and 1956 (three on oil and one on nuclear energy) and none for the following fifteen years, before surging to roughly twice a year from 1971 to 1990, then down to once a year from 1990 to 2010 and back to twice a year since 2010. Although not atheoretical, these articles are written for a wider audience and are generally focused on pressing policy questions such as the challenges facing an incoming US administration or how energy (such as the Nord Stream pipeline or expanding renewables or nuclear power) impinges on the geopolitics of, say, China or Russia.

By contrast, the leading political science journals have published almost nothing that is explicitly on the subject of energy. What little has been published has been either on the subject of nuclear power or was written in the aftermath of the oil crises of 1973 to 1979. Over the past sixty years[2] there have been five articles in the *American Journal of Political Science* (three from 1978 to 1982 and one each in 2004 and 2013), three articles in *American Political Science Review* (in 1952, 1987 and 2008), and

[1] We examined whether the words 'energy', 'oil', 'petroleum', 'coal', 'shale', 'renewables', 'solar', wind', 'nuclear' or 'atomic' appear in the titles of articles in the leading political science journals (as measured according to impact factor in 2017). We did not count any articles that did not deal with energy (e.g., articles on nuclear weapons).

[2] Note that the entire back catalogue of the journals was searched although no articles on energy were found from before 1950. The start dates for the journals reviewed are: *Foreign Affairs* 1922, *American Journal of Political Science* 1956, *American Political Science Review* 1906, *World Politics* 1948, and *International Organisation* 1947.

seven articles in *World Politics* (on energy security in 1961, 1982 and 1987; on oil in 1974, 1985, 2001 and 2015). The leading political science journal with the most energy-related articles is *International Organization*, although here too interest came in waves with five articles (all on atomic energy) between 1959 and 1971, a further fifteen between 1974 and 1989 (primarily on oil but also on other topics such as energy markets, energy R&D and nuclear power) and an additional six since 2010 (all on oil). According to Hughes and Lipscy (2013), who link the rise and fall and rise again of interest in energy in the political science literature to the long-term fluctuation in the oil price, 'The politics of energy is reemerging as a major area of inquiry for political science after two decades of relative quiet.' Although perhaps a generous interpretation, it is clear that there are opportunities for political science to contribute to a better understanding of the forces affecting energy production and consumption.

2.3 ENERGY AND POLITICAL SUBFIELDS

To understand how political science would view 'energy' in its various forms and where it might be able to impart particular insights, it is important to appreciate how the discipline has been divided into subdisciplines, which vary depending on the 'unit of analysis', i.e., is the focus on international organisations, nation states, subnational actors or individual actors such as policymakers or bureaucrats? (Keman and Woldendorp, 2016). This division leads to the major subfields including: (i) international relations as the domain to study international institutions, nation states and multilateral negotiations; (ii) comparative politics to contrast the evolution of similar policy issues in different countries or jurisdictions; (iii) national politics (e.g., American or British or Chinese politics) that will explore in great detail particular national circumstances and institutions or public opinion on energy (e.g., Ansolabehere & Konisky, 2014; Farhar et al, 1980); and (iv) bureaucratic or institutional politics to examine specific agencies such as the United States Environmental Protection Agency or the formation of Chinese energy policy (Lieberthal and Oksenberg, 1986).

There is, however, no single agreed or even dominant approach or methodology within each of the subdisciplines. Rather, there are divergent philosophical approaches that coexist within a single subfield that view the nature of politics through inherently different perspectives. Within international relations, one might contrast different approaches including: realism, constructivism, liberalism (which might be further divided into neoliberalism and regime theory) and Marxism.

The most prominent divide is between analysts who focus on international organisations and those who focus on conflicts among nations. As a bit of a caricature, those studying international organisations tend to be liberal institutionalists who are more optimistic about the role for international norms and conventions. They are optimistic not only about the potential for formal international legal frameworks to constrain behaviour, but about the ability of existing and emergent institutions to shift the calculus of both state actors and subnational actors.

By contrast, as students of international conflict, realists tend to focus on the role of the state and are very sceptical of the potential for non-state actors or non-binding international 'law' to have much influence. Realists view the world as inherently conflictive and often focus on relative gains as more important than absolute gains, whereas liberals (and most economic analysis) implicitly assumes that absolute gains are the primary objective (Powell, 1991). Coercion or the threat of coercion is often needed to obtain a state's desired outcome and state survival can be at stake in such conflicts. Although similar views date back to Plato, modern advocates such as Mearsheimer or Waltz argue that states employ strategies to manage an otherwise anarchic international system.

Constructivists move away from the rational-actor model found in most liberal and realist work and focus on the role of identity and social structures rather than material considerations (such as wealth or power) in driving state interests (Wendt, 1994). From this perspective, the focus is on the emergence of identities or norms, which might affect how both state and non-state actors deal with concerns such as transparency or corruption (Gillies, 2010). By contrast, Marxists focus on who controls the means of production and, in that lens, the overriding role of the state is acting in the interests of the capitalist class. Neo-Marxist approaches include dependency theory and core-periphery models, which describe developing countries as being dependent on wealthier states through a reinforcing web of trade, financial and security arrangements. Resource extraction in developing countries and the export of those resources to wealthier countries where they are transformed into higher value-added goods is a central element in most narratives of dependence (Ross 2001).

Perhaps the most prominent or consistent thread through studies of the politics of energy is the question of energy security or energy independence. The conflict between Ukraine and Russia over gas pipelines would be an appealing case for realists since the context and outcomes fit well into this world-view. The threat of force is omnipresent and realists could trace Ukraine's weakness to its decision to hand over its nuclear weapons at the end of the Cold War. There may be numerous negotiations over terms of bilateral contracts, but these are not primarily driven by markets but by barely veiled efforts to use coercion in different venues. Russia accepts the sanctions and economic damages resulting from its invasion of Crimea and intervention in eastern Ukraine as a necessary cost for maintaining its sphere of influence in its 'near abroad' and demonstrating a credible commitment to a use of force.

By contrast, institutionalists would prefer to focus on the successful institutional interventions. Thus, Keohane (1978) focuses on the emergence of the International Energy Agency in encouraging international coordination and how that coordination spread from a narrow emphasis on strategic petroleum reserves to a wide range of energy topics. It is, of course, not impossible for a realist to analyse the IEA or for a liberal institutionalist to focus on geopolitical conflict in the Russian periphery, but there is inevitably a selection bias.

There are, of course, topics which will be of interest from different perspectives. Consider the proposed part-privatisation of Saudi Aramco. Viewed from a realist perspective, the proposal is being driven by a new leader (Mohammed bin Salman, the current Saudi crown prince) seeking to consolidate power and allow Saudi Arabia to project its geopolitical power more effectively at a time of threat created in part by the advent of American shale oil and gas (and the existential threat posed by Islamic extremists). A liberal institutionalist might look at how greater engagement with markets and national sovereign wealth funds has begun to shift attitudes both towards OPEC and the market discipline created through an IPO. A social constructivist would likely focus more on social identity and challenges to existing norms that the crown prince is trying to foster through greater openness.

The subject of energy tends to arise in political affairs when the market is sidelined and more traditional political actors become involved, as was the case in the rounds of nationalisation (e.g., Gaddafi's Libya or Venezuela under Chavez), liberalisation (e.g., retail markets in the UK or proposed part-privatisation of Saudi Aramco) or government interference in the activities of national champions (such as France in mergers of GdF and Suez or Alstom with GE). One important role for political scientists is in understanding sources of change and inertia in systems and in so doing anticipating flashpoints and transitions (or the lack thereof). A large regional studies literature covers the role of energy, especially oil extraction (Karl, 1997) in different regions, particularly for resource-dependent states, such as in west Africa (de Oliveira, 2007) or the Gulf states, where so-called rentier states developed (Coates Ulrichsen, 2011, Crystal, 1990). Although oil has been the source of the rents, it is striking that a discussion of energy itself plays a relatively small role in most of these studies.

2.4 AREAS OF FUTURE GROWTH: PUTTING ENERGY INTO ENVIRONMENTAL AND CLIMATE POLITICS

In recent years, energy has increasingly emerged as a focus for study in environmental politics. One key reason why a distinct field of environmental politics arose but not a distinct field of energy politics is that energy is often viewed as a technical or technological artefact, whereas the environment is associated with a political ideology about changing approaches to, and an ethos about, consumption and about human interaction with the natural world and its implications for the wider politics (Barry, 1998; Eckersley, 2004). The modern origins of environmental politics in the 1960s and 1970s were not particularly focused on energy, however, and instead research emphasised issues of clean water, clean air, degraded land and endangered species (e.g., Ashby and Anderson, 1981; Hird, 1990). Although the recognition of coal-fired power plants as the major source of emissions and of motor vehicles as the main source of urban air pollution led to major pieces of legislation and rulemaking, these issues were viewed as fairly technical, and changes to the energy system were an outcome of decisions taken on environmental grounds.

The first major international conference (United Nations Conference on the Human Environment) was held in Stockholm in 1972, but its wider political significance was rather minimal. Only two heads of state or government addressed the conference: Olaf Palme, the prime minister of the host Sweden, and Indira Gandhi of India. The relatively narrow impacts of the first summit related to energy were primarily due to concerns by Sweden and others over acid rain, which is primarily caused by nitrogen oxides (NOx) – especially sulfur oxides (SOx) – produced at coal-fired power plants (Bernauer and Koubi, 2009). The resulting Convention on Long-range Transport of Air Pollution (LRTAP) was translated into national plans aimed at reducing emissions through either technology mandates as in Germany or emissions markets as in the United States (Joskow & Schmalensee, 1998).

By contrast, the 1992 Rio Earth Summit (formally the United Nations Conference on Environment and Development) was a far more political event and began to put energy and climate change near the top of the international agenda. At Rio de Janeiro, 108 world leaders attended. Even US President George H.W. Bush, who was initially reluctant to attend, appeared and the United States was one of the first countries to ratify the UN Framework Convention on Climate Change.

Since then, climate negotiations have seen high-level engagement including Al Gore's flying to Japan in 1997 to help ensure the agreement of the Kyoto Protocol, and Barack Obama and other world leaders meeting to negotiate the final agreement, notably at the major summits in Copenhagen in 2009 and in Paris in 2015. Unlike in 1972 when the conference debated population, acid rain and other local or regional impacts, the attention on climate change has inevitably led to a focus on fossil fuels and the challenge of decarbonising the energy sector. The rising attention to these issues in international relations and in domestic politics translates into increased efforts to transform the energy systems.

If, and it is a big if, countries aggressively pursue the ambitions outlined at Paris in 2015 to limit the increase in global temperatures to 2°C or even 1.5°C, the result could be a profound reshaping of not just energy systems but of national economies and polities as well as of international relations and geopolitics, and even the relationship of citizens with the state. Liberal institutionalists would point to the growing adherence to international law and the potential benefits to firms and nations that are supported by evermore capable institutions. Constructivists would point to shifting norms and a growing environmental groundswell exacerbated by worsening weather-related disasters. These more optimistic views would be challenged, however, by dependency theorists sceptical of the potential to change the North–South dynamic and by realists who would challenge as unlikely any significant shift in existing power relationships, shifts necessary to achieve the dramatic move away from fossil fuels that is essential to meeting environmental goals.

2.5 REFERENCES

Ansolabehere, S. & Konisky, D.M. (2014). *Cheap and Clean: How Americans Think about Energy in the Age of Global Warming*. Cambridge, MA: MIT Press.

Ashby, E. & Anderson, M. (1981). *The Politics of Clean Air*. Oxford: Clarendon Press.

Barry, J. (1998). *Rethinking Green Politics: Nature, Virtue and Progress*. Sage.

Bernauer, T. & Koubi, V. (2009). Effects of Political Institutions on Air Quality. *Ecological Economics*, 68(5), 1355–1365.

Coates Ulrichsen, K. (2011). *Insecure Gulf: The End of Certainty and the Transition to the Post-Oil Era*. London: Hurst.

Crystal, J. (1990). *Oil and Politics in the Gulf: Rulers and Merchants in Kuwait and Qatar*. Cambridge: Cambridge University Press.

de Oliveira, R.S. (2007). *Oil and Politics in the Gulf of Guinea*. Columbia/Hurst.

Eckersley, R. (2004). The Green State: Rethinking Democracy and Sovereignty. Cambridge, MA: MIT Press.

Farhar, B.C., Unseld, C.T., Vories, R., Crews, R. (1980). Public Opinion about Energy. *Annual Review of Energy and Environment*, 5, 141–172.

Gillies, A. (2010). Reputational Concerns and the Emergence of Oil Sector Transparency as an International Norm. *International Studies Quarterly*, 54(1): 103–126.

Goodin, R.E. (2011). 'The State of the Discipline, the Discipline of the State' in R.E. Goodin, ed., *The Oxford Handbook of Political Science*, pp. 1–84.

Hird, J.A. (1990). Superfund Expenditures and Cleanup Priorities: Distributive Politics or the Public Interest? *Journal of Policy Analysis and Management*, 9: 455–483. doi:10.2307/3325258

Hughes, L. & Lipscy, P.Y. (2013). The Politics of Energy. *Annual Review of Political Science*, 16:1, 449–469.

Joskow, P.L. & Schmalensee, R. (1998). The Political Economy of Market-Based Environmental Policy: The U.S. Acid Rain Program. *Journal of Law and Economics* 41:1, 37–84.

Karl, T.L. (1997). *The Paradox of Plenty: Oil Booms and Petro-States*. Berkeley: University of California Press.

Keman, H. & Woldendorp, J.J. (Eds.) (2016). *Handbook of Research Methods and Applications in Political Science*. Edward Elgar Publishing.

Kennan, G.F. (1982). *Nuclear Delusion: Soviet-American Relations in the Atomic Age*. New York: Pantheon Books.

Keohane, R.O. (1978). The International Energy Agency: State Influence and Transgovernmental Politics. *International Organization*, 32(4): 929–951.

Lieberthal, K. & Oksenberg, M. (1986). Bureaucratic Politics and Chinese Energy Development, Washington, D.C.: US Department of Commerce, International Trade Administration.

Powell, R. (1991). Absolute and Relative Gains in International Relations Theory. *American Political Science Review*, 85(04), 1303–1320.

Ross, M.L. (2001). Does Oil Hinder Democracy? *World Politics*, 53(3), 325–361.

Victor, D.G., Jaffe, A.M., Hayes, M.H. (2006). *Natural Gas and Geopolitics: From 1970 to 2040*. Cambridge: Cambridge University Press.

Wendt, A. (1994). Collective Identity Formation and the International State. *American Political Science Review*, 88(2): 384–396.

3

Economics – The Proper Valuation of Security and Environment

David Newbery

3.1 INTRODUCTION

Environmental quality, and notably the global climate, are said to suffer from the 'tragedy of the commons' (Hardin, 1968) – what is owned by everyone is looked after by no one and the free market will fail to deliver the right environmental outcomes. Security as it applies to energy supplies is sometimes considered a *public good*, in that if the supply is made secure or reliable for one, it is reliable for all, and thus may be undersupplied by the free market. In both cases it is argued that there is a *market failure*. If we are to assess these claims and their implications for good energy policy, we need to probe more deeply into what economics has to say about markets, market failure and public goods, and the remedies that have been proposed.

Economics is justly proud of its contributions to the understanding of market equilibrium. In their definitive text on *General Competitive Analysis*, Arrow and Hahn (1971) open with the claim that 'There is by now a long and fairly imposing line of economists from Adam Smith to the present who have sought to show that a decentralised economy motivated by self-interest and guided by price signals could be compatible with a coherent disposition of economic resources that could be regarded, in a well-defined sense, as superior to a large class of alternative dispositions… it is important to know not only whether it is true, but also whether it could be true.'

The sense in which this general equilibrium is superior needs careful interpretation. A competitive equilibrium can be shown to be efficient (strictly, Pareto efficient) under restrictive assumptions: a complete set of markets, all agents have full information about all prices and there are no transactions costs. Pareto efficiency means there is no other feasible allocation of goods in which no one is worse off and at least one person is better off.[1] With additional assumptions on production

I am indebted to David Spiegelhalter for information about the health impacts of air pollution and to Marc Ozawa for helpful editing.

[1] A 'better off' alternative is one that would be preferred by the agent, revealed by a choice between the two alternatives.

technologies, Arrow and Debreu (1954) proved the existence of a competitive equilibrium, ensuring that the claims of competitive equilibrium are not vacuous.

3.2 THE ROLE AND LIMITATIONS OF COMPETITIVE MARKETS

Several points need to be made. The particular competitive equilibrium depends on the allocation of endowments – the wealth, assets, skills, abilities and labour power of the agents – and there is no ethical reason to suppose that the resulting equilibrium is just. A reallocation of endowments would clearly make some agents worse off, but taxes on the rich to finance health care for the many have been widely accepted as a step towards a more just society for most countries. The central theorem of welfare economics goes further, and argues that if these endowments could be costlessly reallocated, then different feasible equilibria could be generated, and, with some criterion for comparing them, the social optimum could then be supported as a competitive equilibrium. This would require the Benevolent Dictator to have perfect knowledge of all these endowments and then propose lump-sum taxes on, and transfers to, individuals. Lump sum means that the amounts are independent of any actions taken by those individuals, whereas in practice taxes have to be based on observable attributes (e.g., property ownership) or actions (e.g., earning income, buying goods) of agents and as such likely distort choices. High taxes on goods reduce their demand; high income taxes reduce effort, encourage emigration or distort activities in the pursuit of ways of avoiding or reducing those taxes.

Public economics is concerned with the informational and incentive problems of choosing tax and expenditure policies to reach the best feasible outcome – feasible in the sense of respecting both the constraints on resources and endowments, and the limits set by the information available to the tax authorities when levying taxes. Considerations of equity and fairness are hugely important in almost all policy questions, and certainly in the design of good energy policy. The fact that the authorities are ultimately answerable to the electorate means that popular concepts of fairness may dominate those guiding more philosophically inclined welfare economists.

One of the key theorems in public economics is that in the absence of market failures and externalities, indirect taxes (i.e., taxes levied on goods and services, in contrast to direct taxes levied on income) should fall on final consumers and not distort production (Diamond and Mirrlees, 1971).[2] A Value Added Tax on goods has this desirable property and is the recommended form of indirect taxation, to be supplemented by additional corrective taxes, discussed below. The force of these two theorems is that if market failures can be corrected, then the production side of the

[2] Strictly, there should be no pure profits or rents, or they should be taxed at 100 per cent, otherwise the production side of the economy impacts on incomes, and *may* provide an additional way of taxing final incomes not otherwise available through direct taxation. In a modern capitalist economy with an efficient direct tax system this is unlikely to be material.

economy can be left to the free market. Market failures (potential market power) associated with natural monopolies may need regulation that mimics the operation of a competitive market to deliver efficiency, provided the costs of regulation are less than the costs of the market failure. (A natural monopoly arises where the least-cost way of delivering a service is in a single firm, with the cost of supplying the service from more than one competing firm materially greater.)

Issues of equity and distributional justice are properly the subject of the tax and expenditure system (most redistribution derives from benefits such as health, education and pensions that are closer to equal for all, while most tax systems are roughly proportional, see e.g., Newbery, 1997). Under reasonable conditions indirect taxes should be uniform (Deaton and Stern, 1986) and so taxes on individual goods or sectors would not normally be appropriate vehicles for redistribution. That leaves the pursuit of efficiency at the sectoral level important in the very obvious sense that if a situation is inefficient, then in principle we could find a better alternative in which at least one person is better off and no one is worse off. Apart from envy, what is not to like with that? One objection might be that the person made better off becomes even more rich and powerful and would use that extra wealth to buy influence or subvert the polity, leading to others becoming worse off (which would include feelings of powerlessness or exploitation). Clearly in such cases the change would not be Pareto improving in the sense described above.

This principle of Pareto optimality is more useful than it might seem, for many regulatory changes are impeded because while they may lead to overall small gains, they often entail quite large individual gains and losses on participants. In the run-up to privatisation of the electricity sector in Britain in 1989, transmission charges were seen to be in need of reform to rebalance access charges across Britain, but were put in the 'too difficult' box and left for later adjustment, starting with a consultation in 1992. Access charges are intended to signal where new generation should locate (with low charges) and where not, because of high transmission losses or limited export capacity (signalled with high charges). Clearly, after entry there is no likelihood that a generator will move if the charges change, but as the pattern of demand changes (heavy industry closes in the north, server farms open in the south) and as technology encourages new entry (from gas and wind whose local availability differs from the old coal stations) so these charges need to be rebalanced. Charges in the north should rise and in the south fall, but this shifts huge sums from Scottish generating companies to English ones, and was effectively killed by political intervention.

The solution is to deem the original charges that guided the investment location decisions as long-term contracts to pay for the necessary grid reinforcements (amortised over, e.g., twenty-five years after which no further charges are payable and the access right can be sold on if the generator closes) and new connections have new charges reflecting current conditions. That way there need be no resistance from incumbents, and everyone could become better off.

However, the conditions for market outcomes to be efficient are not only strong – no market manipulation or market power – but not immediately apparent from the list above.

3.3 MARKET COMPLETENESS AND MISSING MARKETS

A complete set of markets means a market for every impact that affects well-being. A market for apples can provide my apple a day and keep the doctor away, but efficiency also needs a market for air quality, or a price on pollution, and markets may fail to exist for such services. When my factory for making widgets emits smoke, or my car emits nitrogen oxides (NO_x), I may not pay the cost of the damage that these inflict on others unless I am taxed, or required to meet optimal emission standards. The design of such taxes or standards represents a major area of economic analysis and policy discourse, and is a key concern of this chapter.

Many such goods are *public goods* in that once produced for one person, they can be made available to others at no additional cost. If I make a radio or TV programme and then broadcast it to you, that broadcast could in principle be made available to everyone within range at no extra cost. If it is an excludable public good, I can restrict access to those who subscribe by encrypting it, and as a result charge for it, but many such goods, such as lighthouses, are not easily excludable and may need to rely on voluntary subscription, or public provision.

Air pollution is a public bad in that sense, as victims cannot avoid their individual consequences by paying the polluter to reduce the pollution just to them and not to others in the locality. In such cases markets will either work imperfectly (for excludable public goods) or not at all, and other social mechanisms are needed. Pigou (1920) argued that producers will pursue their private interests, which, if they cause external damage ('externalities'), will not be aligned with the public interest ('social welfare'). The factory emitting smoke causes damage that harms its neighbours but, unless charged for that damage, will not take the cost-justified measures to reduce the damage. Similarly, beekeepers manage hives to produce honey and beeswax, but their bees provide valuable pollination services to orchards and farmers. Unless compensated, these beneficial externalities risk being undersupplied.

Pigou (1920) argued for a corrective 'Pigovian' tax on damaging actions, or a subsidy for beneficial externalities. These would correct the externality by aligning social and private costs and benefits and so internalise the externality. Producers would be incentivised to minimise all costs, for example, those from air pollutants and greenhouse gases, not just those paid for on markets. Producers of beneficial spillovers, such as the learning-by-doing from deploying immature renewable energy, could be compensated and thereby encouraged to produce their efficient level.

A fuller analysis indicates that there is a 'missing market' for the smoke, greenhouse gases or bee pollination services. Markets have two sides – a buyer who pays and a seller who charges for the good. Harmful externalities would require a negative price (i.e., a charge) on the emission of pollutants, and also a negative charge, i.e. a payment, to the 'buyer' (recipient) of the pollutant, compensating for the damage suffered. Specifically, the payment would equal the marginal cost of the damage caused by the last unit of pollution received (which for greenhouse gases may be distant in time and space).

Coase (1960) argued that Pigou had overlooked an important aspect of externalities, for if transaction costs were sufficiently low, the agent experiencing the externality (beneficial or harmful) would have an incentive to bargain with the agent producing that externality and reach a mutually better outcome. Almond orchards in California thus pay beekeepers to locate their hives in the orchard to ensure pollination,[3] and selling bee pollination services seems well established in many countries. Greenhouse gases may be taxed or priced on markets that have been created to rectify the missing market, e.g. via the EU Emissions Trading System.

Bilateral negotiations when both parties are well informed ought to lead to efficient outcomes, but a lack of information, threats, bluff and a sense of injustice can hamper that process. Economists have studied this in the *ultimatum game*, in which one player offers a division of a reward, which the other can either accept or reject, but if rejected neither gets anything. Experiments reveal that large deviations from a 50:50 split are deemed unfair and are often rejected, even though both parties would be better off agreeing (Henrich et al., 2004; Oosterbeek et al., 2004). If more than a few need to reach agreement and cannot agree on a leader to negotiate on their behalf, inefficiencies may again persist.

Society may agree to set up authorities or governments with powers to tax, charge, regulate, finance or provide the public good, as a solution to such coordination difficulties. A compromise between the Pigovian and Coasian approach that might improve on each was suggested by Farrell (1987), who noted that 'bumbling bureaucrats' might find it hard to determine the right corrective tax, while Coasian bargaining might fail to overcome transaction costs. The compromise is for the state to prescribe a reference or default standard and then allow agents to bargain away from that if mutually advantageous.

This principle of opening central decisions to contestability by private agents (in this case allowing subsequent bargaining) is useful in overcoming a variety of obstacles. In Britain, connections to the electricity distribution system are firm, in that once paid for, the holder has a right to deliver the contracted amount, and if the System Operator needs to curtail injections, the holder must be compensated for lost profit. The cost of providing that firm access, paid for by the generator, can be very high, and it may be much cheaper to use existing assets, but for a small fraction of the time to curtail injections. As a result of an interesting experiment (Anaya and Pollitt, 2015), the local distribution operator offered prospective wind farms the existing expensive connection option or a cheaper connection with guaranteed access for

3 See, e.g., www.pressreader.com/usa/porterville-recorder/20170213/281925952764811

varying levels (94 per cent or higher). The cheaper connection arrangements proved cost effective and in the subsequent conference discussion of the trials, the regulator, Ofgem, and the generating companies were asked if there were any obstacles preventing this arrangement – to which the answer was no.

3.4 CLIMATE CHANGE MITIGATION

Climate change 'is the greatest and widest-ranging market failure ever seen' (Stern, 2007), not only because its solution requires agreement among a large fraction of the world's nations, but they need to act now to prevent damage to future generations. While these future costs are uncertain, there is a very high probability that they greatly exceed the costs of efficient and coordinated mitigation. In one sense the market failure is simple – greenhouse gases (GHGs) are global stock pollutants, meaning that the damage done is the same wherever they are released, and GHGs persist for centuries. Indeed, the timescale for some impacts such as ocean warming is millennia; although at the other extreme arctic sea ice may disappear within decades. That suggests that a single price at each date regardless of the source of the release is sufficient to address the problem. Furthermore, a large fraction of GHGs come from burning carbon, and so taxing the carbon content of the fuel would be the simplest solution. Carbon capture and storage could then be credited with the carbon sequestered. Other GHGs and agriculture admittedly pose more difficult monitoring issues. However, only a few Nordic countries (with no coal) have to date imposed carbon taxes on fuels, with the exception of Britain and its Carbon Price Support discussed below.

The problem is not the lack of an adequate policy measure, but rather that GHGs are either not priced at all or are subject to very low prices per tonne of CO_{2e} (Dolphin et al., 2016). Indeed these actual carbon prices are low relative to any plausible estimate of the marginal damage done (as computed by EPA, 2016 or Stern, 2007).

The fact that GHGs are persistent stock pollutants has a number of implications – the social cost of carbon (GHGs are measured by their carbon or CO_2 equivalent, CO_{2e}) depends not on the rate of release but on the total stock, which only changes slowly with emissions. That means that the social cost of carbon (measuring its damage) should not vary much with emissions, but only with the stock (and new information about future damage). In addition, actions to mitigate climate damage have to persist over long periods of time, and policies therefore may be slow to deliver the perceptible changes that an impatient public demands. The difficulty of action is exacerbated as the source of most of the problem, burning fossil fuels, takes place in highly durable equipment whose stock takes a long time to replace. Coal-fired power stations built now will likely last fifty to sixty years, while inefficient housing stock may only be replaced 1 per cent or less per year in advanced countries. Another implication of a stock pollutant with a low rate of absorption is that the cost of the damage done (the social cost of carbon) will increase over time at the social discount rate as the date of future harm approaches. One of the better aspects of a 'cap-and-trade' system of auctioning allowances to emit that can be banked is that their price will rise at the rate of interest, as a result of arbitrage – if their price is expected to rise faster than the cost of borrowing money, agents will borrow and buy allowances now, driving up their present price, while if not, agents will sell, bank the cash and wait until allowances are cheaper than their accumulated savings.

In terms of global agreement, 142 of the 197 Parties to the Convention on Climate Change (COP 21) had ratified by 5 October 2016, and hence the threshold for entry into force of the Paris Agreement was achieved.[4] However, the agreement is voluntary, and currently falls far short of delivering sufficient, credible and binding agreements to take adequate action. Quite apart from the difficulty of reaching such a commitment, there is the difficult of determining a suitable price for carbon. Stern (2007) and the EPA (2016) both point out that the social cost of carbon today depends critically on three hard-to-measure parameters. The first is the social discount rate, where figures between about 1 per cent and 5 per cent have been proposed (e.g., Nordhaus, 2007). If damage can occur a century from now, the present value of £1 million 100 years hence discounting at 5 per cent is only £7,600, but discounting at 1 per cent is £370,000, nearly fifty times as large and justifying substantially more current investment in mitigation. Second, the economic and social magnitude of the potential future damage is even harder to assess. More severe floods and crop failures are almost inevitable, but their implications for death, diseases, war and mass migration are far less certain, but certainly possible and definitely very costly. Finally, there is the problematic ethics of weighing future impacts against the yardstick of current money (needed to assess the value of mitigation), even if we could predict how many future people would suffer how much equivalent loss in consumption or life expectancy.

One simple and rather naïve approach is to assume that lives are equally valuable in a utilitarian sense, which has the implication that £1 reduction to a person enjoying a level c of consumption is worth n times as much as £1 reduction to a person enjoying nc consumption. This in turn has the implication that the social discount rate is just the rate of growth of consumption per head plus a small addition for the possibility of extinction, which is the way Stern (2007) came up with an estimate of 1.4 per cent. Others, notably Weitzman (1998) and Gollier & Weitzman (2010) have correctly argued that this simple rule only applies if all consumption grows at the same rate, and if, plausibly, some experience far worse futures, or if there are small risks of catastrophic outcomes, then the social discount rate should be considerably reduced.

Economists have made other important contributions to the understanding of policy choices for climate change mitigation, apart from the extensive, welfare-economics

4 See http://unfccc.int/paris_agreement/items/9444.php. However, the future status of the United States under President Trump remains a major concern.

based analysis of the social cost of carbon. A carbon price can be either delivered by fixing the quantity (the cap) and then trading, as in the EU Emissions Trading System (ETS) (2003/87/EC), or fixing the price through some form of carbon tax or charge, such as the Carbon Price Support introduced in the 2011 UK Budget (HMT, 2011). The classic argument for setting a carbon price is based on Weitzman (1974), who noted that in the face of uncertainty, a price instrument (tax or charge) dominates a quantity instrument (a cap or quota) if the marginal benefit of reducing emissions is flatter (i.e., changes less rapidly with emissions) than the marginal cost of abatement schedule. The marginal damage of a tonne of CO_2 now is essentially the same as a tonne emitted in ten years' time, as CO_2 is resident in the atmosphere and oceans for a century or more. Thus the marginal benefit of abatement (which is the marginal cost of damage) is essentially flat (i.e., constant) in the *rate* of emissions, even if the marginal damage is steeply increasing in the *stock* of emissions (Grubb & Newbery, 2008). In contrast the marginal cost of abatement increases rapidly as the low-hanging fruit is plucked early and it becomes increasingly costly to find additional sources of abatement.

Weitzman's original result was derived from a one-period model with uncertainty resolved immediately after abatement choices, and so only suitable for flow, not stock pollutants. Persistent stock pollutants like GHG should properly be studied in a many-period model in which actions (like emissions, or investment in abatement) continue to have impacts in subsequent periods. One-period models and their results may be suitable for addressing short-run operating decisions of existing capacity (whether to run coal or gas-fired plant more intensively), but are not well suited to investment decisions in highly durable capacity. Nuclear and coal power stations have a life of sixty-plus years, even if gas-fired plant and wind turbines have shorter (twenty-plus) year lives, periods that commit to significant lock-in of cumulative emissions and hence a lock-in to a higher and more damaging stock of greenhouse gases (GHGs).

To deal with these lock-in and stock effects, one needs an intertemporal model in which damage depends on the stock of pollutant, not the flow. Newbery (2016) summarises the research done to demonstrate that Weitzman's original argument in favour of taxes rather than quotas remains robust. The evidence of the EU ETS supports this, for after its launch in 2005, the EU Allowance price shown in Fig.1 rose rapidly to nearly €30/tonne CO_2, before collapsing to zero by December, 2007, the end of the first period. Second-period prices similarly rose to €30/tonne CO_2, before collapsing as a result of increased targets for renewable energy and the global financial crisis.

Clearly, the ETS carbon price is neither adequate, credible nor durable, and a poor guide for durable investment decisions in generation. So why, given persuasive arguments, do most jurisdictions choose quotas like the ETS rather than taxes? The simple and persuasive explanation is that quotas can be handed out to the emitting companies, who would otherwise effectively block any attempt

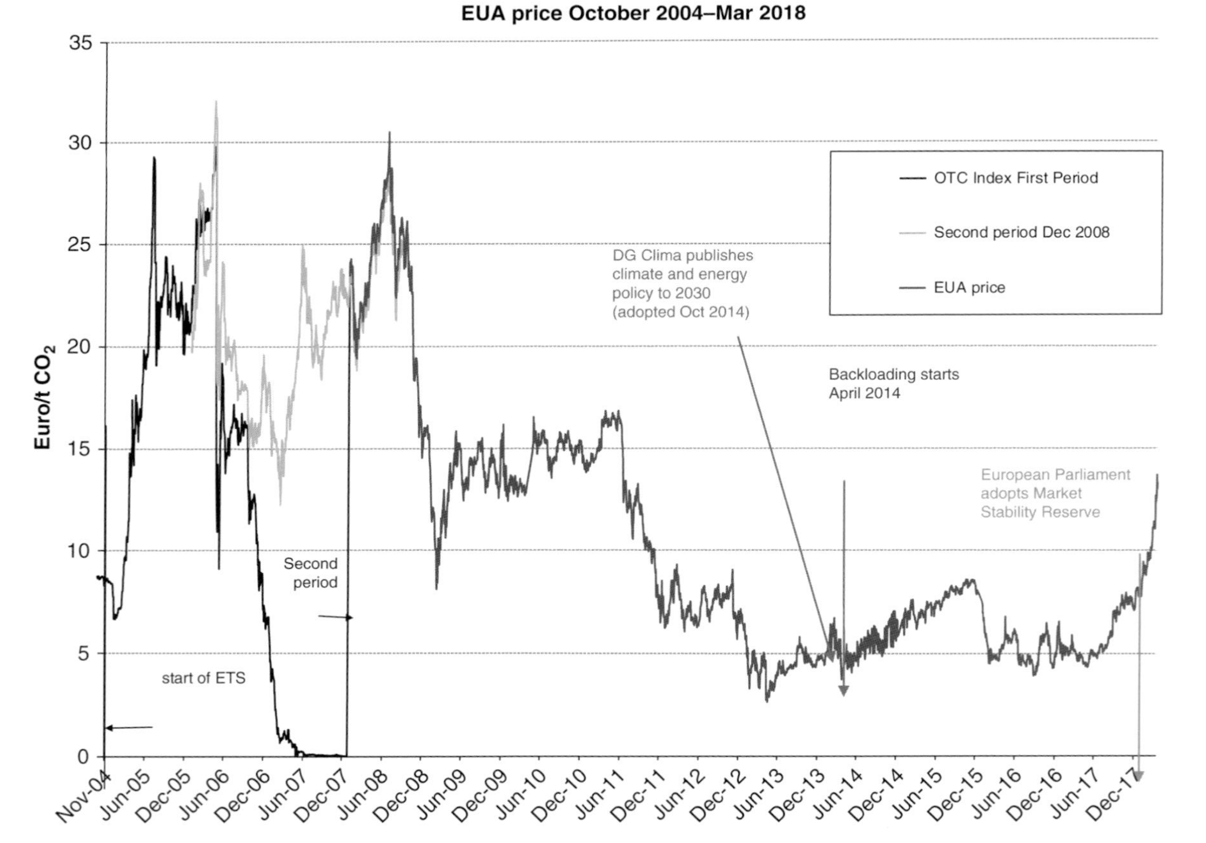

FIGURE 3.1 The EU Allowance (EUA) price for CO_2 in the EU Emissions Trading System
Source: EEX

to tax their emissions, while the voting public, observing such free allocations, believes that they will therefore not increase the prices of the products of the emitting industries. In the case of electricity, the Emissions Allowance Price was immediately added to the cost of generating from fossil fuels, as the allowances had an opportunity cost – they could be sold if not used. The estimated impact of a €20/tonne EUA price on generating company profits in Belgium, France, Germany and The Netherlands varies between €5–13.5 billion per year (Sijm et al., 2006).[5] Fortunately, the EU moved to auctioning permits for the power sector in 2012, so that at least the revenues were available and could be used to subsidise e.g., renewable energy, where subsidies are an efficient (Pigovian) compensation for learning spillovers (Newbery, 2017, 2018).

3.5 SECURITY

Security of energy supply ranks almost at the top of the policy agenda – if the lights go out, oil supplies run short or gas deliveries are threatened, widespread popular discontent will be visited upon policymakers and politicians. Whether there is a market failure is less clear, as if prices are allowed to rise when supplies are scarce, investments in storage and spare capacity could in principle balance the cost of increasing security against the benefit of avoiding the more extreme scarcities. However, the required price rises may be almost as unpopular, and investors may suspect that price rises will be restrained, removing the incentive to improve security. Again, this can be viewed as a problem of missing markets, in this case missing futures and risk or insurance markets in which consumers can buy insurance against shortages, and producers can invest to satisfy those future needs. This may work well in some markets (oil is at least in some countries left to market forces, although the IEA requires governments to hold ninety days of stocks). In other cases, notably electricity, governments have been sceptical that adequate capacity to avoid shortages will be delivered in time, and run capacity auctions to procure the required reserves.

It was suggested in the opening paragraph that some consider reliability as a public good, but for gas and electricity, large consumers can and do sign interruptible contracts that require them to reduce demand when asked, if they are not willing to pay for extra reliability. In a future where everyone has a smart meter that can control which appliances are switched off in response to spot prices, one can imagine consumers indicating how much they were willing to pay for varying levels of supply, the most essential (lighting) with the higher value, time-shiftable appliances with the lowest. This expressed willingness to pay for reliability could be aggregated into a demand for reliability in an auction for capacity, much like the

5 This is based on simulations with the COMPETES model, with the lower values assuming market power and higher demand elasticities.

current British capacity auction, but with consumers determining demand rather than administrators. The auctioned contracts are a remedy for the missing futures and risk markets that cause the original concerns.

3.6 CONCLUSIONS

Economists are sometimes accused of being market fundamentalists, of wishing to get the government out of the marketplace and not caring for the social and distributional impacts that markets may deliver. This chapter attempts to correct that misperception. First, in public finance – and in policy areas in general – instruments are needed that are well targeted to deliver objectives. Intervening in markets is almost always less effective at delivering distributional justice than are more direct methods, targeted public expenditures such as health care, unemployment insurance, pensions and direct taxation. That leaves markets to be corrected for market failures, not as mechanisms for addressing poverty.

There are exceptions to this rule, in that in an imperfect world of Manifesto pledges and the difficulties facing any type of tax reform, intervening in particular markets may be 'third-best' ways of addressing public concerns – hence governments may ask regulators to address fuel poverty rather than addressing it themselves. Indeed, natural monopolies such as transmission and distribution (wires and pipes), by definition are cheaper to provide through one (regional) company than many competitive companies, and a direct implication of that is that their efficient price will not cover their full cost. The balance is collected by regulated tariffs, and is akin to a tax, and it is quite appropriate to consider the distributional impacts of such charges, while, as with all public finance decisions, balancing equity gains against efficiency losses.

Economists do indeed have a well-developed theory of what a competitive market can and cannot achieve – under restrictive conditions (market completeness) it can deliver efficiency, but even then it cannot unaided deliver distributional justice or equity. The concept of market completeness is extremely helpful in designing policies that attempt to remedy market failures, which are pervasive for environmental goods and in energy markets. Policies can also fail, as policymakers often lack the information necessary to effect favourable interventions, and it may be better to define property rights (e.g., in carbon emissions) and use auctions or markets to properly price these rights. The same is true for the delivery of reliability, where auctions have proven more cost effective than bureaucratically determined capacity payments.

3.7 REFERENCES

Anaya, K.L. and Pollitt, M.G., 2015. 'Options for Allocating and Releasing Distribution System Capacity: Deciding between Interruptible Connections and Firm DG Connections', *Applied Energy*, 144, 96–105. DOI:10.1016/j.apenergy.2015.01.043

Arrow, K.J. and Debreu, G., 1954. 'Existence of Equilibrium for a Competitive Economy', *Econometrica*, 22, 265–290.

Arrow, K.J. and Hahn, F.H., 1971. *General Competitive Analysis*. Holden-Day.

Coase, R. H., 1960. 'The Problem of Social Cost', *The Journal of Law & Economics*, 3, 1–44.

Deaton, A. and Stern, N.H., 1986. 'Optimally Uniform Commodity Taxes, Taste Differences and Lump-Sum Grants', *Economics Letters*, 20, 263–266.

Diamond, P.A. and Mirrlees, J.A., 1971. 'Optimal Taxation and Public Production, Part 1. Production Efficiency', *American Economic Review*, 611, 8–27.

Dolphin, G., Pollitt, M., and Newbery, D., 2016. 'The Political Economy of Carbon Pricing: A Panel Analysis', EPRG 1627, at www.eprg.group.cam.ac.uk/wp-content/uploads/2016/11/1627-Text.pdf.

EPA. 2016. *Technical Update of the Social Cost of Carbon for Regulatory Impact Analysis Under Executive Order 12866*, US Environmental Protection Agency, at www.epa.gov/sites/production/files/2016-12/documents/sc_co2_tsd_august_2016.pdf.

Farrell, J., 1987. 'Information and the Coase Theorem', *Journal of Economic Perspectives*, 1(2), 113–129.

Gollier, C. and Weitzman, M.L., 2010. 'How Should the Distant Future Be Discounted When Discount Rates Are Uncertain?', *Econ Lett* 107(3): 350–335.

Grubb, M.G. and Newbery, D.M., 2008. 'Pricing Carbon for Electricity Generation: National and International Dimensions', ch. 11, pp. 278–313 in *Delivering a Low Carbon Electricity System: Technologies, Economics and Policy*, M. Grubb, T. Jamasb, M. Pollitt (eds.). Cambridge University Press.

Hardin, G., 1968. 'The Tragedy of the Commons', *Science*, 162, Issue 3859, 1243–1248. DOI:10.1126/science.162.3859.1243

Henrich, J., Boyd, R., Bowles, S., Camerer, C., Fehr, E., and Gintis, H. (2004). *Foundations of Human Sociality: Economic Experiments and Ethnographic Evidence from Fifteen Small-Scale Societies*. Oxford University Press.

HMT, 2011. *Budget 2011*, Stationary Office, HC 836, at http://webarchive.nationalarchives.gov.uk/20130105112918/http://cdn.hm-treasury.gov.uk/2011budget_complete.pdf.

Newbery, D.M., 1997. 'Optimal Tax Rates and Tax Design during Systemic Reform', *Journal of Public Economics*, 63(2), 177–206.

Newbery, D.M., 2016. 'Policies for decarbonizing a liberalized power sector', *Economics: the Open-Access, Open-Assessment E-Journal*, 12 (2018–40). http://dx.doi.org/10.5018/economics-ejournal.ja.2018-40.

Newbery, D., 2018. Evaluating the case for supporting renewable electricity, *Energy Policy*, 120, 684–696. https://doi.org/10.1016/j.enpol.2018.05.029.

Newbery, D.M., 2018. 'What Future(s) for Liberalized Electricity Markets: Efficient, Equitable or Innovative?' *The Energy Journal*, 39(1), 1–27. DOI:https://doi.org/10.5547/01956574.39.1.dnew

Nordhaus, W.D., 2007. 'A Review of the "Stern Review on the Economics of Climate Change"', *Journal of Economic Literature*, 45(3), 686–702, at www.jstor.org/stable/27646843.

Oosterbeek, H., Sloof, R., and Kuilen, G. V. D., 2004. 'Cultural Differences in Ultimatum Game Experiments: Evidence from a Meta-Analysis'. *Experimental Economics*, 7(2): 171–188. DOI:10.1023/B:EXEC.0000026978.14316.74

Pigou, A.C., 1920. *The Economics of Welfare*. Macmillan and Co.

Sijm, J., Neuhoff, K., and Chen, Y., 2006. 'CO2 Cost Pass-through and Windfall Profits in the Power Sector', *Climate Policy*, 6(1), 49–72. DOI:10.1080/14693062.2006.9685588

Stern, N., 2007. *The Economics of Climate Change: The Stern Review*. Cambridge University Press.

Weitzman, M., 1974. 'Prices vs Quantities', *Review of Economic Studies* 41, 477–491.

Weitzman, M., 1998. 'Why the Far-Distant Future Should Be Discounted at Its Lowest Possible Rate', *Journal of Environmental Economics and Management*, 36(3): 201–208. DOI:https://doi.org/10.1006/jeem.1998.1052.

Weitzman, M., 2012. 'The Ramsey Discounting Formula for a Hidden-State Stochastic Growth Process', *Journal of Environmental and Resource Economics*, 53(3): 309–321.

4

Good Energy: Philosophical Perspectives

Tim Lewens

4.1 GOOD OUTCOMES AND GOOD PROCESSES

This chapter sketches some of the ways in which philosophy, and its various subbranches, illuminate good energy policy. Philosophy's most obvious promise is to give direct answers to questions about which policies we should adopt; questions such as, 'what, exactly, does an equitable energy policy look like?' or 'what weight should energy policy give to the interests of future people, compared to the interests of people alive today?'.

In addition to giving direct responses to questions about the content of specific energy policies, philosophy can also shine a light on the deliberative processes by which policy should be crafted. In this mode we might ask whether policy formulation should rest entirely in the hands of technical experts – and whether it is expertise in natural sciences, engineering, economics, sociology or philosophy itself that counts most – or whether instead various laypeople should have input. Alternatively, we might ask what it means to craft energy policy in a 'precautionary' manner, and whether there is a coherent and valuable interpretation of the 'precautionary principle' that might guide the process of policy formation. Philosophy's contributions to these process-oriented topics are rather less obvious – but perhaps of more immediate practical value – than those made to outcome-oriented issues. Consequently, this overview concentrates more on energy policy process than on outcome.

Needless to say, this short overview can give only a superficial sketch of a subset of philosophy's contributions: important topics for energy policy that are not addressed here include the strengths and limitations of efforts to approach complex and multifaceted policy decisions using quantitative frameworks, the issue of how we should understand and measure the well-being of people affected by energy policies, and a host of vital questions about the implications for privacy and governance of new methods of collecting and analysing data relating to individual energy usage.[1]

[1] For various relevant analyses, see Sunstein, C. (2002) *The Cost Benefit State*. American Bar Association; articles in Lewens, T., ed. (2007) *Risk: Philosophical Perspectives*. London: Routledge; A. Alexandrova

Before proceeding further, it is also important to stress that philosophical analysis should devote at least as much time to exploring scientific and ethical cases for the pursuit of new energy opportunities as it dedicates to placing ethical brakes on these developments. For example, in addition to using human rights and environmental values to place *constraints* on energy use and production, we must also attend to the *positive* cases to be made in favour of developing new approaches to energy extraction, via their potentially beneficial effects on future generations, precarious communities and endangered habitats.[2]

4.2 GOOD OUTCOMES

4.2.1 *Energy Justice*

The production and consumption of energy inevitably raise questions about justice of the sort that have interested philosophers for several decades.[3] Such questions arise in the global context as well as at the local level and include, for example, making decisions about siting new power-generating facilities; considering the effects of energy consumption on climate change; and assessing the impact of biofuels on the workers who cultivate them. In each of these cases, we must trade off the welfare of one population – which might be augmented by the energy deriving from nuclear power, by the unrestrained use of energy in facilitating valuable activities, or by the widespread availability of bioethanol – against the welfare of different, sometimes overlapping, populations that might be harmed – or at least exposed to risk of harm – by a potentially unsafe nuclear facility, by rising sea levels, or by the arduous process of cutting sugar cane.[4]

In practice, more or less all commentators agree that there are limits on the extent to which concern for aggregate welfare justifies subjecting subgroups to disadvantage. But exactly what form these constraints take is by no means agreed upon. Amartya Sen expresses this predicament by suggesting that while theorists of justice agree on equal treatment for all in some sense or another, there is little agreement on how this equal treatment is to be interpreted.[5] A minimalist libertarian framework might understand equal treatment for all in terms of universal respect for individual

(2017) A *Philosophy for the Science of Wellbeing*. Oxford: Oxford University Press; S. Leonelli (2016) *Data-Centric Biology*. Chicago: University of Chicago Press; Nuffield Council on Bioethics (2015) *The Collection, Linking and Use of Data in Biomedical Research and Health Care: Ethical Issues*. London: Nuffield Council on Bioethics.

2 For a valuable discussion of many of these issues in the context of biotechnology policy, see Nuffield Council on Bioethics (2012) *Emerging Biotechnologies*. London: Nuffield Council on Bioethics.

3 See, e.g., Rawls, J. (1971), *A Theory of Justice*. Oxford: Oxford University Press; Dworkin, R. (1981), 'What Is Equality? Part Two: Equality of Resources', in *Philosophy and Public Affairs* 10: 283–345; Roemer, J. (1996), *Theories of Distributive Justice*. Cambridge, MA: Harvard University Press.

4 For details of the biofuels case, see Nuffield Council on Bioethics (2011) *Biofuels: Ethical Issues*. London: Nuffield Council on Bioethics.

5 Sen, A. (1995), *Inequality Re-examined*. Oxford: Oxford University Press.

rights to property. According to the libertarian, the free exchange of property can then result in massive inequalities of resources that are not unjust.[6] More demanding liberal frameworks that advocate redistribution of wealth and other goods from the rich to the poor also differ from each other in considerable ways. Some suggest that all should have equal resources, some require equal well-being and some require equal opportunities. Finally, some frameworks insist that we ensure that everyone can obtain a basic, minimum amount of resources, well-being or opportunity, not that everyone be strictly equal in these respects.

4.2.2 *Future Generations*

Decisions made – or dodged, or delayed – about energy policy do not affect only people alive today. The courses that we set for the reduction or preservation of biodiversity, or for the diminution or persistence of greenhouse gas emissions, have significant repercussions for future generations as yet unborn. In weighing their interests, policymakers often make use of what is called 'discounting'. They give less and less weight to costs and benefits falling on individuals, as those individuals recede further into the future. The question of how, if at all, we can justify discounting is an interesting philosophical one: it requires that we explain why temporal distance is more relevant than spatial distance when it comes to assessing value.[7] The obvious fact that individuals of the future cannot be present to argue their cases, and to highlight relevant features of their situations, further complicates the issue of how to take their interests into account. Without some means of keeping their needs in the foreground, and engaging in an imaginative way with their plausible predicaments, it is likely that they will not receive fair treatment.

4.2.3 *Non-identity*

Our policy decisions do not merely affect what sort of a world these future people will live in, and what decisions they will have to take: Derek Parfit has argued that decisions taken now also affect which future people will exist. To give just one example, decisions regarding large-scale transport policy have knock-on impacts on the global distribution of people, hence on who ends up having babies with whom, and ultimately on which of the infinitely many possible future people are the ones who will in fact populate the world 150 years from now.[8]

Parfit's observation raises problems for how we assess the long-run impact of energy policy. Suppose that in 2170 there will be an individual named Sabbir, living

6 Nozick, R. (1974), *Anarchy, State and Utopia*. New York: Basic Books.

7 See, e.g., Cowen, T. and D. Parfit (1992) 'Against the Social Discount Rate' in P. Laslett and J. Fishkin (eds.) *Justice between Age Groups and Generations*. New Haven: Yale University Press.

8 Parfit, D. (1984), *Reasons and Persons*. Oxford: Oxford University Press. For discussion, see Lewens, T. (2015), *Biological Foundations of Bioethics*. Oxford: Oxford University Press, Chapter 6.

in Dhaka and struggling in a country ravaged by climate change. Parfit conjectures that had we instituted different energy policies that were more beneficial to Bangladesh, we would not have found Sabbir's life any better. Instead (by virtue of our policies' eventual impacts on who has children with whom, and how many children they have), Sabbir would almost certainly not have existed, and Dhaka would have been populated by different people altogether.

Parfit concludes that we cannot use any familiar notion of harm to persons when we assess the long-run impacts of energy policy, and of other policies with similar effects on which people come to exist. It is by no means clear what notion of harm we should use instead. For example, a focus on overall aggregate well-being might lead us to favour policies that produce future people with lives barely worth living, so long as they exist in large enough numbers for their combined welfare to outweigh situations in which fewer, better-off people exist. A focus on average well-being might instead lead us to favour a policy that produces just a handful of individuals, all exceptionally well off.

4.2.4 *Comparing Consequences*

Finally, energy policy raises a series of questions about how we should assess policy decisions when their impacts range over very different types of consequences. In the case of cultivating crops for use in biofuels, for example, we need to consider potential impacts on greenhouse gas emissions, on biodiversity, on the availability of food, on ways of life associated with the cultivation of more traditional crops and so forth.[9] It is hard to know how we are supposed to come to an all-things-considered assessment of a new form of energy production when it has positive impacts in one domain, and negative impacts in another. This assessment is rendered more complex when we introduce uncertainties not just about how to compare the values associated with these impacts, but about the chances of these various outcomes coming to pass.[10]

There is unlikely to be any consensus soon on the complex questions outlined in this section. One option for dealing with all of these energy uncertainties – about the demands of justice and the proper understanding of equality, about our duties to future generations and our methods for understanding harm to future persons, about the relative values of vastly different forms of outcome – would be to press ahead nonetheless in the hope that eventually we will develop a well-defended basic philosophical stance that gives us direct answers to all of these questions. A different strategy, favoured by several philosophical commentators, does not seek to reduce these uncertainties in such a direct manner. Instead, it suggests that good answers to complex questions like these are those that derive from good processes of

9 Nuffield Council on Bioethics (2011) *Biofuels: Ethical Issues*. London: Nuffield Council on Bioethics.

10 See Peterson, M. (2007), 'On Multi-Attribute Risk Analysis' in Lewens, T. (ed.), *Risk: Philosophical Perspectives*. London: Routledge.

deliberation.[11] In this view, it is suitably structured deliberation itself that makes a stance on the comparison of values, or the interests of future generations, a rational and defensible one. It is to these process-oriented issues that we now turn.

4.3 GOOD PROCESSES

4.3.1 *The Role of Experts*

In 2012 the Royal Society and the Royal Academy of Engineering produced a joint report on hydraulic fracturing, a technique for the extraction of shale gas that is more often known under the notorious name of 'fracking'. In the summary notes at the beginning of the report, the authors note what they have, and have not done.[12] They *have* 'analysed the technical aspects of the environmental, health and safety risks associated with shale gas extraction to inform decision making'. They have *not* looked into what they call 'public acceptability' of these risks, although they note that research into this domain will be beneficial. Moreover, they have not 'attempted to determine whether shale gas extraction should go ahead', which the report views as 'the responsibility of the Government'.[13]

Taken together, these comments suggest the following rough picture of how policy decisions should be made about fracking. First, we have a series of 'technical' questions about risk, best addressed by experts with training in the natural sciences and engineering. These experts can tell us the facts about risks from fracking. Such facts do not mandate any particular course of action with respect to policy, but knowledge of them is essential if the people making policy decisions are to be well-informed. Second, there is a set of questions about which risks relating to fracking the public may be prepared to shoulder. Finally, the government is the body with responsibility for coming to a policy decision, perhaps by combining insights about technical risks with insights about what the electorate will, and will not, tolerate.

Several elements of this general image are defensible. It is true, for example, that in many Western democracies government ministers, rather than technical advisers, have final responsibility for policy decisions. It is also true that these ministers are influenced by what they think their electorates will tolerate, and that opinion sampling can thereby be of use to them in their deliberations. But this image of the policymaking process also involves considerable simplification: it is obvious, for example, that 'the public' is a highly heterogeneous collection of people, that

11 For an example of this kind of approach in the medical context, see Daniels, N. and Sabin, J. (2002) *Setting Limits Fairly: Can we Learn to Share Medical Resources?* Oxford: Oxford University Press.

12 Royal Society/Royal Academy of Engineering (2012) *Shale Gas Extraction in the UK: A Review of Hydraulic Fracturing*. London: Royal Society/Royal Academy of Engineering.

13 Ibid., 5.

different individuals tolerate and trade off risks in very different ways and that scientists themselves also differ in how they evaluate risks.[14]

We should also not assume that scientists and engineers make purely factual recommendations which are wholly devoid of the evaluative considerations that influence various public reactions to new technology. As we will now see, it would be a mistake to suppose that values only enter into debates about energy risks *after* the facts about risk have been established by dispassionate scientific experts, and that these values only need to be considered when we ask whether the public can stomach the decisions these facts point towards.[15]

4.3.2 *Inductive Risk*

This last point has been a recurrent theme in philosophical work on the question of whether science is 'value laden'. Heather Douglas has recently revived and strengthened an argument originally put forward by Richard Rudner, which purports to show that all scientists – and a fortiori the scientists and engineers who contribute to reports such as the one on fracking – must make value judgements if they are to act in a responsible and helpful manner.[16] This survey gives special attention to this issue, because the stance we take on it is especially likely to influence the practical detail of how we manage and respond to the policymaking process.

Douglas's version of the 'argument from inductive risk' begins with the banal observation that scientists' empirical claims are never infallible. Assertions about, for example, the impact of fracking on seismic events, are always based on extrapolation from potentially unrealistic geological model systems, on limited historical data that may not be representative of new sites, and so forth. The joint Royal Society/Royal Academy of Engineering report openly acknowledges the difficulties associated with coming to reliable conclusions about induced seismicity from fracking.[17]

In general, if one is attempting to come to a firm conclusion based on shaky evidence, one needs to consider the costs of error. To begin with a gross oversimplification, suppose the joint academies had been charged with telling the UK government in a yes/no manner whether fracking was safe enough to be permitted throughout the UK. Neither answer can be given with certainty: if they erroneously report that fracking is not safe when in fact it is, then this results in considerable costs in terms of lost jobs, a lost source of useful energy and so forth. If, on the other hand,

[14] The very significant degree of uncertainty in risk estimations is stressed by Kristin Shrader-Frechette in the nuclear power context. See, e.g., Shrader-Frechette, K. (1991), *Risk and Rationality*. Berkeley, CA: University of California Press.

[15] For a recent exploration of these themes as they play out in environmental policy, see Owens, S. (2015) *Knowledge, Policy and Expertise*. Oxford: Oxford University Press.

[16] Douglas, H. (2009), *Science, Policy and the Value-Free Ideal*. Pittsburgh, PA: University of Pittsburgh Press; Rudner, R. (1953), 'The Scientist qua Scientist Makes Value Judgments' *Philosophy of Science* 20: 1–6.

[17] *Shale Gas Extraction in the UK*.

they erroneously report that fracking is safe when it is not, then this decision also brings considerable costs in terms of dangers to employees and residents near fracking sites.

Whether these scientists should offer a yes or no answer to questions relating to safety depends not only on the strength of the evidence, but also on the relative moral values they accord to opening up new sources of energy, to the provision of local economic stimulus, to ensuring the safety of workers and residents, and so forth. Douglas suggests that scientists cannot avoid taking stances – either implicitly or explicitly – about the value of these outcomes, and that it is entirely proper that they should give active consideration to these evaluative questions.

One response to Douglas, suggested by several commentators, claims that her argument for the value-ladenness of scientific claims fails once we remove our simplifying assumption that scientific advisors need to give simple yes/no answers to equally simple questions such as 'Will fracking damage environments?'. Instead, scientists can report the uncertainties associated with drawing strong conclusions, and can offer value-neutral statements of likely fact that are framed in probabilistic terms.[18] The joint societies' report does not come to any yes/no conclusion about the safety of fracking. Instead, it considers matters risk by risk, and offers hedged conclusions that describe these risks using qualitative estimations. To give just one example, the report mentions that 'Concerns have been raised about the risk of fractures propagating from shale formations to reach overlying aquifers. The available evidence indicates that *this risk is very low* provided that shale gas extraction takes place at depths of many hundreds of metres or several kilometres.'[19] Moreover, large sections of the report are devoted to drawing attention to the limited body of evidence available, to the need to gather more data about risk, and to recommending strategies for mitigating risk.

Our simplifying assumption about how experts report on risks associated with energy technologies is substantial. Even so, pointing out this simplification does not suffice to dismiss Douglas's underlying argument. Douglas takes the view that a decision to report the probability of an outcome as, for example, 'very low', is also a fallible one, and that it, too, can only be arrived at when the costs of error are considered.[20]

Stephen John boosts Douglas's original argument further by drawing our attention to the evidence base upon which these reports rest.[21] His own illustrative case comes from another domain intimately bound up with energy policy, namely the regular 'Assessment Reports' published by the Intergovernmental Panel on Climate

18 For a recent version of this response, see Betz, G. (2013), 'In Defence of the Value Free Ideal' *European Journal for Philosophy of Science* 3: 207–220.

19 *Shale Gas Extraction in the UK*, 4 (emphasis added).

20 *Science, Policy and the Value-Free Ideal*. See also Steele, K. (2012), 'The Scientist qua Policy Advisor Makes Value Judgments' *Philosophy of Science* 79: 893–904.

21 John, S. (2015), 'The Example of the IPCC does not vindicate the Value Free Ideal: A Reply to Gregor Betz' *European Journal for Philosophy of Science* 5: 1–13.

Change (IPCC). These reports are meant to give policymakers around the world a summary of 'the state of the scientific, technical and socio-economic knowledge on climate change'. This means that the scientists who compile these reports must decide which pieces of potential evidence to draw on in providing their overall synthesis. The IPCC's policy on this matter is that 'priority is given to peer-reviewed scientific, technical and socio-economic literature'. This policy has the obvious attraction of increasing the chances that only well-validated data and analyses inform the reports. But relying solely on peer review is not an unequivocal good; non-peer-reviewed studies may also contain vital pieces of information. We need to consider the costs of scientific editorial policies if they sometimes prevent access to information essential for timely action. Once again, values intrude.

This is not a mere abstract possibility. John draws on sociological work by O'Reilly et al., which looked at the IPCC's handling of data about the Western Antarctic Ice Sheet (WAIS) to illustrate his concerns.[22] Back in 2001 when it published its Third Assessment Report, the IPCC claimed that there was no risk of the ice sheet collapsing before 2100. Only six years later, when its fourth report was published in 2007, this verdict was overturned and the IPCC noted that the WAIS might already be collapsing. In spite of this, the fourth report made no effort to quantify probable rates of ice loss from the collapsing WAIS, and as a consequence the contribution of the WAIS was not included in IPCC estimates of future increases in sea levels.

One of the reasons why the fourth report did not include such quantitative estimates was that while suitable data and models had been produced prior to the report's publication, they had not passed through peer review. This shows us the evaluative decision that the IPCC needs to make when it sets thresholds and policies for the sources of evidence it can turn to. On the one hand, an insistence to use only peer-reviewed results might cause the IPCC to delay incorporating pieces of information with enormous practical utility. On the other hand, a loosening of standards for inclusion might result in governments basing their climate change policies on falsehoods. A body like the IPCC can only decide how to tune its editorial policy on data inclusion by taking a stand on evaluative questions about the practical consequences of these different types of error.[23]

4.3.3 *Participation*

These discussions of the value-ladenness of scientific advice in the context of energy policy help to illustrate two further important themes, namely the topics of precaution and participation. Let us tackle participation first. We saw that the preamble to

22 O'Reilly, Oreskes, J. N., and Oppenheimer, M., 'The Rapid Disintegration of Consensus: The West Antarctic Ice Sheets and the International Panel on Climate Change' *Social Studies of Science* 42 (2012): 709–731.

23 See Lewens, T. (2015), *The Meaning of Science*. London: Penguin.

the joint academies' review of fracking mentions a role for the investigation of public attitudes towards this technology, but it limits this to an estimation of which of a number of known risks the public might find acceptable. We can now begin to appreciate some of the reasons for looking beyond narrow groups of technical experts when we come to determine those risks in the first place.

To begin with we have seen that editorial questions about which forms of information should, and should not, be included in risk assessments rely implicitly on evaluative questions about the costs of error. Here, reasonable people might disagree about (let us say) how to weight damage to different aspects of urban and rural environments, damage to business interests, damage to elements of community culture and so forth.

Second, psychologists have suggested that there are feedback effects between how individuals evaluate different outcomes in terms of their goodness or badness, and the probabilities they assign to how likely or unlikely those outcomes are to issue from a course of action. Some have claimed that *optimism bias*, for example, is a phenomenon whereby people tend to underestimate the probabilities of outcomes they regard as negative, while overestimating the probabilities of outcomes they regard as positive.[24] (There is, admittedly, disagreement among psychologists over the reality of a general phenomenon of optimism bias.[25]) There are also reasons to think that experts, just as much as laypeople, are subject to this bias.[26] The upshot is that if the experts appointed to evaluate the risks of energy technologies share the same forms of optimism and pessimism – perhaps because their past work developing the technology itself, or advising industry, gives them similar sets of enthusiasms and priorities – then we can anticipate that systematic biases will be introduced in their risk assessments when acting collectively. Such biases can be countered by ensuring disciplinary and political diversity in expert advisory groups.

Third, as Brian Wynne's classic case study of nuclear energy makes clear, there are times when laypeople can in fact have forms of relevant specialist knowledge.[27] The Chernobyl nuclear reactor exploded in April 1986. Wynne argues that scientists' lack of attention to the local expertise of Cumbrian sheep farmers helps to explain their wildly inaccurate initial estimations for the time it would take for radioactive caesium levels to drop in upland Britain in the wake of that explosion. When, in June 1986, government scientists first detected caesium in upland Britain, they imposed a ban on the movement and slaughter of sheep that

24 Sharot, T. (2011), 'The Optimism Bias' *Current Biology* 21: R941–R945.

25 Shah, P. et al. (2016), 'A Pessimistic View of Optimistic Belief Updating' *Cognitive Psychology* 90: 71–127.

26 Flyvbjerg, B. (2004), *Procedures for Dealing with Optimism Bias in Transport Planning*. British Department for Transport.

27 See, e.g., Wynne, B., 'Misunderstood Misunderstandings' *Public Understanding of Science* 1 (1992): 281–304. These themes are also repeatedly stressed in the important work of Sheila Jasanoff, e.g., Jasanoff (2005), *Designs on Nature*. Princeton: Princeton University Press.

they thought would last for three weeks. In the end the ban lasted – in some areas – for twenty-six years.[28]

Wynne suggests numerous ways in which farmers' knowledge could have been put to better use. Farmers had an intimate knowledge of the type of soil specific to the area in which their sheep grazed. They understood where they could graze sheep in sustainable ways. They also understood how the sheep would react – in terms of their overall health and condition – to various efforts to reduce the ability of caesium to recirculate from land to animal and back. In all of these ways, the farmers were experts with valuable knowledge even though they lacked formal qualifications.

Wynne's work does not mean that it is always worth attending to the views of arbitrarily chosen laypeople. Instead, it highlights the important knowledge – often relating to specifics of local environments and ways of life that are of enormous relevance to wise policy choices – possessed by suitably placed individuals who are not members of technically qualified elites.

4.3.4 *Precaution*

What is often called the 'precautionary principle' – a principle that has been of great importance for health and environmental policy in the European Union and beyond – is sometimes informally expressed as the view that when considering how to regulate technology (including energy technology) it is better to be safe than sorry. In response, critics often accuse the precautionary principle of being either objectionably anti-technology or simply incoherent.[29]

The charge of incoherence is the stronger of the two. Suppose we think that the precautionary principle tells us to 'err on the side of caution' in situations of uncertainty. Suppose, further, we understand this to mean that we should refuse any course of action if it carries with it the possibility (whether well supported by evidence or not) of causing great harm. Critics then point out that in most cases this leads to contradiction. On the one hand, encouraging the widespread uptake of nuclear power carries the potential for great harm to be done via uncontrolled reactor meltdowns or leakage events from the storage of radioactive waste. On the other hand, a failure to encourage the widespread uptake of nuclear power also carries the potential (perhaps not well supported by evidence, but that is not the

28 *BBC News*, 'Post-Chernobyl Disaster Sheep Controls Lifted on Last UK Farms' (1 June 2012). Available online at: www.bbc.co.uk/news/uk-england-cumbria-18299228 Last accessed 6 September 2017.

29 Sandin, P., Peterson, M., Hansson, S. O., Rudén, C., and Juthe, A. (2002), 'Five Charges against the Precautionary Principle' *Journal of Risk Research* 5: 287–299; Sunstein, C., *Laws of Fear: Beyond the Precautionary Principle*. Cambridge: Cambridge University Press (2005); Sandin, P. (2007), 'Common-Sense Precaution and Varieties of the Precautionary Principle' in Lewens, T. (ed.), *Risk: Philosophical Perspectives*. London: Routledge; Lewens, T. 'Taking Sensible Precautions', *Lancet* 371 (2008): 1992–1993; John, S., 'In Defence of Bad Science and Irrational Policies' *Ethical Theory and Moral Practice* 13 (2010): 3–18.

point here) for great harm, via the continued release of greenhouse gases from fossil-fuel-based energy generation. On this reading, the precautionary principle tells us that we must, and that we must not, encourage the uptake of nuclear power generation.

Although this charge of incoherence is attractive, it fails because it relies on an uncharitable reading of the precautionary principle itself. One of the most frequently cited statements of the principle issued from the 1992 Rio de Janeiro Earth Summit: 'Where there are threats of serious or irreversible damage, lack of full scientific certainty shall not be used as a reason for postponing cost-effective measures to prevent environmental degradation.'[30] This version of the principle does not say that the mere possibility that a course of action may have grave consequences counts as sufficient grounds to veto it. Instead, the Rio Declaration points out that mere uncertainty about the efficacy of proposed measures to reduce risk cannot be enough to reject them. Such risk-reduction measures could include everything from an insistence that fracking be temporarily ceased in the light of adverse monitoring data, to encouragement of renewable energy technologies in an effort to combat greenhouse emissions. There is, then, nothing intrinsically pro- or anti-technology in the Rio Declaration's recommendation: it can sometimes result in measures that hasten the adoption of risk-reducing technologies.

Moreover, while the declaration insists that uncertainty over efficacy should not be a reason to veto these risk-reduction measures, it does not say that uncertainty by itself is sufficient to mandate those measures. Instead, it insists on the further requirement that such measures should be cost-effective. For that reason, the Rio Declaration does not grant power to whimsical and ill-supported concerns about what are sometimes called 'phantom risks'.

While the Rio Declaration helps to codify common sense about the need to tolerate significant uncertainties while making decisions about risk reduction, it does not offer us anything like a recipe or algorithm that tells us how to act in the face of limited information. Partly for this reason, some commentators have suggested we are better off thinking in terms of a precautionary 'approach' – that is, a humble stance that is mindful of the possibilities of costly error, and concerned with the conflicting demands of gathering rich data and acting in a timely way – rather than a decision-theoretic 'principle'.[31] One theme consistently stressed in such a precautionary approach is the need to enact policy choices that are, as far as possible, reversible. This allows future actors, who may have a more nuanced

[30] *Rio Declaration on Environment and Development*, available at www.un.org/documents/ga/conf151/aconf15126-1annex1.htm Last accessed 6 September 2017.

[31] For example: Stirling, A. (2003), 'Risk, Uncertainty, and Precaution: Some Instrumental Implications from the Social Sciences', in F. Berkhout, M. Leach and I. Scoones (eds), *Negotiating Environmental Change: New Perspectives from Social Science*. Cheltenham: Edward Elgar; Stirling, A. (2005), 'Opening Up or Closing Down: Analysis, Participation, and Power in the Social Appraisal of Technology', in M. Leach, I. Scoones and B. Wynne (eds), *Science, Citizenship, and Globalisation*. London: Zed.

appreciation of the moral texture of our energy choices, and who may simply have a better understanding of the risk-related facts, to undo what may with hindsight be regarded as mistaken decisions.

4.4 CONCLUSIONS: SCIENCE, POLICY AND PROCESS

This short overview has focused, for the most part, on a series of procedural questions about how formal, technical expertise should inform policymaking processes, and what the role of informal expertise and moral evaluation should be in those processes. When acting in what we might think of as a purely scientific mode, with no particular thought to practical applications and policy implications, a technical expert's primary role is to contribute to a growing body of reliably generated information about the world around us. This typically involves setting very high burdens of proof before a proposition is included in the established corpus of scientific wisdom. If scientists owe their progress to the fact that they stand on the shoulders of giants, then scientists need to ensure that future generations of researchers will also stand on strong shoulders.

When technical experts are instead asked to provide information and opinion for policy, then the question of where to set the burden of proof becomes more fluid.[32] To have any chance of averting disaster, action sometimes needs to be swift, and very rigorous forms of data gathering and hypothesis testing may take so long that we are all dead before they have been completed. We have already seen that a keen sense of what is valuable is required for experts to strike a balance between action and exploration. Policy trajectories also need to strike a balance between enacting the best confirmed assumptions about (for example) climate change, energy consumption and the availability of renewable sources, while also building infrastructures that can be dismantled or remodelled if those assumptions turn out to be mistaken. Recent philosophical work contains useful material to assist in these fearsomely complex deliberations.[33]

[32] Lewens, T. (2015), *The Meaning of Science*. London: Penguin.

[33] Thanks to Marc Ozawa, and especially to David Reiner, for very useful comments on an earlier draft.

5

Public Theology – 'Grounded': An Energy Policy Rooted in Human Flourishing

Jonathan Chaplin

5.1 THE NATURE OF 'PUBLIC THEOLOGY'

'Public theology' refers to theological or religious reflection addressed to publics, and concerning public issues, existing beyond the confines of religious communities themselves. It is the application or elaboration of religious ideas within potentially any issue of public concern or public policy. Three clarifications of this definition are necessary. First, the term 'public theology' has a distinctly Christian provenance and it should be acknowledged that not all religious traditions would understand the nature of public theology, or indeed the importance of 'theology' at all, in the same way. A wider analysis of how religion might relate to the environment would need to attend, for example, to the role of communal religious practices and institutional behaviours. Second, in UK university departments, 'theology' is increasingly housed alongside 'religious studies', which includes social scientific, cultural and historical studies of the phenomenon of religion. The discipline of religious studies also has distinct contributions to make on 'good' energy policy – for example, social-anthropological work on how religious communities engage in (ir)responsible energy practices – but I will not pursue those here.[1]

The third clarification is that, at least in its Christian manifestations, public theology is presented as a form of religious communication accessible to the diverse audiences making up modern societies that are complexly plural and secular (and, perhaps, increasingly 'post-secular') (Graham 2013). What 'accessible' means has, however, been a subject of vigorous debate within and beyond the theological guild. Minimally, it has been taken to require mere intelligibility to outsiders, thus excluding only the public use of esoteric terminology or forms of reasoning meaningful only within a faith community, while otherwise permitting theological

I am grateful to my co-editors, especially David Reiner, for helpful comments on an earlier version of this paper. The usual disclaimer applies.

[1] See, e.g., the work of Hancock (2015, 2018) which uses social movement theory to analyse the emergence and motivations of Islamic environmental organisations in the USA and UK.

justifications of policy stances in public debates where these are thought necessary. Maximally, it has been thought to mandate that public theologians may only employ language or rely on reasoning that would be immediately recognised as valid by all citizens. The maximal position is similar to that espoused by Rawlsian public reason liberals and it implies that any theological content, even if articulated, must not be decisive in justifying a policy and so, ultimately, be dispensable.

The debate on this question is extensive and complex (Billingham and Chaplin 2019) but the relevant point here is that many religious practitioners regard themselves as engaging in 'public theology' even when some or much of the language and reasoning they employ on a matter like energy policy apparently lack any overtly religious content. Some would describe this kind of language as religious 'ethics' – the moral imperatives flowing from or comporting well with a religious world-view, even when that world-view is not made explicit. But there is often no bright line between 'theology' and 'ethics' in several religious traditions.[2] Most public theologians would claim that their 'ethical' claims could (upon request) be shown to be ultimately grounded in some theological proposition but they would also insist that such ethical claims remain 'religious' in character even when such a proposition is not made explicit.

5.2 ENVIRONMENTAL PUBLIC THEOLOGY

A notable feature of public theology over the last generation is its growing engagement with environmental questions, and indeed its increasing adoption of politically progressive or radical responses to such questions (Chaplin 2016).[3] The best-known recent example is Pope Francis's encyclical *Laudato Si'* (2015), explored further in Chapter 18, which calls for a comprehensive 'ecological conversion' away from environmentally damaging behaviours. This is a particularly evocative example of the new environmental public theology, at least in its Christian expressions. While so far there are few instances of something as specific as a 'public theology of *energy policy*', energy issues are frequently cited as revelatory of the deeper cultural and societal pathologies that make up what public theologians increasingly speak of in the singular as 'the ecological crisis', something afflicting the entire earth (McKibben 2010: 2).[4]

Public theology has long been concerned with broad, interdisciplinary questions such as what makes for a 'good' or 'virtuous' human life, what are the cultural

[2] In Christianity, for example, there has been an increasing tendency to speak of 'moral theology' in order to urge that (even public) expressions of Christian ethical concern not be severed from the underlying theological convictions that alone render them coherent.

[3] For a wide-ranging overview, see Gottlieb (2006). See also the Forum on Religion and Ecology at Yale, a leading global documentation centre on such developments across all the major world faiths (http://fore.yale.edu/). Founded in 2006, the Forum is built on extensive work done at Harvard University since 1996, including a pioneering ten-volume series on religion and ecology (http://fore.yale.edu/publications/books/cswr/).

[4] McKibben has spoken of the Christian motivation behind his leadership of what is a broad-based secular climate change campaign, 350.org. (He is a Methodist.) McKibben, 2012: 28.

conditions for a flourishing human society and what might a responsible relationship with non-human nature entail (Williams 2012, chs. 14–18). So public theology will strongly endorse the assumptions from which this book proceeds, namely that 'good' energy policy cannot just be about getting the technology right nor is it exclusively about energy itself but is as much about good policy.[5] Yet public theologians will also want to assert that proposals regarding 'good' energy policy, even seemingly technical ones, are also likely to presuppose substantive normative assumptions about 'the good life', 'the good society' and the humanity–nature relationship. They will thus tend to affirm, in the particular case of energy policy, what Pope Francis asserts about environmental policy generally, namely that it must be understood against the background of an 'integral ecology', one uniting the environmental, the social and the moral. Such an integral ecology implies both that 'we cannot adequately combat environmental degradation unless we attend to causes related to human and social degradation' (2015 §48) but, more radically, that in confronting such issues, 'one cannot prescind from humanity'. That is, 'there can be no renewal of our relationship with nature without a renewal of humanity itself. There can be no ecology without an adequate anthropology' (2015 §118). The distinctive insights of public theology for energy policy, then, will seek to stretch the bounds of discourse beyond even a laudable academic concern with interdisciplinary approaches, towards a confrontation with fundamental questions regarding the very nature of humanness and the human–nature relationship. Such questions might better be classed as 'transdisciplinary' (Charlesworth 2015).

The extent to which the recent resurgence of religiously inspired environmentalism represents a break with the past remains an important and challenging question for contemporary public theology. Fifty years ago, Lynn White famously argued that the Judeo-Christian doctrine maintaining that humanity had received a divine mandate (in Genesis chapter 1) to exercise 'dominion' over the earth has contributed substantially to the reckless exploitation of nature under modern industrialisation (White 1967). It would not be difficult to garner evidence from theologically influenced sources from the eighteenth and nineteenth centuries that sought to justify the industrial revolution as a shining example of successful 'dominion'. While few today would claim that this position represents an authentically Christian theology of nature, western Christianity as a globally influential historical movement has to acknowledge its own profound complicity in the contemporary ecological crisis, if only by silence or neglect.

In fact, the vast majority of contemporary Christian eco-theologians have long since renounced that version of 'dominion' theology (although not necessarily the concept of 'dominion' itself, suitably modified) as a 'sub-Christian' deviation from the more holistic theologies of nature typical of the patristic, medieval and early

5 On this, see also New Zealand political scientist Ton Bührs' (2009) proposal for 'environmental integration', in which not only all energy policies but all public policies are coordinated to support the goal of environmental protection.

Reformation periods. There remain, however, forceful popular attempts to justify it theologically, most notably in the US, and these continue to have wide appeal among conservative evangelicals. For example, in 2009 the Cornwall Alliance for the Stewardship of Creation published an *Evangelical Declaration on Global Warming*, which dismissed anxieties about anthropogenic climate change and initiated a campaign under the slogan, 'forget climate change – energy empowers the poor!' (Cornwall Alliance, 2009).[6] There are, however, few if any substantial, academically credible theological defences of this position today.

Academic environmental public theology is particularly well-developed in Christianity, yet its concerns are increasingly shared across many of the world's religions.[7] As a case study of the point, it is worth noting that surprisingly convergent statements on climate change were issued by many global religious authorities prior to COP21.[8] These statements reveal considerable agreement on both the diagnosis of the problem and the preferred responses (see Clingerman and O'Brien 2017). Five convergent stances emerge in these documents, each finding growing support in other works of public theology.

First, all operate with a 'holistic' conception of nature, construed not as an infinitely manipulable and exploitable object existing only for the expansion of material wealth, but rather as reflecting a 'divine' ordering of a universe marked by integration, equilibrium, balance and harmony. This is very clear in monotheistic religions which insist on maintaining a sharp ontological distinction between 'God' (the transcendent source of all existence) and 'creation' (the world, construed as dependent upon that source). But the notion of a divinely ordained balance in nature also appears in those Eastern religions which tend to soften the God–creation boundary. They adhere to a reverential or sacralised notion of 'nature' or 'mother earth' in which humans are seen rather as one species among many, perhaps even ontologically continuous with or ethically equivalent to non-human nature.[9]

Second, all favour some version of the notion of a human 'stewardship' or 'trusteeship' of nature (see, e.g., Charlesworth 2015), grounded in an appeal to human accountability to some higher or deeper spiritual authority for the use of scarce natural resources and fragile ecosystems. Secular modernity is then commonly charged with having aspired to a reckless, 'promethean' domination of nature at the expense of respect for non-human nature as bearer of inherent ontological

6 It was published as a rejoinder to a 2006 manifesto from a coalition of progressive American evangelicals called *An Evangelical Declaration on Care for Creation* (Evangelical Environmental Network, 2006).

7 The remainder of this chapter draws on Chaplin (2016).

8 Many such statements are available at http://fore.yale.edu/climate-change/statements-from-world-religions/.

9 Thus a recent Hindu statement asserts that all elements of reality are 'organs of God's body … The Divine is all and all life is to be treated with reverence and respect … The entire universe is to be looked upon as the energy of the Lord' (Oxford Centre for Hindu Studies/Bhumi Project, 2015).

meaning and ethical value.[10] Humans, it is argued, do not 'own' the earth but only hold it on 'trust'. Even in Hinduism, which is sometimes alleged to downplay human agency, one today finds a robust call for responsible, transformative human action. Most religious traditions emphasise that this must begin with significant changes in personal behaviour, brought about by appeals to religiously based ethical norms like stewardship, social justice and contentment. Pollitt proposes that there is a potentially significant resource in religious communities that might bring about the 'personal norm activation' (the term is Vandenbergh's) – a 'spontaneous change of behaviour created by a sense of duty in the absence of explicit sanctions' – necessary if such behavioural changes are to come about (Pollitt 2010: 8).[11]

Third, notwithstanding a critique of 'modernity' in many religious statements, there is a readiness to endorse what modern science is telling us about the ecological crisis, and specifically about the predominant climate science consensus on the causes, scale and consequences of global warming: that it is largely anthropogenic, that it is the outcome of unrestrained exploitation of finite planetary resources, notably fossil fuels, and that this is driven by the pursuit of unlimited economic growth on a neo-liberal model of globalised capitalism.[12] Most religious traditions have found ways to affirm the insights of modern science, at least where they do not directly contradict core religious teaching.[13] In Christianity, for example, 'natural knowledge', even when recognised as debatable, can be seen as indirect revelation from God, mediated through the 'created' faculty of human reasoning. It is in such areas that public theology does not purport to offer any esoteric or specialised knowledge of the world unavailable in principle to others but rather claims to supply a meaningful framing of generally available knowledge and an ethical motivation to act on it.

Thus, an acceptance of the findings of climate science, when combined with the other theologically informed commitments and diagnoses noted here, typically leads on to strong support for the strategic policy stance of seeking drastic reductions in greenhouse gas emissions through an urgent phasing out of fossil fuel-based

[10] Both Christian and Islamic statements embrace the notion that we are now entering an 'Anthropocene' in which the vaunted pride of human irresponsibility towards the environment is plain for all to see. The *Islamic Declaration on Global Climate Change* cites the Qu'ran as warning humans: 'Do not strut arrogantly upon the earth. You will never split the earth apart, nor will you ever rival the mountain's stature' (IICCS 2015).

[11] Charlesworth identifies a 'global virtue tradition' across various faiths and cultures and proposes that its core virtues (prudence, courage, moderation and justice) can inform not only personal behaviour but also institutional action (2015).

[12] Clingerman and O'Brien (2017) identify a distinction between eco-theologians (and secular thinkers) who regard climate change as a wholly unique challenge facing humanity for which unprecedented responses are required and those (such as Pope Francis) who think it can be adequately addressed by developing the existing resources of religious traditions.

[13] Pope Francis's encyclical *Laudato Si'* was substantially informed by the work of leading climate scientist Hans Joachim Schellnhuber (Potsdam Institute for Climate Impact Research).

energy supplies and a substantial shift towards renewables. It is worth noting that several public theologians also insist that the fundamental problem is not control of GHG emissions but the very extraction of fossil fuels at all, since once extracted it is (given the culturally sustained economic pressures noted below) inevitable that they will be used, releasing GHGs (Northcott 2013). They argue that merely pushing for greater energy efficiency, utilising market incentives such as carbon pricing or trading, or working to change consumer attitudes, essential though these may be, will be insufficient to meet the challenge of global warming.

Fourth, it is widely asserted that ecological challenges such as global warming or humanly induced loss of biodiversity disclose embedded societal values – such as unquestioning faith in the prospects for limitless economic growth (defined narrowly in terms of growth of GDP), or addictive forms of 'consumerism' – that support unsustainable energy practices and obstruct needed steps towards better ones. These diagnoses are often informed by a theologically based conviction that human fulfilment consists far more in the quality of human relationships, expressions of generosity, participation in creative activity or the quest for spiritual authenticity (the pursuit of 'virtues') than in the acquisition of greater material resources. Public theologians tend to argue that the pursuit of limitless increases in material prosperity is now producing not only ecological, economic and political damage but also a debilitating spiritual and moral poverty – the 'wages of sin', to cite New Testament language – which further enfeebles the human capacity to make the behavioural changes needed to combat environmental problems generally. In some contributions, these concerns lead on to a wider structural proposal that fossil-based energy is unsustainable not only ecologically but also, at least in the long term, economically (it will eventually become uneconomic even on conventional measurements) and politically (it will increase economic inequality, evoke social unrest, cause mass migration and even feed military strife) (Northcott 2013).

Fifth, there is a common attempt to situate ecological questions within a broader commitment to a just social order. While diverse religions interpret the meaning of 'social justice' rather differently (like secular traditions they differ, for example, on what degrees and kinds of 'equality' it entails), almost all recognise it as a primary religious, and not merely ethical, obligation. Social justice is increasingly taken to imply, first of all, a global distributional corollary. One finds strong endorsement of the view that the major historical emitting nations must bear a fully equitable burden of the costs of the transition to renewable energy, including the costs of mitigation and adaptation that will fall on poorer and ecologically more vulnerable nations. Such claims often rest on an explicit or implicit needs-based conception of justice, sometimes alongside a rights-based conception (invoked by many secular campaigning groups), but rarely on a utilitarian one (implicit in the neoclassical economic models that inform much public policy).

The commitment to a just social order is also sometimes taken to imply, second, an institutional corollary with more concrete implications for energy policy.

Environmental public theologians are increasingly joining others in robustly critiquing energy regimes (such as the UK) dominated by fossil-fuel oligopolies, urging a far-reaching redistribution of economic power in the energy sector, and supporting policies (on subsidy, licensing, infrastructure, etc.) that favour decentralised, localised means of supply employing renewables (community energy cooperatives, Transition Towns and so forth).

In some cases, such stances invoke a broader argument that the exercise of human ecological (and economic) responsibility must be channelled through a balanced diversity of complementary and mutually limiting agencies in order that excessive concentrations of power in any one agency, especially corporations and states, or in carbon markets, be pre-empted. This is an appeal to what might be termed 'environmental subsidiarity'. While the concept of 'subsidiarity' has distinctly Christian origins, echoes in other traditions can be found.[14] In each case, there is a recognition that humans are 'created' to require, and be equipped for, active participation in a plurality of distinct forms of community – that such an arrangement somehow fits 'with the grain of the universe'. Here Christian public theology is particularly well placed to draw on long traditions of reflection and practice in seeking a pluralistic, mutually limiting balance between central government, other layers of government (subnational and transnational), and numerous non-state actors such as households; business, professional and voluntary associations; trades unions; educational institutions; religious organisations; and so forth.[15]

Northcott seeks to push this line of argument further in proposing that energy markets be substantially restructured so as to incentivise suppliers to work with households and businesses to reduce the total amount of energy actually produced. The goal, he proposes, is to make fossil fuel extraction basically uneconomic by means of carbon taxes (e.g., much higher oil sands royalties), ending fossil fuel subsidies (both direct subsidies such as tax or royalty breaks and indirect ones such as provision of energy infrastructure like power grids or roads), and requiring companies to fully internalise the true costs of research, technical innovation, extraction, production and distribution (2013: 143–4, 203).[16]

14 For example, Halpert quotes Arthur Waskow, Director of the Jewish Shalom Center, as asserting that today, 'the Pharaohs are giant corporations: big coal, big oil, and big natural gas . . . The only way to deal with a modern-day Pharaoh is to organize the people' (Halpert 2102). 'Wisdom in Nature', an Islamic document, likewise calls for 'a power-shift – away from large power-hungry corporations . . . from corporate power and privilege, towards corporate constraints, accountability and grassroots cooperative-type movements' (quoted in Hancock, 2015: 111).

15 Extensive policy discussions on this specific theme have emerged out of Christian Democracy (although it is worth noting that this decentralist theme has sometimes stood in tension with the monopolistic pretensions of the Roman Catholic Church prior to the Second Vatican Council and to some societally hegemonic 'national' Protestant or Orthodox churches).

16 The proposal that such costs be internalised is, of course, a goal many mainstream economists would already endorse as a way to enhance environmental responsibility (see Newbery, Chapter 3).

5.3 PUBLIC THEOLOGY AND 'GOOD' ENERGY POLICY

In the light of the foregoing sketch of themes in environmental public theology, let me identify more closely its potential relevance for 'good' energy policy.

First, notions of 'good' or 'just' need to be defined in an energy context. Overly abstracted or generalised accounts of these notions will not be sufficient to inform the details of public policy. As noted in the Introduction, that context is often framed as the familiar 'energy trilemma': how to achieve simultaneously the goals of *efficiency* (yielding affordable energy prices), *security* (understood as reliable long-term supply) and *sustainability* (minimising environmental damage). What public theology might contribute at this point is a critical probing of the underlying conceptual assumptions underlying these three key terms, all of which have proven to be 'essentially contested'. For example, public theology will certainly support the goal of 'affordable' energy, not least because it is essential to equitable access to energy – a key social justice goal. But it will want to question whether 'efficiency' is best understood in terms of the prevailing, utilitarian neoclassical economic definitions, and to propose instead broader definitions taking into account not merely end-user prices but also, for example, qualitative measures of the inherent value of threatened environmental goods (Weatherley-Singh, Branco and Felgueiras 2016)[17], or the intrinsic good of local supply and control, as promoted by community energy, district heating and the like. Or, public theology will seek to interrogate a definition of 'sustainability' in which a commitment to minimising environmental damage in effect turns out, explicitly or tacitly, to be rendered subservient to a higher norm of sustaining continually increasing economic growth as conventionally understood (Charlesworth 2015).

Second, as the Introduction also notes, 'starting points matter'. For example, 'legacy investments' by companies and consumers cannot easily or speedily be dispensed with in favour of new technologies. A salutary note of realism thus needs to discipline public theology's more far-reaching proposals; it could prevent them sliding from a proper radicalism into an unhelpful and paralysing utopianism. Here is one obvious point at which existing energy policy discourse can instruct public theology (there are others). Public theology, then, should join in recognising that the search for better energy policy requires a proper reckoning with inherited local, regional and national preconditions and institutions.

Yet public theology itself ought to engender such a realism from within its own intellectual resources. Religious thought is often able to acknowledge that all human societies, and thus all regimes of public policy, are necessarily conditioned by persisting historical patterns, enduring customary practices and greatly varying

[17] Many eco-theologians would endorse Sagoff's (2008) forceful critique of neoclassical economics' instrumentalisation of such goods (in, e.g., otherwise valuable cost–benefit analyses) and his argument that their inherent value be explicitly honoured in public policy and not merely factored in as another quantifiable, and fungible, 'preference'.

geographical and cultural contexts, and more broadly by the embeddedness of all of these in the vicissitudes of a morally ambiguous human history (to which religion itself has contributed). Augustine's Christian theology of history might be one useful resource here, offering an account of the possibility of morally responsible human action in an 'earthly city' dominated, as was the Roman empire which was his context, by powerful personal and structural forces sustained, he asserted, by an inordinate love of wealth and power. Augustine insisted that one could not wish away the severe constraints imposed on moral action by that city, while arguing that one could nevertheless cultivate different 'loves' that would mitigate its worst aspects and bring about modest improvement.

Christian public theology, at least, thus has reasons of its own to recognise that energy policy cannot simply leap out of its confining present into some imagined future but must be crafted to negotiate the constraints, and leverage the possibilities, of its inherited historical context.[18] Only then can societies advance incrementally towards 'better' energy policy. This is not to mute public theology's potential for a 'prophetic critique' of the present (to invoke a central theme in the Hebrew Scriptures), only to caution it to propose steps that are concretely available to the diverse individual and institutional energy actors which alone can effect change (on which see Chapter 18). Such a caution will also encourage public theology to recognise that 'bad' energy policies persist even long after their deficiencies are fully recognised. Public theology will thus readily acknowledge the need for a proper stance of 'historical patience' – as distinct from passivity or complacency.

Third, public theology will echo the caution against the tendency of technology-based approaches to rely too much on what have frequently turned out to be unreliable predictions about the future; and, more generally, against an overreliance on quantification and scientific argument. Public theology will endorse an appropriate modesty about the capacity of finite humans to exercise future mastery over nature – to 'manage the planet', as Charlesworth puts it (2015). Nature can certainly be scientifically explored, and to a degree, modified and directed towards human goals and it is quite proper that it should be; 'culture', we might say, is 'natural'.[19] But it is also proper to acknowledge that aspects of the non-human realm will always elude our complete intellectual grasp and capacity for technological steering and to caution against what has been termed 'the role of hubris in delivery'.[20] But furthermore, our predictions about future human behaviour will always remain fallible, given that such behaviour is shaped by a highly complex and shifting amalgam of subjective motivations, values and affiliations (some virtuous and some vicious) and

18 Other religions have produced quite different 'theologies of history' and I will not presume to speak for them at this point.

19 The Qu'ran, for example, speaks of nature as being designed by God to be 'tractable' to human action.

20 Nagle's (2010) documentation of how even well-intentioned environmental laws often generate unintended damaging environmental consequences serves as one example of such 'hubris'.

objective societal and environmental factors (some conducive to human flourishing, others obstructive to it).

Such a stance has a powerful bearing on the goal of pursuing policymaking via full stakeholder consultation. Public theology's posture of 'historical patience' will strongly incline its practitioners to support incremental change via participatory democratic processes that make time and space for the articulation of multiple viewpoints, and will lead them to resist the lure of 'being China for a day'. Energy experts, as well as campaigners, will often experience these processes as cumbersome and ad hoc, and their outputs as falling well short of the desiderata of 'rational choice'. Yet the need for democratic legitimacy must surely be factored into the very definition of 'good' energy policy. That will be essential if the goal of nurturing public trust in policy processes and outcomes is to be realised.

The discipline of public theology, then, will bring its own, sometimes distinctive, partly overlapping, concerns to the search for 'good' energy policy. It will desire a 'grounded' energy policy – one that is rooted in a clear understanding of what is conducive to the wider goals of a 'good' society in which humans flourish both as consumers of ample material benefits but also as social, relational, situated, ecologically integrated, and for many in the world, religious beings. In that objective it will find numerous allies in, and should learn from, many other disciplines.

5.4 CONCLUSIONS: FROM THEOLOGY TO ACTION

American philosopher Oelschlaeger ventured controversially that 'There are no solutions for the systemic causes of ecocrisis, at least in democratic societies, apart from religious narrative' (1994, 5). Many would dispute that stark conclusion, yet even if religion is but one narrative among others, it is positioned to play a potentially significant role in preparing the conditions for goals such as 'good' energy policy. Religious narratives would likely appeal to the convergent themes outlined above: a holistic view of nature; a strong conception of human trusteeship of the environment; a critique of consumerist capitalism; a call for reverence for the inherent worth of nature; solidarity with the poor; frugality of lifestyle; and an account of social justice both as equitable distribution and as institutional decentralisation.

Evidently, such narratives will only exert influence if they actually motivate the actions of large masses of religious adherents, and perhaps others, worldwide. Gottlieb reported in 2006 that 'from the United States and Latin America to south Asia and Africa people of faith now make up a vital presence in the global environmental movement ... [T]o a greater extent than at any previous time in history religious people from around the world are active members of a progressively oriented global movement for social change' (2006: 18). Yet the pool of such activists is, globally, small. In May 2014, Cambridge economist Partha Dasgupta and climate scientist Veerabhadran Ramanathan (Scripps Institution of Oceanography,

University of California) convened a workshop on the issue at the Vatican,[21] subsequently venturing optimistically in an article in *Science* that 'religious leaders can instigate the "massive mobilisation of public opinion" needed to stem the destruction of ecosystems around the world in a way that governments and scientists cannot' (St. John's College, Cambridge, 2014). As Pollitt puts it, the issue is 'how to harness both the considerable power of organised religion to bring about social change (by engaging committed adherents *and* other people of goodwill) in order to win hearts and minds to the considerable behavioural changes and economic costs required in tackling climate change' (2010: 11). Reviewing evidence from several Anglophone Western democracies in the early 1990s, he concludes, however, that the correlation between religious affiliation and environmental responsibility was at best 'weakly positive' (2010: 9). The large challenge for environmental public theologians, then, is not only to articulate clear and compelling narratives of ecological responsibility but also to work to ensure that these narratives are actually disseminated and acted upon in religious communities and that such communities not content themselves with issuing platitudinous exhortations but be equipped to shape significantly their members' values and actions.

5.5 REFERENCES

Bell, Colin, Chaplin, Jonathan and White, Robert (eds.) (2013) *Living Lightly, Living Faithfully: Religions and the Future of Sustainability*. Cambridge: Faraday Institute/KLICE.

Billingham, Paul and Chaplin, Jonathan (forthcoming 2019) 'Law, Religion and Public Reasoning'. In *Handbook of the Interdisciplinary Study of Law and Religion*, edited by Norman Doe, Russell Sandberg, Bronach Kane and Caroline Roberts. Cheltenham: Edward Elgar.

Bührs, Ton (2009) *Environmental Integration: Our Common Challenge*. New York: SUNY.

Chaplin, Jonathan (2015) '*Laudato Si*': Structural Causes of the Ecological Crisis', *Comment* (24 September and 1 October).

Chaplin, Jonathan (2016) 'The Global Greening of Religion', *Palgrave Communications Comment* 2 art. no 19047 (July 2016), doi:10.1057/palcomms.2016.47.

Charlesworth, Mark (2015) *Transdisciplinary Solutions for Sustainable Development: From planetary management to stewardship*. Abingdon, Oxon: Earthscan/Routledge.

Clingerman, Forrest and O'Brian, Kevin J. (2017), 'Is climate change a new kind of problem? The role of theology and imagination in climate ethics'. *Wiley's Interdisciplinary Reviews: Climate Change* 8 (September/October), 1–10, accessed 6 December 2017. (WIREs Clim Change 2017, 8:e480. doi:10.1002/wcc.480)

Cornwall Alliance (2009) An Evangelical Declaration on Global Warming, http://cornwallalliance.org/2009/05/evangelical-declaration-on-global-warming/, accessed 15 April 2016.

Evangelical Environmental Network (2006) Evangelical Declaration on the Care of Creation, https://creationcare.org/creation-care-resources/evangelical-declaration-on-the-care-of-creation/, accessed 15 April 2016.

21 'Sustainable Humanity, Sustainable Nature: Our Resposnibility', a 'Joint Workshop of the Pontifical Academy of Sciences and the Pontifical Academy of Social Sciences', http://www.pas.va/content/accademia/en/events/2014/sustainable.html, accessed 18 April 2016.

Gottlieb, Richard S. (ed.) (2006) *Oxford Handbook on Religion and Ecology*. Oxford: Blackwell.

Graham, Elaine (2013) *Between a Rock and a Hard Place: Public Theology in a Post-Secular Age*. London: SCM.

Halpert J. (2012) 'Judaism and Climate Change'. *Yale Climate Connections* 29 February 2012, www.yaleclimateconnections.org/2012/02/judaism-and-climate-change/, accessed 15 April 2016.

Hancock, Rosemary (2015) '"Islamic" Environmentalism in Great Britain', in Peace, Timothy (ed.), *Muslims and Political Participation in Britain*. Abingdon, Oxon: Routledge, 103–123.

Hancock, Rosemary (2018) *Islamic Environmentalism: Activism in the United States and Great Britain*. Abingdon, Oxon: Routledge.

IICCS (Islamic International Climate Change Symposium) (2015) *Islamic Declaration on Global Climate Change*, http://islamicclimatedeclaration.org/islamic-declaration-on-global-climate-change/, accessed 15 April 2016.

McKibben, Bill (2010) *Eaarth: Making a Life on a Tough Planet*. New York: St Martin's Griffin.

McKibben, Bill (2012) 'Preface – the challenge of sustainability'. In Bell, Colin, Chaplin, Jonathan and White, Robert, eds (2013) *Living Lightly, Living Faithfully: religions and the future of sustainability*. Cambridge: Faraday Institute/KLICE: 21–29.

Nagle, John Copeland (2010) *Law's Environment: How the law shapes the places we live*. New Haven and London: Yale University Press.

Northcott, Michael (2013) *A Political Theology of Climate Change*. Grand Rapids, MI: Eerdmans.

Oelschlaeger, M. (1994) *Caring for Creation: An Ecumenical Approach to the Environmental Crisis*. New Haven: Yale.

Oxford Centre for Hindu Studies/Bhumi Project (2015) Bhumi Devi Ki Jai! A Hindu Declaration on Climate Change, www.hinduclimatedeclaration2015.org/english, accessed 15 April 2016.

Pollitt, Michael (2010) 'Green Values in Communities: how and why to engage individuals with decarbonisation targets'. Centre for Business Research, University of Cambridge Working Paper No. 398.

Pope Francis (2015) *Laudato Si': On Care for our Common Home*, http://w2.vatican.va/content/francesco/en/encyclicals/documents/papa-francesco_20150524_enciclica-laudato-si.html, accessed 15 April 2016 http://w2.vatican.va/content/francesco/en/encyclicals/documents/papa-francesco_20150524_enciclica-laudato-si.html, accessed 15 April 2016.

Sagoff, Mark (2008) *The Economy of the Earth: Philosophy, Law, and the Environment* 2nd ed. New York: Cambridge University Press.

St. John's College, Cambridge (2014) 'Partha Dasgupta leads appeal to religion for "mass mobilisation" on environmental change', www.joh.cam.ac.uk/partha-dasgupta-leads-appeal-religion-mass-mobilisation-environmental-change, accessed 18 April 2016.

Weatherley-Singh, Janice, Branco, Tiago and Felgueiras (2016) 'The greening of the EU? A Christian assessment of the EU's environmental policies for biodiversity and nature', in Chaplin, Jonathan and Wilton, Gary (eds), *God and the EU: Faith in the European Project* (Abingdon, Oxon: Routledge, 230–250.

White, Lynn (1967) 'The historical roots of our ecologic crisis', *Science* 155 (3767): 1203–1207.

Williams, Rowan (2012) *Faith in the Public Square*. London: Bloomsbury.

6

Anthropology and Energy Policy

Charlotte Johnson

Energy policy uses tools of the state and market to establish an evidence base – a picture of the world as it is – and then identifies a range of possible futures that can be realised through policy interventions. It is a system of knowing and regulating the world which extends from natural resource extraction to appliance use in the home, which has a time frame covering geological pasts and imagined futures, and a geographical range from the subterranean through the atmosphere into space. Energy and its management through policy, therefore, offer fertile ground for anthropological investigation, impacting on some of the discipline's core theoretical concerns: power, value, identity, symbolism and myth.

Energy anthropology is an emerging field, albeit one which draws on traditional anthropological questions and approaches (Wilhite 2005). Anthropologists find energy can be central to key debates within, for example, political anthropology, economic anthropology and material culture studies. They are also exploring ways that energy policy can be investigated through traditional anthropological methods of participant observation and ethnography, as well as opening up new methodological areas and issues that anthropologists find themselves studying, such as big data, information systems and algorithms.

6.1 INTERESTS

Social anthropology focuses on questions related to culture, society, social reproduction and identity. Its trademarks are cross-cultural comparison and ethnographic investigation. Criticised as relativist, it focuses on understanding the parameters in which meaning can be made and the self can be situated in society. It is a discipline which struggles with the pared-down descriptions of engineering and the assumptions of economics that all things can hold exchange value. Instead it adopts a mode of interrogation that privileges the internal logics of people within their environments, and a mode of analysis that points to the fraying of boundaries and of certainty, the clashes between realities, the power asymmetries and the contested, changing ways of being in the world and of knowing the world. Energy policy has provided anthropologists with an opportunity to explore core anthropological concerns. The following are burgeoning dimensions of exploration within anthropology.

6.1.1 *Anthropology of the State*

The management of energy resources is a key component of statecraft. Resource extraction and distribution build the institutions of the state and enable types of citizenship to come into being. 'Energopolitics' is a term used by anthropologists Dominic Boyer and Cymene Howe to focus on how the control of energy has been fundamental to modern statecraft. Boyer (2011, p. 5) explains this in contrast to the Foucauldian concept of 'biopolitics' arguing that control of energy is as important to the development of modern statecraft and that 'power over energy has been the companion and collaborator of modern power over life and population'. Coal and oil resources have institutionalised forms of power in the modern period, but these are now being challenged as such resources are interpreted as more precarious in terms of their availability and the environmental harm they produce. The transition to other forms of energy resources opens up questions of how existing power structures will be reworked including relations between governments, corporations and citizens; between resource-consuming centres and resource-producing peripheries; or between the global north and south. For Howe and Boyer (2016) low-carbon transition can be an opportunity to rework existing relationships of domination. However, based on their ethnographic study of a wind development in Oaxaca, Mexico, it is one which is being missed as 'green capitalism' pursues large-scale renewable resource extraction using the same political institutions and forms of power as carbon capitalism. Their analysis demonstrates how anthropological research can critically engage with the power plays that support the status quo, as well as prospect for alternatives, by looking at the local, context-specific ways of managing and valuing the environment and its resources.

6.1.2 *Economic Anthropology*

Value is a constant source of anthropological investigation particularly within economic anthropology. This is a subfield which distinguishes between the 'formal economy', a space in which *homo economicus* can operate, and the substantive economy, the socially embedded processes through which people's material needs are met (Polanyi 2001). Energy is a problematic commodity and hard to confine to the 'formal economy'. Although objectified through policy and turned into a commodity, energy is not an object. It is a force that flows and the focus of anthropological research necessarily turns to examine these flows and follow the pipes and wires together with the policies that enable or disrupt them. This approach finds that cities are designed around energy management (Collier 2012) and energy infrastructures cement social contracts that prove hard to disembed when policies change (Johnson 2016). Anthropologists of post-socialism have explored the interaction between the liberalisation of the energy sector and the organisation of urban space, identifying the impacts on social norms and political relations (Collier 2012; Humphrey 2005; Alexander et al. 2007). In the global south the dominant development discourse that associates economic progress with energy access raises questions about neo-imperialist modes of expert knowledge. At the same time, new trends in renewable energy are moving away from universal access, seeking opportunities to decentralise and create 'community energy' systems that match local supply and demand without using national networks. Anthropologists are studying mutual energy exchanges in off-grid communities and learning about the ethics and social relations these exchanges create which exist outside market logics (Singh et al. 2017). In post-industrial countries the transition of households from energy consumer to energy producer, distributor, or asset and equity holder raises questions about the moral economies of grid defection and the new socio-material alliances between people and their IoT-enabled homes that are formed to capture value from dynamic energy flows and prices.

6.1.3 *Material Culture of the Home and Consumption*

Once energy enters the home it opens up a fresh set of anthropological questions. The material culture of the home is a long-standing area of interest, and one which provides scholars of energy policy with analytical tools. Bourdieu's concept of '*habitus*' has been used to examine cultures of cleanliness for example, and how these drive energy consumption through showering habits (Gram-Hanssen 2007; Strengers 2008). Anthropological investigation of consumption is about interpreting the social forces underlying the kilowatt hours consumed, recognising these as expressions of maternal love perhaps, or displays of a cosmopolitan identity. As Wilhite (2008) demonstrates through his analysis of the uptake and use of fridges by middle-class families in Kerala, India, there is a role for anthropology to show how globally ubiquitous appliances are used in different ways and mean different things in different cultural contexts. This line of questioning looks at how internationally derived policies and standards that promote energy efficiency and aim to drive down energy consumption can have unexpected results when they land in local contexts.

With policymakers' interest in demand-side response, energy policy is following energy into the home and hoping to retrain residents in their understanding of what things like laundry, cooking and cleaning mean. Smart energy technologies and the associated visual displays of energy consumption encourage people to interpret domestic chores as energy-consuming activities with ecological and economic impacts. Anthropology can respond by questioning how such products and policies affect the ways that people produce their identities and social relationships through their activities at home. Anthropology can ask how such interventions may intersect with gender, class, ethnic or age divisions, and with what consequences not only for the residents, but also for the policy.

6.1.4 *Digital Anthropology*

Smart energy is a burgeoning area of policy innovation, and of anthropological interest. Digital anthropology has developed to understand the increasing role that digital technologies play in social life (Horst & Miller 2012). Starting from technologies such as mobile phones and social media platforms that explicitly integrate with social life, this form of research is now moving behind the interface into the codes and algorithms of digital systems to identify social forms embedded there, and follow their impacts. For example, the assumption that machine learning is outside the social sphere, and is 'acultural', is demonstrated as incorrect through social analysis which clearly demonstrates that the 'biases' of cultural perceptions of the world enter into algorithms and produce reflections of these worlds (Crawford & Calo 2016). As policymakers place faith in a smart future conducted by technology orchestrating big data, there is a growing role for digital anthropology and critical data studies.

6.2 APPROACHES

Anthropology is known for its method of participant observation and its use of ethnography to give holistic representations of lifeworlds. It is a discipline that has grappled with its colonial past and representational bias, developing tools for reflexive practice and participatory research in response. An anthropological approach suits the study of energy policy because it can examine in detail ways that people's livelihoods, lifestyles, sense of self and ethics can be impacted or directly targeted by energy policy. Traditional ethnographies can and have been written of communities whose experience exemplifies contemporary energy issues, such as coal miners, for example (Rolston 2013), or electricity traders (Özden-Schilling 2015). Multi-sited ethnography is another potential approach, as ethnographers can follow the trails of pipelines between countries exploring upstream and downstream experiences. Or they can move from policymaking communities to the communities of 'policy intervention' and represent both the internal logics of expertise that produce the policies as well as situate the impacts of policy within a specific cultural context, identifying the often unanticipated consequences produced as policy moves from design to implementation. Energy research also prompts new and experimental methods. Sensory ethnography offers a way of understanding how people feel in their environments and is used to explore the sounds, smells and bodily sensations that help create the feeling of home for example (Pink 2015). This kind of approach is being used specifically to understand energy use and to critically engage with the impacts of policy, as well as to offer insights on how policies and products can be better designed (Pink & Leder Mackley 2012; Mackley et al. 2017). Design anthropology also offers new methodological innovation as anthropologists move from their traditional position of observer into a position of active intervention, adopting experimental research designs. 'Intervention ethnography', for example, has been used by Singh et al. (2017) to examine new peer-to-peer energy exchanges by piloting specific technologies in collaboration with off-grid communities.

6.3 COLLABORATIONS

The areas sketched in Section 6.2 intersect with familiar energy-sector divisions: the politics of extraction, distribution and consumption; the dynamics of supply and demand and the social construction of smart- and low-carbon futures. In all these areas, anthropologists find questions that can be explored through anthropological theory and questions that open up spaces for innovative methods. This makes energy anthropology a growing field, but one which is still tentative in how best to engage. Should they collaborate with policymakers and the disciplines on whose evidence they depend or expose their combined lack of understanding of the 'local' and an inability to correctly intervene in it? As an anthropologist working in the field of energy, I find myself caught between understanding the global challenge and the political response required by climate change, while also recognising that policy can be part of the problem. Energy policy, based on narrow (or perhaps not very anthropological) types of evidence, assume neo-imperial frameworks for valuing resources and defining a future that privilege some lifeworlds over others. I find myself, like other anthropologists, questioning how to engage, how to move from critique to intervention, how to apply the insights that anthropological interrogation can provide.

This is a struggle which has been long-running. In the late 1970s American anthropologist Laura Nader led a programme of interdisciplinary research for the Committee of Nuclear and Alternative Energy Systems. Her foreword to the final report provides a wry commentary on the difficulties of constructing energy futures through interdisciplinary collaboration. Critiquing reductive modes of thought, she writes: 'Economists think that price determines everything. Physicists and chemists believe that progress means technological progress. Engineers believe that the language of numbers is somehow more precise than the language of words' (National Research Council 1980, p. v). She paints the anthropologists' role as opening up the range of possible futures based on the knowledge that human societies are flexible and changing. She also sees that the anthropologist's role is to point out how expertise curtails the range of possibilities and how it structures which futures can be achieved through policy. I would argue that today the divisions between disciplines are less stark and interdisciplinary work is more common, but that the anthropologist's role continues to be about opening up the possibilities and pointing to the inventiveness of people. Revolutions come from ideas about what is possible, and although there is a dialectical relationship between the technical and social, each extending and constraining the other, the anthropologist will always seek to show not only the fallibility of expertise and the faith it places in technology, but also the inventiveness and possibilities of lay knowledge. As the need to respond to climate change becomes ever more urgent there will be perhaps more active engagement from anthropologists in the problems and solutions posed by energy policy, but also more interest from the policymaking community in the questions and answers presented by anthropologists.

6.4 REFERENCES

Alexander, C., Buchli, V. & Humphrey, C. eds., 2007. *Urban Life in Post-Soviet Asia*, Abingdon, Oxon.; New York, NY: UCL Press.

Boyer, D., 2011. 'Energopolitics and the Anthropology of Energy', *Anthropology News*, 52 (5): 5–7.

Collier, S.J., 2012. *Post-Soviet Social: Neoliberalism, Social Modernity, Biopolitics*, Princeton: Princeton University Press.

Crawford, K. & Calo, R., 2016. 'There Is a Blind Spot in AI Research', *Nature*, 538(7625): 311–313.

Gram-Hanssen, K., 2007. 'Teenage Consumption of Cleanliness: How to Make It Sustainable?' *Sustainability: Science, Practice, & Policy*, 3(2): 15–23.

Horst, H. & Miller, D. eds., 2012. *Digital Anthropology*, London & New York: Berg.

Howe, C. & Boyer, D., 2016. 'Aeolian Extractivism and Community Wind in Southern Mexico', *Public Culture*, 28(2 (79)): 215–235.

Humphrey, C., 2005. 'Ideology in Infrastructure: Architecture and Soviet Imagination', *Journal of the Royal Anthropological Institute (N.S.)*, 11: 39–58.

Johnson, C., 2016. 'District Heating as Heterotopia: Tracing the Social Contract through Domestic Energy Infrastructure in Pimlico, London', *Economic Anthropology*, 3(1): 94–105.

Mackley, KL. et al., 2017. *Methods for Researching Homes*.

National Research Council, 1980. *Energy Choices in a Democratic Society: The Report of the Consumption, Location, and Occupational Patterns Resource Group, Synthesis Panel of the Committee on Nuclear and Alternative Energy Systems*, Washington, D.C.: National Academies Press.

Özden-Schilling, C., 2015. 'Economy Electric', *Cultural Anthropology*, 30(4): 578–588.

Pink, S., 2015. *Doing Sensory Ethnography* (2nd ed.), London: Sage Publications.

Pink, S. & Leder Mackley, K., 2012. 'Video and a Sense of the Invisible: Approaching Domestic Energy Consumption through the Sensory Home', *Sociological Research Online*, 17(1): 3

Polanyi, K., 2001. *The Great Transformation: The Political and Economic Origins of Our Time* (2nd ed.), Boston, MA: Beacon Press.

Rolston, J.S., 2013. 'The Politics of Pits and the Materiality of Mine Labor: Making Natural Resources in the American West', *American Anthropologist*, 115(4): 582–594.

Singh, A. et al., 2017. 'Towards an Ethnography of Electrification in Rural India: Social Relations and Values in Household Energy Exchanges', *Energy Research & Social Science*, 30: 103–115.

Strengers, Y., 2008. 'Smart Metering Demand Management Programs: Challenging the Comfort and Cleanliness Habitus of Households', *Energy*, 35(4): 9–16.

Wilhite, H., 2005. 'Why Energy Needs Anthropology', *Anthropology Today*, 21(3): 1–2.

Wilhite, H., 2008. 'New Thinking on the Agentive Relationship between End-Use Technologies and Energy-Using Practices', *Energy Efficiency*, 1(2): 121–130.

7

History: A Long View?

Paul Warde

Energy policymakers and analysts have frequently looked to history. Unfortunately, the result has often been bad energy policy.[1] Perhaps energy policymakers would be advised, then, to leave history well alone?

This perhaps surprising assertion in a chapter about energy policy and history is, however, somewhat paradoxical, because it is an observation drawn from the study of the history of energy policy. Repeatedly, policymakers have expected the future to be something like the past, and repeatedly, this has turned out to be wrong. This would seem to be a lesson from history, would it not?

It is important to distinguish from the outset between two kinds of history: we might say 'history' and 'History'. With a small 'h', history can be considered as simply information that comes to us from the past. It can be analysed and deployed using techniques from any discipline or none, but this is usually done using formal procedures specific to the various disciplines to which policy analysts belong. The information is treated no differently from that related to the present. Indeed, such analysts are generally better informed about the present than the past so the more historical their work is, the lower the quality of their analysis is likely to be. This is very different from approaching 'History with a big H', that is, the body of work produced by people trained within the discipline of history. History with a big H is not simply analysis that employs using information from the past, but a particular set of approaches and outputs elaborated by historians. It is this second 'History' that is the subject of this chapter.

Information from the past is a central aspect of the work of many disciplines. Often this information has required the labour of historians to be made accessible.

[1] The simplest and perhaps most frequent examples are the lineal projection of past trends into the future, and the optimism that new technologies will follow a declining cost curve as some past technologies have done. For a particularly egregious example, see Cesare Marchetti and Nebojsa Nakicenovic, *The dynamics of energy systems and the logistic substitution model*, Working Paper RR-79–13, International Institute for Applied Systems Analysis, Laxeburg, Austria; abridged version reprinted in Libby Robin, Sverker Sörlin and Paul Warde, eds., *The Future of Nature. Documents of Global Change*, New Haven: Yale University Press, 2013, 282–6, which applies a Fisher-Pry equation to data on historical mixes to predict patterns of the future energy mix.

But such historical analysis is not the same as an analysis by a historian. If oil analyst Maurice Adelman, for example, (correctly) observes in 1972 that rather than the oil price spike being a signal of diminishing supply it is likely to presage a glut, he is combining historical information with economic theory, but he does not require any engagement with History as a discipline to make the claim.[2] Similarly, if government reports in the post-war period use established trends in the relationship between industrial output and energy consumption to (incorrectly) predict a dramatic overshoot of demand over supply in future decades, no historian had to sit on the panel. In each case the analyst or policy adviser uses techniques normal within their own disciplinary approach and uses history as a means to extend the dataset on which they work.

So let us move away from the idea of history as a repository of wisdom somehow forgotten but waiting to be discovered, and move to History: the kind of contributions that historians can make to the interdisciplinary discussion of energy policy. First we will set out some of the methodological and presentational characteristics of History, although it is important to state from the outset that one of the most distinctive characteristics is the lack of formalisation. We will then proceed to examine some more specific insights that historians can bring to questions of energy policy (which is not to say that such insights are exclusive to historians).

In a world of 'evidence-based' policy, what can History provide? History is a discipline infused with particularity, irony and contingency. Historians like to operate, after all, with hindsight, and a default instinct is to anticipate that a problem is more *complex* than anyone can easily perceive (*complex* does not mean that any individual element is necessarily *complicated*). This may predispose policymakers to regard historical research and historians' comments on current issues as unhelpful, even if an expectation of the unanticipated is, in itself, a potential virtue for policymaking. Because of its inclination towards complexity and hidden significance, historical research also generally *requires time* to produce outputs; often many years. This makes it poor at responding to demands of policy production. Whilst historians may well apply hypothesis testing or statistical analysis as part of their work, the end goal is usually to present a unique synthesis. As with any discipline, the quality of information available – the survival and accessibility of sources – will shape the emphasis of the work. The result is often long, dense, rarely prescriptive, highly qualified and not well suited to digestion and incorporation into policy.

Nevertheless, historians can contribute to policy discussions in three main forms:

a) Firstly, history may provide *analogues* for thinking about problems; tools derived from identifying similar cases, although not necessarily similar topics. Such work is not necessarily done by historians. This is unlikely to be as straightforward as providing a prediction. For example, it seems that uptake of new fuels in domestic households was historically frequently related to the opportunity cost

2 Morris A. Adelman, *The World Petroleum Market*, Baltimore: Johns Hopkins University Press, 1972, 1.

of labour in sourcing and preparing wood, coal, coke or oil, and especially female workforce participation. Although one cannot predict what the balance of opportunity costs would be now, it would be surprising if this insight was not worthy of attention today. Historians, in bringing to bear a deeper contextualisation and attention to detail, can also identify *false analogies*, of the kind that 'This is like the last oil price spike and hence the consequences will be the same', or 'the technology will become cheaper over time'.

b) Secondly, history can provide *direct evidence* of past circumstances, indicating levels of fuel consumption and energy use, their association with other activities, the impact of regulatory change, levels of capital investment and so on. This historical information may well be used in studies by non-historians, but an important consideration should be knowledge of the *quality* of the data. For example, it is not uncommon to see analysis of energy transitions such as the wood-to-coal transition in the United States in the nineteenth century. Analysts may not realise that the century-long time series for firewood consumption contains only one nineteenth-century data point in 1879, and this was based on anecdotes without any attempt at a systematic survey. The 'historical' data is thus in fact the product of a later model, which is of course true of a lot of energy-related data.[3] However, if limited to this view, historians are treated as mere purveyors of 'information' that should be delivered to people who really are in a position to rigorously develop policy. Certainly historians *can* and do play this role.
c) Thirdly, and perhaps most importantly, History provides a specific *style* of thinking about issues. Its approach, as we have already seen, tends to anticipate complexity and work in a broadly synthetic manner, often integrating evidence that is different in kind and developing intelligible narratives. Historians work in theoretically informed ways, but balance this with empirical material woven into an overall chronology, capable of critically assessing change or continuity over time.

This third quality is arguably the most important. Such forms of thinking are often required to synthesise disparate data provided by a range of (sometimes competing) stakeholders and interests. Indeed, such synthesis may be a prerequisite of turning *data* into *evidence* by making causal connections and developing techniques for integration and comprehension. This is precisely what the able policymaker must do; weigh disparate views and forms of data. This openness and eclecticism does not mean that historians are vague in the handling of any particular piece of evidence or in the manner in which a corpus of data is built up. These tasks are often performed with rigor and are subject to a high degree of peer scrutiny. Rather, historians work from the assumption that their evidence base is fragmentary and partial, even when using carefully constructed statistical samples.

[3] Paul Warde, 'Firewood Consumption and Energy Transition: A Survey of Sources, Methods and Explanations in Europe and North America', *Historia Agraria*, 77 (2019).

We can now turn to a more specific example: the history of prediction. Much energy policy implicitly or explicitly involves prediction, and this relates to history both in that we can test the accuracy of previous predictions, and that prediction itself relies on a set of assumptions about the relation of the past and the future. If the future is highly constrained by the past, then the spread of possible futures is very limited, and in principle the information to allow us accurately to predict should already be at our disposal. If the future is not constrained by the past, and what happens is contingent on decisions made now and in the future, outcomes become dependent on information that in principle we cannot have. This is all the more salient in a world where innovation hunts the next 'disruptive technology', which almost by definition is technology whose effects we cannot predict. History may be useful in both cases; in assessing, even in a constrained world, whether it is actually possible to collect the relevant information; or in highlighting whether disruption is a more typical experience than constraint.

For the most part, past predictions about future energy demand, mix, prices and so forth have been quite badly wrong, although varying with sector (whether from governments, firms, think tanks, etc.) and time horizon. Increasingly, prediction has become qualified into 'scenarios'; in the words of the godfather of them all, Herman Kahn of RAND and the Hudson Institute, 'a scenario . . . which puts issues in a new perspective', but that does 'not [seek] to predict the actual course of events'.[4] Arguably this is not really very much different from the older, naïve making of a prediction when the predictor simply said they were working with the best information available. But as a historian, my main interest is not whether past predictions were correct or not (although it's interesting and fun). A historian is not in the business of refining the model to improve the quality of prediction, which historically does not seem to have been very successful. Rather, firstly, *I want to know why people believed particular predictions at the time*. This is partly because there are frequently a range of predictions among which one can choose (all of which may have turned out to be wrong), and one can clearly not test them empirically in advance. Equally, a related issue is *why people thought it was a useful exercise to predict at all*. This might be considered so self-evident a need as to hardly deserve discussion. And yet given that many earlier predictions were done on a basis that we now would consider laughable, and a very high proportion of these are wrong (or at best not much different from those a relatively uninformed person could come up with), it may be worthwhile to reflect on why we feel the need to produce predictions and what *political* (in the very broadest sense) purpose they serve. A general assumption about predictions would be that they should make us better informed. If that turns out not to be the case, or that it is rather hard to adjudicate whether we are better informed or not, this opens up

[4] Herman Kahn, William Brown and Leon Martel, *The Next 200 Years. A Scenario for America and the World*, New York: William Morrow, 1976, vii.

a whole new set of questions about what is actually going on when policymakers demand predictions.

The central aim of History is not to extract knowledge useful for answering present-day questions, but to understand the dynamics of the past in their own distinctiveness. Of course, this can and does generate insights of use to us now, but if we start every inquiry with this goal, we are unlikely to appreciate the distinctiveness of the past. A History of prediction, then, would examine the *processes by which people have demanded, evaluated and used predictions.*

Much energy history has been written by researchers who are not, in fact, Historians. Their studies of energy transition, for example, are more likely to focus on developing a generic model of transition. Studies of historical policy are often evaluations of whether the policy might be judged 'good'. Perhaps unsurprisingly, such works tend to narrate histories of failure.[5] This outcome might be because the policymakers were mistaken, but in fact the reason for 'failure' as defined by the researcher is often because the policymakers had a set of motivations and pressures that were different from those that the researcher thinks they should have had: they were distracted from what she or he considered the 'real' purpose of energy policy. Such judgements are only clearly valid if there is unambiguous agreement as to what would count as success, and it is often rather difficult to have that discussion with the past. Studies of the dissemination of new energy technology such as electrification or the growth of the oil industry have a tendency to become stories of heroic success (with the assumption that the dissemination was generally desirable, rather than testing any kind of counterfactual). Such studies are perfectly valid in their own right, but are not the kinds of questions History (with exceptions) would usually ask. Historians focus more on questions of the interests and habits and institutions involved in energy policy, on questions of distributive effects and costs and benefits (however defined). These concerns are of course not exclusive to History, but the aim is not to adjudicate whether these are good or bad, or indeed to imagine a world where the unequal distribution of costs or benefits could be minimised or eliminated. Nor is there any search within the discipline for any kind of consensus as to what could have constituted an objectively good outcome that everyone could agree on. Of course historians are all capable of taking part in such debates, and like anyone else have opinions about them; but that is not the purpose of their discipline qua discipline.

History as a discipline does not have a monopoly over using information about the past. What the Historian can reasonably claim is that she or he is well-placed to set such information in its appropriate context – and constant contextualisation is what historians engage in. History does engage with specific research questions, but in contrast to many social scientific disciplines that in principle value parsimony and the tradition of *ceteris paribus* as virtues, the historical imagination tends to expect

[5] A recent example, which in many respects is an excellent history, is Peter Z. Grossman, *U.S. Energy Policy and the Pursuit of Failure*, Cambridge: Cambridge University Press, 2013.

that a satisfactory parsimonious explanation of any phenomenon of interest is unlikely, although not impossible. It is not their goal to find one, which others may find perplexing or even annoying.

This is partly because of History's interest in – unsurprisingly – time, and its tendency to take a 'long view' of any problem. In fact, works of History deal with very different timescales, from the length of centuries to very specific short-term events. There is no standard length of time for a historical study, and indeed there is no particular virtue in looking at longer timescales, as if the longer the view, the greater the insight. Rather, in a discipline that seeks to contextualise and explain the distinctive conditions of events, the expectation is that the factors shaping and explaining an event may have been operative on multiple timescales. A choice in favour of expanding nuclear power, for example, that crucially affects the energy mix and response to the Kyoto Protocol in the 1990s, may have been made in the 1970s, and strongly conditioned by norms of behaviour and institutional 'style' set a generation or more earlier.[6] A factor enabling energy transition may be a technological shift in an industry not directly related to energy at all. Or, for example, levels of air pollution might be shaped by the availability of 'coke' rather than more polluting lower grades of coal, which is a by-product of the demand for 'town gas' and in turn competition between technologies of lighting and cooking rather than heating, although the latter is the proximate source of pollution. Consumer choice regarding domestic household technologies may be shaped by the housing market, forms of tenancies, cultural norms and established gendered divisions of labour – and so on. All of these things can be studied in their own right and 'in their own time'. But the conditions generating such patterns, their interrelation, and the way they change, can only be fully contextualised by *ranging across multiple timescales*. It is this synthetic work, of which a 'long view' is but one component, that gives History its distinctive and eclectic approach, and also explains the final preference for the narrative form even though historians may use many more formal techniques of analysis. And it is this understanding of time, and an aversion to treating historical data as if it is 'timeless' and can be analysed in ways that do not take the distinctiveness of historical context into account, that History brings to policy discussion: the fact that the view is not 'long' but 'many'.

6 See, e.g., Chapter 12 in this volume, by Magnus Lindmark.

8

Management – From the Drawing Board to Successful Delivery

Jim Platts

The development of infrastructure is always a major social and technical exploration process. You cannot simply walk into a shop and buy one. It is not a 'choosing'. What is still called 'the drawing-board stage', even in this computerised age, is a long, careful and collaborative process of coming to understand what the real needs are and what potential solutions have to offer, over a future timescale and a physical scale that most people find difficult to imagine, never mind plan around. So the drawing-board stage itself needs careful planning and management – a paragraph on that in a moment – but the execution stage is still a collaborative exploration, because in all civil engineering works there are always major external factors which are unknown at the beginning (what the weather will be like through next year, for instance) that must be responded to by the team during the journey to keep the project progressing fruitfully.

Several years ago as part of its expansion plans, Hong Kong planned a major new railway development to open up a new area inland. This involved several coordinated contracts covering much earth moving, line laying and station building, both in congested parts of Hong Kong and in the more open new zone, and the boring of a major tunnel through a mountain to get to the new zone. The project was running well until, in the middle of the mountain, the tunnelling process hit some bands of rock that were harder than expected, which slowed progress. This was potentially disastrous as, in the overall plan, the new railway line through the tunnel was meant to be the supply route for much of the equipment and material for the development work on the parts of the project that were in the new zone. Relationships began to fray and the project was beginning to become a bear pit of unhappy engineers arguing and blaming rather than collaborating.

In infrastructure projects, the corollary of 'you can't just buy one' is that the project 'owner' has to be a fully involved 'owner', from the beginning and throughout the whole process, being engaged at every step and taking full responsibility all the time for fully understanding what the needs are, what the options are, what the risks are and what has to be done each day to make each new decision work. Wisely, the Hong Kong officials supervising this project saw the need, searched the world and brought in as project manager a man with the personal characteristics, soundness of judgement and engaging leadership to reunite the team and get the people, and hence the project, back on track. Yes, the technology has to work, but the team has to 'work' for that to happen. This is essentially a task of the spirit and he did it well. In no time he had the respect and the trust of all the members of the team, he had them eating together and collaboratively evolving work-around moves that kept the project flowing. It is not just that the project finished on time and on budget. A happy team emerged, proud of what 'we' had done together and with many friendships established which have gone on to be fruitful in other contexts. They had learnt what it means to be 'civil' engineers.

The word 'wisely' appeared in the last paragraph. There is an ancient Chinese saying:

> Wisdom is knowing what to do next.
> Understanding is knowing how to do it.
> Knowledge is embodied in the ensuing action.

The Hong Kong team wisely understood that whilst they had the responsibility of thoughtful oversight, the project also needed someone to give the wisdom day-by-day embodiment 'on the ground', and they went and found that person and brought him to the project. What does embodied wisdom look like when you meet it in the street?

8.1 EMBODYING WISDOM

In looking at the process of good leadership, Kim and Mauborgne[1] made the important observation that in any project, as in any team, the actual function of leadership shifts from person to person from moment to moment and a key skill is knowing how to work in a team, and to be able to pick it up when it needs you to pick it up, to pass it on when it needs you to pass it on and to facilitate when it needs you to do that. Slightly stiffly, they referred to this as 'procedural justice' – what might be more informally called 'fair play' – but they outlined three key characteristics of a good leadership process, and in doing so identified the 'role' of a wise leader as being essentially about facilitating this process, and 'listening' as being the main tool of facilitation. The three essential characteristics of the process are:

Engagement – the opportunity for individuals to have input into a decision and be able to collectively discuss the merits of one another's ideas and assumptions.

Clarity of expectation – a shared understanding amongst the involved group of each other's responsibilities and what is individually expected of them.

Explanation – an understanding by everyone involved as to why a certain decision has been taken.

[1] Kim, W. C. & Mauborgne, R. 'Fair process: Managing in the knowledge economy', *Harvard Business Review*, Vol. 75(4): 65–75 (1997).

This is a flow process and above all a team process, not a hierarchical 'giving of orders'. It recognises the particular psychological role that emotions play in thinking, especially in the search process that 'understanding the problem' involves. Good managers understand that the psychological role of the emotions is as messengers. The 'task' of emotions is to flag up to consciousness things that need or deserve attention because they are problems or opportunities. The core requirement that follows from this understanding is that there is always some insight lying behind that emotion and you need to understand what that insight is, or you will not have a complete understanding of what is in play. So you must create a non-judgemental safe space for the emotion to flow out, so that you can get to the piece of understanding that is on the far side of it. It is the creating of this safe space that is the task of a wise leader. Wise leaders make it possible for the team to get to understand each other and also the totality of the problem, and then – and only then – to be able to work together to develop a whole and wholesome solution that works for everybody. The saying is 'emotions are messengers, so honour them as messengers and listen to the message. If you treat emotions as masters they become monsters'. The wise project managers in Hong Kong recognised this emerging problem and moved to fix it before it got too late.

8.2 DEVELOPING AN INDUSTRY

Developing a whole new industry, as is needed in the development of renewable energy technologies, is more than a project and the multidimensional nature, scale and timescale of this task must be understood if it is to be achieved successfully. To take wind energy as an example, forty years ago a handful of people across the planet began exploring if it could be technically possible and economically viable to generate electricity from wind. The answer was positive and the global wind industry now employs over a million people and could possibly employ over ten million people in a decade's time[2]. Progress in the development of offshore wind energy in recent years demonstrates what is involved in doing this, but it is first helpful to set out what the industry looks like which produces, installs and operates the wind turbines erected on land.

This global industry is currently installing (as of 2017) some 50 GW of electricity-generating capacity every year, comprising some 25,000 wind turbines each year, mostly with rotor diameters between 80 m and 100 m and generating between 1.5 MW and 3 MW each at full power[3]. This is serious quantity production. To take one company as an example, Vestas, the largest wind turbine manufacturing company globally, with the help of the many companies in its supply chain who make many of the large and small components, itself employs some 20,000 people

[2] Bailey, D. 'Paying lip service, or getting nervous?', *Windpower Monthly*, Vol. 33(12): 22–27 (2017).

[3] 'Complete country-by-country guide to installed wind capacity', *Windpower Monthly*, Vol. 34 (1): 36–37 (2018).

and makes and installs several thousand wind turbines a year – around ten turbines a day – in its several factories around the world and has done so for several decades.

This is a very stable industry with large factories housing long-established workforces that make these turbines. Whilst a company like this is in one sense very capable of developing and making the larger wind turbines appropriate for installing offshore, it cannot do so in these factories because the factories are not physically big enough to make these much larger wind turbines and also the teams of people working in them are fully occupied doing what they are doing now. So, developing new turbines for installation offshore involves also developing new factories with new workers, and this is not a small task.

What is attractive about installing wind turbines offshore is that the wind speeds are higher and also more constant and it is possible to capture something approaching twice the amount of wind energy that a similar turbine might capture if installed on-shore. But it is not easy to do. A cost estimate developed in 2015 for a possible wind farm development far offshore in the North Sea gives an indication of the nature of the problem as it appeared at that time[4]. The turbines are what we see and think about, but as wind energy moves offshore, they become the small part of the story.

8.3 DEVELOPING NEW INFRASTRUCTURE

The estimates for this wind farm suggested that, offshore, the subsea foundations needed for the wind turbines would cost as much as the wind turbines, the subsea electrical power system required to collect the electricity and convey it back to the grid onshore would cost as much as the turbines and foundations together, and the offshore installation costs and then the offshore maintenance and operating costs would be as much again. Moreover, in 2015, all these technologies were 'in development'; they were not 'established technologies'. So 'offshore' was the central technical issue, not the wind turbines. But more than that, the whole exercise was seen as very risky and investment capital was only on offer at an 11 per cent interest rate for something judged to be this risky. Thus, the finance alone was creating 44 per cent of the projected project cost, which was suggesting a price for the eventually produced electricity of some $200.00 per MWh – a very high price for electricity.

8.4 INSIGHTFUL LEADERSHIP IDENTIFIES THE RISKS AND REMOVES THEM

It is always important to remember that 'prices' are first and foremost a signalling system and need to be treated as such. Here, the suggested 11 per cent interest rate is not a rate you should pay for the capital, it is an indication that, in 2015, offshore wind

4 Milborrow, D. 'Offshore wind', *Windpower Monthly*, Vol. 31(9): 59 (2015).

projects such as this were still far too risky for anyone to build a business around and you needed to greatly reduce the level of risk if you wished to proceed successfully. The Netherlands proceeded to do exactly this by directly tackling all the big unknowns themselves[5].

First, the government established a forward plan of five offshore wind farms, all of a standardised size of 700MW capacity, to be built progressively over a period of five years. 700MW is roughly one hundred large wind turbines, so each wind farm is a large project giving a year's work to the successful bidding team. All previous offshore wind farms had been far smaller and gave no continuity of work, so this step introduced the prospect of steady workflow – a key issue, as will be shown in Section 8.5. The government also made a commitment to a secure long-term payment agreement for the electricity produced, which again produced a secure future cash-flow environment for the successful bidding team, which had not previously existed. The creation of this stable environment was a transformational step.

They then removed two of the risks. First, the Dutch government themselves commissioned complete seabed mapping and soil surveys of the sites selected for these five offshore wind farms and made the data available to all bidders. Then, secondly, the government committed to the creation of the subsea electrical infrastructure necessary to deliver the power from the wind farms back to the onshore grid and undertook to have it available in time for the wind farms to have the necessary access to the electricity market as soon as the wind farm was completed and ready to generate power. These were significant risks and their removal enabled the bidders to focus on developing their bids for the wind farms. The resulting winning bids for the first two were, for the first, (Dong) €72.7 per MWh and for the second (Shell) €54.5 per MWh, in each case with the additional cost of paying for the subsea electrical infrastructure, which added approximately €14 per MWh to the total electricity price. These organisational moves by the client had finally made offshore wind projects an economically viable business prospect for the bidders. But the wind industry too had been making progress, and it is important to understand that aspect as well.

8.5 DEVELOPING BIGGER WIND TURBINES

One of the difficulties in wind turbine development is, as the size of wind turbines increases, the cost to develop and prototype a new turbine increases dramatically. Using round numbers to indicate the scale of cost, if a 2 MW wind turbine in mass production costs €2 m, a 10 MW wind turbine similarly in production will cost €10 m. But to develop and prototype it will cost well in excess of €100 m and it is

5 Weston, D. 'Dong wins Borselle tender at record low €72.70/MWh', *Windpower Monthly*, Vol. 32(8): 17 (2016).

likely that fewer of them will be made over the lifetime of the design. At the same time, you need to build larger factories in which to build the turbines and you need to create and train a completely new workforce to do the manufacturing. Accomplishing this costs several hundred million euros. Moreover, the usual consensus is that it takes three years of steady production before a new workforce is completely settled in, fully skilled, smoothly competent, confident in their 'ownership' of the technology and feeling secure in their jobs. Achieving all this is no small undertaking. How do you minimise the risks?

The steps taken by Vestas illustrate one company's route over a fifteen-year period. Since the early 1980s a steady stream of leading-edge innovation in wind turbine blade design and manufacture has come from the Solent area in the UK. Each time the blades got bigger the company involved had to move its location because it needed more space. Coming into the 2000s, in moving from making 23 m long blades to developing 40 m long blades, Vestas moved into a specially designed factory on the Isle of Wight beside the water's edge for ease of transporting the blades. The change also included a substantial development of the manufacturing process, reducing it from 21 steps and two days to 13 steps and a 24-hour production cycle, making these blades very cost effective indeed.

The 82 m-diameter turbine – the Vestas V82 – was a very successful machine, particularly in America, where a second blade factory was built. As blade sizes continued to increase, the Isle of Wight factory – which had been tightly planned around the 40 m blades – could not make bigger blades. Production ceased and shop-floor employment fell. But the engineering creativity was recognised and Vestas made a £79 m investment to create a global blade technology development centre, with a building big enough to make and test blades up to 100 m in length, and it increased the development staff to 200 engineers. Many longer blades were developed and prototyped there, but made in other Vestas blade factories, until the development of the 80 m blades for the 164 m-diameter Vestas V164 turbine intended for offshore use.

This was a major development investment for what was then a tentative offshore market. The cost of a new factory large enough to make these blades, along with the development of a team skilled enough to do so, was a formidable challenge. Insightfully, Vestas recognised that the building on the Isle of Wight was big enough to house modest production of 80 m blades whilst still continuing to develop and test other blades, and the workforce had the skills to do so. So that is what they have done, maximising the technical reach whilst minimising further investment.

8.6 MAKING IT HAPPEN

A new industry does not just 'happen'. As outlined in Section 8.5, there has to be innovation at every step. The conundrum that all work on infrastructure illustrates is that when an infrastructure project has been completed successfully and it all works, people become used to its presence and simply use it without thinking about it, i.e., the very measure of success of the myriad competencies that, moment by moment, decision by decision, made it so, is their invisibility. Failures hit the headlines. Success becomes invisible as it becomes ubiquitous. The wisdom of good leadership – which is always in short supply – lies not only in being able to see, but in caring over, watching for, developing and managing these necessary competencies which are the salt of the earth, yet are invisible to the average eye.

9

Legal Aspects of Energy Policy

Tibisay Morgandi and Jorge E. Viñuales

9.1 INTRODUCTION

Law, understood as legislation and regulations, both domestic and international, as well as their implementation and enforcement, plays a major role in signalling and prompting or, conversely, preventing social change. Law is the language through which energy policies are formulated and enacted. An analysis of the transition towards a more affordable, clean, efficient and secure energy matrix must therefore recognise both the enabling and the limiting functions of law.

As a language, law uses different words to translate what from an economic or modelling perspective may be seen as the same policy. Yet the choice of such words can have significant practical implications. A basic example is the policy of putting a price on carbon. This policy could take the form of a tax, an emissions trading system, a regulation imposing a ceiling on certain types of emissions or the use of certain technologies. It could also be expressed through a wider set of policies such as removing fossil fuel subsidies, setting renewable energy targets or supporting renewable energy through a variety of schemes (e.g., feed-in tariff schemes).

This is already a complex set of options for the expression of carbon pricing. But from a legal perspective even this detailed level of analysis is still oversimplified. A tax, for example, can be legally structured in many different ways depending on what is taxed (e.g., certain fuels, electricity consumption, emissions beyond a set cap, and income), how it is taxed (e.g., through an indirect tax on a certain unit of the taxed object, and through direct taxation of benefits in a certain sector) and why it is taxed (e.g., merely to internalise negative externalities, to provide a (dis)incentive-inducing behavioural change, to penalise certain activities beyond what is required for behavioural inducements, and to raise revenue for certain activities). Moreover, the tax instrument must rest on a sufficient legal basis (e.g., a constitutional provision, a provision in a statute or a regulation implementing a statute), which, in turn, raises questions about the devolution of powers and proper implementation as well as, more generally, the consistency of the implementation of the policy with a broader set of norms ranging from constitutional guarantees to human rights law, investment agreements and trade disciplines. Similar complexities are found in the legal means by which a price can be put on carbon through instruments other than a tax and, more generally, in the legal means of effecting other energy policies, such as entitlements over energy resources, the (de)regulation of energy markets, or liability for damage arising from energy activities.

It is puzzling that this complexity is largely overlooked in technological and mainstream economic approaches to energy policy.[1] To continue with the carbon price example, mainstream models simply assume that a 'carbon price' can be set at a certain level and the entire economy will rearrange itself on the basis of that price. But little attention is paid to the daunting task of translating the idea of a carbon price into an appropriate legal form. Most often, it is assumed that a carbon price amounts merely to a tax or trading scheme, whereas it is likely to take much more than that to have even an approximation of a carbon price in real life.

The purpose of this chapter is to explain in more detail the importance of the legal aspects of energy policy. The answer is relatively simple and can be summarised in two main propositions: (A) different legal expressions have different implications for the effectiveness and overall impact of a policy, and (B) the choice of legal expression (the choice of words to convey the same idea) is highly constrained by (i) law as a technology (i.e., the tools available to translate a policy into legal terms), (ii) the need to fit the policy within a broader legal framework and, of course, (iii) the underlying economic, social and political considerations affecting the choice of certain legal expressions. This chapter illustrates these two propositions by reference to three case studies relating to the extraction of shale gas in the EU (Section 9.2), decarbonisation in the United States (Section 9.3) and state support for renewable energy in India (Section 9.4).

9.2 EXTRACTION OF SHALE GAS IN THE EUROPEAN UNION

During the last fifteen years, the extraction of gas from shale formations through hydraulic fracturing or 'fracking' has become widespread in the United States. There are several reasons for this, including energy security considerations.[2] More recently, and for similar reasons, European countries – particularly Poland, the United Kingdom and Germany – have also taken an interest in shale gas as an alternative energy resource.[3] The European Parliament, in a resolution adopted in 2012, has

1 See, however, J.-F. Mercure et al., 'Modelling Complex Systems of Heterogeneous Agents to Better Design Sustainability Transitions Policy', (2016) 37 *Global Environmental Change* 102.

2 G. Erbach, 'Shale Gas and EU Energy Security', European Parliament – European Parliamentary Research Service, (2014) Members' Research Service, PE 542.167, p. 2.

3 Ibid., pp. 5–6.

expressly recognised the relevance of shale gas (among other unconventional fossil fuels) as a low-carbon source of energy supply in Europe.[4]

This interest in fracking has required European policymakers to consider what legal means are most appropriate to govern the risks associated with this activity, in particular methane emissions and leakage of drilling fluids containing chemicals into soils and into surface and ground waters.[5] In 2012, the European Commission conducted an online consultation open to individuals, national authorities and public and private organisations to seek their views on unconventional fossil fuel production in Europe, including the suitability of the current legal framework.[6] Although the stakeholders participating in the survey expressed divergent views on the topic, they unanimously considered that the current legal framework was not 'well adapted' and that 'the EU should take some action'.[7] Accordingly, in 2014, the commission adopted a set of standards (so-called minimum principles) for the safe and environmentally friendly conduct of fracking.[8] One of the recommendations made by the standards advises each member state to prepare a strategic environmental assessment (SEA) of its fracking policies.[9] The standards also recommend the preparation of an environmental impact assessment (EIA) before member states grant fracking licences, and monitoring of fracking operators by member states on an ongoing basis throughout the different stages of shale gas exploration and production.[10]

It is notable, from a legal standpoint, that the commission's recommendation are not formally binding. The commission merely 'invites' member states to implement its minimum principles and report back to the commission on an annual basis.[11] It is often thought that a non-binding legal instrument is necessarily a less effective means of pursuing policy goals than enforceable law. There is certainly some truth in this proposition, although practice shows that a non-binding instrument can provide a reason for action when there is a will to do so.

For example, following the commission's recommendation, the UK carried out a SEA before granting any new licences to operators.[12] The UK thus complied with

4 European Parliament Resolution 2011/2308 (INI) concerning the environmental impacts of shale gas/oil extraction activities (21 November 2012), point (C).

5 L. Cremonese et al., 'Shale Gas and Fracking in Europe', (2015) IASS Potsdam, Fact Sheet no. 1, pp. 2–3.

6 For further information on the questionnaire and the results of the consultation, see http://ec.europa.eu/environment/consultations/uff_en.htm.

7 F. Cohen et al., 'Analysis and presentation of the results of the public consultation "Unconventional fossil fuels (e.g., shale gas) in Europe"', Final Report for the European Commission DG Environment (2013), 14.

8 European Commission Recommendation on minimum principles for the exploration and production of hydrocarbons (such as shale gas) using high-volume hydraulic fracturing (hereinafter Recommendation) (22 January 2014), 2014/70/EU.

9 Recommendation, point 3.1, p. 75.

10 Recommendation, point 3.3 and points 6 to 11, pp. 75–77.

11 Recommendation, point 16.1, p. 78.

12 Report from the Commission to the European Parliament and the Council on the effectiveness of Recommendation 2014/70/EU on minimum principles for the exploration and production of

this requirement regardless of the recommendation's non-binding character. By contrast, Poland continued to grant licences without conducting an SEA of its fracking policies, contrary to the recommendation.[13] In such a situation, it makes a difference whether an instrument is binding or non-binding. Thus, while Poland's non-compliance with an obligation to conduct an EIA under binding EU law resulted in the European Commission commencing infringement proceedings against Poland before the EU Court of Justice,[14] there is no possibility of similar action for its failure to comply with the recommendation.

This example suggests that whether an instrument implementing a policy is binding or not can have significant impacts on the successful implementation of energy policies insofar as the implementation of non-binding instruments depends to a greater extent upon political will. At the same time, there are reasons for the selection of a non-binding instrument to govern a certain issue. In the present case, the Commission's decision to adopt a non-binding instrument[15] was driven by the need 'to act urgently'[16] on a matter on which member states had shown divergent positions.[17] The urgency of the adoption of this measure can be appreciated in the light of the growing practice established by some member states (e.g., Poland and the UK) of granting shale gas prospecting and exploration licenses even in the absence of a comprehensive EU-wide regulatory framework.[18] The commission also sought to adopt a measure that would provide 'a reference action at national level'.[19] This also occurred in practice. For example, Lithuania set out requirements concerning monitoring of shale gas exploration and exploitation activities that are more detailed than those established by the recommendation.[20]

hydrocarbons (such as shale gas) using high-volume hydraulic fracking (hereinafter Report) (15 December 2016), COM(2016) 794, point 3.1, p. 3.

13 Report, point 3.1, p. 3.

14 Report, point 5, p. 8. For more information about the infringement procedure brought against Poland, see European Commission Press Release on 'Environmental Impact Assessment: Commission refers Poland to the Court of Justice of the EU over inadequate assessment of exploratory mining drillings' (28 April 2016), at http://europa.eu/rapid/press-release_IP-16-1454_en.htm.

15 The Commission considered several types of legal instruments to establish an EU-wide regulatory framework on fracking, including a legally binding instrument (i.e., a directive). See European Commission Impact Assessment concerning the exploration and production of hydrocarbons (such as shale gas) using high volume hydraulic fracturing in the EU (hereinafter Impact Assessment) (22 January 2014), SWD (2014) 21 final, pp. 44 ss. In the end, however, it adopted a non-binding instrument (i.e., the recommendation).

16 European Commission Memo on questions and answers on the shale gas initiative (hereinafter Memo) (22 January 2014), MEMO/14/42, p. 2.

17 Impact Assessment, pp. 44 ss; Cohen, note 7, pp. 67–83.

18 Impact Assessment, p. 34. Countries such as Poland consider their shale gas reserves as a means for emancipating their markets from gas imports from Russia and for effectively addressing energy security issues. See C. Johnson, T. Boersma, 'Energy in(security) in Poland: the case of shale gas', (2013) 53 *Energy Policy* 389, at 394–397.

19 Memo, p. 2.

20 Report, point 3.1, p. 4.

In other words, the commission preferred to adopt a non-binding instrument rather than delay a decision on a pressing issue or fail to adopt any instrument at all. Furthermore, a non-binding instrument, such as the shale gas recommendation, may serve to prepare the ground for the adoption of a binding instrument in the future. And in all events, a non-binding instrument has certain effects (e.g., the UK's uptake of the recommendation) that may suggest 'best practices' and provide a signal to the industry about the direction of travel, thereby triggering a self-reinforcing process.

9.3 LOW-CARBON POLICIES IN THE UNITED STATES

Political conditions can also affect the legal design of the instrument by which energy policies can be implemented. This is well illustrated by the case of the United States. As was widely reported at the time, the efforts of the Obama administration to adopt climate legislation at the national level (the 'Clean Energy and Security Act' or 'Waxman-Markey Bill') could not overcome Republican opposition in the US Senate. The shadow of such opposition (which a decade earlier had equally blocked the ratification of the Kyoto Protocol) also affected the strategy of the United States in international climate negotiations leading to the Paris Agreement.[21] Legal design was a particularly important aspect on both the domestic and the international fronts, and the two are closely related.

The adoption of the Paris Agreement rested upon a prior understanding between the world's two main emitters of greenhouse gases, namely, China and the United States. In order to reorient the domestic energy production trajectory, the Obama administration sought to tackle emissions from power plants by way of regulation, namely the Clean Power Plan (CPP) of 2015.[22] The CPP was a way of overcoming domestic opposition through the selection of a specific legal form as well as of providing a credible basis for an international agreement. However, the choice of a specific legal instrument has implications for the viability of the energy policy it is designed to pursue. In the absence of nationwide legislation on climate change,[23] the administration turned to another avenue, a legal enabler, the decades-old Clean Air Act (CAA), which authorises regulations to fight air pollution.[24] By interpreting the concept of 'air pollutants' in the CAA to include carbon dioxide,[25] it became legally possible to adopt the CPP under the CAA. What to a non-lawyer may look like a hardly noticeable difference in legal form is, in practice, very important for the

[21] The Paris Agreement was adopted, as an Annex to Decision 1/CP.21, on 12 December 2015. For further information on the agreement, see http://unfccc.int/paris_agreement/items/9485.php.

[22] EPA, Carbon Pollution Emission Guidelines for Existing Stationary Sources: Electric Utility Generating Units, 80 Fed. Reg. 64,662 (October 23, 2015).

[23] This discussion relies on J. E. Viñuales, 'Law and the Anthropocene' (2016) *C-EENRG/Collège de France Joint Working Paper Series* 2016–4.

[24] CAA, 42 U.S.C. §7401 et seq. (1970).

[25] *Massachusetts* v. *EPA* 549 US 497 (2007).

possibility of overcoming political opposition, as well as for the prospects of the CPP. This became manifest when in early February 2016 the US Supreme Court suspended the implementation of the CPP following legal action from a group of adversely affected parties.[26]

The legal strategy followed by the Obama administration at the domestic level also influenced the legal strategy that was pursued in international climate negotiations. To appreciate the importance of legal form, it is useful to refer to a detail that made newspaper headlines suggesting that a mere word (namely the use of 'shall' instead of 'should' in Article 4(4) of the draft Paris Agreement) could have derailed the entire negotiation. In its final formulation, the first sentence of Article 4(4) states that 'developed country Parties should continue taking the lead by undertaking economy-wide absolute emission reduction targets'.[27] Given the absence of economy-wide climate legislation – a consequence of the failure of the Waxman-Markey Bill to pass the US Senate – accepting the verb 'shall' in this provision would have meant that the United States was going beyond the scattered (hence, not economy-wide) legal authority provided by legislation such as the CAA. Moreover, going beyond such authority would have meant that the Paris Agreement would have contained emission-reduction obligations that were binding as a matter of international law but not of domestic law (e.g., under the sole authority of the CAA). Under Article 2, section II of the US Constitution, that would have made the Paris Agreement a 'Treaty' (rather than an 'executive agreement') that required the approval of the Republican-dominated Senate.

It is for this reason that what appears to be a mere word had deep legal and political roots. Secretary of State John Kerry – who led the negotiations on behalf of the United States – expressly and successfully conditioned the support of the United States to the agreement as a whole on the use of the word 'should' instead of 'shall' in Article 4(4).[28] The use of the word 'should' allowed Kerry to maintain that the Paris Agreement 'doesn't need to be approved by the Congress because it doesn't have mandatory targets for reduction, and it doesn't have an enforcement compliance mechanism'.[29] A similar point can be made in connection with Article 15 of the Paris Agreement, which, unlike the Kyoto Protocol, does not provide for a compliance mechanism with an enforcement dimension.[30]

Furthermore, legal design was also used to lock in, at least to some extent, the climate policies adopted during President Obama's second term. Articles 28(1) and 28(2) of the Paris Agreement serve this purpose.[31] They provide that State Parties may

[26] Order in pending case, *West Virginia et al.* v. *EPA et al.* (February 9, 2016), 577 U.S. 15A773.

[27] Paris Agreement, Article 4(4).

[28] J.E. Viñuales, 'The Paris Agreement on Climate Change: Less is More', (2017) 59 *German Yearbook of International Law*, 11.

[29] Quoted in D. Wirth, 'Cracking the American Climate Negotiators' Hidden Code: United States Law and the Paris Agreement' (2016) 6 *Climate Law* 152, at 168.

[30] Paris Agreement, Article 15.

[31] Paris Agreement, Articles 28(1) and 28(2).

withdraw in writing from the agreement only after three years from the date of its entry into force and that such withdrawal takes effect upon expiry of at least one year from the date the depositary receives the notification of withdrawal.[32] This means that the agreement is, from a legal standpoint, immune from any repudiation for at least four years, which is, not coincidentally, the duration of a first-term US President. The relevance of this clause can be seen in the announcement of President Trump in June 2017 that the United States would withdraw from the Paris Agreement.[33] That modicum of legal resistance may suffice, together with the wealth of scientific and socio-economic indications encouraging the transition towards a low-carbon economy, for the private sector to refrain from making investment decisions on the mere basis of a presidential announcement, even if eventually the withdrawal were to take effect.

9.4 RENEWABLE ENERGY SUPPORT IN INDIA

A third case study illustrates the constraints imposed on energy policies by legal regimes with other objectives, such as the regimes governing international trade and investment. These regimes essentially require government policies to follow due process standards, to be proportionate to the goal being pursued and to be non-discriminatory as between foreign and domestic producers and investors. Energy policies that do not meet these conditions can be challenged before an international trade or investment tribunal.

How this works in practice can be seen in the example of a subsidies scheme introduced by India to support the production of renewable energy (solar) equipment.[34] The key point in this case is that India limited its support to domestic producers. Indeed, the Indian renewable energy support scheme (the National Solar Mission adopted as part of India's National Action Plan on Climate Change) included local content ('buy local') requirements (LCRs).[35] This meant that a producer of electricity from renewable sources had to purchase equipment from Indian manufacturers in order to participate in the government electricity purchase programme.[36] India introduced LCRs to support its renewable energy equipment

32 Paris Agreement, Articles 28(1) and 28(2).

33 See 'Trump Will Withdraw U.S. from Paris Climate Agreement', *New York Times*, 1 June 2017, available at www.nytimes.com/2017/06/01/climate/trump-paris-climate-agreement.html.

34 This example draws upon the discussion on the function of law in promoting or hindering the transition towards sustainable energy systems carried out by Viñuales in 'Law and the Anthropocene', note 25, pp. 55–56.

35 The text of the Jawaharlal Nehru National Solar Mission (hereinafter National Solar Mission) launched on 11 January 2010 is available at www.mnre.gov.in/file-manager/UserFiles/mission_document_JNNSM.pdf.

36 National Solar Mission, point 6, pp. 7–10.

industry as well as to garner political support for the introduction of a feed-in-tariff scheme. Many other countries have introduced LCRs for the same reasons.[37]

The difficulty, however, is that LCRs are, as a rule, illegal under international trade disciplines. Indeed, following legal action from the United States and others, a WTO trade panel found India in breach of its international trade obligations.[38] Underlying this ruling – and the trade rules on which it is based – is the idea that trade must be liberalised to promote efficiency, based on the principle of comparative advantage. If a foreign producer of solar energy equipment abroad is more efficient (it produces and sells at a lower price) than an Indian producer, then its advantage must not be neutralised by governmental interference (protectionism). The policy question that arises is whether this imperative – justifiable from the perspective of international economics – should override other concerns, including energy security (by diversifying energy sources and strengthening the local energy industry), environmental protection (by reducing emissions) and inclusiveness (by creating work and supporting nascent industries).

But even if the introduction of LCRs in an energy policy is vulnerable to legal challenge in the long term, in the short term it can encourage local industry to do its utmost to adjust to new conditions. It is worth noting that, under international trade law, the damage caused by an unlawful policy is not compensated. The obligation of a state in breach is only to bring its laws back into compliance with trade disciplines. Therefore, states and their industries may consider the time it will take for a challenge to be brought and the duration of the procedure as breathing space for a domestic industry to be supported. The nature of the legal regime for enforcing constraints on climate-friendly energy policies is therefore another relevant piece in the regulatory puzzle.

9.5 LEGAL ASPECTS OF 'GOOD' ENERGY POLICY

The illustrations provided in this chapter demonstrate the relevance of legal form in promoting or hindering energy policies. The final and broader question that needs to be addressed is how legal analysis may contribute to 'good' energy policy. The basic answer is that energy policies have a higher chance of being introduced (overcoming certain political constraints) and being effective (harnessing socio-economic buy-in) if they are enshrined in a legal form that is both adaptive to existing political conditions and resilient to future legal challenges or amendments.

37 See J.-C. Kuntze and T. Moerenhout, 'Local Content Requirements and the Renewable Energy Industry: A Good Match?', *ICTSD Study* (May 2013).

38 *India – Certain Measures Relating to Solar Cells and Solar Modules, Report of the Panel*, 24 April 2016, WT/DS456/R. This decision was subsequently confirmed by the WTO Appellate Body, *India – Certain Measures Relating to Solar Cells and Solar Modules*, AB Report (16 September 2016), WT-DS456/AB/R.

Different legal forms can be used for different purposes and within specifically defined legal, economic and political constraints. The non-binding recommendation used at the EU level to govern fracking is flexible enough to accommodate different national circumstances and, at the same time, it enjoys some level of effectiveness. The complex legal strategy followed by the Obama administration both to overcome domestic opposition and to command sufficient credibility in international climate negotiations relied on the specific legal nature of 'regulations' under previously reinterpreted legislation (the CAA) as well as on the technical difference between a 'treaty' and an 'executive agreement'. Although not developed in this chapter, similar considerations of design can be used to make LCRs more difficult to challenge under international trade law.

However, adaptability has a price, particularly in terms of resilience to subsequent legal changes. In some cases, the legal form selected may promote such resilience, as suggested by the withdrawal provisions of the Paris Agreement. But this is not always the case, as can be seen in the challenge against the CPP in the US Supreme Court, and the challenge to India's LCRs. But even then, a short-term gain can override a long-term loss, whether politically or strategically (if an infant industry is thereby given the time to become internationally competitive).

The purpose of these remarks is not to take a stance on the desirability of specific energy policies. It is simply, and more fundamentally, to show that the legal form of energy policies as well as the analysis of this form are important considerations in designing 'good' energy policy.

PART II

Cases and Multidisciplinary Responses

10

The Ethics of Nuclear Energy: Its Past, Present and Future[1]

Behnam Taebi and Sabine Roeser

10.1 INTRODUCTION

On 11 March 2011, a large earthquake struck off the coast of the Fukushima prefecture in Japan. Less than an hour later, a massive tsunami wave rumbled off Japan's north-western coast and damaged, among other things, the nuclear energy reactors in Fukushima-Daiichi. The nuclear disaster in Japan has let several countries to reconsider their nuclear energy policies. Not surprisingly, the largest impact was visible in Japan, where the entire nuclear fleet (reactors) was eventually shut down. Yet other countries have also decided to not expand or to phase out nuclear energy, most notably Germany that immediately shut down eight of its older reactors; the other seven German reactors are scheduled to shut down in 2022.

These setbacks by no means mark the end of the nuclear era. Nuclear energy is still growing, but mostly in other parts of the world; i.e., the nuclear landscape is tilting towards Asia, with China and India as the new leaders in the field. In the same vein, many fast-growing developing countries, most notably emerging economies, are interested in this source of electricity that could help them meet their vastly growing electricity demands. Furthermore, even if nuclear energy production would stop as of today, several issues associated with the decommissioning of the reactors and the treatment and disposal of nuclear waste will last for at least several decades. As a result, the societal and ethical issues associated with nuclear energy production and waste disposal will remain relevant for at least the same period or perhaps even longer, considering the longevity of nuclear waste's lifetime. A revival of the field of 'ethics of nuclear energy' is needed in light of the new global developments (cf. Taebi and Roeser 2015b).

In this chapter, we will review the evolution of the field of 'ethics of nuclear energy'. In Section 2, we will briefly review the history of this field over the previous four decades, while explaining the crucial distinction between nuclear

[1] This chapter is partly drawing on the following piece (Taebi and Roeser 2015a). It is, however, in the focus of the argument a substantially expanded version of that piece.

safety and security. The chapter will review several new and emerging challenges of nuclear energy production and waste disposal, in light of several important developments. We will here list four of the most pressing ethical challenges, while discussing the state of the art and future questions associated with each challenge. These ethical challenges will be discussed in more depth in the remainder of our chapter.

First, most operating reactors worldwide were built in the 1960s and 1970s. Since then, the technology has improved substantially. Both new reactor technologies and new fuel cycles could help us meet several of the old challenges (e.g., nuclear meltdown), while posing new challenges. What will be a morally 'acceptable' nuclear energy production method if we consider the existing and possible new technologies? Future key challenges of nuclear energy could best be understood within the framework of intergenerational justice; these will be discussed in Section 3.

Second, and related to the previous problems associated with nuclear waste disposal, there is a new tendency to consider nuclear waste disposal in several countries. This could be a joint collaboration of countries that all possess some amount of nuclear waste – small nuclear energy producers, for instance in Europe (Salzer et al. 2012) are interested in such proposals – or as an international host repository that could accept waste from other countries, as in the ongoing developments in South Australia (Scarce 2016). These multinational collaborations pose new ethical and governance challenges. More specifically, they create various problems of justice (both spatially and temporally) that need to be specifically addressed. This will be done in Section 4.

Third, the new geographical distribution of nuclear energy around the globe will pose several new safety challenges i.e., current nuclear safety governance regimes are based on strong notions of national sovereignty while – to quote the former Director General of the International Atomic Energy Agency, Hans Blix – 'a nuclear accident somewhere is a nuclear accident everywhere' (Blix 1986). Moreover, and somewhat connected to the previous concern, multinational collaborations for nuclear waste disposal (but also for nuclear fuel provision purposes as the Russian fuel leasing programs) pose new challenges. New and more stringent forms of supranational governance are needed for the future of nuclear safety, which will be discussed in Section 5.

Fourth, nuclear energy projects, most notably nuclear disposal facilities, engender highly emotional controversies. As with other siting questions, a typical pattern can be observed: society is alarmed and worried about its risky aspects, whereas experts assure them that the risks are negligible. Policymakers typically respond to this in two ways: either they ignore the emotions of the public or they take them as a reason to prohibit or restrict a technology. We call these responses the technocratic pitfall and the populist pitfall, respectively (Roeser 2018), and argue that neither is helpful for nuclear waste governance. Instead, new methods are needed that address and include people's emotional responses, as those indicate their deeper moral concerns. Section 6 deals with these challenges.

In Section 7, our concluding section, we wrap up our discussion concerning these challenges and their relevance for the future governance of nuclear energy production and waste management, and we also provide a few suggestions for further research on the topic.

10.2 THE ETHICS OF NUCLEAR ENERGY: WHERE WE COME FROM

In academic research on nuclear technology, one distinguishes between nuclear safety and nuclear security. Safety usually refers to preventing unintentional harm or harm as a result of a nuclear accident, while security refers to safeguarding against intentional harm. The latter refers to risks of theft of nuclear material for the purpose of nuclear sabotage or manufacturing a so-called nuclear dirty bomb, as well as any other way of exposing a large number of people to harmful radiation. Proliferation means the dispersal of both the knowledge that could lead to manufacturing of nuclear weapons and to dispersal of the weapons themselves.

In previous decades, discussions of nuclear non-proliferation and arms control have been the main focus of the ethical analyses associated with nuclear energy. However, some research has focused more on ethical issues associated with nuclear energy, mostly from the perspective of whether it is morally justified to produce nuclear energy. This is a question to which Kneese (1973) unequivocally responds in the title of his essay 'The Faustian Bargain'. Routley and Routley (1979) argue that considering the longevity and the toxicity of nuclear waste, nuclear energy production is morally unacceptable. A number of other authors reflected on the desirability of nuclear energy and unanimously reached the conclusion that it is ethically unacceptable to produce nuclear energy because of the inability of victims to control their fate (Hollyday 1991) and the unacceptable radiation risk that arises from nuclear energy for both the public and radiation workers (Bertell 1991). Kristin Shrader-Frechette did pioneering work on this topic in the 1990s. In addition to editing the first collection that addressed the ethical issues of nuclear energy (Shrader-Frechette 1991), she wrote several influential articles and books that address various ethical aspects of nuclear energy and nuclear risk (Shrader-Frechette 1980, 1991, 1993, 1994, 2000). Among other things, she questioned the ethical acceptability of nuclear energy because of its inequitable distribution of risks (Shrader-Frechette 1991) as well as environmental justice concerns associated with different steps in the production of nuclear energy (e.g., Wigley and Shrader-Frechette 1996). In a more recent book, she argues that renewable energy, rather than nuclear energy, is the answer to addressing the challenges posed by climate change (Shrader-Frechette 2011a).

There are a number of other recent works that address ethical issues associated with nuclear energy production and nuclear waste disposal (Löfquist 2008; Gosseries

2008; Doyle II 2010; Taebi 2011; Roeser 2011b; Taebi, Roeser, and Van de Poel 2012; Taebi 2012; Oughton and Hansson 2013; Taebi and Roeser 2015b; Taebi and Van de Poel 2015).[2] This chapter focuses on four of the most pressing ethical challenges and their relevance for the future governance of nuclear energy production and waste management, as well as for future academic research on the topic.

10.3 NEW NUCLEAR TECHNOLOGY: OLD AND NEW CHALLENGES

One important reason why we need new thinking about the societal and ethical issues of nuclear energy is that the technology has seriously advanced throughout the last decades. Most operating reactors worldwide were built in the 1960s and 1970s, but both new reactor technologies and new fuel cycles could help us meet several of the old challenges. A good example is the problem of nuclear meltdown, or uncontrolled heat production that could lead to the melting of a nuclear fuel. The horrifying consequences of nuclear meltdown have been most visible in the Chernobyl accident. However, since then, nuclear reactors have substantially improved; i.e., new generations of reactors have reduced substantially the probability of a meltdown. Moreover, even newer reactors have been proposed that could make a meltdown physically impossible due to the shape of the reactor and the materials with which the nuclear fuel is fabricated.[3] This, however, does not mean that there are no risks – nuclear risks or otherwise – involved in these types of reactors. Even without a meltdown, ionising radiation could leak from a reactor, which could pose serious health and safety risks. This means that the current governance paradigm that relates to reactor safety in terms of melt-down probabilities has to be adjusted. Moreover, reactors are not only designed for safety; there are a number of other ethically relevant values that play a key role in the design of new reactors; i.e., the Best Achievable Nuclear Reactor must be affordable, use nuclear fuel efficiently, and leave behind little and short-lived nuclear waste. It must also be designed so as to reduce the possibility of nuclear proliferation (Taebi and Kloosterman 2015). These criteria are, however, not always compatible, which means that the safest reactor is not the most resource-efficient one and the most affordable reactor is not necessarily the most secure one. This means that choices

[2] In addition, substantial work has been done by various national and international organisations in establishing ethical principles for governing the risk of nuclear energy and nuclear waste disposal. In particular, the work done by the following organisations should be acknowledged: the International Commission on Radiological Protection (ICRP 1977, 2007), the International Atomic Energy Agency (IAEA 1997; IAEA et al. 2006), the Nuclear Energy Agency (NEA-OECD 1995), the National Council for Nuclear Waste in Sweden (KASAM 1988, 2005, 2007) and the Canadian Nuclear Waste Management Organization (NWMO 2005); see also (Wilson 2000).

[3] This requires a radically new design of nuclear reactors from scratch. The High Temperature Reactor Pebble bed Module (HTR-PM) has passive core cooling (due to its shape as a long cylinder with a small radius) and it uses a type of fuel cladding (which surrounds nuclear fuel) that melts at higher temperatures than the temperature that the reactor could maximally achieve. For more information, see (Taebi and Kloosterman 2015).

need to be made that also involve ethical considerations, which in turn must inform the governance of nuclear risk.

The type and specific design of a nuclear reactor is a key component for nuclear energy production, but there are also governance issues associated with nuclear technology, which must be addressed at the level of the nuclear fuel cycle, or the production method for generating nuclear energy. The question that needs to be addressed is: what is a morally 'acceptable' method of nuclear energy production if we consider the existing and possible new technologies? This also involves considerations of intergenerational justice. In what follows we will discuss the notion of intergenerational justice in the context of nuclear energy technology.

In producing and consuming nuclear energy we are essentially creating a problem of justice for posterity since we are depleting a non-renewable resource (i.e., uranium) that will eventually be unavailable to future generations. Furthermore, the phenomenon of long-lived radiotoxic waste adds another intergenerational dimension to the problem. We argue that since we – the present generation – will enjoy the lion's share of the benefits created by nuclear energy, we have a moral obligation also to deal with its burdens. This gives rise to the question as to which fuel cycle is most desirable from the perspective of intergenerational justice.[4]

Nuclear energy is currently produced using either the open or the closed fuel cycle. These fuel cycles are similar until the first uranium irradiation phase in the reactor is reached. Precisely how the remaining *spent fuel* is dealt with determines the nature of the fuel cycle and therefore also the distribution of burdens and benefits between generations. In an open fuel cycle, spent fuel is viewed as waste and is supposed to be disposed of underground and isolated from the biosphere for 200,000 years. The open fuel cycle variant is mainly associated with short-term advantages, as it creates relatively less radiological risk and thus fewer public health and environmental concerns; larger radiological risks take the form of long-term waste disposal. On the other hand the closed fuel cycle could be linked to long-term resource durability because spent fuel is seen as a resource that can be reprocessed to extract deployable materials (uranium and plutonium), which then re-enter the fuel cycle. A closed fuel cycle is further capable of reducing the waste lifetime by a factor of twenty (to 10,000 years). Reprocessing is, however, a very complex chemical process. It is very costly and only available in a very few countries in the world. More importantly, during reprocessing plutonium is separated and that creates serious concerns in relation to the proliferation of nuclear weapons.[5]

In short, the choice between the two existing fuel cycles involves considerations of justice between generations. These insights are indeed relevant for retrospective (*ex post*) reflections on the choices made by each country to pursue the open or the closed fuel cycle. Perhaps more importantly, these insights could guide policy

[4] Both questions have been extensively dealt with in (Taebi 2010).

[5] For an extensive discussion of these fuel cycles, see Taebi and Kloosterman (2008).

decisions on future choices for a fuel cycle, hence for an *ex ante* analysis. When doing so, it is of course important not only to include current technology but also its future promises because, as mentioned earlier, nuclear reactors – but also several other associated technologies – are continuously being further developed (Taebi, Roeser, and Van de Poel 2012; Taebi and Kloosterman 2015).

Following our argument that the present generations have the responsibility to deal with the remaining nuclear waste, we can reflect on the choice for a nuclear fuel cycle. As mentioned above, the closed fuel cycle scores best from the perspective of reducing the waste lifetime, which is better from the perspective of future safety. A recent fuel cycle could – in principle – enable us to reduce the waste lifetime after recycling from 10,000 to about 1,000 years. This fuel cycle is an extension of a closed fuel cycle and it is based on two new technological advancements. First, a new type of reactor is needed (a so-called fast reactor) for deactivating the isotopes and, second, a new reprocessing technology must be introduced to repeatedly reprocess this new type of spent fuel coming from the new reactor. The scientific feasibility of both these technologies has been shown at the lab level; their further development and industrialisation would, however, require a few decades' time and substantial investments. Moreover, in addition to the short-term burdens of the closed fuel cycle, this *extended* closed fuel cycle will create even more short-term radiation risk (both for human beings and the environment) as well as economic burdens (for the further developments of these technologies). This gives rise to the same essential question of intergenerational justice: i.e., what level of protection should we guarantee for future generations and to what extent does that justify additional burdens for the present generations (Taebi 2011). The question of what constitutes desirable – or acceptable – nuclear energy should explicitly address these considerations.

Including these considerations in decision making has implications for the type of fuel cycle a country might consider for nuclear energy production. But it also has important bearing on the choices for nuclear waste management, i.e., when disentangling the implications of waste management choices for future generations, we see that an option could be good for the immediately following generation while it scores less well for distant future generations (Kermisch 2016; Kermisch, Depaus, and Labeau 2016; Kermisch and Taebi 2017). The conceptual clarification of the notion of future generations is again important for the governance of nuclear energy and nuclear waste disposal.

10.4 MULTINATIONAL NUCLEAR WASTE DISPOSAL AND PROBLEMS OF JUSTICE

Yet another important new development that is highly relevant to consider for the good governance of nuclear energy is the quest for multinational disposal. An increasing number of countries are developing an interest in such repositories.

The arguments most often heard in favour of multinational repositories are strategic arguments, including the following three. First, building a disposal facility costs a few decades of research and development and its implementation is expected to spawn serious controversies, as has been shown in many countries around the world. For countries with small nuclear energy programs, say one or two nuclear reactors, it makes sense to join forces and embark on these costly and technically difficult activities collaboratively. Second, from the perspective of enhancing safety and security, it is expected that when countries join forces and (financial) efforts, this could lead to safer and more secure disposal facilities (IAEA 1998). Third, some countries do not have very suitable geological places for hosting a repository; the host geology is very important for the period in which radioactivity could be kept away from the biosphere. Joint disposal facilities could then, potentially, increase long-term safety of repositories, which could be beneficial for future generations.

In addition to these strategic arguments, there are also ethical considerations that one needs to take into account. On the one hand, one could argue that multinational repositories could be supported from the perspective of intergenerational justice; i.e., when we concentrate the number of facilities holding risks for the future this decreases the risk of human intrusion in the event of knowledge about the location of repositories being lost. To illustrate this with a simple example, future generations in Europe would be better off if the fifteen current European nuclear power-producing countries were to dispose of their nuclear waste in, for example, five rather than fifteen separate locations.[6] On the other hand, multinational repositories can create an instance of injustice for the present generations as they involve one country hosting another country's nuclear waste. Some scholars argue that the decisions to host a multinational repository should involve an economic transaction – that is, a country should receive funds to take care of another country's waste – claiming that we should guarantee that there is social acceptance in the receiving country (Boutellier, McCombie, and Mele 2006). Considering multinational disposal merely in terms of economic transactions can, however, obscure the created injustice between countries (Taebi 2012, 2017). For one thing, it disregards the economic starting positions of countries and their sensitivity to economic incentives. For another, the fundamental ethical issue remains unanswered as to why it is justified for one country to accept another country's waste. What exacerbates the situation is the fact that international injustice issues will be perpetuated into the future, creating a problem of intergenerational injustice, which cannot straightforwardly be overcome by economic compensations; moreover, future generations cannot be asked for their consent in such a transaction.

This type of international injustice that multinational nuclear waste repositories create is comparable to the chemical waste exports from industrialised to non-industrialised countries in the 1970s and 1980s. This situation was mainly

[6] See (Taebi 2012) for a detailed defence of the last argument.

attributable to the tightening of environmental laws in developed countries, which led to enormous domestic waste disposal costs. For companies, it became a cheaper option to export most of their waste to African states where no such laws existed. In order to avoid such injustice, the Basel Convention on the Control of the Transboundary Movements of Hazardous Wastes and their Disposal was agreed upon. This convention restricts countries in exporting hazardous chemical waste to other countries. Interestingly enough, nuclear waste is not included in the Basel Convention. The Convention could be revised to also address issues of multinational nuclear waste disposal. Decision making about this should go beyond a mere pursuit of social acceptance in the receiving country, rather, it should take into account issues of inter- and intragenerational justice and fairness. This emphasises the need to elevate questions of nuclear risks governance above nation states, which will be elaborated in Section 10.5.

10.5 THE NEED FOR GLOBAL GOVERNANCE OF NUCLEAR ENERGY

As mentioned in Section 10.4, multinational repositories urge us to consider questions of nuclear risk governance beyond the current focus of national governance. Moreover, the new geographical distribution of nuclear energy will pose several new safety challenges that should be considered at the supranational level, for pragmatic as well as moral reasons. Current nuclear safety governance regimes are, however, strongly based on notions of national sovereignty. This is problematic for future governance of nuclear energy and nuclear waste management.

Nuclear energy technology is essentially an international technology insofar as only a handful of countries have the capability of manufacturing nuclear reactors and a limited number of countries have the facilities to enrich uranium for energy production purposes. Moreover, if a country chooses to reprocess its waste in a closed cycle, currently, that country would likely depend on the only two commercial reprocessing plants in the world, which are located in France and the UK. Yet, there are very strong national sentiments attached to this technology; in the 1950s and 1960s, nuclear energy was considered a matter of national prestige, prosperity and pride (Bergen 2016). In the current state of the world, countries increasingly consider themselves as technologically advanced when they host a nuclear energy reactor. Moreover, the need for more electricity is increasingly felt in many developing countries and emerging economies, which helps explain the growing interest of these countries in nuclear energy. This is particularly the case if countries have committed themselves to the Paris Agreement and to not using carbon-intensive electricity such as coal power plants. Current nuclear energy production is showing a shift towards countries that have had less experience with this technology. While it is a commonly heard argument that the major nuclear accidents have been in countries with considerable experience – the most recent example is the Fukushima-Daiichi accident that occurred in Japan, considered a very advanced nuclear country – the new distribution of nuclear energy, together with the increasing attention for multinational disposal, emphasises the need for global governance of nuclear safety. To be sure, emphasising the need for global governance does not mean national governance by national legislators and regulators becomes obsolete. A global regime of nuclear governance should strive for a balance of rights and obligations between individual countries as well as taking into account the well-being of humanity as such, also concerning future generations. Furthermore, such a global governance regime requires international oversight and monitoring (Taebi and Mayer 2017). Such a proposal will, of course, create new challenges and questions that need to be addressed in order to achieve good governance of nuclear energy.

10.6 NUCLEAR RISK, VALUES AND EMOTIONS

A main challenge for policymaking about nuclear technology on a national as well as on a global level is that nuclear power plants as well as nuclear disposal facilities engender tremendous controversies that are often highly emotional. Members of the public are often concerned about a possible meltdown of a nuclear reactor, and that the storage of nuclear waste may also have unforeseen risks. Policymakers, nuclear experts and proponents of nuclear energy usually see these emotional responses as a sign of irrationality and lack of understanding by the public. They refer to quantitative, probabilistic risk assessments that show that the risk of, for example, a nuclear meltdown is extremely unlikely. In other cases, a lack of societal support has been seen as a reason to phase out nuclear energy, as happened in Germany after the Fukushima accident. We can call these responses a technocratic versus a populist approach, respectively (Roeser 2018). In both kinds of responses, there is no genuine debate about the moral desirability of nuclear energy. This is due to several assumptions: 1) that decision making about risky technologies such as nuclear energy is a purely technical matter; 2) that such decision making does not involve any ethical considerations; and 3) that the emotional responses of the public are irrational. In what follows we will argue that all three of these assumptions are mistaken. We will argue that decision making about risky technologies, and specifically about nuclear energy, is highly value laden and should hence also take into account emotional responses, as these can point to important ethical considerations.

We already mentioned ethical aspects of nuclear energy in the previous sections. Here we will analyse in more detail what the relationship is between quantitative and ethical aspects of nuclear energy and concomitant risks. The standard approach to risk is to define it in terms of probability of an unwanted effect. This is typically measured in terms of annual fatalities, and then a cost–risk benefit analysis is applied to compare different options. This is considered to be a purely quantitative approach. However, this approach faces severe methodological and ethical problems.

The probabilistic approach to nuclear safety is methodologically highly problematic as it systematically leaves out events that are hard to quantify, such as human failure, because such events are unique and hard to predict, but these are often the cause of (near) accidents (Downer 2015). Furthermore, the standard approach to risk is highly value laden. First of all, what counts as an unwanted effect is an ethical decision. Should it only include fatalities, or also long-term illness, or maybe also the loss of one's home or an emotional attachment to a region? Arguably, the latter cannot simply be replaced in the form of financial compensation or a new home. This is highly relevant for people who had to leave, for example, the Chernobyl and Fukushima areas after the nuclear disasters that took place there. After each accident some areas became exclusion zones, which means that they have become uninhabitable, at least for a substantial period of time. In the case of Chernobyl, many people suffered long-term health effects. Furthermore, there are impacts on nature that may be considered morally problematic in themselves, irrespective of effects on human well-being.

How should these very different kinds of impacts be measured and balanced? Usually a cost–risk benefit analysis is used to address impacts of risky events. However, it is unclear how one can compare these different kinds of damages on a common scale. Furthermore, cost–risk benefit analysis resembles a consequentialist approach in ethics. According to such an approach, the ends justify the means, and negative and positive effects should be assessed on an overall, aggregate basis. However, other ethical theories have criticised consequentialist approaches since some actions are bad in themselves, irrespective of their consequences (either good or bad), such as intentionally harming people. An overall, aggregate assessment of positive and negative effects overlooks important ethical issues of autonomy, fairness and equity, since it could justify the exploitation of minorities against their will. In short, the standard approach to risk is far from value neutral, and it leaves out important ethical considerations; see (Krimsky and Golding 1992; Shrader-Frechette 1993; Asveld and Roeser 2009; Roeser et al. 2012) for criticisms of the quantitative approach to risk from a variety of disciplines. Rather, technological risk involves quantitative and ethical considerations at the same time; see (Möller 2012) on risk as a so-called thick concept, i.e., a concept that is descriptive and normative at the same time.

Empirical research has shown that laypeople's risk perceptions do include such additional considerations (Slovic 2000) that can be justified on ethical grounds (Roeser 2007). Also, lay risk perceptions tend to be emotional (Slovic 2010), which leads numerous scholars to argue that the emotions of individuals should not play a role in decision making about risk, as emotions are usually seen as contrary to rational decision making (Sunstein 2005). However, emotion research shows that emotions are crucial to ethical decision making (Frijda 1987; Damasio 1994; Nussbaum 2001; Roberts 2003; Roeser 2011a). These insights about emotions are highly relevant for decision making about risk: emotional responses to risk, such as fear, concern, indignation and feelings of care and responsibility can highlight important ethical aspects of risk such as justice, fairness and autonomy that are excluded from the standard, quantitative approach to risk (Roeser 2006, 2018).

In short, the three assumptions mentioned at the beginning of this section do not hold. These assumptions underlie the idea that one should not include public concerns in decision making about nuclear energy. In direct contrast, our argument emphasises that it is actually of vital importance to include the public and their emotional responses in decision making about nuclear energy, as these responses help to point out important ethical issues. Of course, in doing so, quantitative information should not be excluded from decision making. Indeed, such information is necessary; however, it is not sufficient for decision making about nuclear energy. Legitimate decisions also require ethical thinking, which in turn involves attention to emotions as a source of insight into what morally matters (Roeser 2011b; Taebi, Roeser, and Van de Poel 2012; Nihlén Fahlquist and Roeser 2015).

Here are a few examples of how emotions can help draw our attention to ethical considerations in the context of nuclear energy. The standard approach to risk in terms of probability times an unwanted effect does not distinguish between high-probability, low-impact events and low-probability, high-impact events, in case the product of probability and effect is similar. However, emotionally and morally these could be substantially different. Even if a nuclear disaster is highly unlikely, if it happens, its effects can have an impact that is incomparable with any other technology, as in the case of the Chernobyl disaster, which had effects way beyond the direct region. The Chernobyl disaster has further made a large region uninhabitable for generations to come, not to speak of the people who died and who have suffered severe long-time illness, stigma and loss of home. The Fukushima accident may not have had as severe consequences in terms of fatalities, but here as well people may suffer long-term illness and they will not be able to go back to their homes and will have to start new lives. The moral impact of this may be hard to measure in quantitative terms, but emotionally we can grasp what this means by seeing images of people who have to leave their homes, or by putting ourselves in their shoes in order to imagine what this must mean for them. Furthermore, the impact in terms of cleaning up the site is tremendous, an impact that one might only start to grasp when witnessing it with one's own eyes, as here we start to feel the intense and long-term impact of the accident. Indeed, emotions can provide us with much more direct experiences of moral impact than abstract theorising (Roeser 2018).

Furthermore, there are ethical considerations involved in the management of nuclear waste, as mentioned in previous sections. Can we burden future generations with the effects of our lifestyle and well-being in which they did not have a share? From a purely rational approach, future generations may be too easily dismissed, as indeed happens in economic approaches to intergenerational considerations, where future generations are simply 'discounted', by being assigned a lower numerical value. Discounting may make for a smooth mathematical model that serves our own self-interest too well, but from a moral perspective, this can be seen as utterly unjustified. Feelings of care, guilt and responsibility can help to make such considerations of intergenerational justice much more tangible and strong. We have discussed the questions of nuclear waste and intergenerational justice in more detail in Sections 10.4 and 10.5. Here we only highlight the fact that these important ethical considerations do not figure (appropriately or not at all) in quantitative approaches to risk, and that emotions can help to be more aware of such considerations.

These arguments are not meant as a refutation of nuclear energy. Rather, they are meant to show that emotional resistance to nuclear energy is not irrational and is not due to a lack of understanding of the technology or its risks, as is usually portrayed by policymakers and proponents of nuclear energy. Rather, these emotional considerations draw our attention to important ethical considerations that are currently insufficiently addressed in the standard approaches to risk and decision making about nuclear energy. This also means that the public should be directly involved in public debates, and that emotions should not be seen as problematic but rather as a fruitful starting point for critical decision making.

10.7 CONCLUSIONS

In this chapter, we argued that for good governance of nuclear energy technologies, we need to understand and include several important ethical considerations. The first sections spelled out several important ethical challenges of nuclear power production and nuclear waste management. Awareness about these challenges would require a profound analysis from the perspective of ethics, but it would also urge us to seriously engage stakeholders in the decision making. Engaging stakeholders can be justified on ethical grounds in terms of procedural justice, but it can also help to identify important ethical values and dilemmas (Taebi 2017). When it comes to stakeholder involvement, there is the tendency to dismiss some voices, assuming that they reflect *emotional and hence irrational* responses. However, as we argue in Section 6, it is wrong to assume that emotional responses are irrational. To the contrary, at the heart of these emotional responses there can be important ethical concerns that need to be explicitly addressed. Of course, paying attention to emotional and ethical resistance to nuclear energy does not entail dismissing it as a future energy system. Rather, the potential use of nuclear energy highlights that decision making on the subject should not be made in isolation. Instead, it should be part of a larger public debate about a responsible energy mix. Most energy technologies give rise to public resistance, while at the same time most people are not willing to reduce their energy consumption. So here emotions such as feelings of responsibility and care can play an important role in asking the public to reflect on which trade-offs and concessions they are willing to make, and how we could develop energy technologies in a more responsible way, in order to do justice to ethical considerations. It should be an open question as to what the role of nuclear energy may be in such an energy mix, and whether nuclear energy can be produced in a way that is considered sustainable and socially responsible. But addressing these questions cannot and should not be left to experts and quantitative approaches alone, rather, they involve ethical questions that should be deliberated upon in a public debate; they also involve emotions and underlying values, in order to make ethical considerations explicit and to put them at the core of the deliberation.

Lastly, understanding the complex future of nuclear technology also has implications for future academic research on the topic. As with many other technologies, nuclear energy technologies could follow different paths into the future, depending on how quickly different countries introduce nuclear energy into their electricity grids, which technologies they choose for energy production and waste management and whether there will be major setbacks (e.g., a major nuclear disaster) to stop the developments. What makes nuclear energy technology a peculiar example is the fact that these different *future scenarios* could have serious international and intergenerational implications. Academic research should consider these future scenarios and anticipate, evaluate and steer – to the extent possible – their implications in a morally responsible way, taking into account present as well as future generations.

10.8 REFERENCES

Asveld, L., and S. Roeser, eds. 2009. *The Ethics of Technological Risk*. London: Earthscan.

Bergen, J. P. 2016. 'Irreversibility and Reversibility of Nuclear Energy Production Technologies: A Framework and Three Cases'. *Ethics, Policy and Environment* 19 (1): 37–59.

Bertell, R. 1991. 'Ethics of Nuclear Option in the 1990s'. In *Nuclear Energy and Ethics*, edited by K. S. Shrader-Frechette, 161–81. Geneva: World Council of Churches Publications.

Blix, Hans. 1986. 'The Influence of the Accident at Chernobyl. Lecture Delivered at Round Table No. 7, on "The Future for Nuclear Power" at the 13th Congress of the World Energy Conference'. Cannes, France: International Atomic Energy Agency, Division of Public Information.

Boutellier, C., C. McCombie, and I. Mele. 2006. 'Multinational Repositories: Ethical, Legal and Political/Public Aspects'. *International Journal of Nuclear Law* 1 (1): 36–48.

Damasio, A. 1994. *Descartes' Error*. New York: Putnam.

Downer, J. 2015. 'The Unknowable Ceiling of Safety: Three Ways That Nuclear Accidents Escape the Calculus of Risk Assessments'. In *The Ethics of Nuclear Energy: Risk, Justice and Democracy in the Post-Fukushima Era*, edited by B. Taebi and S. Roeser, 35–52. Cambridge: Cambridge University Press.

Doyle II, T. E. 2010. 'Reviving Nuclear Ethics: A Renewed Research Agenda for the Twenty First Century'. *Ethics & International Affairs* 24 (3): 287–308.

Frijda, N. 1987. *The Emotions*. Cambridge: Cambridge University Press.

Gosseries, A. 2008. 'Radiological Protection and Intergenerational Justice'. In *Ethics and Radiological Protection*, edited by G. Eggermont and B. Feltz, 167–95. Louvain-la-Neuve: Academia-Bruylant.

Hollyday, J. 1991. 'In The Valley of the Shadow of Three Miles Island'. In *Nuclear Energy and Ethics*, edited by K. S. Shrader-Frechette, 136–60. Geneva: World Council of Churches Publications.

IAEA. 1997. 'Joint Convention on the Safety of Spent Fuel Management and on the Safety of Radioactive Waste Management (Information Circular)'. Vienna: IAEA.

1998. 'Technical, Institutional and Economic Factors Important for Developing a Multinational Radioactive Waste Repository'. Vienna: IAEA.

IAEA, Euratom, FAO, IAEA, ILO, IMO, OECD-NEA, PAHO, UNEP, and WHO. 2006. 'Fundamental Safety Principles'. IAEA Safety Standards Series No. SF1. Vienna: A joint publication of Euratom, FAO, IAEA, ILO, IMO, OECD-NEA, PAHO, UNEP, WHO.

ICRP. 1977. 'Recommendations of the International Commission on Radiological Protection'. Publication 26. Vol. 1 (3). Ann. ICRP. Oxford: Pergamon Press.

2007. *The 2007 Recommendations of the International Commission on Radiological Protection. Publication* 103. Vol. 37 (2–4). Ann. ICRP. Oxford: Elsevier.

KASAM. 1988. 'Ethical Aspects of Nuclear Waste'. Report No. 29. Stockholm: National Council for Nuclear Waste (KASAM-SKN), Sweden.

2005. 'Nuclear Waste State-of-the-Art Reports 2004'. SOU 2004:67. Stockholm: National Council for Nuclear Waste (KASAM), Sweden.

2007. 'Nuclear Waste State-of-the-Art Report 2007 – Responsibility of Current Generation, Freedom of Future Generations'. SOU 2004:67. Stockholm: National Council for Nuclear Waste (KASAM), Sweden.

Kermisch, C. 2016. 'Specifying the Concept of Future Generations for Addressing Issues Related to High-Level Radioactive Waste'. *Science and Engineering Ethics* 22 (6): 1797–1811.

Kermisch, C., C. Depaus, and P. E. A. Labeau. 2016. 'A Contribution to the Analysis of Equity Associated with High-Level Radioactive Waste Management'. *Progress in Nuclear Energy*, no. 92: 40–47.

Kermisch, C., and B. Taebi. 2017. 'Sustainability, Ethics and Nuclear Energy: Escaping the Dichotomy'. *Sustainability* 9 (3): 446.

Kneese, A. V. 1973. 'The Faustian Bargain'. *Resources* 44: 1–5.

Krimsky, S., and D. Golding, eds. 1992. *Social Theories of Risk*. Westport: Praeger Publishers.

Löfquist, L. 2008. 'Ethics beyond Finitude, Responsibilities towards Future Generations and Nuclear Waste Management' (PhD diss.). Uppsala: Uppsala University.

Möller, N. 2012. 'The Concepts of Risk and Safety'. In *Handbook of Risk Theory. Epistemology, Decision Theory, Ethics and Social Implications of Risk*, edited by S. Roeser, R. Hillerbrand, P. Sandin, and M. Peterson, 55–85. Dordrecht: Springer.

NEA-OECD. 1995. 'The Environmental and Ethical Basis of Geological Disposal of Long-Lived Radioactive Wastes: A Collective Opinion of the Radioactive Waste Management Committee of the Nuclear Energy Agency'. Paris: Nuclear Energy Agency, Organisation for Economic Co-operation and Development.

Nihlén Fahlquist, J., and S. Roeser. 2015. 'Nuclear Energy, Responsible Risk Communication and Moral Emotions: A Three Level Framework'. *Journal of Risk Research* 18 (3): 333–46. https://doi.org/10.1080/13669877.2014.940594.

Nussbaum, M. 2001. *Upheavals of Thought*. Cambridge: Cambridge University Press.

NWMO. 2005. 'Choosing a Way Forward; The Future Management of Canada's Used Nuclear Fuel (Final Study)'. Ottawa (Ontario), Canada: Nuclear Waste Management Organization. www.nwmo.ca/studyreport.

Oughton, D., and S. O. Hansson. 2013. *Social and Ethical Aspects of Radiation Risk Management*. Amsterdam: Elsevier.

Roberts, R. C. 2003. *Emotions: An Essay in Aid of Moral Psychology*. Cambridge: Cambridge University Press.

Roeser, S. 2006. 'The Role of Emotions in Judging the Moral Acceptability of Risks'. *Safety Science* 44 (8): 689–700. https://doi.org/10.1016/j.ssci.2006.02.001.

2007. 'Ethical Intuitions about Risk'. *Safety Science Monitor* 11 (3): 1–30.

2011a. *Moral Emotions and Intuitions*. Basingstoke: Palgrave Macmillan.

2011b. 'Nuclear Energy, Risk, and Emotions'. *Philosophy & Technology* 24: 197–201.

2018. *Risk, Technology, and Moral Emotions*. London: Routledge.

Roeser, S., R. Hillerbrand, P. Sandin, and M. Peterson, eds. 2012. *Handbook of Risk Theory. Epistemology, Decision Theory, Ethics and Social Implications of Risk*. Dordrecht: Springer.

Routley, R., and V. Routley. 1979. 'Against the Inevitability of Human Chauvinism'. In *Ethics and Problems of the 21st Century*, edited by K. E. Goodpaster and K. M. Sayre, 36–59. Notre Dame, IN: University of Notre Dame Press.

Salzer, P., J. Pritrsky, A. Mrskova, and P. Richardson. 2012. 'The Status of Multinational Waste Management Solutions'. Deliverable 3.3. of the IPPA (Implementing Public Participation Approaches in Radioactive Waste Disposal).

Scarce, K. 2016. 'Nuclear Fuel Cycle Royal Commission Report'. Adelaide: Government of South Australia. http://nuclear.yoursay.sa.gov.au/system/NFCRC_Final_Report_Web.pdf.

Shrader-Frechette, K. 1980. *Nuclear Power and Public Policy: The Social and Ethical Problems of Fission Technology*. Dordrecht, Netherlands: D. Reidel Publishing Company.

Shrader-Frechette, K., ed. 1991. *Nuclear Energy and Ethics*. Geneva: World Council of Churches Publications.

Shrader-Frechette, K. 1993. *Burying Uncertainty: Risk and the Case against Geological Disposal of Nuclear Waste*. Berkeley: University of California Press.

1994. 'Equity and Nuclear Waste Disposal'. *Journal of Agricultural and Environmental Ethics* 7 (2): 133–56.

2000. 'Duties to Future Generations, Proxy Consent, Intra- and Inter-generational Equity: The Case of Nuclear Waste'. *Risk Analysis* 20 (6): 771–8.

2011. *What Will Work: Fighting Climate Change with Renewable Energy, Not Nuclear Power*. Oxford: Oxford University Press.

Slovic, P. 2000. *The Perception of Risk*. London: Earthscan.

2010. *The Feeling of Risk: New Perspectives on Risk Perception*. London: Earthscan.

Sunstein, C. R. 2005. 'Cost Benefit Analysis and the Environment'. *Ethics* 115: 351–85.

Taebi, B. 2010. *Nuclear Power and Justice between Generations. A Moral Analysis of Fuel Cycles* (PhD diss.). Vol. V. Simon Stevin Series in the Ethics of Technology. Delft: Delft University of Technology.

2011. 'The Morally Desirable Option for Nuclear Power Production'. *Philosophy & Technology* 24 (2): 169–92.

2012. 'Multinational Nuclear Waste Repositories and Their Complex Issues of Justice'. *Ethics, Policy & Environment* 15 (1): 57–62.

2017. 'Bridging the Gap between Social Acceptance and Ethical Acceptability'. *Risk Analysis* 37 (10): 1817–27.

Taebi, B., and J. L. Kloosterman. 2008. 'To Recycle or Not to Recycle? An Intergenerational Approach to Nuclear Fuel Cycles'. *Science and Engineering Ethics* 14 (2): 177–200.

2015. 'Design for Values in Nuclear Technology'. In *Handbook of Ethics, Values, and Technological Design: Sources, Theory, Values and Application Domains*, edited by J. Van den Hoven, P. Vermaas, and I. Van de Poel, 805–29. Dordrecht: Springer.

Taebi, B., and M. Mayer. 2017. 'By Accident or by Design? Pushing Global Governance of Nuclear Safety'. *Progress in Nuclear Energy* 99: 19–25.

Taebi, B., and S. Roeser. 2015a. 'The Ethics of Nuclear Energy: An Introduction'. In *The Ethics of Nuclear Energy: Risk, Justice and Democracy in the Post-Fukushima Era*, edited by B. Taebi and S. Roeser, 1–14. Cambridge: Cambridge University Press.

eds. 2015b. *The Ethics of Nuclear Energy: Risk, Justice and Democracy in the Post-Fukushima Era*. Cambridge: Cambridge University Press.

Taebi, B., S. Roeser and I. Van de Poel. 2012. 'The Ethics of Nuclear Power: Social Experiments, Intergenerational Justice, and Emotions'. *Energy Policy*, no. 51: 202–6.

Taebi, B., and I. Van de Poel, eds. 2015. 'Socio-Technical Challenges of Nuclear Power Production and Waste Disposal in the Post-Fukushima Era: Editors'. *Overview* 18 (3): 267–72.

Wigley, D., C. and K. Shrader-Frechette. 1996. 'Environmental Justice: A Louisiana Case Study'. *Journal of Agricultural and Environmental Ethics* 9 (1): 61–82.

Wilson, L. 2000. *Nuclear Waste: Exploring the Ethical Dilemmas*. Toronto: United Church Publishing House.

10.9 RESPONSE TO 'THE ETHICS OF NUCLEAR ENERGY – ITS PAST, PRESENT AND FUTURE'

By Alexandra C. H. Skelton

As explained by Behnam Taebi and Sabine Roeser, the ethical debate over nuclear power is rooted in concerns over non-proliferation and arms control in the Cold War period. These concerns persist today in a different form, with the escalation of threats between the United States and North Korea, President Trump's intention to increase tenfold the nuclear arsenal of the United States, and the list of countries with nuclear capabilities expanding to include India, Pakistan, Israel and North Korea. Whether the nuclear deterrence argument (that nuclear weapons will not be used due to the potential for mutually assured destruction), which averted nuclear Armageddon at the peak of the Cold War in 1962, will still hold with current leaders who flippantly tweet 'fire and fury' and compare the size of their nuclear buttons, remains to be seen and raises new ethical challenges. In keeping with the focus of this book, Taebi and Roeser are less concerned with these issues regarding arms and focus instead specifically on the (at times related) ethical issues resulting from the use of nuclear fuels as a source of energy.

In their chapter they identify four key new pressing ethical issues relating to nuclear energy. These are: (1) that technological change reduces the risk of nuclear meltdown (a key ethical concern in the past) but raises new ethical questions regarding the waste implications of fuel cycle choices; (2) that collaborative transnational disposal arrangements reap economies of scale and reduce the risk of unintentional future human intrusion on nuclear repositories but raise questions regarding the morality of paying less developed countries to take on this waste; (3) that geographic shifts in the nuclear landscape towards Asia and fast-growing developing countries raise questions about the global governance of nuclear power that may conflict with the national pride sentiment that underpins some nuclear ambitions; and (4) that public emotional responses (such as the German response to the nuclear catastrophe in Fukushima in 2011 that is described by Growitsch and Höffler in Chapter 11) should not be denigrated as purely irrational as these responses embody some of the underlying philosophical concerns that cannot be captured by traditional economic risk analysis.

Taking the chapter as a whole, what is clear is that the question 'Is nuclear energy ethical?' quickly fragments into a multitude of questions that range from the more philosophical (e.g., relating to intergenerational justice in the creation of nuclear waste that must be isolated from the biosphere for 10,000–200,000 years, or questioning whether countries that have developed nuclear capabilities can morally restrict other countries from doing so) to the more practical (regarding what precisely the most preferable method of nuclear energy generation would be). Assessing where traditional economics sits within this hierarchy leads to questions regarding which aspects of the problem economics is best suited to answer, and which philosophical assumptions economists must rely upon in addressing these questions.

Economists have a well-rehearsed vocabulary that can helpfully be used to explain some of the ethical issues raised in Taebi and Roeser's chapter. Nuclear waste is an 'externality' as the costs and risks associated with nuclear waste are not fully borne by the individuals who benefit from nuclear energy. There are 'spillovers' between nuclear energy R&D and nuclear weapons, e.g., uranium enrichment. 'Diminishing returns' to income means that developing countries may be willing to accept nuclear waste that carries risks that are unacceptable to citizens of more developed countries. There is an 'opportunity cost' to developing nuclear capabilities. Whilst the vocabulary may be helpful, the methods used and solutions proffered by traditional economists are less well suited to the questions raised by Taebi and Roeser: you cannot trade property rights with future generations to tackle externalities; probabilistic risk models (that multiply the probability of an event by the unwanted effects) fail to adequately account for low-probability, catastrophic impact ('black swan') events; and, discount rates, which assume that future generations will be better off and that environmental impacts are reversible, quickly erode the value of costs placed on future generations.

As explained by Taebi and Roeser, key normative questions regarding the definition and assessment of unwanted effects are neglected by economists. Should only fatalities be counted or long-term illness, too? Is one person's life worth more than another's because that person earns more or is more loved? Should environmental impacts only be taken into account to the extent to which they affect humans? How should costs be shared? The economists' search for Pareto efficiency (trading to the point at which it is not possible to make one person better off without making another worse off) is itself value laden as it is based on utilitarian principles and protects the initial distribution of resources. Translating different environmental and social impacts into monetary units and comparing them is a metaphysical scandal in the eyes of Aristotle. The problem with using economics to address the questions raised by Taebi and Roeser is partly that many of the questions lie outside the remit of economics, and partly that traditional economics itself, often unconsciously, relies on normative philosophical assumptions that may be disputed.

Despite these shortcomings, a more self-aware form of economics can helpfully be used to structure arguments, to set and compare benchmarks, to inform decisions about trade-offs and to tease out 'no regrets' policies in a complex, uncertain world. This is particularly important if we see the economist as a 'modern missionary', enabling society to make a decision in a field where otherwise 'wrangling would go on indefinitely with no decision ever taken' (Beckerman, 1956). Whilst economics might be best suited to making recommendations on the practical end of the spectrum of questions raised by Taebi and Roeser (in particular marginal questions about affordability and efficiency raised by Taebi and Kloosterman, 2015), such a role can only be effective with a greater emphasis on assumptions and greater humility regarding ultimate recommendations. Finally, in order to be more effective, economics must engage more openly with constraints imposed by physical reality, including environmental constraints and limits to efficiency improvements.

It is a shame that Taebi and Roeser isolate the ethical debate on nuclear energy from wider environmental constraints and in particular from the ethical debate relating to climate change given nuclear energy's potential contribution as a low-carbon, base-load energy source. Climate change raises intergenerational justice questions not just because its impacts will be greatest on future generations but because inaction now constrains the climate mitigation options available to future generations as temperature increases depend on cumulative stocks (not annual flows) of emissions. Globally, continued use of fossil fuels, industrial activity and land use change will reduce the permissible stock of emissions that would be consistent with the 'less than 2°C' target set by the international community in the Paris Accord by 3 to 6 per cent each year, meaning that the total stock of permissible emissions will be exhausted in sixteen to thirty-three years (Anderson and Peters, 2016). Inaction today (including turning away from nuclear power) imposes the requirement on future generations to achieve net-negative emissions with technology that is as yet unproven at scale. Isolating questions relating to the ethics of nuclear power from the climate change debate and relying on public emotion to convey underlying philosophical arguments risks not just NIMBYism (Not In My Back Yard) but going BANANAs (Build Absolutely Nothing Anywhere Near Anyone). Public engagement on difficult issues may be helpful but perhaps rational political debate would be preferable. Either way, ethical debate regarding 'good energy policy' must be caged in the language of 'plans that add up' (MacKay, 2009) if we are to have a hope in meeting our climate change commitments.

10.9.1 *References*

Anderson, K., Peters, G., 2016. 'The trouble with negative emissions'. *Science* 354, 182–183.

Beckerman, W., 1956. 'The Economist as a Modern Missionary' *Econ. J.* 66, 108. https://doi.org/10.2307/2227407

Fuss, S., Canadell, J.G., Peters, G.P., Tavoni, M., Andrew, R.M., Ciais, P., Jackson, R.B., Jones, C.D., Kraxner, F., Nakicenovic, N., Others, 2014. 'Betting on negative emissions'. *Nat. Clim. Change* 4, 850–853.

MacKay, J.C., 2009. Sustainable Energy – Without the Hot Air. UIT Cambridge Ltd.

Taebi, B., Kloosterman, J.L., 2015. Design for Values in Nuclear Technology, in: Van den Hoven, J., Vermaas, P., Van de Poel, I. (Eds.), Handbook of Ethics, Values, and Technological Design: Sources, Theory, Values and Application Domains. Springer, Dordrecht, 805–829.

11

Fukushima and German Energy Policy 2005–2015/2016

Christian Growitsch and Felix Höffler

11.1 THE IMMEDIATE EFFECT OF FUKUSHIMA[1]

11.1.1 The Political Consequences

On March 11, 2011, an earthquake in the Pacific Ocean caused a tsunami which hit the Japanese coast. This tidal wave caused severe damage at the nuclear power plant Fukushima Daiichi, operated by the Tokyo Electric Power Company (TEPCO). As a result, large amounts of radioactive material were emitted into the environment.[2]

Though without any direct effect on Europe, this tragic accident at the (literally) opposite side of the globe triggered strong reactions in the German energy policy debate. It led to an accelerated phase-out of nuclear power in Germany, with decommissioning of the last plants by 2022 and an immediate shutdown of Germany's seven oldest nuclear power plants on 14 March 2011.

In Germany, the controversy over the use of nuclear power in the electricity system had been long and fierce. Resistance against nuclear power was one of the founding elements and building blocks of the Green Party in Germany in the 1970s. Support for environmental issues, but in particular the fight against nuclear power, allowed this political movement to enter the previously extremely stable German political party landscape. Since the early days of the German Federal Republic in the 1950s, Germany was essentially a three-party system, with two large parties, Conservatives (CDU) and Social Democrats (SPD) and a small liberal party (FDP). The Conservatives and Liberals held, by and large, positive views of nuclear power. By contrast, the SPD had sought the decommissioning of some nuclear power plants ever since the Chernobyl accident in 1986.

[1] The following section is partly based on: Christian Growitsch and Felix Höffler, Impact of Fukushima on the German Energy Policy Debate, IAEE Policy Brief 4/2011, pp. 13–15.

[2] Official report of the Fukushima Nuclear Accident Independent Investigation Commission (NAIIC Report), 2012, pp. 12–14.

Just prior to the Fukushima accident, in 2010, the then-ruling Conservative-Liberal government had prolonged the use of nuclear power. It granted a life extension of more than ten years for newer nuclear power plants.[3] In doing so, the government overruled its predecessor's faster phase-out plans. In 2000, a coalition of the Social Democratic Party and Green Party had established a 'nuclear consensus' with the nuclear power plant operators, which meant a decommissioning of all nuclear power plants by the early 2020s.[4] The coalition of Social Democrats and Conservatives, ruling from 2005 to 2009, did not change this plan. However, overruling the 'nuclear consensus' and prolonging nuclear power use had explicitly been a core element of the Conservatives' political campaign in the 2009 election, which they had won and which had also put the Conservative-Liberal government in office at the time of the Fukushima accident.

Fukushima drastically changed the Conservative-Liberal government's view on nuclear power, in particular the position held by Chancellor Merkel. As a reaction to the events of Fukushima on 11 March 2011, the government, anticipating a strong revival of anti-nuclear sentiments, and facing an important election in one of the federal states (Baden-Württemberg), was quick to revise its nuclear power-friendly position. Within three days after the Fukushima accident, by 14 March, the Conservative-Liberal government established a three-month 'Moratorium on nuclear power' to evaluate and reflect on the risks of this technology. This meant the immediate shutdown of the 5 GW generation capacity of older nuclear plants (another 3.5 GW of nuclear capacity was not running due to technical revisions).

On 6 June, even before the end of the moratorium (planned for three months, i.e., up to 14 June), the very same government that had overruled the phase-out plans of its leftist predecessors now committed to an accelerated phase-out. The government now proposed (again) a total decommissioning by 2022. Due to Fukushima, nuclear power lost the support of all main political parties and the overall German population.

11.1.2 *Short-Term Market and Quantity Reactions*

Before the Fukushima accident, nuclear power was a very important component of German electricity generation. In 2010, 22 per cent (140 TWh) of German electricity generation stemmed from nuclear power plants. There was an installed nuclear capacity of 21.5 GW, 13 per cent of a total installed capacity of 171 GW in 2010 (Figure 11.1).

3 Elftes Gesetz zur Änderung des Atomgesetzes, 8 December 2010, Bundesgesetzblatt Jg. 2010, Teil I, Nr. 62, 1814–1816.

4 For the background on the phase-out plans of the SPD-Green government, see, for instance, Miina Kaarkoski, 'Energiemix versus Energiewende. Competing Conceptualisations of Nuclear Energy Policy in the German Parliamentary Debate of 1991–2001', *Jyväskylä Studies in Humanities* 290, 2016, 60–67.

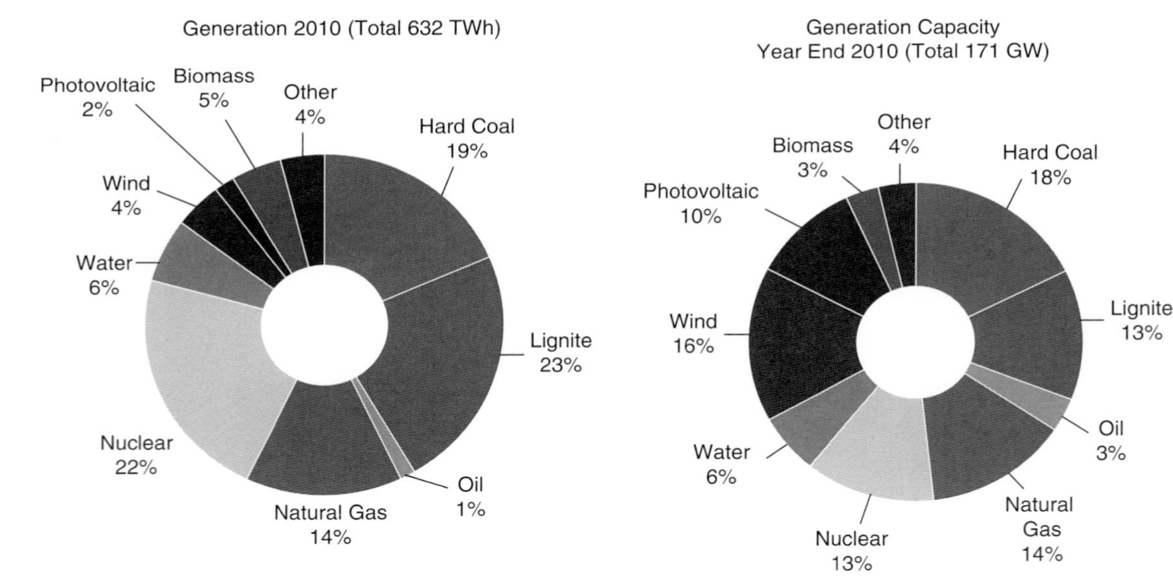

FIGURE 11.1 Electricity generation and capacity 2010[5]

[5] Source: BMWi. Zahlen und Fakten. Energiedaten. Last updated October 4, 2017. (Energy data published by the German Federal Ministry of Economic Affairs and Energy.) www.bmwi.de/Redaktion/EN/Artikel/Energy/energiedaten.html.

Hence, the moratorium affected a significant part of total power generation: almost a quarter of all nuclear installations had to be shut down immediately.

The shutdown of 5 GW of nuclear capacity by 14 March 2011 was completely unexpected and constitutes a textbook example of a negative supply shock. It is therefore interesting to investigate how the markets reacted to this event. Thoenes[6] shows that the markets reacted quickly, and correctly anticipated that the decommissioned power plants would not come back and that the accelerated nuclear phase-out was irrevocable.

Since short-term electricity prices are highly volatile, it is unsurprising that for the day-ahead prices an effect of Fukushima is hardly discernible. Figure 11.2 (left) depicts the day-ahead base and peak price on the German electricity exchange before and after the announcement of the moratorium.

While it is harder to identify price increases in the spot market,[7] Figure 11.2 (right) immediately reveals that future prices reacted. On the German electricity exchange, future prices increased sharply and – after some 'overshooting' – stayed at a significantly higher level than before the moratorium.

Did the markets expect that the moratorium was only transitory and that the 4 GW capacity would come back on the market? Or did they immediately foresee that the U-turn of the conservative government regarding nuclear power was irreversible? Figure 11.3 elicits from market prices the quantity effects which the market expected (Thoenes, 2011).[8] It illustrates which changes in the merit order (i.e., reduction of nuclear capacity) would support the price changes of Figure 11.3, i.e., the 'capacity effect' (in MW). It shows that the market immediately accounted for the reduction of the 5 GW capacity but quickly adjusted to a level of about 3 GW. This reflects the fact that the market (correctly) anticipated that part of the withdrawn nuclear capacity was to be replaced by fossil power plants and imports. Looking at long-term expectations beyond the end of the moratorium in June 2011, Figure 11.3 (which depicts the futures for the fourth quarter of 2011) shows that the market anticipated that the nuclear power capacity would not come back, but that the capacity effect remained stable at about 3 GW.

The fact that removing 5 GW base-load capacity did not destabilise the electricity system in Germany is due, to a large extent, to the strong interconnection of the electricity grid in continental Europe. Imports quickly increased as a reaction to the moratorium. Figure 11.4 highlights that soon after the moratorium, Germany became a net importer of electricity, reaching a maximum by May 2011. This atypical constellation continued well into autumn 2011.

[6] Thoenes, Stefan: 'Understanding the Determinants of Electricity Prices and the Impact of the German Nuclear Moratorium', *Energy Journal* 35 (4), 2014.

[7] Grossi et al. (2017) show that indeed the supply reduction had the expected price-increasing effect on the spot market. Grossi, Luigi, Heim, Sven, and Waterson, Michael: 'The Impact of the German Response to the Fukushima Earthquake', *Energy Economics* 66 (2017), 450–465.

[8] See also Thoenes (2014), pp. 69–75 for the derivation and discussion of the capacity effect.

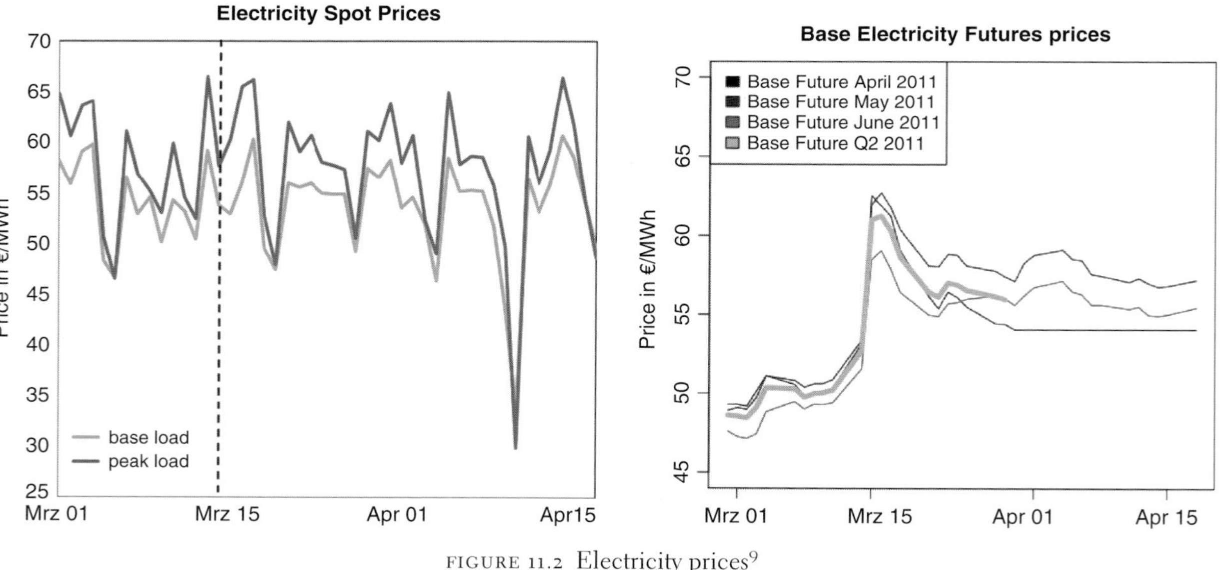

FIGURE 11.2 Electricity prices[9]

9 Source: Left – European Electricity Exchange (EEX); right – Thoenes, Stefan, 'Understanding the determinants of electricity prices and the impact of the German nuclear Moratorium in 2011', EWI Working Paper, 11/06, 2011.

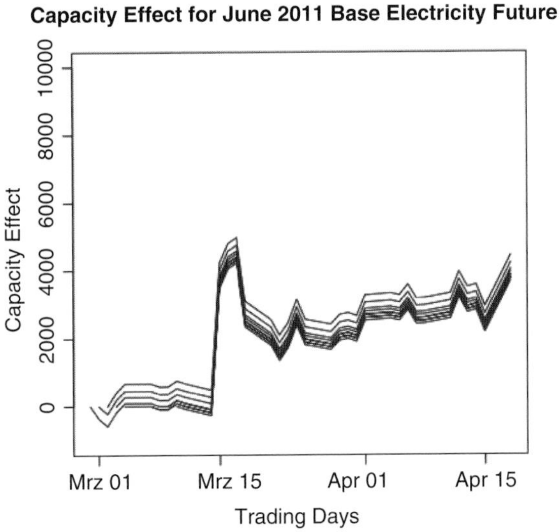

FIGURE 11.3 Capacity effects (in MW) for June 2011[10]

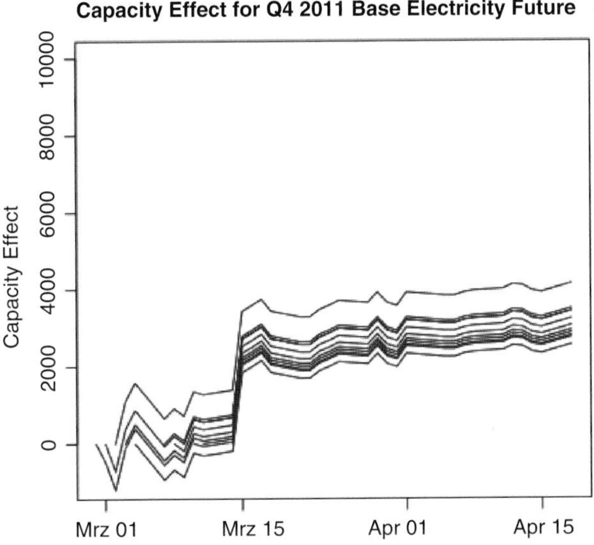

FIGURE 11.4 Capacity effect (in MW) for after the end of the moratorium[11]

[10] Thoenes, Stefan: Understanding the Determinants of Electricity Prices and the Impact of the German Nuclear Moratorium in 2011, EWI Working Paper, 11/06 (2011).

[11] Thoenes (2011), p. 24.

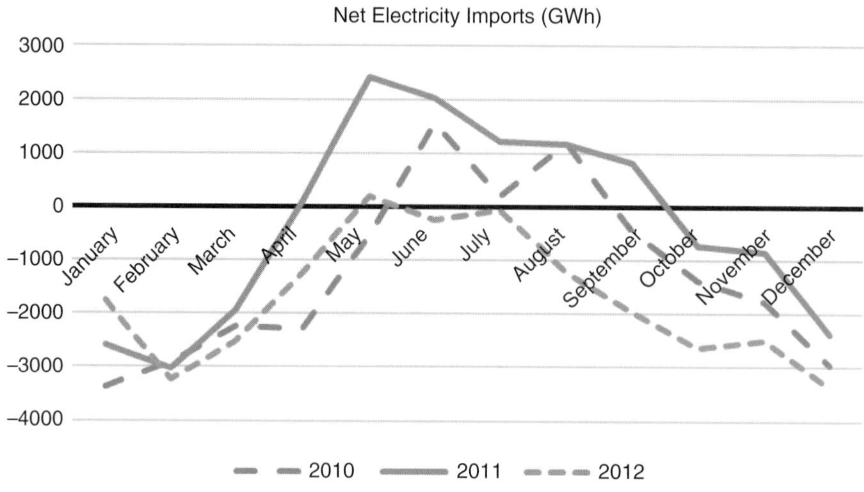

FIGURE 11.5 Electricity exports and imports[12]

A closer look into the data reveals that France and the Czech Republic had increased their exports to Germany, while German exports to Austria, Poland, Switzerland and the Netherlands had declined.

Figure 11.5 also illustrates that the substitution of nuclear by imports was only a temporary phenomenon. Net imports came back to (or even below) pre-Fukushima levels by 2012. The reason was fuel switching. By comparing pre- and post-Fukushima fuel mixes, Figure 11.5 shows that the significant cut back in nuclear generation (41 TWh of 629 TWh total generation, i.e., 7 per cent of total generation) was compensated by various domestic sources, while total generation stayed almost constant. Lignite directly substituted for nuclear baseload generation (+ 15 TWh), and also renewables increased significantly (by a total of 37 TWh). The decrease in generation from natural gas is to a large extent due to the increase in the gas price by 40 per cent;[13] however, gas generation never returned to pre-Fukushima levels, an indication of merit order effects due to increased renewable production, discussed in Section 3.

[12] Source: Destatis, GENESIS Datenbank, Monatsberichte über die Elektrizitätsversorgung, 43311–0003, Ein- und Ausfuhr von Elektrizität, (German Statistical Office, Monthly Reports on Electricity Supply, Imports and Exports) www-genesis.destatis.de/genesis/online/data;jsessionid=DBAFDCA2FCEC2C9D82155AE7FC12CC41.tomcat_GO_1_1?operation=statistikAbruftabellen&levelindex=0&levelid=1496249610018&index=4.

[13] The average import price for gas ('Grenzübergangspreis') increased from 5.7 €/TJ in 2010 to 8.1 €/TJ in 2012. Source: Bundesamt für Wirtschaft und Ausfuhrkontrolle, BAFA, (Federal Office for Economic Affairs and Export Control), www.bafa.de/DE/Energie/Rohstoffe/Erdgas/erdgas_node.html.

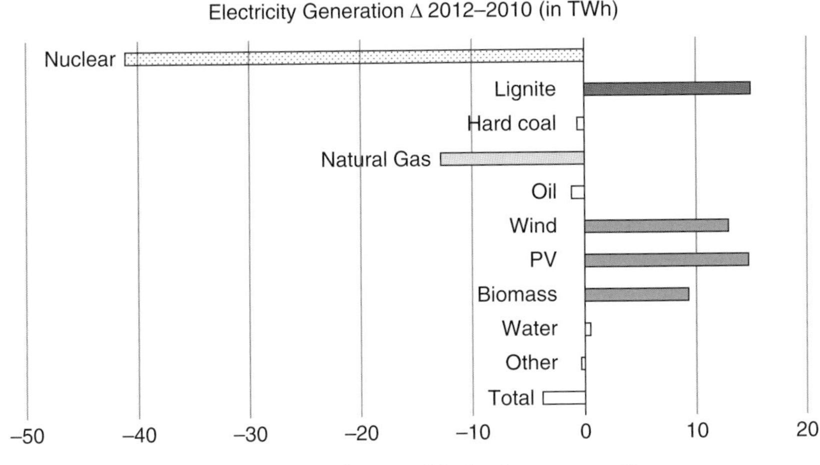

FIGURE 11.6 Change of fuel mix 2010–2012[14]

11.2 LONG-TERM EFFECTS OF THE ACCELERATED PHASE-OUT

The federal government reacted to Fukushima not only with the moratorium on nuclear power, but also published a new 'energy concept' on 6 June 2011.[15] In thirty-nine paragraphs the document describes adjustments to the German energy policy in reaction to Fukushima. It starts out with the aim of an accelerated decommissioning of nuclear power plants (§ 3) and supporting measures to ensure short-term generation adequacy. The concept paper also includes many other topics and policy aims, like reducing greenhouse gas emissions by 40 per cent in 2020 (compared to 1990).

Most notably, the proposal defines as a cornerstone a rapid expansion of renewable energy sources (§ 11). Though the text starts by speaking generally of renewable energy, almost all subsequent measures and initiatives refer to the electricity sector. For instance, the 'energy concept' sets forth an explicit target for the maximum fee for financing renewable electricity sources, which should not exceed 3.5 €-Cent/kWh for household customers (§ 12). Important targets and areas of activity named in the concept paper include electricity grid expansion, and energy savings in the housing sector. Eight legal acts were initiated by the energy concept in June 2011.

Nothing of the 2011 energy concept was fundamentally new. Clearly, the decommissioning of nuclear power was accelerated, though essentially only brought back to the phase-out trajectory that was previously negotiated in 2000 by the leftist government in the 'nuclear consensus' with the energy industry. However, the

14 BMWi. Energiedaten. Table 22.

15 BWMi, Der Weg zur Energie der Zukunft, www.bmwi.de/Redaktion/DE/Downloads/E/energiekonzept-2010-beschluesse-juni-2011.html.

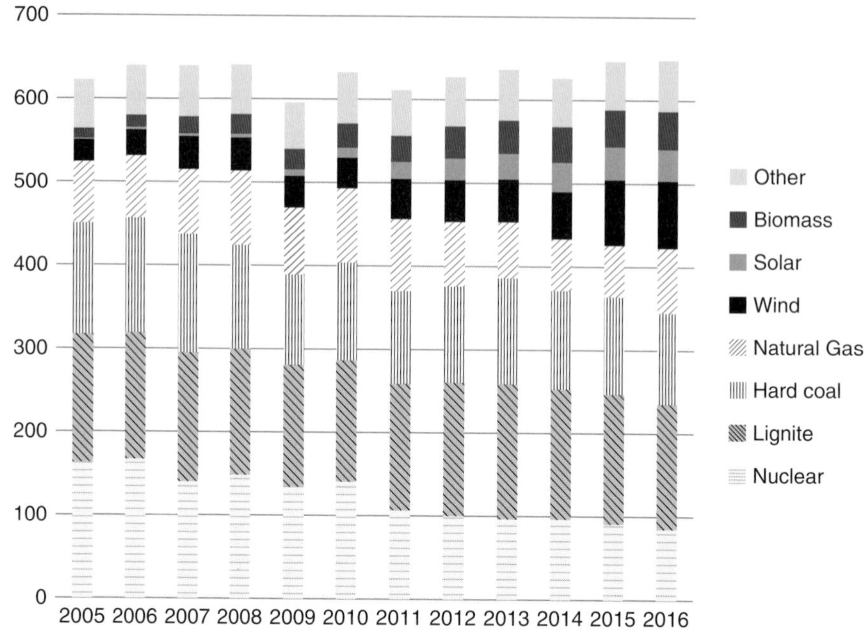

FIGURE 11.7 Gross electricity generation (TWh)[17]

'energy concept' stabilised the political energy agenda. Although the 'energy concept' has seen various adjustments, the core elements are still guidelines for the German energy policy and monitored biannually by a standing committee of energy market experts. Still, the core elements are 1) decommissioning of all nuclear power plants by 2022; 2) increasing the share of renewables in electricity generation (2017 target: 40–45 per cent by 2025); 3) reduction of greenhouse gas emissions (2017 target: by 40 per cent in 2020, compared to 1990); and 4) reduction in primary energy consumption (2017 target: by 20 per cent by 2020, compared to 2008).

The part of the German energy system that has changed most in the last one to two decades is clearly the electricity sector. The generation mix nowadays differs substantially from that before Fukushima. Nuclear power has been substituted mainly by lignite as a base-load technology. The enormous increase in renewable electricity sources[16] has, whenever available, driven the most expensive technologies (in the sense of variable cost) – namely gas and, in part, hard coal – out of the merit order (see Figure 11.7).

However, these changes had already started well before 2011. Nuclear power was already on the decline, and renewables already had increased significantly before 2011. Nevertheless, the growth rate increased after 2011, to a large extent driven by

[16] Wind, solar and biomass accounted for 6 per cent in 2005 and 25 per cent by 2016 of gross German electricity production.

[17] BMWi, Table 22.

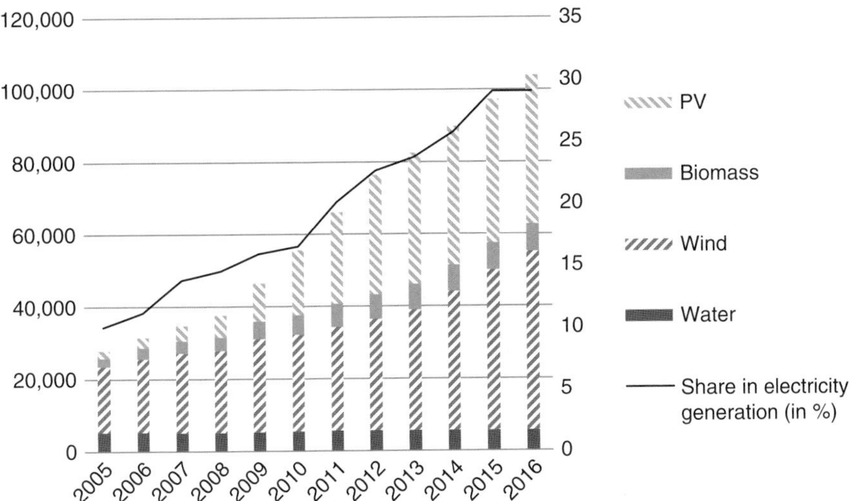

FIGURE 11.8 Renewable electricity capacities (in MW)[20]

solar energy. In the five years before Fukushima (2006–2011), the share of renewables in electricity consumption[18] increased on average by 1.8 percentage points p.a., while the increase from 2011 to 2016 was on average 2.3 percentage points p.a.[19] Figure 11.8 shows renewable capacities and their share in overall electricity generation from 2005 to 2016. Wind installation doubled, and PV capacity increased by a factor of almost twenty. Total renewable electricity capacities tripled in this decade, and so did the share in total electricity generation.

While the generation mix significantly changed, overall electricity generation stayed roughly constant at 600–650 TWh (consumption: about 530 TWh[21]) for the period 2005–2016. Within the generation mix, lignite generation was stable at about 150 TWh, and also hard coal remained constant at about 110 TWh since 2009, while natural gas, peaking at 89 TWh in 2010, has been declining since then.

The sum of different changes in the generation mix (much more renewables, less nuclear power and gas, stable coal) explains why despite the sharp increase in renewables, the CO_2 emissions from electricity generation remained almost unchanged for the whole decade at a bit more than 300 mt CO_2 p.a. A slight

18 This refers to the figures reported by the federal government for its (current) target of 35 to 40 per cent share of renewables by 2025. It divides gross domestic electricity generation from renewables by gross domestic *consumption* of electricity. Germany is a net exporter of electricity (8.6 per cent of total generation exported in 2016), in particular in hours with high renewable generation (and hence low German prices). Therefore, this figure does not really measure 'how green' is the electricity consumed in Germany.

19 BMWi, Energiedaten, Table 22.

20 BMWi, Energiedaten, Table 20.

21 Net of network losses and self-consumption. BMWi, Energiedaten, Table 21.

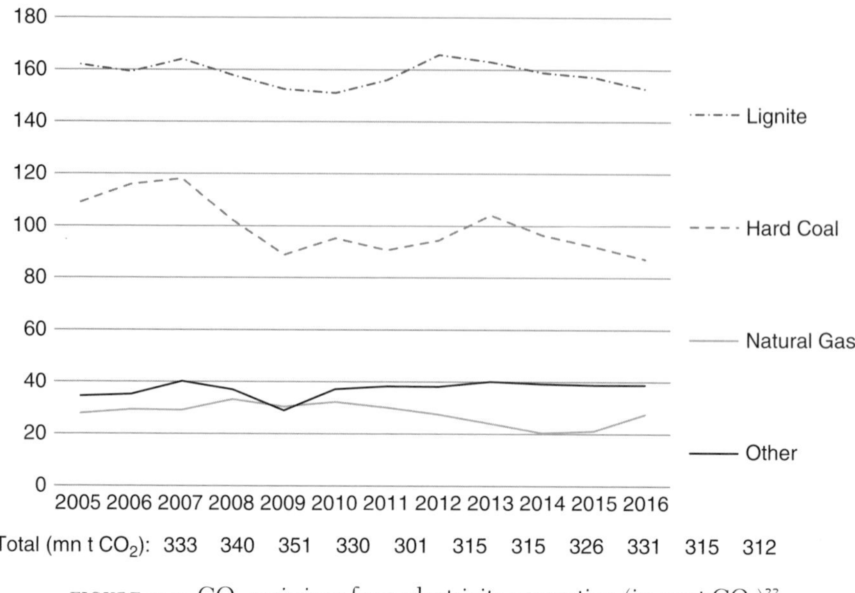

FIGURE 11.9 CO_2 emissions from electricity generation (in mn t CO_2)[22]

decrease of 5 to 10 per cent took place, but this occurred primarily in the five years before 2011.

While CO_2 emissions from the electricity sector decreased only slightly in the last decade (and not at all since Fukushima), overall emissions, i.e., from all sectors (including electricity) did. Figure 11.10 illustrates a decrease of total greenhouse gas emissions, particularly in the five years before Fukushima. The decrease stems mainly from the energy sector (– 60 mt CO_2 equivalent), with contributions from the energy industry (– 27 mt) and the industrial sector (– 10 mt), where these reductions certainly reflect the economic downturn after the global financial crisis. The household sector reduced emissions by – 23 mt, mainly due to more efficient heating and insulation. Little changed after 2011 in terms of overall emissions.

While Germany saw (moderate) real growth in the period after Fukushima (+1.2 per cent GDP p.a. from 2011 to 2016), total energy consumption stayed almost constant (+0.6 per cent p.a. from 2011 to 2016) in this period. It had decreased in the five years before Fukushima, mainly due to less energy consumption in the housing sector.

As a result, energy intensity, and also emissions intensity kept on declining after 2011, though at a slightly lower rate (Figure 11.12, (left). Electricity intensity reduced from 0.23 kWh/€ GDP in 2006 to 0.174 kWh/€ GDP in 2015 (– 22 per cent)). Again, all of this reflects long-term trends in which 2011 does not feature prominently.

22 BMWi, Energiedaten, Table 11.

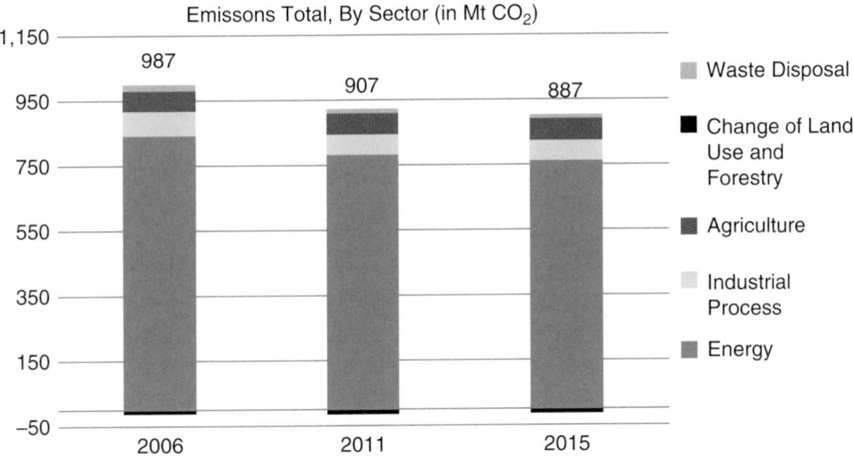

FIGURE 11.10 Total CO_2 emissions (in mn t CO_2 equivalent)[23]

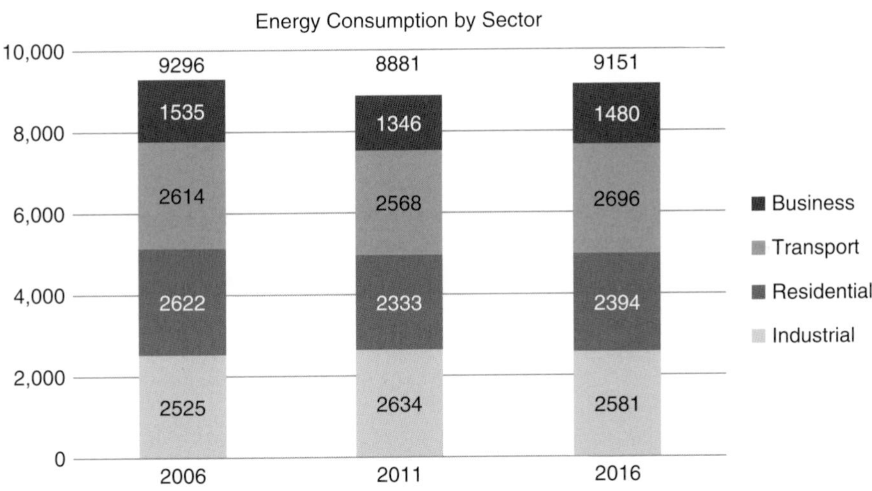

FIGURE 11.11 Primary energy consumption (in PJ)[24]

One might expect that the policy change may have had a significant effect on the business model of the (incumbent) energy companies. Indeed, the four major incumbent companies have undergone dramatic changes. For instance E.ON, which had been the largest German energy company, has actually split its business

[23] BMWi, Energiedaten, Table 10. The data in this data source are not fully consistent with the data for Figure 11.10 (which are based on Table 11) due to different calculation methods and conversion factors. See the footnote for Table 11 in the data source.

[24] BMWi, Energiedaten, Table 6a.

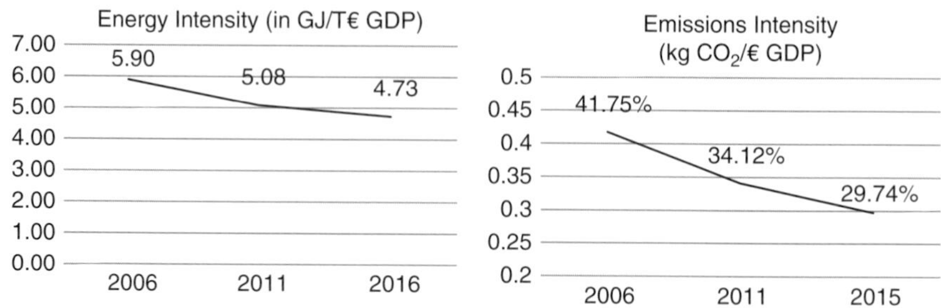

FIGURE 11.12 Energy intensity and emission intensity[25]

into an incumbent part (including all conventional generation assets) and a 'new' E.ON company, focusing on renewables, trade and services.[26] The two major players, RWE and E.ON, faced a dramatic loss in stock market value after Fukushima. From 2011 to 2016 each of the two companies lost about 60 per cent of its market capitalisation, a combined loss in value of 28 bn €.

However, taking a long-term perspective reveals that the year 2011 does not appear as a turning point. Figure 11.13 illustrates that both German energy incumbents already had lost value pre-2011, and performed significantly worse than energy industry indices, or the stock market on average (Euro Stoxx, or the German DAX).

11.3 SOME TENTATIVE INTERPRETATIONS

There is a common perception that 'Fukushima' drastically changed the German energy policy, or that it at least significantly accelerated the different elements of the '*Energiewende*'. The shutdown of the older nuclear power plants as a reaction to the Fukushima accident of 2011 certainly was a supply shock for the electricity system. The market, however, accommodated this shock quickly and efficiently. For most major elements of the '*Energiewende*', the year 2011 nevertheless does not stand out.

- Total primary energy consumption stayed almost constant after 2011, after a slight decrease in the years before Fukushima.
- The same holds true for emissions; in particular, emissions from the electricity sector stayed almost constant.
- Energy efficiency slightly increased, but this process did not accelerate after 2011.
- Renewables kept on growing, at a slightly higher speed than before Fukushima.

25 BMWi, Energiedaten, Tables 1, 4 and 10.

26 It also includes the nuclear power plants. Political pressure insisted on keeping the liabilities from nuclear power within the E.ON company.

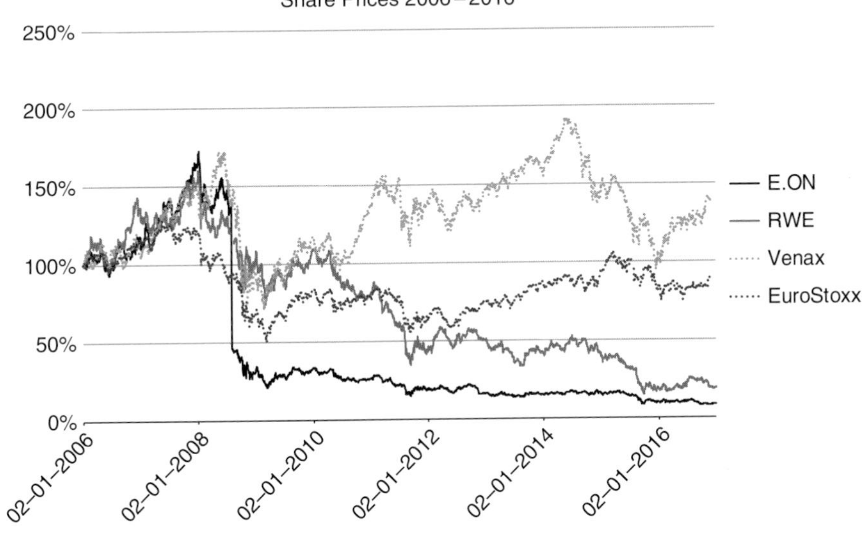

FIGURE 11.13 Energy company valuations[27]

- Nuclear decommissioning was accelerated, but usage of nuclear power had already declined significantly before Fukushima. Indeed, the phase-out plan from 2011 is rather similar to an earlier plan from 2000.
- The large incumbent electricity companies suffered from the *Energiewende*, and Fukushima decreased the value of their nuclear assets; but these companies had already lost significant value before 2011.

Rather, the decades from 2005 to 2015/16, with Fukushima in the middle, appear rather to have been an ongoing process of change, as opposed to a system that was shocked in the year 2011. Obviously, we do not know if all or some of these processes of change would have slowed down or stopped without Fukushima. The data just make it hard to argue that Fukushima constitutes a drastic change in German energy policy.

At the core of this change process, and for many the big success of the *Energiewende*, is the dramatic increase in the utilisation of wind power and solar power in electricity generation and the decommissioning of nuclear power. We propose, tentatively, three possible reasons for this.

- First, environmental and climate policy issues had already featured prominently in the German public debate for a long period.

[27] Company data, yahoo.finance.com.

- Second, there is widespread sympathy for 'technological' solutions instead of market economy solutions in Germany.
- Third, there was weak opposition by incumbent firms and strong public opposition against these major energy companies.

These arguments may at the same time help to explain the lack of support for more mechanism- (economics-) based approaches, like emission trade of carbon pricing. And the 'success' in terms of renewables and the decommissioning of nuclear power may overshadow the lack of progress on other fronts, in particular in reducing greenhouse gas emissions.[28]

As mentioned earlier, environmental issues had been important in the public debate since the 1970s, giving rise to a strong Green Party, which entered state government in 1985 (in Hessen) and the federal government in 1998. All other parties have reacted and included environmental politics in their agendas. And already in the 1990s, the conservative administration of Chancellor Kohl had formulated a national greenhouse gas target to reduce emissions by 25 per cent by 2005, compared to 1990.[29]

The key mechanism that drove the expansion of renewable electricity sources is the subsidy scheme introduced by the renewable support act (EEG) in 2000. Despite the strong support from the left-green government (Social Democrats and Green Party), the act itself had a much broader backing and originated from an initiative by members of parliament from all major political parties.[30] Targets or quotas for renewable energies became a rarely disputed instrument for 'greening the economy' and often appeared to become ends in themselves. Part of the scheme's success in Germany was the financing mechanism. Subsidies were financed by a levy on electricity consumption, mainly for households. The levy is now (2017) substantial (almost 7 €-Cents per kWh, comparing to a wholesale price of 3 to 4 €-Cents/kWh), amounting to payments with an average of almost 300 € per year for the average household. However, the levy increased only gradually, from 2.1 €-Cent/kWh in 2010 to 6.7 €-Cent/kWh in 2017, i.e., on average by less than 0.7 €-Cent/kWh per year. The levy is distributed across all consumers (exemptions being made for energy-intensive industries). Important beneficiaries are the wind and PV industries, investors in wind turbines, and households with PV rooftop installations. Although this means that the number of beneficiaries is substantial, it is still much smaller than the

[28] Germany is part of the European emission trading system. In particular, the electricity industry is covered by this cap-and-trade system. National greenhouse gas reductions therefore have little (direct) climate effect. Nevertheless, national contributions remain an important policy topic, not least within the Paris accord.

[29] Fischer, Severin, *Die Energiewende und Europa*, Springer VS, Wiesbaden 2017, p. 276. There were, however, few effective instruments installed to realise these targets. The largest contribution towards accomplishing this came from the shutdown of large parts of the industrial sector of the former GDR (East Germany) after 1990 that had caused large emissions but was non-competitive in the global market.

[30] Fischer, Energiewende, p. 227.

number of contributors – which, by the 'logic of collective action' (Olson 1965)[31] facilitates political implementation of this regime.

Given this broad support, it is not surprising that even after the conservative party took over, this agenda was kept widely unaltered. The then-new chancellor, Angela Merkel, played an important part when a renewable target was included in the European energy target system in 2007, and when the EU formulated the 20–20–20 agenda (which includes a target quote of 20 per cent renewables by the year 2020).[32]

Germany has a reputation for engineering. It is therefore probably not by chance that early efforts in wind generation research were realised in Germany, and they were realised as large-scale technology solutions.[33] There probably was always sympathy across all political parties for identifying 'green technologies' as promising for future industrial development, and worthy of political and financial support.

The combination of the perceived importance of environmental and climate policy aspects in the public debate, and the widespread sympathy for technological solutions and industrial policy may have served as important drivers for the *Energiewende*. Both aspects support a 'green industrial policy', which promises to combine the idea of technological progress (and growth and wealth) with the desire for sustainability. 'Greening the economy' is advocated not as a costly sacrifice to use less resources, but as a means of improving 'national competitiveness' in a global competition in promising fields of industrial development and, in addition, to avoid imports from countries with governments that are considered, in Germany, as undemocratic. This logic promises growth, employment and fuel independence as an additional dividend of the *Energiewende*.

The *Energiewende* policy agenda clearly cut into the business model of the major incumbent energy companies and therefore triggered their opposition. That the incumbents were not successful in defending their position is due to many different factors. Johannes Teysse, E.ON CEO since 2010, looking back in an interview in 2017, said: '*Yes, we knew it: the feeling of being invulnerable . . . Didn't we have close – perhaps too close – relations with politics?*'[34] One interesting detail may illustrate the misperceptions of their own strength, or even arrogance. In 2008, E.ON, then the largest German energy company and seeking to expand further in Europe, faced a cartel investigation by the European Commission. To accommodate the Commission, the company agreed to sell off its network business, and in return

31 Olson, Mancur, *Logic of Collective Action: Public Goods and the Theory of Groups* (Harvard University Press, 1965).

32 Fischer, *Energiewende*, p. 139.

33 The 'Growian' project in Germany was realised in the 1980s. It built the largest wind turbine at that time (3 MW capacity). The turbine itself faced considerable technical problems, and had to be shut down after a runtime of less than twenty days. Nicole Kronenberg, 'Schleswig-Holstein – Geburtsland der Windenergie'. In: Dominik Collet, Manfred Jakubowski-Tiessen (ed.): *Schauplätze der Umweltgeschichte in Schleswig-Holstein*, pp. 95–103.

34 The delusive perception of being invulnerable. Interview with Johannes Teyssen. Der Tagesspiegel. Background Energie und Klima, 6.9.2017 (own translation).

the Commission settled the cartel investigation. However, other German energy incumbents were also vertically integrated and had fiercely opposed any unbundling attempts. The federal government strongly supported their case in Brussels. It so happened that E.ON announced its deal with the Commission on the very same day on which the German secretary of state had, once more and in line with the incumbents' official position, argued in Brussels against any separation of network and generation. This situation does not bode well for the building of future political support for the energy incumbents.[35]

Fukushima certainly did have an effect on German energy policy. Over a longer time horizon, however, the impression of major change fades away and is dwarfed by more fundamental changes in German energy policy. Two of these fundamental trends were slightly accelerated, namely, growth of renewable electricity sources and the decommissioning of nuclear power plants. The reasons for these developments are rooted much deeper in the German (energy) political landscape and require a comprehensive political economy analysis.

11.4 RESPONSE TO 'FUKUSHIMA AND GERMAN ENERGY POLICY 2005–2015/2016'

By Marc Ozawa

Growitsch and Höffler present a well-grounded and in-depth account of Germany's reaction to the Fukushima nuclear disaster of 2011. Perhaps owing to pre-existing German energy policy goals that were fundamentally different from those of neighbouring countries, combined with German politicians' dramatic public statements on Fukushima, Growitsch and Höffler paint a picture of perception being greater than facts, at least over the long term. It is true that compared to neighbouring countries, the aims of Germany's energy transition policies (or the German *Energiewende* that has entered English vernacular) appear drastic, namely the two-pronged aims of phasing out nuclear power and building up renewables while at the same time cutting down carbon emissions. German policy did change after Fukushima, and there was indeed a German reaction to Fukushima, but it was neither as dramatic nor as simply explained as portrayed in the media. Growitsch and Höffler's main argument is that Fukushima did not have a substantive effect on German energy policies. The changes taking place were already underway in 2011, and at best, they represent a continuation of policies instigated as early as 2000. The origins of the *Energiewende*, according to Growitsch and Höffler, were in place by the time Fukushima Daiichi exploded, and the concerns of environmental and climate issues had 'featured prominently in German public debate already for a long period'. The authors also explained that German culture was predisposed to

[35] Fischer, *Energiewende*, pp. 184–187.

technological solutions, which complimented the development of renewable energy resources like wind and solar. And finally, they suggest that incumbent companies were, perhaps out of arrogance, 'weak' in reacting to changing policies against a backdrop of strong public opposition to incumbent firms.

Growitsch and Höffler begin by situating the *Energiewende* into an historical and political-economy context. The argument they advance is made all the more compellingly because they do not rely solely on market indicators or economic theory. In fact, they do not invoke any theory, leaving the numbers and historical events to speak for themselves. This simple yet sound approach opens up the analysis to a broader audience beyond economists. From a political perspective, the authors also offer insights into the politics of the *Energiewende*, perhaps just the tip of the iceberg, but insights nonetheless.

A reading from the disciplinary perspective of politics, however, raises some important questions that go unaddressed in the analysis. The first is why the market incumbents failed to respond effectively to changes if it was in their interests to do so. The analysis implies that their 'weak' reaction was partly attributed to a perceived arrogance, but if this is the case, what was it about previous interactions with government that made these companies think that they did not need to do more? Was it purely due to public opposition about which incumbents were caught off guard?

Related to this point, prominent political scientists, such as Robert Gilpin, have described Germany as a 'corporatist' state, a term that ascribes a type of industrial-state coordination.[36] This coordination was clearly demonstrated between energy incumbents and the state in previous German energy transitions, prominent among those was the transition away from coal in the Ruhr region.[37] The *Energiewende* case raises a valuable question. What has changed since then, and given the experience of the *Energiewende*, is it still useful to think about modern Germany in terms of corporatism?

Although the authors mention the history and importance of environmental and climate issues in German political debates, they neglect to offer an explanation for the public salience of these issues. How did environmental and climate factors rise to prominence in the public's awareness, and why would events on the other side of the world (Japan) under unimaginable circumstances for Germany (earthquake coupled with tsunami) resonate with the German public? Is there something about the fact that this happened in Japan that contributed to the political and public reaction? These questions concerning the salience of issues would be critical to an understanding of the German reaction to Fukushima from the disciplinary perspective of politics.

36 Robert Gilpin, *Global Political Economy: Understanding the International Economic Order* (Princeton University Press, 2011).

37 Martin F. Parnell, *The German Tradition of Organized Capitalism: Self-Government in the Coal Industry* (Oxford University Press, 1994), https://ideas.repec.org/b/oxp/obooks/9780198277613.html.

Another issue the chapter only mentioned in passing without further explanation is the impact of domestic party dynamics on the *Energiewende*. Although the origins of the policies trace back to 2000 when the Social Democrats (SPD) were still in power, for the past thirteen years, Angela Merkel has been chancellor with her party's union, CDU-CSU, at the helm of government. What effect has this conservative government had on the trajectory of energy policy development and would things have turned out differently under SPD leadership?

Expanding beyond domestic politics, the discipline of politics is also concerned with the impact of international factors on policies. As an example, one observer of German federal politics commented that the Ukraine crisis, which began in November 2013, raised politics over commerce with respect to energy policies, international trade and Russia.[38] Although the Ukraine crisis took place after Fukushima, instability in the EU's eastern border region began with the 'colour revolutions' in 2005 and continued through the war in Georgia in 2008. As Tomas Maltby has argued, with each geopolitical conflict in the eastern countries of Europe, the arguments of those advocating energy independence from Russia and supply diversification away from fossil fuels received more weight.[39] Have geopolitical events, then, had an effect on the shape and development of the *Energiewende*?

In summary, Growitsch and Höffler present a compelling explanation of the origins of the German *Energiewende* and the limited impact that Fukushima has had on German energy policies despite significant media attention. True to the authors' discipline, the analysis draws on market developments to stipulate historical effects on the *Energiewende*. Anyone reading from the perspective of politics should applaud the authors for including some non-market factors in the analysis. However, the chapter tends to neglect certain questions that political analysis would be more likely to emphasise, such as the salience of Fukushima in German political debates, the apparent shift away from 'corporatist' industrial-government interactions, domestic party factors and the impact of geopolitical developments. On the other hand, the political analyst might not have highlighted the importance of long-term market developments in framing the analysis. In this way the chapter demonstrates that energy policy is a fruitful ground for multidisciplinary collaboration drawing from both economics and politics.

38 Tomas Maltby, 'European Union Energy Policy Integration: A Case of European Commission Policy Entrepreneurship and Increasing Supranationalism', *Energy Policy*, special section: Long Run Transitions to Sustainable Economic Structures in the European Union and Beyond, 55 (1 April 2013): 435–444, https://doi.org/10.1016/j.enpol.2012.12.031.

39 Tomas Maltby, 'Between Amity, Enmity and Europeanisation: EU Energy Security Policy and the Example of Bulgaria's Russian Energy Dependence', *Europe-Asia Studies* 67, no. 5 (28 May 2015): 809–830, https://doi.org/10.1080/09668136.2015.1046817.

12

Rethinking the Environmental State: An Economic History of the Swedish Environmental Kuznets Curve for Carbon

Magnus Lindmark[1]

12.1 INTRODUCTION

The low levels of Swedish carbon dioxide emissions, both emissions intensity (per unit of GDP) and per capita, has been noticed in the scholarly world (e.g., Schipper et al. 2001) and in domestic political debate (e.g., SOU 2000:23, p. 136). Historical data covering the period prior to official data reporting to the UN, in other words, before the 1990s, also show that the transition from relatively high to relatively low emissions occurred primarily in the 1970s and 1980s (Kander 2002). Viewed over an even longer time frame, the Swedish carbon emissions therefore resembles an Environmental Kuznets Curve or EKC (Lindmark 2002; Johansson and Kriström 2007). Sweden was indeed an early mover in recognising global warming as a problem that necessitated political action, including the carbon tax in the early 1990s, which can be seen as the starting point of an active climate policy. Since then, the carbon tax has been raised on several occasions, and has been accompanied by Swedish ratification of the Kyoto agreement in 2002 and membership in the EU-ETS carbon emission trading from 2005. Sweden has currently the highest effective carbon price – average price across all GHG emissions – in the world at $80 per tonne of CO_2 equivalent (Dolphin et al. 2016).

Still, important steps in the transition to reduce carbon intensity had already taken place during the 1970s and 1980s. Most studies of Swedish climate policy focus on the period from 1990 and onward, which is not strange as such. Climate policy did not exist before the 1990s, and the relevant economic and environmental data mainly cover this period. Low-carbon emissions and their continuing decline has contributed to a confident self-image and Swedish ambitions for greater climate policy leadership. The self-image rests upon an idea of extraordinary environmental responsibility and the idea that other countries could, and should, learn from

[1] The author recognises the valuable comments by Prof. Lena Andersson-Skog, Dr. Martin Eriksson and the participants at the 'Good' Energy Policy seminar at the University of Cambridge. The usual disclaimer applies.

Swedish experiences and solutions. Contemporary climate policy in Sweden has adopted very ambitious targets, including a fossil-free vehicle fleet by 2030 but also other steps that take Sweden beyond negotiated international burdens. Current climate policy goals state that by 2045, Sweden will produce zero net greenhouse gas emissions into the atmosphere, and achieve negative emissions thereafter (Regeringskansliet 2017b).

Still, Swedish emissions are only a tiny fraction of global emissions, and further cuts would not contribute in any important respect to the global total. Instead, Sweden's ambition is to act as a pathfinder; action demonstrates the possibility of becoming a carbon-free welfare state. As the government put it in early 2017, 'By taking responsibility for our climate impact at home, we show leadership for the world's countries' (Regeringskansliet 2017a). An important part of the self-image which can be seen as the ideological foundation of the pathfinder strategy is certainly the low level of carbon emissions, not merely the reduced emissions after 1990. One implication of this is that it is important to explain why the carbon emissions were so low already when the climate policy was introduced.

The aim of this chapter is to analyse this process of transitional change, focusing on key political strategies in response to exogenous drivers, and taking into account that energy issues, despite having environmental consequences, were mainly driven by other policy fields, most importantly, economic policy. The setting of stabilisation policy in a fixed-exchange rate regime with low unemployment as one key target in combination with the mutual labour and capital interests in a competitive export industry, as well as energy security in a Cold War setting, are central to the analysis. The evolution of carbon emissions over time should also be seen as the outcome of a process characterised by historical contingency – a contingent sequence of actions from various actors that reflects the expectations, assumptions and self-reinforcing decisions that shaped the process (Andersson-Skog 2009, p. 73; Lipartito 2003, p. 75ff). This is to say that historical contingency creates certain development paths, which tend to converge at key conjunctions in time, and which create a process with several open-ended or even unintended outcomes. Such processes are intrinsically evolutionary by nature and therefore not deterministic nor possible to copy as such. It is only after the convergence of several such paths, including accidental outcomes of decisions, that the contemporary, highly ambitious Swedish stance in climate policy issues emerged. The study mainly covers the period from 1973 to 1990, aside from occasional (justified) deviations.

12.2 THE OIL CRISES AND THE DEVELOPMENT OF CARBON EMISSIONS

Swedish carbon dioxide emissions declined by approximately 40 per cent between the early 1970s and the late 1980s, which should be compared with the 6 per cent cut between 1990 and 2005. As previously pointed out, and as seen in Figure 12.1, this

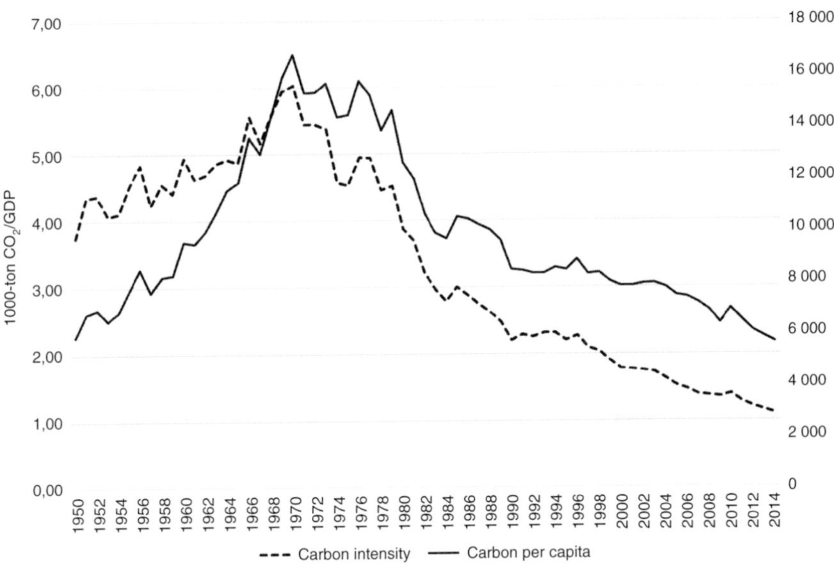

FIGURE 12.1 National per capita carbon dioxide emissions (kg per person) and carbon dioxide intensity. Sweden 1950–2014
Source: Lindmark and Andersson (2010) and Statistics Sweden after 1990

means that the largest cuts in carbon dioxide emission took place prior to the implementation of an active climate policy.

Swedish carbon intensity – the amount of carbon per constant-price GDP – increased throughout the 1950s and 1960s, while it fell from the 1970s, apart from a period during the early 1990s when intensity was relatively flat. It can also be established that the intensity has closely followed the development of absolute carbon emissions, and that both curves reveal an overall EKC pattern. Moreover, the decoupling of emissions and GDP was stronger than the reduction of emissions during both the period 1970 to 1990, and from the period after 1995. Clearly, the falling intensity primarily can be explained by the absolute emission cuts.

Understanding the EKC starts with the fact that the Swedish primary energy supply in the early 1970s was characterised by a large proportion of imported oil, as shown in Table 12.1. Indeed, Sweden was one of the top five most oil-intensive countries in the Western world in 1973.

In 1972, Sweden's oil intensity was 95 per cent of Canada's, the highest in the Western world (versus a developed world average of 68 per cent of Canadian intensity). By 1991, Swedish oil intensity had fallen to 33 per cent of the Canadian intensity in 1973, and was actually lower than the Western world average. This suggests a strong convergence in terms of oil intensity. This phenomenon may be measured as the β-convergence, the relationship between the initial oil intensity and the change in oil intensity over the period. A higher initial oil intensity is expected to

TABLE 12.1 *Oil intensity in Western world countries 1973, 1979 and 1991. Index. Canada 1973=100*

COUNTRY	1973	1979	1991
CAN	100	77	52
FIN	98	78	39
SWE	95	82	33
IRE	93	82	40
DEN	91	75	30
USA	89	75	47
BEL	81	65	35
NOR	74	60	37
FRA	67	55	31
NET	66	57	28
AUS	62	51	40
ITA	62	51	37
GER	60	52	35
GRB	57	45	29
ESP	53	56	35
AUT	52	45	31
GRE	49	49	44
SWI	47	40	31
NEZ	42	34	28
POR	33	38	36
Average	68	58	36
Stand. dev.	20	15	6

Note: Oil intensity is calculated as oil consumption for energy uses in relation to PPP-adjusted GDP volumes.
Source: Author's calculations based on the Maddison project historical GDP data and carbon emissions from liquid fuels, adopted from Boden et al. (2013).

be negatively related to the change, implying that a higher oil intensity also leads to a larger relative decrease in intensity. Thus, oil prices as an exogenous factor acting upon economic and political decisions are compatible with β-convergence if all countries face the same world oil market price and if the countries face similar technical conditions for oil substitution. Countries with larger reductions than expected, given their initial oil intensity, are in this respect overachievers. For such countries it is reasonable to find some kind of cutting-edge energy technological development, new forms of organisation, and changes in infrastructure or

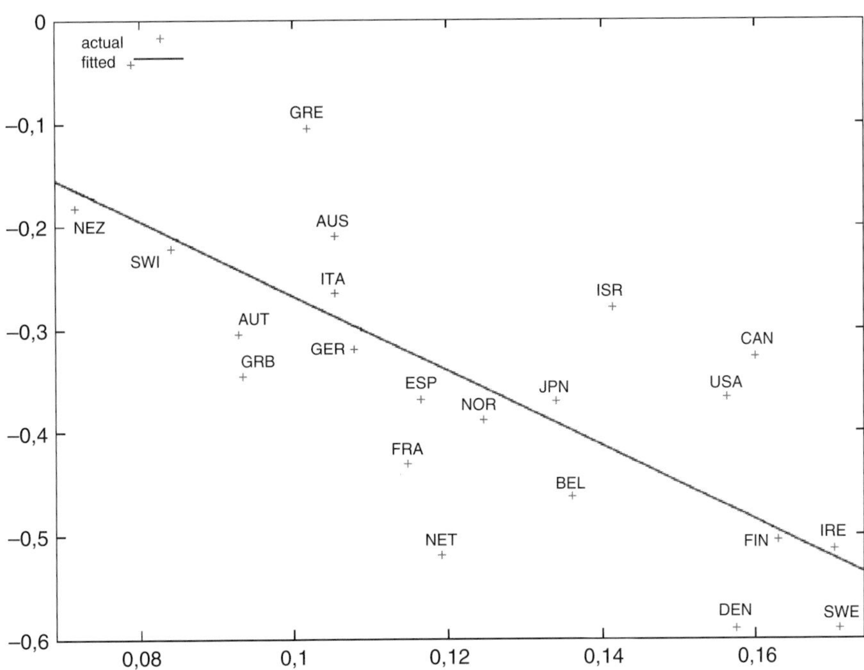

FIGURE 12.2 Oil intensity β-convergence 1979–1991 in Western economies – actual observations and fitted regression line
Source: Acar and Lindmark (2016)

perhaps some type of unique change in the production structure. Therefore, it is also plausible that there are unique features in such countries that can be identified through actor-level or firm-level studies. It would be possible to identify differences in terms of how, for instance, other countries implemented their energy policies or how companies developed their oil saving strategies or special features of national innovations systems. Figure 12.2 shows a basic cross-plot of oil intensity β-convergence for a sample of OECD countries over the period from 1979 to 1991, the period with the largest changes in intensity. It is clear that the Swedish reduction was among the largest in the Western world.

Given the intensity in 1979, the β-convergence suggests that Sweden would have been expected to reduce its oil intensity by 50 per cent, while it was in reality reduced by 60 per cent. Thus, 5/6 of the reduced intensity can be explained as a response to the initially high Swedish oil intensity. The remaining 1/6 can be attributed to specific Swedish ambitions. It is only in this sense that Sweden can be seen as a pathfinder; i.e., from a strict oil intensity perspective. A number of other countries, including the Netherlands, France, the UK, Denmark, Austria and Belgium achieved even larger reductions in the 1980s, given their initial oil intensity. The internationally uniform pattern also has an institutional side of importance.

Carlsnäs (1988) has pointed out that Swedish responses to the first oil crisis of 1973–1974 (OPEC I) included increased emergency storage capacity and the implementation of international oil disruption programs. This became a cornerstone in International Energy Program's (IEP) post-OPEC I policies. Furthermore, the IEA was established in 1974 on the initiative of Sweden and Denmark, with the main tasks of maintaining oil reserves and allocating oil consumption rights among its members. Thus, there was international coordination of oil policy, almost as if Sweden and Demark had started an oil consumers' cooperative. Still, the reduced oil-intensity issue does not explain why Sweden did not substitute the oil with other carbon-emitting fuels.

12.3 WHY THE OIL INTENSITY WAS SO HIGH IN 1973

The high Swedish oil dependency evolved during the 1950s and 1960s, and can be traced to political decisions taken immediately after the Second World War. The disruptions of international trade during the 1940s had caused immense energy problems due to the collapse of the Polish coal supply and dwindling American oil deliveries. Another significant problem was the outbreak of the Cold War in a situation where Sweden's position in the emerging NATO cooperation remained unclear. After the collapse of the Nordic defence pact initiative, Sweden and Finland were left outside the major military alliances. Against this background, the Swedish government therefore decided to investigate the prospects of developing a military nuclear weapons program in the fall of 1945 (Jonter 2010).

The military program was accompanied by a civil counterpart based on domestic uranium deposits (SOU 1956:46; Larsson 1987). A main reason for launching the civil nuclear program was energy security supplemented by commercial motives. The abundance of hydropower had framed a high electricity-intensive export industry, depending on cheap electricity. It could be foreseen that the full exploitation of hydropower would be reached in the 1970s. Also, a nuclear program would benefit from high competence in electrical engineering and energy technology primarily through ASEA (the Swedish industrial concern, which would later merge to form ABB) and the state-owned utility Vattenfall. The strategy of energy self-dependence became known as the Swedish Line. While the military part of the nuclear program was abandoned in the mid-1960s, the civil program continued, and the first large commercial reactor began operations in 1972. In the meantime, Sweden had developed one of the Western world's most oil-intensive economies. This was, however, part of the plan. It was already recognised in the 1950s that nuclear power necessitated electrification of energy consumption, which had previously been covered by imported fuels. Electrification involved space heating outside urban districts, but also further development of certain electricity-based manufacturing processes, such as electro-steel. It was therefore concluded that steam-generated electricity would first need to expand before nuclear power could be an option (SOU 1956:46).

Since it would take decades to develop nuclear technology, however, relatively low-cost oil plants were scheduled, although these plants were generally not part of government investment schemes, but more often owned by conglomerates made up of private and municipal power companies. This also included the development of district heating systems, the first of which began operation in 1948. A more rapid build-up of district heating started in the 1960s (Werner 1991). Oil thus became the main fuel. Indeed, coal had never fully returned as an important fuel after the Second World War, and the city gas production in Stockholm (and other cities) culminated by the mid-1950s.

The number of private cars increased and public investments in roads rose significantly during the 1950s and 1960s. As demand for petrol produced in Swedish refineries rose, so too did the supply of heavier fuel oils obtained as more or less by-products of the primary petrol and diesel production. Low prices boosted demand for fuel oils in the residential sector (Bladh 2012; Levin 2014).

The transformative pressure of OPEC I and II coincided with economic problems in Sweden's heavy export industry, reflecting the end of the post-war catch-up growth relative to the United States (Temin, 2002). The ultimate driver was slow productivity growth, which was already being felt from the mid-1960s. As the country with one of Western Europe's highest per capita incomes, this effect was felt from rather early on. For example, Finland did not experience an end of catch-up growth until the early 1990s (Svanlund 2010).

This was felt and interpreted as a structural crisis in the export industry, which emphasised the need for structural rationalisation. Sweden was, of course, not unique in this. Throughout the twentieth century, Sweden had developed into an open economy, highly dependent on foreign trade. The rising oil bill therefore threatened Swedish macroeconomic stability (Vedung 1982; Bergman 2014), and the energy debate therefore concentrated on direct economic impacts (e.g., Kall 2011). In short, imported inflation drove up the costs in export industries, which meant falling market shares and rising unemployment.

Another important macroeconomic event was the collapse of the Bretton Woods system in 1972. The Swedish currency, in relation to a depreciating dollar, appeared as overvalued. This, in combination with the adaptation to the new European fixed exchange rate regimes in October 1973, meant that the oil prices became a factor with direct implications for monetary policy, which had as its primary goal defending the fixed exchange rate.

The main pressures were import-led inflation, a rapidly deteriorating balance of trade and a slowdown in underlying productivity growth. This effect was, however, not immediately fully appreciated by the political and economic actors, while over the 1970s it did become evident that the investments in manufacturing were too low. Due to the high levels of oil dependency, the combined transformation pressure was

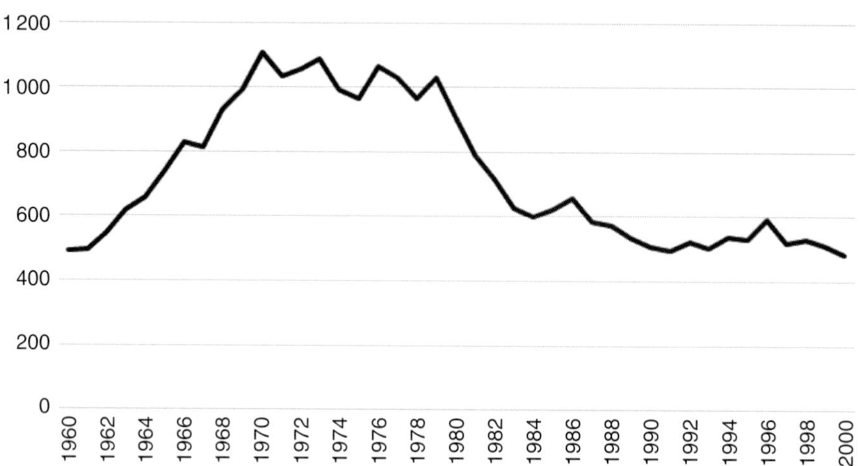

FIGURE 12.3 Swedish oil consumption 1960–2000. PJ
Source: Kander (2002)

among the highest in the Western world. A trade deficit would also make it difficult to defend the fixed exchange rate without rising unemployment. A primary goal was therefore to find quick, domestic solutions to the oil problem. One strategy was given by the nuclear power program, which had already begun, while another strategy lay in the plentiful resources of the Swedish forests for biofuels.

As seen in Figure 12.3, we can conclude that Swedish oil consumption already had levelled out before OPEC I, but also that the 1970s only saw a modest decrease of oil consumption. There is, for instance, no obvious break in the trend in 1973.

Rather, it was between 1979 and 1984 that the most dramatic reduction took place with a decrease of around 40 per cent. Also, the period from 1986 to 1991 saw a further pronounced decrease of almost 30 per cent. Comparing Figure 12.2 with Figure 12.1 also indicates that Swedish carbon emissions were mainly driven by oil consumption, reflecting the fact that coal played only a minor role in the story. Indeed, there was no readily available infrastructure for coal, apart from the coke used in the steel mills, in the 1970s. As a matter of fact, coal had more or less disappeared already in the mid-1950s, which along with nuclear power, helps to explain why Sweden did not turn to coal on a massive scale.

The modest increase in coal is clearly seen when changes in the national energy mix over the period from 1973 to 1990 are studied. As demonstrated in Table 12.1 showing changes in the primary energy supply, oil energy decreased by 456 PJ over the period. The total change in energy consumption was only −1.6 PJ, which is to say that substitution dominated over energy savings. Around 36 per cent of the decrease in oil in primary energy supply is explained by substitution of biofuels, including black liquor and other fuels used in the pulp and paper industry, an additional

TABLE 12.2 *Changes in the Swedish primary energy supply by energy carrier 1973–1990.*

Energy carrier	Change PJ (1973–1990)	Share of change in oil
Firewood	106	−23 %
Black liquor and other internal biofuels in pulp- and paper industry	59	−13 %
Coal	34	−8 %
Peat	10	−2 %
Natural gas	24	−5 %
Hydro and nuclear electricity	220	−48 %
Total energy	−1.6	0 %
Oil	−456	

Sources: Kander (2002) and Lindmark, Bergqvist, Andersson (2013) for new estimates of black liquor and internal biofuels.

8 per cent from substitution by coal and an additional 5 per cent due to substitution by natural gas.

The dramatic reduction of Swedish carbon emissions and the resulting EKC for carbon is therefore largely explained by the modest substitution by coal and gas. Instead, hydropower and nuclear power (with nuclear power accounting for the lion's share of the change) explain an additional 48 per cent of the reduced oil energy supply, completing the picture of reductions in oil consumption as a consequence of substitution by non-carbon emitting energy sources, which were the main driver behind the falling carbon emissions. This had, however, little to do with environmental concerns, but rather depended on historical decisions, macro-economic concerns and, as we will see, some very open-ended political decisions.

12.4 THE ROLE OF TAXES AND SUBSIDIES

Economic theory holds that the marginal utility of consumption and the marginal cost to produce what is consumed equals a perfect market price. Emissions of pollutants such as carbon dioxide, do, however, cause disutility which is not reflected in market prices. This is known as a negative externality and is evidence of market failures, which should be corrected by taxes. This has been a central position in Swedish climate policy since the early 1990s, when the carbon and other environmental taxes were first introduced. The first Swedish energy taxes were the petrol tax, introduced in 1924 (SFS 1924:137), the electricity tax of 1951 (SFS 1951:374) and the general energy tax of 1957 (SFS 1957:262). Energy taxes were therefore active policy tools during the late 1970s and 1980s.

An intended effect of environmental and energy taxes is to push technological development towards lower emissions and increased technical energy efficiency.

Still, the role of environmental regulation in innovation is a complex issue, as shown in a recent survey by Berek et al. (2014). Policy instruments can be divided into those that address the entire economy (general controls) and instruments that address specific technologies. Near-term energy and carbon targets can be reached with general policy instruments (Sandén and Azar 2005). This is possible if the targets can be reached with technologies that can be 'picked off the shelf', in other words, existing technologies that require relatively modest efforts to be developed into viable alternatives. The energy taxes of the 1970s and 1980s were general controls, targeting the entire economy, which suggests that the taxes were aimed at promoting quick solutions, using 'off the shelf' technology. On the other hand, the government launched a very ambitious research program as part of its 1975 political energy decision. This is compatible with Sandén and Azar's argument that technology-specific policy actions are relevant for bringing new technologies to the shelf. These types of policy measures are more complex and involve public research as well as development and demonstration facilities. Investments in infrastructure was also needed, as demonstrated in the case of district heating, which also included joint projects on utilising waste heat between process industries and municipalities (Grönquist and Sandberg 2006). Similar approaches, involving close cooperation between the government and the manufacturing industry, were a main strategy in the oil policy after 1975, particularly concerning the pulp and paper industry (Bergquist and Söderholm 2014), but also other manufacturing sectors such as steelworks, ironworks and energy (SIND 1979). Still, it is important to recognise that increasing market prices constituted the bulk of the energy transformation pressure during the 1970s. The subsidies directed to the whole business sector amounted to 1100 mn SEK during the period from 1974/75 to 1978/79 (SIND 1979:1, p. 22), to be compared with a total increase of the manufacturing industry's oil expenditures by approximately 6500 mn SEK in relation to the oil expenditures in 1973 over the same period.[2] In total, the various projects financed by subsidies during the period were estimated to have saved 401,700 toe in the manufacturing industry (SIND 1979:1, p. 59), amounting to approximately 25 per cent of the total cut in oil consumption between 1974 and 1978. In practice, it is also evident from Figure 12.4 that the tax rate was comparatively modest until the early 1980s.

Indeed, taxes were less important in the early 1980s than during the era of active climate policy from the 1990s and onward. Oil tax revenues were also used for building up an oil fund for the purpose of financing the aforementioned subsidies. It is therefore safe to say that the oil and energy taxes were primarily introduced for fiscal reasons with the purpose of financing subsidies that would kick-start the transformation. The oil product price increases were approximately of the same magnitude during the OPEC II crisis of 1979–1980 as during the OPEC I oil price shock, and taxes did little to change this. However, beginning in 1982 taxes came to

[2] Calculated as the sum of oil expenditure changes over the period. Data from SOS *Industrin*.

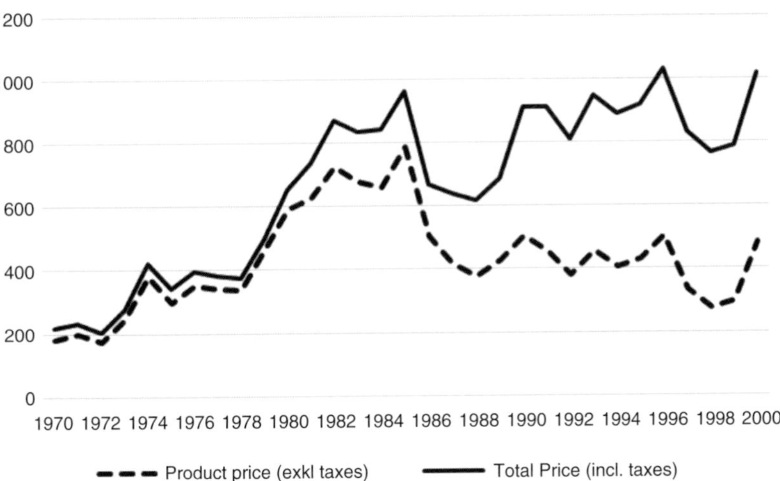

FIGURE 12.4 The Swedish real fuel oil (EO-1) total and product prices 1960–2000. Fixed 1970 prices.
Source: Oil prices from Svenska Petroleuminstitutet. GDP-deflator obtained from Schön, L. and Krantz, O. (2012), *Swedish Historical National Accounts 1560–2010*, Lund Papers in Economic History 123, department of Economic History, Lund University. Note: the GDP deflator is used for fixed-price calculation.

constitute a higher share of the oil price, thus reinforcing the transformation pressure emanating from world market prices. These tax increases, however, served to dampen the falling oil prices during the second half of the 1980s, and can only be understood in the context of the fixed exchange rate regime and the great devaluation of the Swedish currency in 1982. The whole idea behind the devaluation and the 'third way politics' was to kick-start investments with a 'once and for all' devaluation. Low inflation should be maintained through wage moderation, enabled by the close links between the Social Democratic government and the Labour Union movement. Still, this was easier said than done, and by 1984 inflation had picked up speed. It was foreseen that falling petrol prices would further boost private consumption, leading to new trade deficits that threatened to undermine the fixed exchange rate (Feldt 1991).

12.5 ENERGY AND THE 'THIRD WAY' ECONOMIC POLICY

One of the effects on the Swedish economy of the OPEC I crisis was a sharply deteriorating trade surplus, as shown in Figure 12.5. By 1976, the balance of trade had even become negative.

Certainly, the trade deficit was not solely a result of the higher oil prices, but even more a reflection of falling foreign demand in the wake of the economic hardships of

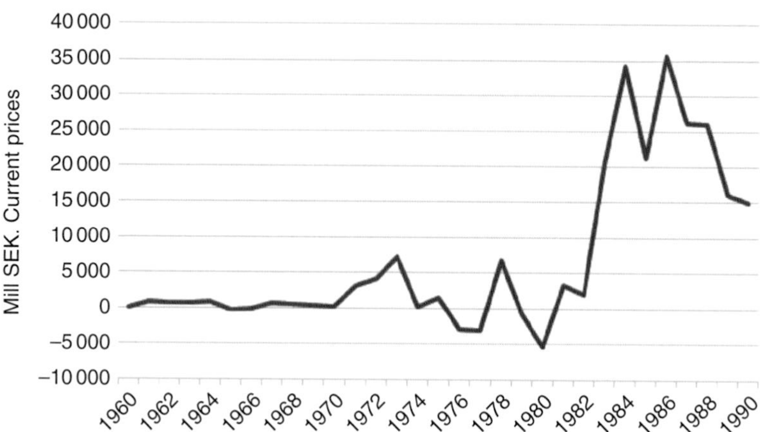

FIGURE 12.5 The Swedish balance of trade 1960–2000. Current prices.
Source: Schön, L. and Krantz, O. (2012), *Swedish Historical National Accounts 1560–2010*, Lund Papers in Economic History 123, Department of Economic History, Lund University.

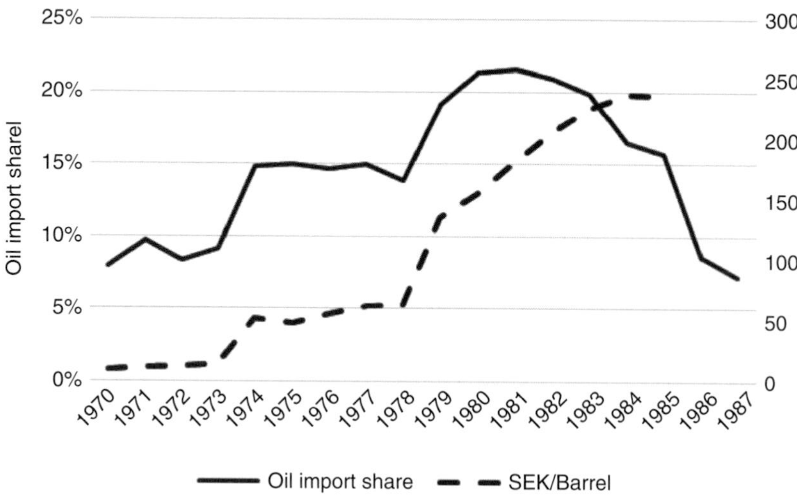

FIGURE 12.6 The oil share of imports and the oil price. Sweden 1970–1990.
Sources: Author's estimates based on Schön, L. and Krantz, O. (2012) *Swedish Historical National Accounts 1560–2010*, Lund Papers in Economic History 123, department of Economic History, Lund University and *BP Statistical Review of World Energy* June 2014.

the period. Still, the cost for oil imports jumped from around 10 per cent of total imports in 1973 to 15 per cent in 1974, which, along with the oil prices, is seen in Figure 12.6.

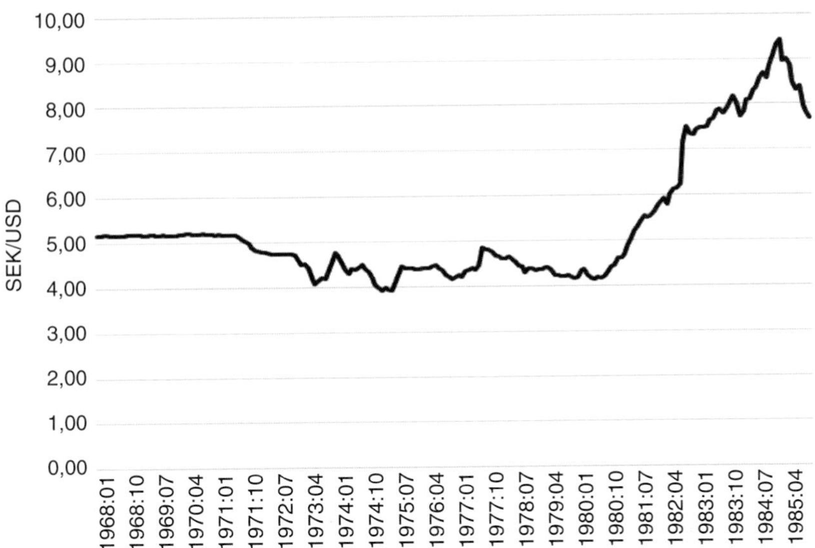

FIGURE 12.7 The SEK/USD exchange rate January 1968 to December 1985
Source: Edvinsson, R., Jacobson, T., Waldenström, D. (2010). *Exchange rates, Prices and Wages, 1277–2008*, Sveriges Riksbank, Ekerlids Förlag. Data downloaded from Riksbanken

The oil price shock explains roughly half of the deteriorating balance of trade in these years. The balance of trade did not, however, become negative until 1976, which was after the immediate effects of the oil price shock. Rather, the negative balance reflected the ongoing recession in the Western world, to which the oil crisis contributed, while it was not the sole, or perhaps not even a main, explanation for the economic hardship of the era. It is also clear that the deficit again rose with the OPEC II crises, but the deficit this time can almost entirely be attributed to the oil price shock. The deficit was again sharply reversed in 1982, which is partly explained by the great devaluation of the Swedish currency in the same year. Still, it is necessary to look closer at the dynamics of oil consumption and the devaluation to understand the series of events which eventually led to the rise of a low-carbon economy.

A devaluation is certainly a double-edged sword if the economy is heavily dependent on oil imports. A sharp devaluation intended to increase profits in the manufacturing industry through lower prices and export-led growth has the obvious drawback that oil imports become more expensive. However, by 1982 the manufacturing sector had undertaken substantial cuts in its oil consumption, which in principle facilitated the devaluation. As evident from Figure 12.7, the Swedish

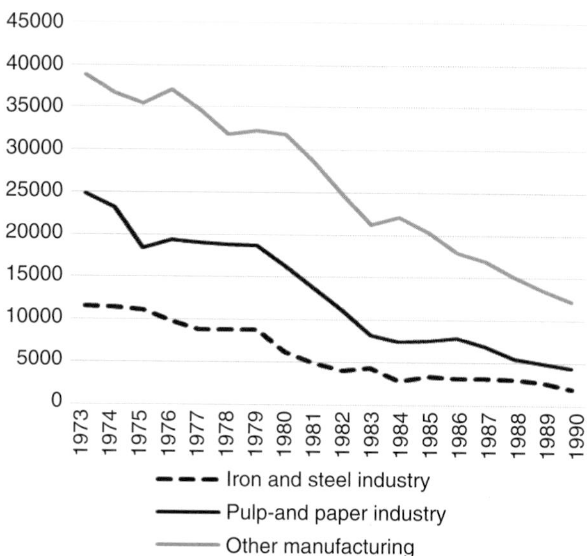

FIGURE 12.8 Oil consumption in the Swedish manufacturing industry 1973–1990. TJ. Source: Author's estimates based on SOS *Industrin*.

currency had appreciated against the US dollar through the fall of 1971 to the spring of 1972, but then stabilised.

However, from January until the summer of 1973, the SEK appreciated once more as a consequence of the final collapse of the Bretton Woods system. The appreciated currency became a major obstacle for the export industry, while the appreciation at the same time tended to dampen the effects of rising oil prices. Through a period of volatile exchange rates and a series of smaller Swedish devaluations, the exchange rate was back to 1970 levels by early 1977. The small devaluation in August 1978 marked, however, the beginning of a new period of Swedish currency appreciation, which lasted until September 1980. However, the US monetary policy now changed with an upward adjustment of the interest rate, leading to a steadily depreciating Swedish currency from the first half of the 1980s.

By 1982, oil consumption had significantly reduced in the manufacturing sector. The evolution of oil consumption in the Swedish manufacturing industry from 1973 to 1990 is seen in Figure 12.8. The pulp and paper industry was the single most important sector in this respect (Lindmark et al. 2011), while it is also true that the absolute reductions in the rest of the manufacturing sector were equally large. One of these sectors was the heavily oil-consuming steel industry, where the reduced oil consumption included a discarding of the Bessemer and Thomas processes in the 1970s, and the oil-intensive Martin process in the early 1980s, followed by the introduction of continuous casting (STEM 2000). The cuts in oil consumption in the steel industry were, to a high degree, interwoven with the industrial crisis and the reconstruction of the bankrupted privately owned steel industry under the newly formed state-owned Swedish Steel (SSAB) (Schön 2011).

The reduced oil consumption in manufacturing was an important condition for the great devaluation of the Swedish currency in 1982 and the so-called third way economic policy of the 1980s (Feldt 1991, 72–77, 84; Ahlström and Carlsson 2009). Since oil consumption in manufacturing, which comprised the bulk of Swedish exports, had been reduced at a much faster rate than overall oil consumption, a major downside of a devaluation had been significantly reduced. A devaluation in an oil-importing economy would lead to a corresponding increase in the oil bill, which would have partly offset the intended boost of international competitive power. The substantial reduction of oil consumption in the manufacturing industry up to 1982 meant that a devaluation had smaller effects on the cost structure in the manufacturing industry than if a similar devaluation had been attempted in the 1970s. It is therefore suggested that the reduced oil consumption in the manufacturing sector constituted a structural condition that paved the way for the general economic policy of the decade. That the oil consumption had not fallen as quickly in other sectors was less important, since it was the performance in the export industries that was the real economic target of the policy. The switch from oil to other fuels had started in the late 1970s. While the largest changes in the economy mainly took place after 1982, the transition to biofuels in the energy sector mainly took place in the 1990s (Eriksson 2009). This was certainly not a self-evident choice since biofuels competed with the raw material supply of the important pulp and paper industry.

12.6 FROM THREE MILE ISLAND TO THE CARBON CEILING AND BEYOND

To fully understand why biofuels were preferred over coal and gas, it is necessary to recall the political debate over nuclear power. The environmental movement had been enthusiastic over nuclear power in the 1960s, and the Swedish Natural Protection Association (SNF) nourished a vision of a '. . . pearl necklace of reactors along the Norrland coast'. This was how the rivers should be saved from hydropower exploitation. Indeed, the protection of river landscapes and environments was probably the most important issue for the environmental movement during the 1960s. Environmentalists also won an important victory in 1970 as the government decided to abandon its plans to establish hydropower plants in the Vindel River (Nilsson 1970). In practice, four major rivers in northern Sweden were exempted from hydropower, a decision which was confirmed in 1987 (SFS 1987:12).

However, by the early 1970s, the tide was also turning for nuclear power. Hannes Alfvén, professor in physics and member of the agricultural and rural-based Centre Party (C), had become more sceptical over nuclear power, and pointed at the risk of meltdowns, problems of radioactive waste disposal and, above all, the threat of a diffusion of nuclear weapons (Afvén 1975). The opposition against nuclear power soon evolved into a main issue for the Centre Party. Nuclear power was also a major issue in the 1976 election, in which the Social Democrats (S), for the first time since the 1930s, lost power to a non-socialist coalition led by the 'greenish' Centre Party. The Social Democrats had traditionally been in favour of nuclear power, but more sceptical voices with connections to the peace movement had gradually become more important within the party. The right-wing opposition was also divided, with the Centre Party clearly opposing nuclear power and the Liberals (Fp) and Conservatives (M) in favour. The Three Mile Island accident in 1979 accentuated the issue and led to a referendum in 1980, as a way to solve the split within the Social Democrats and within the non-socialist opposition.[3] A simple yes or no question in the referendum would, however, have meant that the Social Democrats and the Conservatives would have ended up on the same side, which was politically impossible. The Social Democrats therefore launched a third position in the nuclear referendum. It was neither a no, nor a yes, but rather an in-between position according to which nuclear power should be phased out in a 'responsible manner', over a twenty-five-year period. This latter option won in the referendum, while in practice the difference between the Conservatives' and the Social Democrats' positions should not be exaggerated. However, disagreements and tensions between the Centre Party and the coalition partners over nuclear power plagued the non-socialist government until the Social Democrats returned to government in 1982.

Nuclear power seemed to have lost some of its political edge. This came to an abrupt end in the spring of 1986 as what was at first suspected to be a radioactive leak at the Forsmark plant in the Stockholm region turned out to be a major nuclear disaster in the USSR. In the immediate aftermath of the Chernobyl accident and with references to the referendum, the Social Democratic government therefore decided to shut down two reactors. Natural gas linking Western Sweden to the Norwegian gasfields and the construction of two coal power plants were the intended replacement power. Indeed, if these projects had been realised, Sweden would have experienced considerably higher carbon emissions in the 1990s and the emission pattern would have resembled a tilted S and not the familiar inverted U. The Conservatives, however, had an unexpected ace up their sleeves, and in the summer of 1988 they proposed a carbon-emission ceiling in the Parliament – carbon emissions should not be allowed to increase above present levels. References were made to the 1988 Toronto conference. Probably, the Conservatives' sudden interest for climate change was only half-hearted (TT 1990). For one, the Conservatives never discussed carbon emissions from road traffic in this context, and secondly, the carbon ceiling served as a major stumbling block for the government's plans to close two nuclear reactors. The Conservative proposal was supported by all other parties,

3 The socialist opposition consisted of the Communists (VPK). It is important to realise that Swedish referendums are only advisory; the parliament still decides at its own discretion. A Swedish referendum is therefore to be seen as a strong statement from the voters.

even though the Green Party (MP) hesitated as they realised that the carbon ceiling would make it difficult to dismantle nuclear power. As the government was defeated in the Parliament, the consequence was that the plans for coal and gas power had to be abandoned. Still, the defeat was accepted by the Social Democrats. It did not lead to a government crisis even though Swedish energy politics was locked in a self-induced full nelson.

Hydropower had been stopped, two reactors were scheduled to be closed down and carbon emissions were not to increase. It was effectively a punctuated equilibrium situation and Sweden was set on a path towards biofuels, energy efficiency and low-carbon emissions. This was enforced by other converging political decisions with historical roots. The Conservatives and Liberals had from the mid-1980s advocated taxes as a primary environmental policy tool. In short, Pigouvian taxes – or environmental fees as they were called at the time – had first been advocated in the Swedish debate by the economist Eric Dahmén in the late 1960s (Dahmén 1968). The Liberal Party under the leadership of Dahmén's famous colleague, Bertil Ohlin, proposed environmental fees in 1969 but the idea was met with little enthusiasm (Lindblad 2013:300). The environmental movement saw the taxes as an environmental letter of indulgence and the Social Democrats put their trust in administrative tools while the Conservatives distrusted new taxes. Environmental taxes were among the policy tools subject to an official investigation initiated in 1971, but even though the report (SOU 1974:111) was positive about the use of environmental fees, the issue basically lay dead in the political water until the latter part of the 1980s. As environmental issues became more politically important in the mid-1980s and the Green Party, an offshoot of the anti-nuclear campaign of the 1970s, seemed to gain parliamentary seats, the conservatives picked up the idea of environmental taxes. The idea did soon gain a broader popularity and the Social Democratic government proposed a commission on economic instruments in environmental policy to investigate the use of taxes as tools in environmental policy (prop. 87/88:85). This investigation eventually came to be coordinated with a much bigger political issue at the time.

Over the course of the 1980s it became clear that the Swedish tax system was in need of major reform. The problems included overly high marginal taxes and the general hotchpotch tax system that had evolved over the previous decades. The settlement of the tax system was a broad parliamentary agreement involving the Social Democrats and the Liberals (Fp). The general competence in economic theory was remarkably high at the time. The Prime Minister, Ingvar Carlsson, had a degree in economics from Northwestern University and Bengt Westerberg, the leader of the Liberals, had studied economics at Stockholm University. The economic spokesperson of the Liberals, Anne Wibble, was the daughter of Bertil Ohlin and a former student of Eric Dahmén, and accordingly well acquainted with the concept of environmental taxes. As the tax reform focused on income tax cuts, it became essential to broaden the tax base and for this purpose environmental taxes were also considered, although the purpose of a Pigouvian tax is to partly erode its own tax base.

Indeed, the Commission on Economic Instruments in Environmental Policy did discuss a carbon tax in its first preliminary report (SOU 1989:22). While the sulphur tax in particular was expected to erode the tax base as emissions declined, the revenues from the carbon tax were foreseen to be much more stable (SOU 1989: 83, p. 28). The carbon tax was therefore seen as a way to finance the tax reform while also having an environmental policy purpose. The carbon tax was designed as a relatively high tax, which was possible since the general energy taxes were simultaneously removed in turn, and, as a tax that was levied before VAT, the carbon tax would still be powerful enough to discriminate between different fuels.

At the same time, subsidies to encourage oil substitution were abolished as well as the carbon ceiling. To dampen the negative effects of the carbon tax on the export industry, the tax was highly differentiated with exceptions for the energy-intensive manufacturing industry and rather directed towards domestic land transports and the domestic heating and municipal power sectors. Several studies have shown that the carbon dioxide tax became an important policy tool for achieving a decoupling of emissions and GDP after 1990 (Johansson, 2001; Ds 1997:26; Ds 2005:55; Scrimgeour et al., 2005) and that the tax contributed to removing coal from local district heating and oil from domestic heating (ER 2006:06). As previously noted, VAT was introduced on energy as the energy taxes were removed. Since VAT is only paid by final consumers, this meant that the tax burden for energy was shifted from businesses to households and consumers, while the carbon tax mainly hit domestic oil- and coal-consuming sectors, including household heating, road transport and the energy sector. The pressure for a tax-driven energy transformation was therefore lifted from the export industry to the household sector, domestic heating and private transport.

In praising the Swedish carbon tax it is important to recognise that the carbon tax was implemented in favourable circumstances as the carbon emissions were already at historically low levels, coal played a minor role in the energy sector and the tax could be linked to a major tax reform which needed the fiscal benefits of the tax. Unique as it is, so was the window of opportunity.

12.7 CONCLUSIONS

The Swedish EKC for carbon, generally low carbon emissions and continuously falling carbon intensity, has been recognised in both the political and academic spheres. It is, however, important to appreciate that this achievement was initially the result of a series of historical decisions, macroeconomic circumstances and ordinary political kicks on the shin with accidental outcomes. It was only when several political processes had converged that the highly ambitious Swedish climate policy of today could emerge, standing on the shoulders of the accidental outcomes of yesterday's decisions and often dressed in narratives of stewardship and pathfinding. Key components that explain the development of Swedish policy on carbon emissions include the military nuclear weapons program decided on in the late 1940s, followed by a civil counterpart in the 1960s. Coupled with the fact that coal, apart from coke in the steelworks, had never really returned as a fuel after the Second World War, nuclear power necessitated the creation of one of the Western world's most oil-intensive economies during the 1960s. Thus, OPEC I hit Sweden when it was highly dependent on imported oil and lacking infrastructure for coal. In addition, the Swedish export industry had experienced faltering productivity and growth since the mid1960s, reflecting the end of catch-up growth, and the need for a new investment cycle despite falling profits. Just as this was happening, there were nine nuclear reactors more or less ready to be charged with uranium and a well-developed infrastructure for wood. At the same time, Swedish monetary policy aimed at maintaining a fixed exchange rate without jeopardising employment. In these circumstances high priority was given to the task of reducing oil consumption in manufacturing. This was mainly done through ordinary price signals reinforced by subsidies both for the rapid implementation of off-the-shelf technologies and for basic energy research and the development of new technology.

As oil dependency in manufacturing decreased, the scene was set for a major devaluation in 1982, which kick-started the export industry and shifted the burden of the oil bill to the domestic sector. When oil prices again started to fall in the mid-1980s, while at the same time inflation slowly went out of hand, oil taxes were raised to dampen the risk for trade deficits and an undermining of the exchange rate. Around the same time a new situation arose as the environmental issue converged with the long-time need for a major tax reform, where the environmental issue was totally dominated by nuclear safety, while other issues gained greater prominence in public opinion.

The Social Democrats had won the 1980 referendum over nuclear power on a 'go-stop' position, something that annoyed both the Conservatives, in favour of nuclear power, and the environmental movement. This led to the introduction of a carbon ceiling in 1988, effectively stopping the Social Democrats' plans to replace a few of the reactors with gas and coal power. The Conservatives slammed the door shut in the face of the government in an unholy alliance with the Greens and the left-wing party. As the environmental issue gained more attention, the Conservatives also had embraced environmental taxes, Pigouvian taxes, as their main position on the environmental question. This was hardly an election winner, but came in handy in the broad negotiations around tax reform. Environmental taxes, including the carbon tax, were introduced in the tax reforms of 1991, partly as a way to broaden the tax base, partly as a way to avoid future increases of carbon emissions. The accidental outcome of these historical processes was the carbon EKC and low-carbon emissions, achievements which in turn have affected the pathfinding strategy of contemporary Swedish climate policy. The accidental nature of past events, the operation of normal market forces and improvised strategies have transformed into a project to become the first carbon-free welfare state.

There is, however, another point to be made of the story, which in a more down-to-earth manner can be used as a learning example. Acemoglu et al. (2012) as well as Rezai and van der Plough (2013) used optimisation models to show that an optimal policy mix for a transition to low-carbon technologies can begin where the carbon-free technology is initially less efficient than the dirty technology and initially high subsidies for technological development are followed by the introduction of carbon taxes. The subsidies are initially 'aggressive', but rather quickly dismantled, while the carbon taxes are gradually increased. This is also the broad picture of Swedish energy policy. The 1950s and 1960s saw heavy subsidies for research and development in nuclear technology (however not yet quantified). The government's 1975 energy decision saw heavy subsidies for both renewables and for implementation of 'off-the-shelf' technologies. Taxes were still modest, but they still increased. The tax reform of 1991 saw the introduction of carbon taxes at an initially low level, at the same time as many of the subsidies were dismantled. Contemporary carbon taxes are four times as high as in 1991. Thus, in conclusion, Sweden somewhat accidently followed a path which resembles the strategies that Acemoglu, Rezai and van der Plough have recently suggested. As we have argued, this happened out of chance and path dependency, but still offers an intriguing example of transformative change in a setting of subsidies and taxes. Copy and paste for the future to come?

12.8 REFERENCES

12.8.1 *Official Publications*

Departmentsstencilier (Ds)

Ds 1997:26 *Sveriges andra nationalrapport om klimatförändringar* (Sweden's Second National Report on Climate Change)

Ds 2005:55 *Sveriges fjärde nationalrapport om klimatförändringar* (Sweden's Fourth National Report on Climate Change)

ER 2006:06 *Ekonomiska styrmedel i energisektorn. En utvärdering av dess effekter på koldioxidutsläppen sedan* 1990. (Economic policy tools in the energy sector. An evaluation of their impact on carbon emissions since 1990) Swedish energy agency

Statens Offentliga utredningar (SOU)

SOU 1956:46 *Bränsleförsörjningen i atomåldern*

SOU 1989:22

SOU 1989:89

SOU 2000:23 *Förslag till svensk klimatstrategi*

SOU 2014:37 *Långtidsutredningen*

Svensk författningssamling (SFS)
SFS 1924:137
SFS 1951:374
SFS 1957:262
SFS 1987:12
SFS 1990:587
Sveriges Officiella Statistik (SOS)
SOS *Industrin*

12.8.2 *Online Resources*

BP Statistical Review of World Energy June 2014: www.bp.com/statisticalreview

Maddison-Project. Available at: www.ggdc.net/maddison/maddison-project/home.htm

Regeringskansliet (2017a) Fossilfria transporter och resor: Regeringens arbete för att minska transporternas klimatpåverkan (Fossil-free transportation and travels: the governments work to reduce climate impact from transports). 7 Feb 2017. www.regeringen.se/regeringens-politik/regeringens-prioriteringar/sverige-som-foregangsland-for-minskade-klimatutslapp/fossilfria-transporter-och-resor-regeringens-arbete-for-att-minska-transporternas-klimatpaverkan/

Regeringskansliet (2017b) Det klimatpolitiska ramverket (The climate policy framework). 12 June 2017. www.regeringen.se/artiklar/2017/06/det-klimatpolitiska-ramverket/

Svenska Petroleuminstitutet: http://spbi.se/statistik/priser/mer-prisstatistik/arsmedelspriser-uppvarmningsbranslen/

12.8.3 *Newspaper Articles*

TT, Tidningarnas Telegrambyrå, 1990–03-07 *Koldioxidmålet klaras inte säger Statens Energiverk i ny rapport* [The Carbon Dioxide Goal not to be Reached Claims Swedish Energy Authority in New Report]

12.8.4 *Literature*

Acar, S. and Lindmark, M. (2016), 'Periods of Converging Carbon Dioxide Emissions from Oil Combustion in a Pre-Kyoto Context', *Environmental Development* 19: 1–9.

Acemoglu, D., P. Aghion, L. Bursztyn and D. Hemous (2012), 'The Environment and Directed Technical Change', *American Economic Review* 102: 131–166.

Ahlström, G., Carlsson, B. (2009), 'Superdevalveringen 1982: Sverige under IMF-luppen' [The super devaluation of 1982: Sweden under the IMF microscope], *Ekonomisk Debatt* 37 (5): 5–15.

Alvén, H. (1975), *Kärnkraft och atombomber*, Stockholm: Aldus.

Andersson-Skog, L. (2009), Revisiting Railway History: The Case of Institutiuonal Change and Path Dependency, in Lars Magnusson and Jan Ottosson (Eds.) *The Evolution of Path Dependence*, Cheltenham (UK): Edward Elgar, 70–86.

Bergek, A. and Berggren, C. (2014), 'The Impact of Environmental Policy Instruments on Innovation: A Review of Energy and Automotive Industry Studies', *Ecological Economics* 106: 112–123.

Bergman, L. (2014), *De svenska energimarknaderna – en samhällsekonomisk analys*. Bilaga till SOU 2014:37.

Bergquist, A.-K. and Söderholm, K. (2014), 'Industry Strategies for Energy Transition in the Wake of the Oil Crisis', *Business and Economic History* 12: 1–18.

Bergquist, A.-K., Söderholm, K., Kinneryd, H., Lindmark, M. and Söderholm, P. (2013), 'Environmental Compliance and Technological Change in Swedish Industry 1970–1990', *Ecological Economics* 85: 6–19.

Bladh, M. (2012), 'Energy Consumption and Stocks of Energy Converting Artefacts', *Energy Policy* 43: 381–386.

Boden,T.A., Marland, G. and Andres, R.J. (2013), *Global, Regional and National Fossil-Fuel CO2 Emissions*. Carbon Dioxide Information Analysis Center, Oak Ridge National Laboratory, US Department of Energy, OakRidge, Tenn., USA (available at http://cdiac.ornl.gov/trends/emis/meth_reg.html).

Brännlund, R. and Lundgren, T. (2009a), 'Environmental Policy without Costs? A Review of the Porter Hypothesis', SIRP WP 09–01.

Brännlund, R. and Lundgren, T. (2009b), 'Environmental Policy without Costs? A Review of the Porter Hypothesis', *International Review of Environmental and Resource Economics* 3: 75–117.

Brockwell, E. (2014), 'State and Industrial Actions to Influence Consumer Behavior' (diss.), Umeå economic studies 894, Department of Economics, Umeå University.

Carlsnäs, W. (1988), *Energy Vulnerability and National Security*, London: Pinter Publishers.

Dahmén, E. (1968), *Sätt pris på miljön*, Stockholm: SNS.

Dahmén, E. (1987), 'Miljön och marknaden', *Svensk Tidskrift* 1987: 391–397.

Edvinsson, R., Jacobson, T. and Waldenström, D. (2010), *Exchange Rates, Prices and Wages, 1277–2008*, Stockholm: Ekerlid: Sveriges Riksbank.

Eriksson, K. (2009), 'Introduction and Development of the Swedish District Heating Systems - Critical Factors and Lessons Learned'. D5 of WP2 from the RES-H Policy project, Lund.

Feldt, K.-O. (1991), *Alla dessa dagar … I regeringen 1982–1990*. [All these days … In the government 1982–1990] Stockholm: Norstedts.

Grönkvist, S. and Sandberg, P. (2006), 'Driving Forces and Obstacles with regard to Co-operation between Municipal Energy Companies and Process Industries in Sweden', *Energy Policy* 34: 1508–1519.

Johansson, B. (2001), 'Economic Instruments in Practice: Carbon Taxes in Sweden', Naturvårdsverket rapport 8, Stockholm: SNV.

Johansson P.O. and Kriström, B. (2007), 'On a Clear Day You Might See an Environmental Kuznets Curve', *Environmental and Resource Economics* 37: 77–90.

Jonter, T. (2010), 'The Swedish Plans to Acquire Nuclear Weapons, 1945–1968: An Analysis of the Technical Preparations', *Science & Global Security* 18: 61–86.

Kall, A.-S. (2011), *Förnyelse med förhinder: Den riksdagspolitiska debatten om omställningen av energisystemet 1980–2010* (diss.), Linköping Studies in Arts and Science.

Kander, A. (2002), 'Economic Growth, Energy Consumption and CO2 Emissions in Sweden 1800–2000' (diss.), Lund Studies in Economic History 19, Lund, Almqvist & Wicksell International.

Larsson, K.-E. (1987), Kärnkraftens historia i Sverige, *Kosmos* 64: 125–126.

Levin, M. (2014), *Att elda för kråkorna? Hushållens energianvändning inom bostadssektorn i Sverige 1913–2008* (diss.) Umeå studies in Economic History 46, Umeå University.

Lindblad, H. (2013), *Kärlek, tbc och liberalism: en biografi om Sven Wedén* [Love, TB and Liberalism: a biography of Sven Wedén], Stockholm: Ekerlid.

Lindmark, M. (2002), 'An EKC-Pattern in Historical Perspective: Carbon Dioxide Emissions, Technology, Fuel Prices and Growth in Sweden 1870–1997', *Ecological Economics* 42: 333–347.

Lindmark, M. and Acar, S. (2015), 'Periods of Converging Carbon Dioxide Emissions from Oil Combustion 1973–2004'. CERE WP 2015-1, Umeå University.

Lindmark, M. and Andersson, L.-F. (2010), 'Unintentional Climate Policy: Swedish Experiences of Carbon Dioxide Emissions and Economic Growth 1950–2005'. CERE WP #14/2010, Umeå University.

Lindmark, M., Bergqvist, A.-K. and Andersson, L.-F. (2013), 'Energy Transition, CO2 Reduction and Output Growth in the Swedish Pulp and Paper Industry: 1973–2006', *Energy Policy* 39: 5449–5456.

Liparito, K. (2003), 'Picturephone and the Information Age. The Social Meaning of Failure', *Technology and Culture* 44: 50–81.

Newell, R., Jaffe, A. and Stavins, R. (1999), 'The Induced Innovation Hypothesis and Energy-Saving Technological Change', *The Quarterly Journal of Economics* 114: 941–975.

Nilsson, M. (1970), *Striden om Vindelälven: makten, människorna och verkligheten kring ett beslut* (The Fight over the Vindel River: The power, the people and the realities of a decision) Stockholm: Bonnier.

Popp, D. (2002), 'Induced Innovation and Energy Price', *American Economic Review* 92: 160–180.

Porter, M. and van der Linde, C. (1995), 'Toward a New Conception of the Environment Competitiveness Relationship', *Journal of Economic Perspectives* 9: 97–118.

Radetzki, M. (2004), *Svensk energipolitik under tre decennier: en studie i politikermisslyckanden*, Stockholm: SNS Förlag.

Rezai, A. and van der Plough, F. (2013), 'Abandoning Fossil Fuel: How Fast and How Much?' OxCarre Research Paper 123.

Sandén, B.A. and Azar, C. (2005), 'Near-Term Technology Policy for Long-Term Climate Targets. Economy Wide versus Technology Specific Approaches', *Energy Policy* 33: 1557–1576.

Schipper, L., Murtishaw, S., Khrushch, M., Ting, M., Karbuz, S. and Unander, F. (2001), 'Carbon Emissions from Manufacturing Energy Use in 13 IEA Countries: Long-Term Trends through 1995', *Energy Policy* 29: 667–688.

Schön, L. (2011), *Sweden's Road to Modernity: An Economic History*, Stockholm: SNS Förlag.

Schön, L. and Krantz, O. (2012), 'Swedish Historical National Accounts 1560–2010', Lund Papers in Economic History 123, Department of Economic History, Lund University.

Scrimgeour, F., Oxley, L. and Fatai, K. (2005), 'Reducing Carbon Emissions? The Relative Effectiveness of Different Types of Environmental Tax: The Case of New Zealand', *Environmental Modelling & Software*, 11: 1439–1448.

SIND (1979), *Utvärdering av statsbidragen till energibesparande åtgärder i näringslivet*, Utredning från Statens industriverk, SIND 1979: 1, Stockholm: LiberFörlag.

Söderholm, K. and Bergquist, A.-K. (2011), 'Green Innovation Systems in the Swedish Pulp and Paper Industry 1960–2011', *Scandinavian Economic History Review* 60: 183–211.

STEM (2000), *Effektiv energianvändning. En analys av utvecklingen 1970–1998*. ER 22:2000.

Svanlund, J. (2010), *Svensk och finsk upphinnartillväxt: faktorpris- och produktivitetsutjämning mellan Finland och Sverige 1950–2000* (diss.), Umeå Studies in Economic History, 38, Umeå University.

Vedung, E. (1982), Energipolitiska utvärderingar 1973–81, Stockholm.

Werner, S. (1991), 'District Heating in Sweden 1948–1990', *Fernwärme International* 20: 603–616.
Wolfson, D.J. and Koopmans, C.C. (1996), 'Regulatory Taxation of Fossil Fuels: Theory and Policy', *Ecological Economics* 19: 55–65.

12.9 RESPONSE TO 'RETHINKING THE ENVIRONMENTAL STATE: AN ECONOMIC HISTORY OF THE SWEDISH ENVIRONMENTAL KUZNETS CURVE FOR CARBON'

By Michael G. Pollitt

The historical background to the adoption of high carbon taxes in Sweden, as described in the chapter by Magnus Lindmark, is a fascinating one. The Swedish case is important globally for two reasons. First, Sweden is one of the few countries globally to have actually achieved a significant absolute decarbonisation of its economy. As Lindmark describes, carbon dioxide emissions fell 40 per cent from the early 1970s until the late 1980s. Second, Sweden currently has the highest effective carbon price – average price across all GHG emissions – in the world (at $80 per tonne of CO2e)[4]. Lindmark discusses the imposition of carbon taxes at around this level in 1991, significantly ahead of the EU ETS (2005) and every other country except a handful of near neighbours.

The chapter makes three points which I wish to highlight below.

First, although it is possible to characterise Sweden's history as a triumph of environmentalism, this is not a true reflection of the underlying economic drivers. Environmental arguments played a limited role in both the decarbonisation and the imposition of high carbon taxes. The reduction in CO2 emissions was a consequence of the fortunate arrival of nuclear power plants that were already under planning/construction (which explains around half of the reduction) and policies to support reduction in oil use brought about by the Oil Crises of 1973–79. The chapter makes it clear that reducing oil use itself was thought to be essential given the initial dependence of Sweden's export-oriented manufacturing sector on oil imports and the balance of payments crises following the oil price shocks. The imposition of high carbon taxes in the 1990s was the result of a major tax reform which sought to find politically acceptable and effective new sources of tax revenue, against a background of very high marginal income taxes.

What is striking is that macroeconomics played such a strong role. The desire of oil (and gas) import-dependent countries to reduce their exposure to commodity price fluctuations is a strong motivator behind nuclear policy, local biofuel policy and energy efficiency measures. The Swedish case demonstrates this very clearly. Reducing import dependence on fossil fuels allows for more effective devaluations –

[4] See Dolphin et al. (2016).

for middle-income export-oriented developing countries this might now be very important.

Second, if the end point of Sweden is extreme, so was the starting point. This is a central point in Lindmark's paper, where he emphases the long-running cycles in history (the environmental Kuznets curve of the title). Sweden was the second most oil-dependent country (after Canada) – in terms of consumption – in the OECD in 1973. While its reductions in oil dependency and carbon emissions were impressive relative to its starting point, this actually only reduced its oil dependency to just below the OECD average in 1991. All OECD countries reduced oil dependence and absolute oil dependency converged substantially. While Sweden's performance was very good, other countries had relatively better (if not absolutely better) reductions in oil dependency. Lindmark suggests 5/6 of Sweden's reduction in oil dependency is explained by its starting point.

Starting points do matter for energy policy. If we are looking for candidates for radical energy policy we should look to countries/jurisdictions with high energy consumption or energy dependence on a single fuel. California has led on energy efficiency policy in the United States because it was initially one of the highest priced energy states[5]. France has led on nuclear policy because it had one of the most oil dependent electricity systems in the early 1970s[6]. The UK has championed decarbonisation of its economy because it has seen one of the most rapid deindustrialisations of any advanced economy[7].

Third, while environmentalism alone cannot explain Sweden's adoption of high and relatively comprehensive carbon taxation in 1991, environmental economics did play a role. Pigouvian environmental taxes (first advocated in 1920 by the economist A.C. Pigou[8]) were sold as a solution to the fiscal crisis and the basis for tax reform. Lindmark's discussion makes clear that the logic of Pigouvian taxation was an idea that was picked up by the political process and that the incidence of the taxes was thought about rather carefully. Export sectors were largely exempted and the tax burden fell mainly on households. Reading his description of the imposition of Pigouvian taxes I was reminded of Keynes who wrote: 'The ideas of economists and political philosophers, both when they are right and when they are wrong are more powerful than is commonly understood. Indeed, the world is ruled by little else. Practical men, who believe themselves to be quite exempt from any intellectual influences, are usually slaves of some defunct economist'.[9]

It is somewhat reassuring that energy and environmental economists are sometimes listened to, especially when the political process is looking for 'new' ideas. As Keynes so aptly points out above, what looks like a new idea in politics is often

5 See Joskow (1997).
6 See Chick (2007).
7 See Rowthorn and Wells (1987).
8 See Pigou (1920, part II, chapter IX).
9 See Keynes (1936, p. 383).

actually an old idea in economics. Thus, energy policies worked out in academia (and extensively tried in pilot jurisdictions) are ready to be lifted into legislation when political windows of opportunity come along. Lindmark highlights the fact that not only was carbon heavily taxed, but so were emissions of nitrogen and sulphur oxides, as part of the 1991 tax reform.

However, it is important to see taxing carbon as part of the tax system if it is significant. This has important implications. Taxing carbon has provided a relatively stable source of tax revenue for the Swedish government and an alternative to higher income taxes or VAT. High carbon taxes need to work as taxes otherwise other elements of taxation will have to adjust to meet the government's requirements to raise revenue. The lack of a stable tax base for carbon and its negative distributional consequences explain the general reluctance of governments to impose high carbon taxes. A good recent example of a failed carbon tax is that of Australia, where a failure to appropriately adjust other taxes (to make a majority better off) was thought to be a significant factor in its subsequent removal.[10] By contrast, British Columbia's relatively high and stable carbon tax[11] (at $30 per tonne) is probably helped by the fact that the tax base has not changed that much.

12.9.1 *References*

Ares, E. and Delebarre, J. (2016), 'The Carbon Price Floor', House of Commons Library Briefing Paper, No. CBP05927, 23 November 2016.

Chick, M. (2007), *Electricity and Energy Policy in Britain, France and the United States since 1945*, Cheltenham, UK: Edward Elgar.

Dolphin, G., Pollitt, M. and Newbery, D. (2016), 'The Political Economy of Carbon Pricing: A Panel Analysis', EPRG Working Paper No. 1627.

Elgie, S. and McClay, J. (2013), 'Policy Commentary/Commentaire BC's Carbon Tax Shift Is Working Well after Four Years (Attention Ottawa)', *Canadian Public Policy* 39 (Supplement 2): S1–S10.

Joskow, P. L. (1997), 'Restructuring, Competition and Regulatory Reform in the U.S. Electricity Sector', *Journal of Economic Perspectives*, 11(3): 119–138.

Keynes, J. M. (1936), *The General Theory of Employment, Interest and Money*, London: Macmillan.

Pigou, A. C. (1920), *The Economics of Welfare*, London: Macmillan.

Robson, A. (2014), 'Australia's Carbon Tax: An Economic Evaluation', *Economic Affairs*, 34: 35–45.

Rowthorn, R. E. and Wells, J. R. (1987). *De-Industrialization and Foreign Trade*, Cambridge: Cambridge University Press.

10 See Robson (2014).

11 See Elgie and McClay (2013).

13

Fossil Fuel Systems to 100 Per Cent Renewable Energy-Based Smart Energy Systems: Lessons from the Case of Denmark, 1973–2017

Frede Hvelplund, Søren Djørup and Karl Sperling

13.1 INTRODUCTION

Since the 1973 oil crisis, the Danish energy system has undergone a range of changes. In the beginning of the 1970s and 1980s, the main goal was to become independent of oil by replacing it with coal and natural gas. At the same time, policies for development and implementation of renewable energy, energy conservation and more district heating were emerging.

The initial years of development and implementation of renewable energy were characterised by a conflict-laden process between the proponents of renewable energy, green energy grassroots organisations, and the opponents, power companies, the Ministry of Finance and the Association of Danish Industries. This development happened in a system in which the Danish power production and distribution system and all district heating systems were owned by either municipalities in the large cities or consumers in the small cities and countryside areas. In 2004, the power plants were 'privatised' and sold mainly to the Swedish and Danish state-owned energy companies, Vattenfall and DONG, respectively.

The result of Danish energy policy in the period 1975–2017 has been that in 2017 Denmark has: 43 per cent electricity consumption from wind power; 30 per cent of total energy consumption from renewable energy; 60 per cent of heat market from district heating; 35.8 per cent reduction in CO_2 emissions since 1990; and an export of green energy equipment and energy services of around 50 billion DKK[1][2]. These results showed renewable energy to be a serious opportunity and contributed to a normative breakthrough, as demonstrated by a majority in the Danish parliament declaring their support for a 100 per cent renewable energy supply target by 2050.

In 2018, Danish energy policy is in a process of a turnaround, where the deeper effects of the paradigmatic change from fossil fuels available on demand to fluctuating renewable energy technologies are becoming increasingly evident.

In the first phase of the transition to renewable energy and energy conservation, the focus was on the development and implementation of technical and economically efficient renewable energy technologies, such as wind turbines, photovoltaic units, solar heating, and geothermal energy. This first phase was characterised by renewable energy as a supplement to a fossil fuel system that, from a governance point of view, was a 'sector-based system'.

By 2018, several technologies have passed this first phase and are technically efficient and economically feasible technologies. At the same time, we are entering a second phase, where fossil fuels are gradually going from being the main energy source to becoming a supplement to renewable energy, and where a sector-based energy system is in transition to an integrated smart energy system [3][4].

This turnaround encompasses fundamental *technical, political and economic* changes:

It is *technically fundamental*, because a growing share of fluctuating renewable energy technologies increases the fluctuation challenge[5]. We cannot any longer just build more and bigger wind turbines and cheaper photovoltaic plants. We have to establish systems that can deal with periods with insufficient wind and sun, as well as periods with too much production from these sources. In 2017, wind power in Denmark produced 43 per cent of electricity consumption. This has resulted in systematic reductions in wind power kWh prices, hampering the economics of existing wind parks and threatening future plans for wind power expansion, thereby impeding one of the basic pillars of a 100 per cent renewable energy target for 2050. In this transition the role of district heating is changing from a fossil fuel-based system to a system based on renewable energy, heat pumps and heat storage, where district heating is changing from playing mainly a heat-sector role to having an important role in smart energy systems[3][6][7].

The turnaround is *politically* and *economically* fundamental, because we have to deal with the rising tension between, on the one hand, local and regional ownership and, on the other, distant and large power company ownership[8]. This tension is increasingly intense, as local and regional ownership, to a large extent, is needed in order to get acceptance for participation in the development of new renewable energy power plants (wind turbines, photovoltaic, etc.) and to develop and coordinate the integration infrastructure[9][10] (heat pumps, heat storage, biogas/gasification plants, electrolyzers, EVs, etc.). And different institutional conditions hamper the implementation of local smart energy systems[11].

On the one hand, renewable energy is the only 'horse left' for the survival of the large power companies in a 100 per cent renewable energy scenario. This brings the models of local and regional ownership versus distant energy corporation ownership into conflict. A predominantly distant and large energy company ownership scenario may result in a lack of acceptance of, and participation in, the innovative process of developing new renewable energy plants and smart energy systems. On the other hand, a larger local and regional ownership share will reduce the profit base of the major energy companies. This rather locked-in clash of opposing interests creates a battlefield that might threaten the renewable energy transition and also hamper an efficient climate policy.

Concretely, the 'battle' also concerns which technical and governance system should be established in order to deal with the fluctuating character of the main technologies in the transition to renewable energy.

There are different solutions to this challenge. The two archetypal solution scenarios can be described as either the local and regional integrative *smart energy system scenario* or the export/import *transmission line scenario*.

Meanwhile it should be noted that an increase in the transmission capacities can only supply a limited part of the needed integration of the fluctuating renewable energy sources[12]. Metaphorically, we are comparing a transmission line alternative, which is convenient but a blind alley, with a smart energy system, which is inconvenient, but more akin to a gravel road that can lead to long-term sustainable solutions.

We therefore are dealing with two scenarios where there are no clear alternatives. In the smart energy system scenario there will still be a need for transmission lines, but requiring only a very limited expansion of the existing transmission system. And the transmission line scenario can only cope technically and economically with a fraction of the renewable energy fluctuations without considerable back-up capacity[12].

In reality, the question is to find the right balance between investing in an integrative smart energy system versus investing in further transmission line capacities. And the problem at present is that there are strong transmission system operators (TSOs) that have the political influence and economic capacity to invest large amounts in the transmission line scenario[13], whereas potential investors in the integrative smart energy system scenarios are relatively weak.

The *smart energy system* solution copes with the present fluctuating challenge by means of local and regional integration between the power sector, the heat sector, the transportation sector, wind to gas systems, etc. So, instead of exporting surplus wind power via transmission lines to neighbouring countries, wind power is used for heat in the local and regional heat markets, and in later phases for electric cars and wind-to-gas systems. To the extent that this integration is not sufficient to cope with wind power fluctuations, importing and exporting wind power by means of transmission lines can be used as a last resort. Because many of the wind power integration solutions, such as district heating, heat pumps, heat storage and solar heating are locally and regionally owned, they tend to represent a political urge to establish locally owned integrative smart energy systems[14][15].

In Denmark, we are in the midst of a political competition between these two scenarios. The problem seems to be that expansion of *transmission capacities*, which we see as mainly a 'non-solution'[16] [17], at present has the upper hand, whereas the *Smart Energy Solution*[18], which requires a set of investments that should be coordinated both with regard to the investment dimension and sustainable operation and management, is hampered by a set of unfavourable institutional conditions[19].

Based on our analysis, the least sustainable scenario is set to be a winner, and the most sustainable is set to be the loser. This is the problem we analyse in this chapter. We also develop *policy ideas* that may open doors for the smart energy system scenario.

13.2 THE SOCIAL ANTHROPOLOGICAL GOING CLOSE APPROACH

It is our understanding that the consequences of the two competing scenarios cannot be analysed within one single subject area such as an econometric or a technical analysis. Such analyses are often based on the extrapolation of historical institutional and technical conditions and are thus analytically black boxing concrete details of potentials for change within existing institutional and technical conditions. In the present energy transition this is a very problematic approach because in a fundamental transition process, it is precisely these technical and institutional conditions that need to be changed. Therefore they should be studied and dealt with at the adequate[1] level of aggregation as determinants of possibilities in a political process.

Therefore, in order to open the black box of extrapolations we use here, and historically have been using in almost all our analysis[20][21][22][23], what could be called a social anthropological method of GOING CLOSE to the *situation of the actors and the ecological, technological and institutional contexts we see as relevant for the area being studied.* This approach encompasses *both a precise and adequate description of the technical and institutional area and its unsolved problems by putting oneself as an observer in the context of the decision-making actors involved.* In this case, the main contexts involve the policy and consumer communities. The authors either have drawn from their direct experiences and ethnographic observations or have referred to observations of those in these contexts that are publicly available. Such a holistic analytical process is well suited to produce policy recommendations.

In the following sections we will:

1. Analyse what we can learn from the historical developments on the energy scene since 1973.
2. Describe the competing alternative technical scenarios with their concrete technologies, and their localisation processes in relation to relevant actors, by GOING CLOSE to the technologies at the 'potential actor' level.

[1] We define the adequate level of aggregation as the level of analysis that makes policy actions in accordance with policy goals visible and possible.

3. Describe ownership models and the value-added distribution of the smart energy system scenario and the transmission line scenario. Where and to whom does money flow in the two scenarios? What are the consequences for transaction costs and ownership models?
4. Describe the incentive structure at the level of the actors.

13.3 WHAT CAN WE LEARN FROM THE 1975–2017 HISTORY OF THE DANISH ENERGY SECTOR?

In general, the 1975–2017 transition period has been a success story including: more than 60 per cent district heating, 53 per cent of power production based on renewable energy, 30 per cent reduction in CO_2 emissions compared to 1990 and the creation of a new renewable energy export sector with a turnover of around 50 billion Danish crowns, or around 10 per cent of Danish exports[24].

13.3.1 *From 1975 to 2001*

At the *normative* level, there was a discussion in Denmark regarding whether renewable energy supply was a realistic future strategy, and at the beginning of this period power companies, the parliament and large industrial organisations were against renewable energy and for coal and nuclear energy. The green energy NGOs from the beginning of around 1975 supported the development of renewable energy technologies. At the end of the period there was massive support from a majority of stakeholders for renewable energy becoming an important *supplement* in the energy supply.

At the *cognitive* level, around 1993 it became increasingly recognised that it was possible to have an energy system without both coal and nuclear energy production. But at the same time, there was little discussion about the need for the establishment of an integrated smart energy system to handle the fluctuation challenge. We will examine this point in the next section.

At the *regulatory* level, concrete rules for the sale of electricity from wind turbines based on a fixed price were already established in the late 1970s. These were accompanied by rules supporting local ownership of wind turbines. This resulted in a broad common ownership structure with around 130,000 owners of small 2kW wind turbine shares by around 1990.

In the 1990s, new rules for small co-generation plants and decentralised power production were established. Around 400 small flexible co-generation plants were built. They presented a potential infrastructure for future fluctuating renewable energy due to their flexibility, although such result was unintended.

13.3.2 *From 2001 to 2017*

In 2001, a right-wing government came to power, and the majority in parliament shifted from a green to a black majority that did not support renewable energy at all. Financial support for green NGOs was removed, the renewable energy section in the ministry of energy was drastically reduced and the feed in/fixed price support level for wind power was reduced. As a result of this, almost no new wind power capacity was built from 2003 to 2008, and CO_2 emissions increased during this period.

However, in 2007 the right-wing prime minister made a policy U-turn, and declared that Denmark should be fossil free by 2050. As a consequence, policy support for renewable energy improved in the following years.

In the end, what this period from 2001 to 2017 demonstrates is that there was some *normative* and *cognitive* support for integrated smart energy systems, but this has not, so far, resulted in any substantial *regulatory* support for these systems.

What can we learn from the period 1975–2017?

Lesson 1: An *innovative democratic* governance system[25][26] historically has been the basis of the Danish green transition. It is important to understand that at the normative, cognitive and regulatory levels there has been continuous support for renewable energy from independent green NGOs[27]. NGO pressure and dialogue in democratic forums combined with independent researchers and the ongoing publication of alternative energy plans[20][21][28][22] constitute what we here call an 'innovative democracy' [29]. The innovative element of a democratic process is a strong mobilisation of democratic forces that are independent of economic interests linked to fossil fuels. From 1985 to 2001, these forces combined with support for renewable energy from a green parliamentary majority. This support was, as mentioned, removed by the right-wing government in 2002, but then re-established by the same government in 2007. Most of the time there has been opposition from existing power companies and their trade association, Danish Energy, and the association of industries, Danish Industry. In the 1990s, this opposition was partly replaced by support for large renewable energy systems mainly owned by the members of Danish Energy.

Lesson 2: *An active population that is responsive to incentives* historically has been an important precondition for the development of Danish green transition technologies. In the 1980s, when the institutional conditions for owning a wind turbine share were in place, between 120,000 and 140,000 people bought small wind power shares over a period of ten years. At the beginning of the 1990s, the incentives for small co-generation units were put in place and within a few years, from 1990 to 1995, around 400 decentralised co-generation plants were established by consumer-owned district heating companies. This demonstrates that as soon the right incentives were in place, the Danish public reacted. They have the knowledge to react both as consumers in ownership cooperatives and as active participants in a technological innovation process, just like companies.

Lesson 3: *The parliament and legislation matter.* Parliament's role in setting policy has been essential for the success of the Danish green transition. If there is no active communication between the parliament and the public in an innovative democratic process, the necessary policies will not be developed and implemented. When a right-wing government came to power in 2001, support for renewable energy needed to be re-established, and consequently almost no new wind power capacity was built for a period of around four years.

The general lesson here is that for a country to be able to change its path, it is important that the parliament, educational institutions and other institutions be independent agents on the existing path. It is also important that the population be responsive to economic incentives, even if monetary gains are only minor, as was the case with the 120,000 to 140,000 small wind power shareholders.

In the forty-two years since 1975, a set of new renewable energy technologies has been developed to a level that is both reliable and profitable. But the aim of transitioning from 100 per cent fossil fuels to renewable energy resources presents new and fundamental difficulties. Already in 1987, smart energy systems integrating heat and power with heat pumps and heat storage systems were being discussed in Denmark[30] (KI). But today, thirty years later, despite normative and cognitive recognition of the need for integrated energy systems, regulatory reform is still lacking.

The interesting feature in the ongoing Danish debate is that actors in the political process seem to have forgotten the strong forces linked to mobilising local consumers and consumer-organised developers as demonstrated in lessons 1 to 3.

These forces are even more essential today because the transition to integrative smart energy systems relies precisely on local support for innovation from the population. This support was historically what drove the development of renewable energy. At present, there are widespread initiatives regarding the establishment of smart energy systems in several district heating companies.[2] The transition to smart energy systems is being dealt with through extensive discussions as part of the Danish energy debate. Furthermore, the Danish Ministry of Climate and Energy is aware of the need for establishing smart energy systems, where heat and electricity are integrated[31]. Consequently, the Danish Energy Agency is providing active consulting advice to district heating companies on the use of heat pumps, as well as investment subsidies of around 20 per cent for heat pumps in district heating systems. So far eight small district heating companies have received this subsidy and are establishing heat pumps for the integration of

[2] Blarke, M. (2013). Om SmartVarme, 23 December. http://www.smartvarme.dk/index.php?option=com_content&view=article&id=4219&Itemid=85.

electricity and heat[32]. Two hundred twenty district heating companies have been interviewed regarding their interest in getting advice from the Danish Energy Agency consulting team, and fifty of these have expressed interest. A much larger proportion were interested in heat pumps but were unsure about the future institutional framework[32]. At the municipal level, interest in active municipal energy planning has also increased; forty-nine out of ninety-eight Danish municipalities now employ strategic energy plans, twelve have strategic energy plans under development, thirteen have some sector energy plans and only twenty-four have no municipal energy planning[33][23].

All of this activity demonstrates that there is a persistent and growing interest in the establishment of integrated smart energy systems but the regulatory framework is not yet in place.

13.4 THE DEVELOPMENT AND IMPLEMENTATION OF INTEGRATED SMART ENERGY SYSTEMS[18]

13.4.1 *The Smart Energy System Scenario[34]*

A transition from fossil fuels to renewable energy is a paradigmatic change from *stored fossil fuels* – to *fluctuating renewable energy* technologies. In a smart energy system scenario, a first step of handling an increased share of fluctuating energy is to establish smart energy systems by integrating the sectors of power, heat and transportation, and by integrating these with geothermal energy, power to gas and biomass technologies[35][36][37].

In a transition to a 100 per cent renewable energy smart energy system, the rationale behind district heating has changed from being an infrastructure for saving fossil fuels through co-generation of heat and electricity to becoming a way of handling an increased share of fluctuating renewable energy, and to making economic use of a variety of industrial waste heat, renewable energy-based fuels and geothermal energy[3]. In this system, a large part of the fluctuation challenge can be solved by integrating electricity and heat in a district heating system with heat pumps and hot water storage systems, where, for instance, surplus wind power can be stored as hot water for district heating. This is economical as a first step of integrating fluctuating renewable energy, as hot water storage systems are one hundred times cheaper than battery storage systems[38].

The first step in the creation of a rational base for the wind power economy is to increase its market by integrating electricity and heat into an integrated smart energy system[39]. This way a wind power economy may improve to a level where it pays to build the needed wind power capacity for a 100 per cent renewable 2050 scenario[40]. This can only happen by modifying taxation policy, where taxes on wind power for heat are at the same level or lower than taxes on scarce biomass for heat[41].

13.4.2 *The Transmission System Scenario [42][43][44]*

The main proponents of the *transmission system scenario* are the TSO (Transmission System Operator) and the trade association of power sector companies (Danish Energy) and energy companies originating from the legacy fossil fuel system[42]. The main idea of this paradigm is to cope with the renewable energy fluctuation challenge by establishing more transmission line capacity for trade with neighbouring countries. For instance, the Danish transmission line company, Energinet.dk, has decided to build transmission lines from southern Denmark to Germany, the Netherlands and the UK[13][45]. This 'solution' is sector based and tries to cope with the fluctuation challenge by sending wind power to Germany, the UK and the Netherlands when we have surplus, and by importing electricity from these countries when there is insufficient power production in Denmark.

The reasons why the Danish TSO, Energinet.dk, is attracted to the transmission line paradigm is understandable, as Energinet.dk is not in a position to build smart energy systems, but bound by existing legislation to build and organise transmission lines. They are dependent on a legislative path where their task is to build transmission lines as the solution to fluctuating renewable energy[46]. This legislation perceived the grid system to be a neutral transportation system that serves free and neutral connections between buyer and seller within the electricity sector. The grid system is not viewed as a competitor with the integrated infrastructures needed to further a smart energy system. The main investment, operation and management actions of Energinet.dk are dealing with power grids, but not by supporting and building infrastructures that support 'free trade' across the borders of various sectors, as between, for instance, heat and electricity. Therefore, new legislation for Energinet.dk is needed that not only creates a network for trading electricity, but also opens the door for free trading between the heat and the electricity sectors.

With path-dependent policies that are deeply rooted in the grid system, the transmission line scenario is currently the dominant policy solution in Denmark. The Danish TSO, however, is arguing for a 'we do both' model, professing support for both the local and regional integration smart energy system model and the transmission line scenario. But in reality, we see that TSOs cannot deliver on this because the assumption behind the investments in transmission lines only includes around 5 per cent of the integrated heat market in 2020 and 15 per cent in 2035[45]. This represents only 20–30 per cent of the total power and heat integration potential.

13.5 THE OWNERSHIP DISCUSSION AND THE TRANSITION TO SMART ENERGY SYSTEMS

Who should own and organise the transition to smart energy systems? As a basis for this discussion we will look at the changes in the value-added chain in transition from fossil fuels to smart energy systems.

The fossil fuel supply chain consists of extraction, transportation and refining, where the share of the value add, or electricity prices linked to the fuel consumption is between 25 per cent and 40 per cent depending on the fuel types and prices.

In a 100 per cent renewable energy-based smart energy system, the fossil fuel share is replaced by investments in the renewable energy and integration system consisting of wind turbines, district heating systems, heat pumps, solar panels, heat storage, energy conservation, electric cars, wind-to-fuel systems, etc. The boreholes, coal fields, oil transportation ships, etc. that are owned by the large oil companies are replaced by investments in district heating, heat storage systems, integration of electricity and transportation, geothermal energy, solar heat plants, seasonal storage of heat and power-to-gas systems.

In a smart energy system the storage facility of the distant fossil fuel system is replaced by an integration infrastructure that, to a large extent, is a superstructure consisting of heat pumps, hot water storage, solar heating, etc. Smart energy systems may be built as additions to already existing district heating systems owned by either municipalities or consumers.

Thus, smart energy systems are prone to local ownership, operation and management for many of the reasons outlined below.

1. It is our understanding based on historical experiences [32][47][11] that initiatives for such coordination and integration activities are more likely to take place locally due to possibly lower transaction costs in a decentralised system than in a centralised model due to the transaction cost characteristics described below. The consumers and municipalities already own the district heating systems. This gives a very important advantage to local ownership for smart energy system integration technologies, and makes the transactions of adding heat pumps, heat storage and solar heating relatively low.
2. Almost all new investments in smart energy systems, such as district heating, heat storage, house insulation, etc., are much closer to the consumer than the oil/gas/coal supply systems. These investments are near the consumers and probably can be coordinated with the lowest transaction costs by local actors such as consumers and municipalities.
3. Operation and management of smart energy systems is between local actors and requires a high level of rather detailed local coordination. It is a valid assumption that this operation and management integration and coordination is done with the lowest transaction costs in energy systems with a large share of local ownership and active participation.
4. We are dealing with systems with a high share of natural monopolies. The governance transaction costs of price control are lower when the owners of the natural monopoly are the consumers who do not have an interest in high prices. Consequently it can be argued that consumer ownership, and in some

cases municipal ownership, is the most efficient way to manage natural monopolies.

5. New investments in smart energy systems are made close to the consumers, especially when we are dealing with onshore wind power. This results in the visibility of the energy plants, and therefore also potential local resistance against wind power owned by distant owners. Consumer ownership, therefore, may generate less resistance and lower transaction costs and even new transaction gains with active local participation in new integrated energy systems [9][11].
6. Any energy system has costs and profits. If the profit mainly goes to the consumers and local funds, then the probability of acceptance and local support is increased considerably, lowering the protest and resistance transaction costs linked to new investments.

If we compare the relationship between ownership model and transaction costs found above in points 1 through 6, local consumer/municipality ownership seems likely to have the lowest transaction costs in a transition to an integrated 100 per cent renewable energy-based smart energy system compared to a smart energy system with a more distant owner (e.g., a large power company like Vattenfall, DONG or E.ON[3]).

Historical experience from the development of wind power, district heating and co-generation illustrates that the Danish population reacts to incentives, and they want to own and build their own power and district heating systems. Until 2004, the total power system was owned by the consumers and municipalities. In the 1990s, around 400 consumer-owned co-generation systems were built within a period of five years, when the incentives were in place. From 1980 to 2000, around 130,000 Danes owned shares in small wind cooperatives[48]. In the late 1800s, cooperative dairies and cooperatives within a broad spectrum of other areas were founded[49]. More recently, innovative ecological dairy cooperatives were established in the late 1990s.

Without going into too much detail here on ownership models, it is clear that large investments in transmission lines are comparatively difficult to organise by local consumers. In a transmission line scenario, transmission lines are replacing local integration in smart energy systems, and a large share of the value added will be allocated to distant owners, like in the Danish case, the governmentally owned transmission system operator (TSO). Furthermore this centralised transmission infrastructure is furthering a more centralised model for wind power expansion with large offshore parks. This includes the prospective wind farm at Dogger Bank, where the Dutch TSO Tennet and the Danish TSO Energinet.dk are discussing the construction of an artificial island 150 km west of the southern part of the UK[51].

[3] No initiatives to establish local integrative smart energy systems have so far been taken by large power companies/distant owners.

This tentative plan, in combination with others, would create a wind power capacity of up to 70 GW with power production potential equivalent to fifty 1000 MW nuclear power plants. If this type of plan, which appeared to be a fantasy until recently, was developed and implemented, the value-add moves further away from consumers, and presumably the wind power system will, due to financial risks, tend to be owned by very distant owners such as large incumbent power companies.

But as explained in arguments 1 through 6 above, large power companies seem to have clear comparative disadvantages in an integrated smart energy system. It is reasonable to foresee that incumbents will push for the transmission line scenario combined with a very centralised wind power offshore strategy as a way of constructing a technological path, while the large power companies will have strong comparative ownership advantages. But this path has proven neither plausible nor economic from the standpoint of being a stable supplier of energy in accordance with environmental concerns in the North Sea, where large parts of the potential offshore wind power are Natura 2000 areas. This incumbent favourable scenario is a blind-alley alternative with regard to the need to integrate surplus fluctuating wind power into a 100 per cent renewable energy scenario[12].

Thus, we are left with the following main questions regarding the possible transition to a 100 per cent renewable energy-based smart energy system:

- Will the smart energy systems be able to politically and economically compete with the transmission line paradigm under the present institutional regime?
- Will the lower transaction cost linked to consumer/municipality ownership become internalised and result in consumer/municipality ownership of smart energy systems?

13.6 THE COORDINATION OF SMART ENERGY SYSTEMS VERSUS THE COORDINATION OF THE TRANSMISSION LINE PARADIGM

13.6.1 *Will Smart Energy Systems Be Able to Politically and Economically Compete with the Transmission Line Paradigm under the Present Institutional Regime?*

The goals of a smart energy system infrastructure are to:

- integrate fluctuating energy
- do it in an economically sustainable way
- supply energy when needed in the right amount and quality
- make sure there is a stable energy supply

To make this happen in a smart energy system scenario a *double-incentive system* should be established. See Figure 13.1.

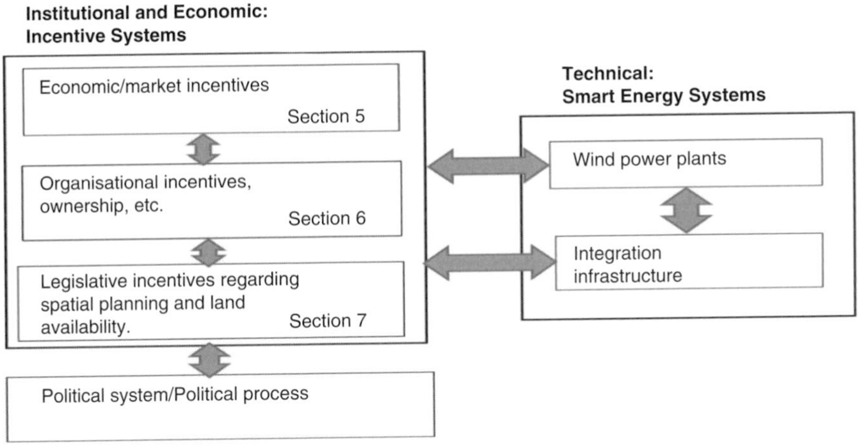

FIGURE 13.1 The need for a double-incentive system to further both wind power plants and an integration infrastructure[27].

There is a need for a double-incentive structure, visualised by the two horizontal arrows in Figure 13.1.

Conclusion: The governance system should systematically include a double-incentive system where one incentive system is directed towards individual renewable energy technologies and the other incentive system towards the establishment of an integrating infrastructure.

But so far this double-incentive structure is not being systematically implemented in the Danish system. In GOING CLOSE to the functioning of the double-incentive system, the present problems in this system can be seen as follows:

- There is a trend towards an increasing wind power capacity, due to wind power's very low marginal costs to lower the electricity price in the Nordpool market[52]. These low prices erode the economics of small backup co-generation plants.
- Wind power for heat in a system with heat pumps and heat storage is hampered by high taxes on electricity for heat, and, conversely, biomass for heat is supported by a zero-tax regime. This keeps the price of wind power low.
- The potential flexibility of infrastructure for the roughly 400 small CHP plants is threatened for two reasons. One, power prices are falling all the time, making it uneconomic to produce electricity from these units. Two, biomass for heat is becoming much cheaper due to the zero tax applied to this fuel. So CHP units turn to biomass for fuel.
- Biomass is, to an increasing degree, used for power production in Copenhagen and Aarhus. This reduces market forces for integration of wind power and heat.

These institutional conditions present serious obstacles for the establishment of smart energy systems. However, this might be in the process of changing because the government is lowering the rate of the electricity tax, improving the economics of integrating wind power into the heat market.

13.6.2 *If the Conditions for Smart Energy Systems Improve, Will These Systems Be Consumer- or Municipality-Owned?*

It should be underscored that the traditional ownership model in the Danish energy system was for power plants, transmission lines and district heating systems to be owned by consumers and municipalities rather than private companies. It therefore is a deviation from the Danish norm for wind turbines to be owned by non-local power companies replacing fossil fuel-based power plants that are traditionally owned by the municipality or consumers.

There are several concrete examples of district heating companies that tried to establish smart energy systems[32].

First, in Hvide Sande[9], a small town on the west coast of Denmark, the local consumer-owned district heating company, founded in 1964, supplies 1,500 consumers with 31,000 MWh of heat. This is done from a 6 MW co-generation plant and a 9576 m^2 solar plant. In 2016, the company decided with a clear majority of its consumers/owners to buy three nearby 3MW wind turbines to supply the district heating system. It was possible to use the electricity from the three wind turbines because they were less than 1 km away from the district heating plant and the company could build its own electricity grid connecting the wind turbines and district heating plant, and in this way avoid paying electricity tax.

Second, Dronninglund is a town with 3,500 inhabitants on the east coast of Northern Jutland[47]. There the consumer-owned district company has four employees and supplies around 30,000 MWh heat annually through a 46 km district heating network. This is done by means of 37,573 m^2 of solar heating in combination with 60.000 m^3 seasonal storage, supplying 40 per cent of the heat, with co-generating units supplying the rest. The system is going through a transition and the companies have invested in heat pumps, which use wind power. In this way they are reducing the fossil fuel share of heat production.

Third, in Aalborg[53], a city of 113,000 inhabitants, the municipality has bought the nearby coal-fired power plant from Vattenfall and intends to use the plant for fossil fuel power production within smart energy systems in combination with heat pumps, heat storage systems, etc. The strategy aims to achieve a renewable energy supply of 60 per cent of heat by 2030, and 100 per cent by 2050.

There are many more examples[32] illustrating that there are social and technological forces working towards the establishment of smart energy systems, and that a large city like Aalborg not to mention small cities like Hvide Sande and Dronninglund have employees that are able to establish innovative solutions.

The above cases show the ability of strong individuals and boards in consumer-owned district heating systems to implement their own smart energy systems despite the current relatively hostile institutional conditions. As pioneer companies they are both an important showcase for technical possibilities and play a part in the innovation process improving technical solutions. At the same time they are also front runners that put pressure on the Ministry of Energy, Supply and Climate and the parliamentary process, and thereby help improve the conditions for smart energy systems. This could be described as the 'standard' model of change:

1. Both the Dronninglund (district heating) and the Hvide Sande (initially wind power) cases have been pioneering companies for twenty to thirty years.
2. They are motivated by the same individuals and small groups that have their own visions, knowledge and stamina to pursue the goals of their district heating or wind power cooperative.
3. Due to these pioneers, technology is developed and the institutional framework improved.
4. Based on their pioneering work, the next round of investors can evolve in the next few years if their track record is successful. It should be emphasised that the process can develop very fast once it has started and surmounted the first hurdles, and that consumer-owned, consumer-profit companies can be very innovative in their search for profit through lower heat prices.

Nevertheless, the current trend leans more towards the realisation of the centralised offshore transmission line scenario combined with distant ownership of wind power plants and biomass heat. But as the above examples also indicate there is a growing countermovement that is developing and implementing smart energy solutions based on renewable energy both in small and larger cities. Moreover, these examples of decentralised and local solutions are more attuned to the social and historical conditions in Denmark. Once the first institutional hurdles are overcome, there is strong evidence that supports rapid development of smart energy systems that will not only meet the 100 per cent renewable energy targets but also provide greater benefits to local consumers.

13.7 POLICY SUGGESTIONS

We mentioned in the beginning of this chapter that it was a serious problem that the present institutional conditions were supporting transmission line solutions and hampering smart energy system solutions. We also argued that for Denmark, this is tantamount to supporting the worst solution while hampering the best solution.

The following institutional reforms would help change this in a positive direction:

- Introduction of a *subsidiarity principle*, with first priority for local and regional integration in smart energy systems, and second priority to large transmission lines. We suggest that this subsidiarity principle be implemented in coming EU directives.

- Establish a change in the role of the Danish TSO, Energinet.dk, so that it is encouraged to promote smart energy system integration and implement a Danish version of the subsidiarity principle. This means that long-distance interconnectors should only be built when local and regional integration of fluctuating renewable energy cannot cope with fluctuations.
- Equalise the level of EU subsidies received by decentralised smart energy system infrastructures up to the high subsidies currently offered to transmission interconnectors. Today, there are massive EU subsidies for transmission interconnectors but none for local and regional integration solutions for fluctuating renewable energy.
- Change the tax regime on wind for heat to the same level or lower than that on biomass for heat. Today, there is no tax on biomass for heat while there are high taxes on wind power for heat.
- Establish wind power tender procedures to make it possible for local citizens to participate where the profits are used for solving local and regional problems. Today, the tender procedures favour large corporate bidders and hamper consumer based cooperative bidders.
- Establish legislation whereby any wind power project is compelled to sell *at least 50 per cent* of the project to a local foundation for the purpose of using its profits for the common concerns in the local area.
- Create user-based transmission tariffs. Payment for the use of transmission lines should be changed from the present principle, where users only pay for transmission in situations of bottleneck limitations. Power transmission tariffs should be dependent on the degree to which a consumer uses the transmission system.

13.8 CONCLUSIONS

In this chapter we have used a social anthropological approach of GOING CLOSE to the area analysed or we have used references that are grounded in concrete local analysis. We and most of our references draw from interdisciplinary perspectives between technical and social sciences, and we have tried to discuss the transaction questions linked to an energy transition that incorporates a smart energy system model.

The economic and technical steps towards a 100 per cent renewable energy-based smart energy system have been theoretically well documented for many years and also practiced in several district heating companies, but systems with large heat pumps and heat storage systems based on wind power have not yet entered into full-scale implementation. This is unfortunate because this model has the potential to be the first step towards the establishment of a new economic rationale for district heating that can make geothermal heat and wind fuels possible in the future. The smart energy system model also gives more value and a higher price to wind power, which will help to solve the current and pressing problem of constantly decreasing wind power prices on the Nordpool market. The model seems to be able to solve many of the problems involved in a transition to a 100 per cent renewable energy scenario, and in that way also contributes to the needed reduction in CO_2 emissions. *But its realisation requires systematic institutional changes both at the EU level and at the Danish energy policy level.*

[1] Energistyrelsen. Energistatistik 2015. 2016.

[2] Fogh Hansen, K, Weise, K, Therkelsen, J, Fuglsang N. Grøn Industri bag næste generation af velstandsdanmark. CEVEA; 2017.

[3] Lund H, Werner S, Wiltshire R, Svendsen S, Thorsen JE, Hvelplund F et al. 4th Generation District Heating (4GDH). Integrating smart thermal grids into future sustainable energy systems. Energy 2014;68:1–11.

[4] Lund H. Renewable Energy Systems: A Smart Energy Systems Approach to the Choice and Modeling of 100 Renewable Solutions: Second Edition. Elsevier Inc.; 2014.

[5] Hvelplund F. Wind Power at a turning point: Key political challenges in Denmark and worldwide. WWEA Q Bull 2012;4:16–20.

[6] Thellufsen J, Lund H. Roles of local and national energy systems in the integration of renewable energy. Appl Energy 2016;183:419–29. doi:10.1016/j.apenergy.2016.09.005.

[7] Lund H, Østergaard PA, Connolly D, Ridjan I, Mathiesen BV, Hvelplund F et al. Energy Storage and Smart Energy Systems. Appl Energy 2016;(Pending).

[8] Brejnholt K. Vindmøller som løftestang for lokal udvikling i udkantsområder. Rambøll/Nordic Folkecenter; 2013.

[9] Dansk Fjernvarme. Nærdemokrati Hvide Sande køber vindmøller 2013.

[10] Jensen LK, Sperling K. Who should own the nearshore wind turbines?: A case study of the Wind & Welfare project. Aalborg: Department of development and planning, Aalborg University; 2016.

[11] Davidsen H. Udfordinger i praksis. Problemer/udfordinger med at bruge egen el fra en vindmølle, Hvide Sande Fjernvarme; 2017, p. 28.

[12] Becker S, Rodriguez RA, Andresen GB, Schramm S, Greiner M. Transmission grid extensions during the build-up of a fully renewable pan-European electricity supply. Energy 2014;64:404–18. doi:10.1016/j.energy.2013.10.010.

[13] Energinet.dk. Energinet.dk offentliggør Netudviklingsplan 2013. https://energinet.dk/Om-nyheder/Nyheder/2017/04/25/Energinet-dk-offentlig gor-Netudviklingsplan-2013 (accessed 7 April 2017).

[14] Mathiesen BV, Lund H, Connolly D, Wenzel H, Ostergaard PA, Möller B et al. Smart Energy Systems for coherent 100% renewable energy and transport solutions. Appl Energy 2015;145:139–54. doi:10.1016/j.apenergy.2015.01.075.

[15] Connolly D, Lund H, Mathiesen BV. Smart Energy Europe: The technical and economic impact of one potential 100% renewable energy scenario for the European Union. Renew Sustain Energy Rev 2016;60:1634–53. doi:10.1016/j.rser.2016.02.025.

[16] Lund H, Mathiesen, BV, Hvelplund, F, Djørup, S, Madsen H. Professorer advarer mod Viking link. Fremlæg de hemmelige beregninger og få alternativerne belyst. Altinget 2017:2.

[17] Wittrup S. Varmepumper er en langt bedre forretning end milliard kabel til England. Ingeniøren 2016:2.

[18] Lund H, Hvelplund F, Østergaard P, Möller B, Mathiesen BV, Connolly D et al. Renewable Energy Systems. Elsevier; 2014. doi:10.1016/B978-0-12-410423-5.00006-7.

[19] Hvelplund F, Djørup S. Multilevel Policies for Radical Transition: Governance in a 100% Renewable Energy System. Environment and Planning C: Government and Policy 2017.

[20] Blegaa S et al. 1976. Skitse til alternativ energiplan for Danmark. OOA and OVE; 1976.

[21] Hvelplund F, Illum K, Jensen J, Meyer Niels, Sørensen B. Energi for fremtiden. Borgen; 1983.

[22] Hvelplund F, Lund H, Serup K, Mæng H. Demokrati og forandring. Aalborg Universitets Forlag; 1995.

[23] Sperling K, Hvelplund F, Mathiesen BV. Centralisation and decentralisation in strategic municipal energy planning in Denmark. Energy Policy 2011;39: 1338–51. doi:10.1016/j.enpol.2010.12.006.

[24] Danish Energy Agency. Master Data Register of Wind Turbines May 19 2016 | Danish Energy Agency n.d.

[25] Hvelplund F. Electricity reforms,Democracy and Technological Change. Department of Development and Planning,Aalborg University; 2001.

[26] Hvelplund F. Innovative Democracy, Political Economy, and the Transition to Renewable Energy. A full-Scale Experiment in Denmark 1976–2013. Environ Res Eng Manag 2014;66:5–21. doi:10.5755/j01.erem.66.4.6158.

[27] Hvelplund F, Sperling K. From Stored fossil fuels to fluctuating Renewable Energy, Clayes and Casteels Publishing; 2017.

[28] Mathiesen B. IDAs energivision 2050: et intelligent 100% vedvarende energisystem for Danmark: sammenfatning 2015.

[29] Hvelplund F. Innovative Democracy, Political Economy, and the transitioin to Renewable Energy: a full scale experiment in Denmark 1976–2013. Aplink Tyrim Ir Vadyb 2013;66:5–20.

[30] Illum K. Lokale Kraftvarmesystemer med vedvarende energi. 1987.

[31] Energistyrelsen. Store varmepumper i fjernvarmeforsyningen. Energistyrelsen; 2016.

[32] Energistyrelsen. Varmepumpe rejseholdets indsats i 2016-aktiviteter. 2016.

[33] Petersen J.-P. The application of municipal renewable energy policies at community level in Denmark: A taxonomy of implementation challenges. Sustain Cities Soc 2018;38:2005–218.

[34] Lund H, Mathiesen BV, Connolly D, Østergaard PA. Renewable Energy Systems – A Smart Energy Systems Approach to the Choice and Modelling of 100 % Renewable Solutions. Chem Eng Trans 2014;39:1–6. doi:10.3303/CET1439001.

[35] Lund H, Kempton W. Integration of renewable energy into the transport and electricity sectors through V2G. Energy Policy 2008;36:3578–87. doi:10.1016/j.enpol.2008.06.007.

[36] Mathiesen BV, Lund H, Connolly D, Wenzel H, Østergaard PA, Möller B et al. Smart Energy Systems for coherent 100% renewable energy and transport solutions. Appl Energy 2015;145:139–54. doi:10.1016/j.apenergy.2015.01.075.

[37] Ridjan I, Mathiesen B, Connolly D. Terminology used for Renewable liquid and gaseous fuels based on the conversion of electricity: a review. J Clean Prod 2016:3709–20.

[38] Lund H, Østergaard PA, Connolly D, Ridjan I, Mathiesen BV, Hvelplund F et al. Energy Storage and Smart Energy Systems. Int J Sustain Energy Plan Manag 2016;11:3–14. doi:10.5278/ijsepm.2016.11.2.

[39] Maxwell V, Sperling K, Hvelplund F. Electricity cost effects of expanding wind power and integrating energy sectors. Int J Sustain Energy Plan Manag 2015;6:31–48. doi:10.5278/ijsepm.2015.6.4.

[40] Hvelplund F, Möller B, Sperling K. Local ownership, smart energy systems and better wind power economy. Energy Strateg Rev 2013;1:164–70. doi:10.1016/j.esr.2013.02.001.

[41] Hvelplund F, Djørup S. Multilevel policies for radical transition: Governance for a 100% renewable energy system. Environ Plan C Polit Sp 2017;35. doi:10.1177/2399654417710024.

[42] Energinet.dk. Strategi 2018–2020. Energi over grænser. 2017.

[43] EnerginetDk. Electricity interconnections 2014.

[44] Energinet.dk. Analyseforudsætninger 2014–2035. 2016.

[45] Energinet.dk. Energinets analyseforudsætninger 2016. 2016.

[46] Energi-FK. Bekendtgørelse af lov om Energinet. Denmark: 2018.

[47] Fjernvarme D. http://www.dronninglundfjernvarme.dk/; 2017.

[48] NIssen, Povl-Otto; Quistgaard, Therese, Thorndahl, Jytte;Christensen, Benny MBT, Hvidtfelt Nielsen K. Wind Power -The Danish way. The Poul La Cour Foundation, Askov; 2009.

[49] Manniche P. Denmark-A Social Laboratory. 1 first. London: Pergamon Press; 1969.

[50] Eikeland PO, Inderberg THJ. Energy system transformation and long-term interest constellations in Denmark: can agency beat structure? Energy Res Soc Sci 2016;11:164–73. doi:10.1016/J.ERSS.2015.09.008.
[51] Energinet.dk. Kæmpe kunstig ø midt i Nordsøen: Tre lande undersøger om fremtidens havmøller kan kobles på sandø på Dogger Banke 2017.
[52] Hvelplund F, Möller B, Sperling K. Local ownership, smart energy systems and better wind power economy. Energy Strateg Rev 2013;1:164–70. doi:10.1016/j.esr.2013.02.001.
[53] Odgaard L. Strategi for fossilfri varmeproduktion. 2017.

13.9 COMMENTS ON DANISH HEATING POLICIES SINCE 1950: A SOCIAL SCIENCE PERSPECTIVE ON DANISH HEAT SYSTEMS

By Paul Warde

The social anthropological tradition in which this chapter places itself insists on the importance of GOING CLOSE, as the authors put it. There are many potential benefits to this. The behaviour of actors can be observed and understood in a rounded and non-reductionist way. The observer may notice that factors ostensibly unrelated to the matter of study (a topic like 'energy policy') may in fact be rather important for the behaviour and motivations that people exhibit. One may discover differences rooted in institutions or traditions set up for other purposes, such as those of municipal ownership or the relatively small communities examined in this chapter, or note the importance of gender, religion or other categories for shaping action. Engaging with actors over prolonged periods of time can bring insight that is not gained through methods such as a snapshot survey or interpreting data such as responsiveness to price changes that infer actors' priorities from models (such as rational choice theory) that are applied to such data. GOING CLOSE equally gives opportunities to appreciate the role that particular institutional cultures, training or background may play in the shaping of action and path dependencies. As a historian, I see many of the preoccupations of the anthropological or ethnographic approaches being close to my own. However, aside from the opportunities offered by oral history – usually a retrospective exercise based on interviews shaped with hindsight – other disciplines just do not have the kind of access to everyday behaviour that we might like.

There are however risks. One cannot follow people all of the time. People may not be good assessors or even conscious of their own motivations, and some patterns of behaviour may well be phenomena best observed on a more aggregate and statistical scale. Equally, the limited capacity of any one anthropologist, and the number of anthropologists in the world, means that it is difficult to scale up analyses and conclusions. As with so much else, the initial choice of the level of analysis may well determine what you find.

There are further risks that have long preoccupied anthropologists more widely, although not discussed in the chapter. How can the information gathered be presented in a plausible and reliable way – and in a way that does justice to the subjects of analysis? How close is UP CLOSE? These are difficult questions to answer, and not always clear in the presentation of results. Clifford Geertz's famous injunction to practice 'thick description' remains, in itself, a matter of subjective judgement, especially when one works across disciplines.[4] The danger in setting up the observer/author as the sole authority in conveying information is that much then rests directly on their personal authority, rather than on the demonstration of how proficiently they handled the evidence. Many of these anxieties have been discussed by anthropologists in the context of writing justly about post-colonial or indigenous societies, where the gap between the analyst and the analysed can be rather wider than in the study of Danish heating systems by a native. But analytically, the issue is the same. How do you present evidence in a way to make it believable to others? And why should they believe you?

These questions are germane here because the chapter presents us with many normative judgements. Offshore wind arrays are a 'fantasy'. Decentralised smart systems are better than centralised systems relying on international interconnection. Municipal ownership is better and will lead to better decision-making outcomes, and coordination is easier at a local level. All these might be true: they are expressly indicated to be 'assumptions'. But they might also be untrue. One thing I observe as a historian is that such disputes have existed throughout the history of energy use, and indeed in many cases the data, which tends to be about periods extending out into the future, is very hard to verify. This has meant that policy success is often not so much based on the quality of information as the strength of political networking and institutional power that can be deployed in support of a particular position ('energy policy is made in the minds of men', to paraphrase a famous statement about oil). This Danish case seems to bear that out, offering one form of path dependency (traditions of municipal ownership and localised activism) against another (fossil fuel regimes). It does not tell us much about which is 'better', however, unless you already have opinions about such things.

However, it is not *necessarily* the case that the collection of actors involved in key decision making in centralised systems is much different than those in decentralised ones. Clearly, the latter have more sets of actors, and the potential influence of the former is greater. But they can be studied in identical ways. Liking the local and getting CLOSE UP might incline us to examine how energy policy can be forged at a municipal level. But even without large-scale, centralised actors, policy can be

4 Clifford Geertz, 'Thick Description: Toward an Interpretive Theory of Culture'. In *The Interpretation of Cultures: Selected Essays*. New York: Basic Books, 1973, 3–30.

forged by relatively small numbers of people interacting in a particular milieu. There is nothing to prevent ethnographic examination of these groups too – we might find that their motivations and drivers are more similar to those who work locally. An exemplar of such work is Gabrielle Hecht's study of the French nuclear industry.[5]

The chapter also raises questions for me of the links between advocacy and analysis. The authors clearly advocate a particular position. They identify a problem with the cleaving of many interests to the fossil fuel industry, which cannot or will not take the imaginative leap to develop a different energy system. This is probably true, but it is not evidence that other suggestions are therefore necessarily better (or on what criteria being better is judged). Green energy NGOs doubtless suffer from their own biases and blind spots and certainly have their own interests (as do academics who have invested much of their careers in advocating particular positions, and for whom changing direction in that sunk intellectual capital is as difficult as for any politician). And what is 'rational' or should be included in 'transactions costs' will depend very much on perspective. Some might consider democratic participation virtuous and an end in itself. But others might simply perceive it as a cost. Methods and analysis can, in the end, enlighten us as to reasons for such views and their consequences, but they do not provide a means to adjudicate between them. What anthropology can do, UP CLOSE, is make more vivid and comprehensible how means of *persuasion* or criteria for *consensus building* emerge, and their consequences. That is a contribution no serious engagement with policy can ignore.

[5] Gabrielle Hecht, *The Radiance of France. Nuclear Power and National Identity after World War II*, Cambridge, MA: MIT Press, 2009.

14

The Politics of Carbon Capture and Storage: How Interests Have Outstripped Economics in Shaping the Evolution of a Technology

David M. Reiner

14.1 INTRODUCTION

What role do interests play in shaping the efforts to introduce new energy technologies to address climate change? Most energy technology studies focus on the potential for improvements in terms of technological characteristics and cost. For example, learning-curve studies describe how costs respond to expanding deployment.[1] 'Technology roadmaps' portray paths forward, almost entirely from a technological perspective.[2] Nevertheless, it is often impossible to explain how or why a technology is adopted without understanding the broader social and political forces shaping support for CCS (both in the sense of public and stakeholder attitudes and in the sense of the financial incentives).

Burning fossil fuels such as coal, oil and natural gas normally releases significant volumes of carbon dioxide, which is, by far, the single largest contributor to climate change, accounting for almost two-thirds of emissions.[3] The traditional view of mitigating CO_2 emissions from the energy sector involves a combination of energy conservation, energy efficiency and substituting fossil fuels (in power generation, transport, heating, cooling and industrial processes) with non-fossil fuel technologies. In the power sector, widely seen as one of the easiest to decarbonise, that means greater reliance on renewable energy sources (wind, solar, hydro, biomass, tidal, etc.) or nuclear power.

Non-fossil sources have historically been very costly relative to fossil fuels and many of the most viable options such as wind and solar power are intermittent sources of energy, which means that they cannot be used to reliably provide base-load power or flexibly respond to changing demand on, say, a cold, windless night in January. For

1 Jamasb, T. (2007). Technical change theory and learning curves: patterns of progress in electricity generation technologies. *The Energy Journal* 28(3), 51–71.

2 International Energy Agency (IEA) (2013). *Technology Roadmap: Carbon capture and storage*. Paris: OECD. www.iea.org/publications/freepublications/publication/TechnologyRoadmapCarbonCaptureandStorage.pdf

3 US Environmental Protection Agency (2017). Global Greenhouse Gas Emissions Data. https://www.epa.gov/ghgemissions/global-greenhouse-gas-emissions-data

variable renewable energy (VRE) sources, the options have been seen as either (a) coupling with energy storage, which has, to date, been limited by cost, or (b) limiting the scale of VRE deployment to some percentage of the overall system that would not be overly disruptive (such as perhaps 30 per cent of overall generation).[4] Nuclear power, the other major low-carbon option, although available for over a half-century, has a long and somewhat tainted history involving major accidents (Sellafield, Three Mile Island, Chernobyl and most recently Fukushima); concerns over proliferation of nuclear weapons, which start under the guise of nuclear power ambitions (Israel, India, Pakistan and lately, Iran and North Korea);[5] long construction delays (Finland and USA);[6] cost overruns and public opposition (California and Germany).[7]

Faced with this set of less than salubrious options, there has been an understandable appeal of maintaining a role for fossil fuels in the economy, while simultaneously addressing the growing imperative of global climate change. Carbon capture and storage (CCS) technologies – capturing carbon dioxide (CO_2) from fossil fuels (before or after combustion), usually at a large centralised-point source such as a power plant and then transporting it to long-term storage underground – seemed to offer the potential to address many of the concerns created by other low-carbon options.

The different components (capture, transport and storage) are all established techniques in themselves and have been used in industry for decades. Capturing CO_2 from combustion processes has been carried out as a way of producing CO_2 for use in different industrial processes such as those in the food industry, welding and steel manufacture, greenhouses and fire suppression.[8] Independently, CO_2 has been injected into geological formations since the early 1970s, primarily for enhanced oil recovery (EOR) in West Texas, although little effort was made to monitor the fate of the millions of tons injected. Moreover, existing EOR has not reduced emissions since rather than capturing anthropogenic CO_2, natural sources of CO_2 such as McElmo Dome in Colorado were tapped and pipelines built to transport CO_2 over hundreds of kilometres. With more of an eye to intentionally storing CO_2, Statoil has been injecting one million tons per year of CO_2 into the Sleipner field in the North Sea for over twenty years and there are many other smaller (10kt-100kt CO_2) storage projects, primarily in the United States.[9]

4 Lund, P. D., Lindgren, J., Mikkola, J., & Salpakari, J. (2015). Review of energy system flexibility measures to enable high levels of variable renewable electricity. *Renewable and Sustainable Energy Reviews*, 45, 785–807.

5 Sagan, S. D. (1997). Why do states build nuclear weapons? Three models in search of a bomb. *International Security*, 21(3), 54–86.

6 Stapczynski, S. (2017). Next-Generation Nuclear Reactors Stalled by Costly Delays, Bloomberg, 2 February.

7 Sovacool, B. K. & Valentine, S. V. (2012). *The national politics of nuclear power: economics, security, and governance*. Routledge.

8 Folger, P. (2010). Carbon Capture: A Technology Assessment, Congressional Research Service, CRS Report R41325, 19 July.

9 International Energy Agency (IEA) (2016). *20 Years of Carbon Capture and Storage: Accelerating Future Deployment*. Paris: OECD.

The components needed for CCS may all exist, but the real questions are the extent such utilisation projects can assist in scaling up CCS[10] and, more generally, what path would facilitate a shift from small commercial projects and heavily subsidised demonstration projects to a viable large-scale industry that would have an impact on national efforts to address climate change.[11]

Section 14.2 explores how CCS has been perceived as a crucial if not indispensable element in any portfolio of mitigation options to achieve deep reductions in emissions moving towards net-zero emissions. We then trace a short history of CCS policy as the issue moves from largely unknown pre-2005 to virtual panacea (2005–2009), followed by a period of disappointment and a persistent difficulty in getting projects funded and launched. Rather than focusing exclusively on costs and technology, stakeholder interests are discussed in more depth to understand why support has been so tepid. Finally, in conclusion, the reasons why the politics of CCS have been so difficult are summarised.

14.2 A PRE-HISTORY OF CCS: THE ANALYSTS' (AND STAKEHOLDER?) FAVOURITE

Although hindsight is often 20:20, viewed from the perspective of an observer in, say, 2005, there were many reasons to expect that the technologies (since CCS is a suite of technologies rather than a single alternative) would be successful. CCS is the rare option that could address many important policy goals simultaneously. Indeed there are some half-dozen reasons that could be enumerated as to why CCS might be expected to be attractive. As a flexible, dispatchable end-of-pipe technology applicable to coal, gas or biomass, CCS could:

(i) address concerns over security of supply in a low-carbon world by providing both baseload non-nuclear power and flexible low-carbon power;
(ii) enable a low-carbon transition with minimal disruption in terms of the existing power system and business models;
(iii) allow for the possibility of decarbonising both existing infrastructure and future supply growth in major developing countries such as China and India;
(iv) provide options for hard-to-abate sectors including heat and process industries such as chemicals, cement and steel;
(v) offer potential learning pathways for negative emissions technologies (NETs) with biomass energy (BECCS); and finally,

[10] Kolster, C., Masnadi, M. S., Krevor, S., Mac Dowell, N., & Brandt, A. R. (2017). CO2 enhanced oil recovery: a catalyst for gigatonne-scale carbon capture and storage deployment? *Energy & Environmental Science*, 10(12), 2594–2608.

[11] Herzog, H. J. (2011). Scaling up carbon dioxide capture and storage: From megatons to gigatons. *Energy Economics*, 33(4), 597–604.

(vi) facilitate energy security by allowing for continued consumption of fossil fuels thereby potentially offering coal-rich countries a path to continue to burn coal in a carbon-constrained world.

All six justifications would be attractive to analysts and policymakers, but the first two reasons would have particular appeal for major industrial (and regulatory) stakeholders. CCS required the least change in the model for how the power system functions at a technical level. In one hundred-plus years, electricity grids, whether reliant on hydroelectric, coal, natural gas, nuclear power or a combination for base-load power, have generally operated with a small fraction of intermittent generation. Security of supply (in the sense of reliability and avoiding blackouts) is complicated by VRE sources, which impose costs on the grid and may not be available in peak demand periods.[12] High penetration of VRE sources will stress the high-voltage grid increasing costs and reserve requirements,[13] and increasingly has led to capacity markets to help support conventional dispatchable plants.[14] This growth in VRE penetration has also posed serious problems for existing electric utility business models.[15]

Nevertheless, in the face of ever-cheaper renewables and mounting concerns over climate change, there have been some tentative efforts by traditional oil and gas firms to shift away from fossil fuels. Notable initiatives include BP seeking to move 'Beyond Petroleum' in the 1990s, when they began investing in biofuels and renewables[16] or more recent investments by RWE, Statoil and others in offshore wind.[17] Recently, Total, the large French energy company, has pledged that 20 per cent of its assets will be invested in low-carbon projects by 2035 and has already begun to make major investments in solar, wind and hydro.[18] At the extreme, the small Danish firm DONG Energy transitioned from being an oil and gas firm in the 1990s to moving completely out of fossil fuels in 2017 and renaming itself Ørsted A/S. Although these few examples have been cited at length in the media, they are the exception and the overall shift in investment away from fossil fuels by these firms is still marginal at best.

12 Brouwer, A. S., Van Den Broek, M., Seebregts, A., & Faaij, A. (2014). Impacts of large-scale Intermittent Renewable Energy Sources on electricity systems, and how these can be modelled. *Renewable and Sustainable Energy Reviews*, 33, 443–466.

13 Joskow, P. L. (2012). Creating a smarter US electricity grid. *The Journal of Economic Perspectives*, 26(1), 29–47.

14 Newbery, D. (2016). Missing money and missing markets: Reliability, capacity auctions and interconnectors. *Energy Policy*, 94, 401–410.

15 Richter, M. (2013). Business model innovation for sustainable energy: German utilities and renewable energy. *Energy Policy*, 62, 1226–1237; Anon (2013).

16 Kolk, A. & Levy, D. (2001). Winds of change: Corporate strategy, climate change and oil multinationals. *European Management Journal*, 19(5), 501–509.

17 Higgins, P. & Foley, A. (2014). The evolution of offshore wind power in the United Kingdom. *Renewable and sustainable energy reviews*, 37, 599–612.

18 Stothard, M. (2016). Total aims to be 20% low-carbon by 2035. *Financial Times*, 24 May.

The challenge for conventional energy firms seeking to move away from fossil fuels, however, is both one of business model and human resources. A switch from fossil fuels to renewables (or nuclear power) requires more capital-intensive investment and a completely different risk profile and approach to shareholders and profitability. Technologies such as wind and solar are the domain of electrical engineers and material scientists rather than the geoscientists and petroleum engineers who populate the ranks of oil and gas supermajors. A solution that allows firms to retain existing staff and business models is thus inevitably more attractive. CCS could allow the oil and gas sector to move away from an exclusive focus on extraction – if CCS were scaled up to the gigatonne-level it would require an industry roughly the same scale as current oil and gas production.[19]

From an environmentalist perspective, CCS offers the possibility of addressing hard-to-reach sectors and allowing aggressive climate targets to be met (addressed in objectives (iii)–(vi) listed at the top of this section). Many countries have adopted long-term targets to reduce emissions dramatically to keep global temperature rise below 2°C with an aim for 1.5°C as laid out in the 2015 Paris Accord. The UK Climate Change Act commits the government to reduce greenhouse gas emissions by 80 per cent below 1990 levels by 2050 and Sweden has gone even further in its recent Climate Act by setting a target of net-zero emissions by 2045. If a country were to genuinely adopt a policy of deep decarbonisation, it would need to move beyond the low-hanging fruit of simply decarbonising the power sector and deal with industrial processes such as those in the cement, steel and chemicals industries as well as heating in buildings, in which case CCS could be vital. There are many approaches to reduce emissions from the power sector but CCS is one of the few options that is seen as capable of enabling dramatic reductions in heat or process industries.[20] Moreover, to get to net-zero emissions (or to address potential overshoot), then bioenergy plus CCS (BECCS) could play an important role since sustainable biomass should have zero emissions, in which case capturing and storing CO_2 from burning biomass would result in net-negative emissions. Finally, a resurgence of coal in the early 2000s was seen as ominous and had the potential to undermine the then-recently signed Kyoto Protocol.[21]

Analysts have long championed the attractiveness of the technology. Studies by leading organisations such as the Intergovernmental Panel on Climate Change (IPCC) and the International Energy Agency (IEA) find that carbon capture and storage (CCS) is essential in keeping down the costs of deep reductions in carbon

19 Benson, S. M. & Surles, T. (2006). Carbon Dioxide Capture and Storage: An Overview with Emphasis on Capture and Storage in Deep Geological Formations, *Proceedings of the Institute of Electrical and Electronics Engineers (IEEE)* 94(10), 1795–1805.

20 Department of Business, Innovation and Skills (BIS) & Department of Energy and Climate Change (DECC) (2015). *Industrial Decarbonisation and Energy Efficiency Roadmaps to 2050*, March. www.gov.uk/government/publications/industrial-decarbonisation-and-energy-efficiency-roadmaps-to-2050.

21 Clayton, M. (2004). New coal plants bury 'Kyoto', *Christian Science Monitor*, 23 December.

dioxide emissions.[22] The last IPCC report synthesises all available economic modelling efforts and finds that if CCS were unavailable, costs would be more than double (138 per cent) under an ambitious scenario to keep atmospheric concentrations below 450 ppm. By contrast, overall costs would rise by a mere 7 per cent if nuclear power were to be omitted, by 8 per cent if solar and wind were limited in their penetration and 64 per cent with constrained bioenergy supply.[23] More strikingly, the IPCC reports that for such a scenario only five economic models can even find a feasible solution without recourse to CCS, compared to thirty-six models when CCS is included. In the industrial sector, only three models could solve (compared to twenty-two with CCS). In large part, this is because of the versatility of CCS and its potential role in addressing 'hard-to-reach' sectors such as heat- and energy-intensive industries such as steel, cement and chemicals where costs would be much higher if CCS was removed as an option. By contrast there are many options in the power sector. Similarly, UK studies by non-partisan organisations such as the Committee on Climate Change (CCC) have found CCS to be critical to efforts to meet aggressive decarbonisation targets at least in terms of cost – without CCS, the cost of meeting the UK's 2050 targets would be twice as high than if CCS was to be included.[24]

14.3 A BRIEF GOLDEN ERA OF CCS (2003–2009)

Yet despite the many signs that might augur well for CCS, it has had, at best, a chequered track record over the past decade (Reiner, 2016). In the mid-2000s, many diverse forces seemed to presage a major push to support CCS. In 2005, at the G8 summit in Gleneagles, Scotland, CCS was put on the international agenda with the International Energy Agency (IEA) tasked with conducting analysis and convening major workshops on the subject. BP advanced a first CCS project at Peterhead north of Aberdeen for which it sought UK government support on the scale of existing support for renewables and was proposing additional 'Decarbonised Fossil' (DF) plants including ones in California and the Persian Gulf (numbered DF1 through DF3). The World Economic Forum included sessions on CCS in its meetings in Davos and Moscow in 2004. Even the NGO umbrella group CAN-Europe produced a major study and a position paper on CCS that was generally positive.[25]

In 2003–2007, as oil prices rose in the wake of the Iraq War and the ensuing quagmire, there was also an upsurge of interest in coal-fired power stations. In the

22 International Energy Agency, *Carbon Capture and Storage: The solution for deep emissions reductions*, 2015.

23 Intergovernmental Panel on Climate Change (IPCC), *Fifth Assessment Report (AR5) Synthesis Report*, 2014.

24 Committee on Climate Change (CCC), *Power Sector Scenarios for the Fifth Carbon Budget*, 2015.

25 Climate Action Network Europe (2006). *Position Paper CO2 Capture and Storage*, www.caneurope.org/docman/climate-energy-targets/2692-2006-oct-can-europe-ccs-position-paper/file.

United States, there had been no significant new coal-fired plants added since 1995, largely as a result of the growth in efficient natural gas combined-cycle power plants. Yet the 2005 Annual Energy Outlook projected that from 2012, the United States would begin to ramp up new coal capacity beginning in 2012 and that by the 2020s, new coal-fired capacity would be increasing by 10 to 12 GW per year – Socolow describes the potential for 260 GW of new coal.[26]

The potential for a coal boom also loomed in Europe. Although currently justified on grounds of the nuclear phase-out and/or the rapid growth of renewables, Germany committed to a new wave of coal projects in the early 2000s long before decisions on nuclear energy and renewables were taken. Instead cross-party support for coal can be traced to defending the 20,000 lignite miners in a relatively poor region.[27] In the UK, there were credible proposals for at least a half-dozen new coal plants. Companies proposing projects included E.on, which proposed a major new coal plant at Kingsnorth of six 300 MW units, of which one would have had CCS (if funded through the government's first CCS competition). Italy, the Netherlands, Spain, Poland and others all proposed new plants. The rush towards coal led to concerns about the clear and present danger posed to the climate.[28] In response, in 2007, European heads of government set a goal of having 'up to 12' CCS projects in operation by 2015.[29] Of course, all this paled against China steadily increasing its coal-fired capacity by 50–100 GW per year over the course of the 2000s.

There was widespread agreement across government, industry and NGOs that it is important to move forward with the first CCS plant(s), that learning by doing is necessary to reduce costs and it is necessary to build large plants and oversized infrastructure to benefit from scale economies over the long term. Yet, the political economy of CCS has never been so straightforward. There was never agreement within industry or governments, for example, on whether to push aggressively for large-scale demonstration projects and associated infrastructure that would minimise costs versus a longer-term emphasis on experimentation and learning. The scale of the investment meant that realistically it was always difficult to steer between the Scylla of rapid expansion to gain from scale economies and the Charybdis of cost reduction.

26 Landler, M., 2006. Europe's Image Clashes with Reliance on Coal. *New York Times*, 20 June, p. 20.

27 Hockenos, P. (2017). Germany Is a Coal-Burning, Gas-Guzzling Climate Change Hypocrite, Foreign Policy, 13 November.

28 Hawkins, D. G., Lashof, D. A. & Williams, R. H. (2006). What to do about Coal, *Scientific American* 295(3), 68-75. Special Issue: Energy's Future: Beyond Carbon (September).

29 EU (2007). *Brussels European Council 8/9 March 2007 Presidency Conclusions*, Council of the European Union.

14.4 MOVING BEYOND RHETORICAL SUPPORT (2009–): A MORE SCEPTICAL VIEW OF INTERESTS

Earlier, we describe some of the reasons why interest groups might support the deployment of CCS, but perhaps less observed at the time were equally valid reasons why stakeholder groups might be either opposed to CSS or at least indifferent or tepid in their support. Mancur Olson long ago noted that organised vested interests will lobby effectively and diffuse actors will not.[30] Policy is not about 'general' support, but about taking action on specific policy measures. There has, however, been little consensus on: (a) the overall level of support; (b) the regulatory and licensing requirements; (c) the size of the plants; (d) the geographical scope; (e) the nature of the support mechanism; (f) how many plants should be supported; (g) what is being demonstrated (e.g., proof of concept and economies of scale/scope); and (h) the implications of CCS support for other technologies. Moreover, generalised support does not necessarily translate into advocacy or more active lobbying on behalf of a technology.

14.4.1 *Government*

A few national (or in some cases subnational) governments have embraced CCS, but that support has not been unwavering. Support has waxed and waned depending on the flavour of government or the vicissitudes of different policies. Supportive governments in Australia, Alberta, Saskatchewan and Norway have all been challenged (from both right and left) for championing CCS.

Consider the case of the UK – after the initial approach from BP in 2004, the Blair government did not want to 'pick winners', so it set up a £1 billion competition to only allow CCS project proposals from coal-fired projects that used post-combustion capture technologies, because that was seen as the most likely to be useful to the Chinese.[31] According to the National Audit Office (NAO), this first competition failed, in part because of the government imposing unnecessary constraints on top of a poorly designed procurement process.[32] The second £1 billion UK Competition advanced to the final two projects, but was cancelled in November 2015 with no obvious repercussions to the government for the cancellation. Indeed, £250 million was then earmarked for small modular nuclear reactors, which stood to benefit from Rolls Royce, a UK national champion. The governing Conservative Party has opposed onshore wind power in response to traditional Conservative voters' fear of spoiling the 'green and pleasant land', but in government they supported generous subsidies

30 Olson, M. (1965). *The Logic of Collective Action: Public Goods and the Theory of Groups.*

31 Dixon, P. & Mitchell, T. (2016). *Lesson Learned: Lessons and Evidence Derived from UK CCS Programmes, 2008–2015*, Carbon Capture and Storage Association.

32 National Audit Office (NAO) (2012). *Carbon capture and storage: lessons from the competition for the first UK demonstration*, 16 March.

for both offshore wind in the North Sea and nuclear power.[33] Although they had never opposed CCS in principle, the interests had never coalesced to make a compelling case in both political and economic terms.

In many countries, CCS has been increasingly marginalised to the corners of the policy debate. The EU went from heralding CCS as a leading technology to be supported across the EU, to a minor issue garnering interest in a small handful of countries. The Energy Union, launched in 2015, advanced 'Four Core' Priorities: (i) renewable energy technologies, including biofuels and energy storage; (ii) smart grids/appliances/cities; (iii) efficient energy systems; and (iv) more sustainable transport systems. Nuclear power (a long-standing point of division among member states) and CCS were relegated to additional research priorities meriting 'a much greater level of collaboration between the Commission and those Member States who want to use these technologies' even as CCS was acknowledged as 'critical to reaching the 2050 climate objectives in a cost-effective way'.

The European Commission, through its European Economic Programme for Recovery (EEPR) stimulus package and latterly through the New Entrants Reserve (NER300) programme, has failed to deliver a single CCS project.[34] More success has been enjoyed in North America where EOR was available as an additional revenue stream, including one-million-ton-plus projects in Saskatchewan (Boundary Dam), Alberta (Quest), Illinois (Decatur) and Texas (Petra Nova).

14.4.2 *Energy Industry*

Many firms have an interest in the long-term success of CCS and some even view climate change as an existential threat to their future since, as noted at the start, they are not well suited to shift to other low-carbon technologies. Nevertheless, there have been a number of barriers that have restrained most firms from a wholesale embrace of CCS.

Among energy firms, integrated oil and gas majors have shown the most long-standing interest. As noted above, BP led the first major effort to support CCS, but other firms took an interest, most notably Statoil (Sleipner and Snohvit storage projects in the North Sea and the Mongstad capture test facility) and Shell (Quest in Alberta and Peterhead in Scotland, which was cancelled at the last moment by the UK government in 2015), but also firms such as Chevron (primarily through its Gorgon project in Australia), Total (Lacq project in southern France), and ExxonMobil (largely focused on research and development). These firms have a depth of expertise in geoscience that places them in a strong position and many also have an interest in power generation technologies and even in CO_2 separation.

33 Carter, N. & Clements, B. (2015). From 'greenest government ever' to 'get rid of all the green crap': David Cameron, the Conservatives and the environment. *British Politics*, 10(2), 204–225.

34 Lupion, M. & H. J. Herzog (2013). NER300: Lessons learnt in attempting to secure CCS projects in Europe, *International Journal of Greenhouse Gas Control*, 19, 19–25.

For example, Shell's patented CANSOLV technology uses an aqueous amine solution to absorb CO_2 from post-combustion flue gas and is being used at several large facilities such as Boundary Dam. Without strong government support, however, firms simply cannot justify to stakeholders why they should abandon their emphasis on highly profitable exploration and production for CCS projects that are, at best, marginally profitable.

Similarly, other major players with an interest in CCS have been turbine manufacturers such as GE, Alstom, Mitsubishi Heavy Industries and Siemens, but these firms tend to be less involved in advocacy and are as happy to sell a gas turbine for a non-CCS project as for a CCS project and many have now begun to sell thousands of wind turbines, so will have no strong incentive to support CCS.

Electric utilities had taken some interest, especially before 2009, but they have been hesitant and lack the human resources to even assess opportunities – large electric utilities are unlikely to have a single geoscientist on their payroll. The greatest efforts have been by firms such as Vatenfall (in Germany); American Electric Power (AEP) and Southern Company in the United States; RWE and E.on (in the UK and Germany) and Huaneng Group (in China). The only successful large project led by an electric utility, however, has been the Boundary Dam project in Saskatchewan, which was championed by a crown corporation not subject to market forces. By 2014, Vattenfall, one of the utility leaders, had completely abandoned CCS[35] and most others had dramatically scaled back any plans.

Despite some notable but small achievements, a major shift in expectations resulted from the US 'shale gas revolution', draining much of the near-term pressure for action on CCS. Although the shale gas boom was already well underway in the early 2000s, its implications had not fully dawned on policymakers in the United States and elsewhere until later in the decade. Throughout the 2000s, estimates of overall production levels exploded and the associated price of natural gas dropped dramatically. By 2007, many companies that had bet on coal failed catastrophically – for example, Texas Utilities (TXU) was headed to bankruptcy and in the process of terminating its eleven proposed coal plants.[36] By 2010, coal was effectively dead as a source of electricity generation in the United States and Europe other than a few plants still in the pipeline in countries such as Germany.

14.4.3 NGOs

For NGOs, even the initial consensus documents were carefully balanced, with great concern expressed for the impact that CCS funding would have on other technologies. For some low-carbon technologies like solar or wind energy, non-governmental organisations (NGOs) are some of the most effective and ardent

35 Tweed, K. (2014). Vattenfall Ditches Carbon Capture and Storage Research, *IEEE Spectrum*, 9 May.

36 Ratcliffe, R. G. & Babineck, M. (2007). TXU fights for 11 new coal plants at $10 billion tab, *Houston Chronicle*, 11 February.

advocates. By contrast, other established technologies, notably nuclear power, inspire environmental groups to organise in opposition, but as an established technology, at least nuclear power already had its own network of advocates.[37]

A few NGOs have placed CCS as central to addressing climate change. The most determined advocate has been Bellona, which is a Norwegian NGO that has been a strong advocate across the European Union and has been an active player in Brussels and within the European debate.[38] In other countries, some NGOs have also taken a generally positive view of CCS including WWF at the international level; Green Alliance and E3G in the UK;[39] and Natural Resources Defense Council (NRDC), Clean Air Task Force, and Environmental Defense Fund in the United States.[40] A number of NGOs have been decidedly sceptical. In the UK, most NGOs adopted a relatively positive (or fairly neutral) stance towards CCS. For example, the Greenpeace International report, *False Hope*,[41] was supported by NGOs across Europe led by Greenpeace Germany, but not a single UK NGO signed on to the accompanying policy recommendations document.

Despite the many appealing aspects of CCS, continued reliance on fossil fuels was deeply problematic to many NGOs because: (i) fossil fuels involve not just production of CO_2 but local and regional pollutants such as sulphur dioxide (SO_2), nitrogen oxides (NOx), mercury and particulates; (ii) fossil fuel combustion creates damage during the process of extraction and transport, such as mountaintop coal mining or oil spills such as the Exxon Valdez or Deepwater Horizon; and (iii) CCS ensured the continuation of business as usual, in terms of large central generation and the existing large energy companies. Thus, the very appeal of CCS to the energy industry and pro-fossil politicians such as George W. Bush in the early 2000s undermined its credibility among NGOs despite its many positive characteristics.

14.5 CONCLUSIONS: WHY HAVE THE POLITICS OF CCS BEEN SO DIFFICULT?

There are four general themes that help explain why what had seemed to be a straightforward logic for a successful deployment of CCS has proven to be so problematic. The first is that we are not on a trajectory to 2°C and there is no pressure for politicians or other stakeholders to seek the more efficient solutions that would

37 Hickman, L. (2012). Nuclear lobbyists wined and dined senior civil servants, documents show, *The Guardian*, 28 November.

38 Meadowcroft, J. & Langhelle, O. (2009). The politics and policy of carbon capture and storage, in Meadowcroft, J. & Langhelle, O. (eds), *Caching the Carbon. The Politics and Policy of Carbon Capture and Storage*. pp. 1–21.

39 Corry, O. & Riesch, H. (2012). Beyond 'for or against'. *The social dynamics of carbon capture and storage: Understanding CCS representations, governance and innovation*, pp. 91–108.

40 Johnson, J. (2013). Striving to Capture Carbon. *Chemical & Engineering News*, 91(47), 24–25.

41 Greenpeace International (2008). *False Hope: Why carbon capture and storage won't save the climate*, www.greenpeace.org/international/Global/international/planet-2/report/2008/5/false-hope.pdf.

need to be pursued if there was a genuine imperative to address the sectors needed for deep decarbonisation. The second related problem is that there has never been a coherent logic or overarching narrative to support CCS as a solution except perhaps in a few isolated locations such as Norway, Scotland, Western Canada and Australia and, even there, progress has been patchy at best. The third challenge is that the nature of CCS requires a much larger initial investment than other low-carbon options (apart from nuclear power). Finally, the appeal of CCS in the early phase was driven in part by a panic from the looming threat of a resurgence of coal and disruption to existing business models in both oil and gas and electric utility sectors. The threat of coal in most of the West has dissipated whereas the last decade has indeed wreaked havoc with existing business models, but CCS has not done much to mitigate those impacts.

The logic for supporting CCS is to drive down overall costs, but that does not translate into specific support for the technologies. Despite the initial optimism about the alignment of factors that should have justified support for CCS, the lack of advocates has, to date at least, determined its fate. As long as climate ambition is modest and implicit or explicit carbon prices are relatively low, the logic of CCS as a 'low-cost option' for decarbonising heat- or energy-intensive industry does not kick in when there is no pressure to decarbonise those sectors and there are many alternatives to address the low-hanging fruit. Perhaps the leading political problem has been that CCS has been what Lord Oxburgh described in the House of Lords as an 'orphan' technology with 'numerous well-meaning aunts and uncles but no parents'.[42] Unlike nuclear power (or onshore wind), there are no strong opponents, but equally there are few if any advocates willing to lobby strongly since amongst the most supportive actors almost uniformly their preferred alternative is continued unabated use of fossil fuels.

Industrial Policy. Another potentially serious impediment is the disconnect that CCS generally has from any sort of industrial policy rationale. By contrast, nuclear power (France and Japan), wind (Denmark) and PV (Germany and China) can all be seen as technologies where national governments have assisted specific national champions (e.g., Areva, Vestas or Siemens) or a variety of firms (e.g., for Chinese PV). Few efforts to think seriously about CCS and industrial policy, e.g., the UK process, have been driven by the logic of cost reduction rather than industrial policy as motivation.[43] The projects that seek to link up industrial sources from clusters (e.g., Teesside in North East England and the Rotterdam Climate Initiative in the Netherlands) can more credibly make the case that they are providing an opportunity for 'green industrial clusters', which may make a more politically palatable

[42] Clark, P. & Pickard, J. (2015). Energy groups face UK bill for pollution Parliament considers proposal to impose charge for carbon capture and storage, *Financial Times*, 9 September.

[43] UK Carbon Capture and Storage Cost Reduction Task Force (2013). *The Potential for Reducing The Costs of CCS in the UK* Final Report May.

proposition. Only recently, for example, has CCS tried to engage actively with trade unions,[44] which has been a long-standing supporter of nuclear power.

'Sticker price' or 'lumpiness' has been a major disincentive for governments and investors. A 'commercial-scale' CCS project is usually cited as being of a scale 300 MW and above (equivalent to a single unit of a large coal- or gas-fired power plant) and so the cost of any CCS project almost inevitably involves one million tons of CO_2 or more. That scale is desirable in terms of its impact in making a significant dent into a region's overall emissions, but problematic because of the high initial costs, particularly when compared to other low-carbon technologies such as wind turbines and solar photovoltaic panels, which come in a scale of kilowatts to megawatts for individual units. Of course, offshore wind (and even large solar farms) now come on a much larger scale of 50 MW–5 GW, but that is only because the technologies have been able to pass through these smaller scales, which has helped investors build confidence and experience, which in turn has driven down costs.

Changing business models and structures. Over the past decade, some of the factors that worked in favour of CCS have eroded. In 2005, E.on was the most profitable company in Europe with annual profits of almost $9 billion and the next four largest and most profitable utilities (all based in Europe) had average profits of $2.5 billion.[45] By 2015, eleven of the top twenty European utilities reported a net loss (compared to five in 2014 and three in 2013), 'led' by E.on at €7bn.[46] Thus, pre-existing business models for electric utilities have been undermined and the entire industry thrown into upheaval making large investments in a new technology such as CCS especially difficult.

In an early study of analogues to CCS, one of the main lessons from the evolution of other technologies was that 'early failures are not easily overcome'.[47] Von Hirschhausen, Herold and Oei identify possible explanations for the 'lost decade' of CCS, including wrong technology choices, over-optimistic cost estimates, a premature focus on energy projects instead of industry, underestimating transport and storage issues and incumbent resistance to structural change.[48] Ultimately, in the 2000s, CCS arose as a solution to a crisis of coal (that vanished) in an industry that was undergoing dramatic transformation and support for CCS when it was not the first choice of any major stakeholder. The need to address emissions from outside the power sector has not disappeared however and as climate action becomes

44 TUC (2014), *The economic benefits of carbon capture and storage in the UK*, Carbon Capture & Storage Association (CCSA) & Trades Union Congress (TUC).

45 Forbes (2006). The World's Biggest Public Companies, Available at: www.forbes.com/lists/2006/18/Utilities_Rank_1.html

46 Prospex Research (2016). Europe's Top Twenty Power Industry Players 2016. www.prospex.co.uk/LiteratureRetrieve.aspx?ID=140423

47 Reiner, D. M. & Herzog, H. J. (2004). Developing a set of regulatory analogs for carbon sequestration. *Energy*, 29(9), 1561–1570.

48 Von Hirschhausen, C., Herold, J., & Oei, P. Y. (2012). How a 'Low Carbon' innovation can fail: tale from a 'Lost Decade' for carbon capture, transport, and sequestration (CCTS). *Economics of Energy & Environmental Policy*, 1 (2), 115–123.

evermore pressing, ultimately the problem of how to find sufficient support for CCS to emerge as a major option will need to be addressed.

14.6 RESPONSE TO 'THE POLITICS OF CARBON CAPTURE AND STORAGE: HOW INTERESTS HAVE OUTSTRIPPED ECONOMICS IN SHAPING THE EVOLUTION OF A TECHNOLOGY'

By Jim Platts

Concerning technical progress, there are always four questions that have to be answered. Three are factual 'how' questions – does the science work, does the engineering work and does the economics work? The fourth is an emotional 'if' question – does anybody want it? This chapter very nicely highlights not only the difference between these two sets of questions but the significance of the difference.

Concerning carbon capture and storage, the chapter lays out the evidence that the science certainly works and it is also possible to engineer systems that do it at reasonable scale, because examples already exist. If we were wanting to pursue the 'how' questions in earnest we would want to develop the 'does the economics work' question further and also expand it.

When what is being considered is at infrastructural scale, there is a very difficult progression from what is still 'demonstration' scale even though it is already physically big and expensive, through to the very much larger and all-pervasive scale that would be necessary to match the global scale of fossil fuel power plants generating electricity and heat around the planet. On the one hand, early 'demonstration' projects, which are essentially both technical and social-learning processes (in how to plan such a thing, in how to engineer it and in how to keep it operational over time) are very expensive because they are always one-off projects. They are disconnected from any other similar experimental projects in other places and they are not large enough as projects, nor is there enough sight of possible continuity of work on other such projects, to make investment in efficient specialised equipment and the establishment of a stable and experienced team of people viable. The issue with projects of this sort is not 'are they technically and economically efficient projects' but 'are they efficient learning processes?'. They are expensive, but their purpose is to find the way to create cost-effective ways of doing what needs to be done at large scale in the near future.

But when the subject under scrutiny is carbon capture and storage, there is a second and deeper analysis necessary. An assessment in terms of financial cost is important but it is not the actual driver that matters. The reason for wanting to create carbon capture and storage technology is because all fossil fuel-burning plants that deliver energy as heat or as power also create carbon dioxide that needs to be captured and stored if we are to have a healthy future. All the infrastructure that needs to be made and operated and maintained to do this itself requires a very significant investment of energy in its manufacture and installation and also continuously in its operation (pumps, etc.) and in its maintenance. So in its making and in its operating it itself creates a carbon dioxide 'overhead cost' that it needs to 'pay off' before it is actually able to contribute at all to a net reduction of carbon dioxide production on the planet.

It is far from clear that this is possible and we would be in a far better state if this 'energy accounting' or 'carbon dioxide accounting' was not only in public awareness but at the centre of public debate.

But this 'how' question pales into insignificance in the face of the 'if' question of 'does anybody really want it anyway?', to which the answer appears to be a definite 'no!' What is interesting – and the chapter lays it out very well – is that there appears to be almost universal agreement on 'the facts' and 'evidence-based policy' appears to be going way beyond simply saying that 'this is a good idea' and is more-or-less delivering an ultimatum along the lines of 'if you don't do this, bye-bye mankind'. Yet nobody moves.

What is clear is that the 'if' question has nothing to do with any kind of technical evidence-based policymaking, it is being taken as an entirely emotional question – and is being handled selfishly. One of the phrases intrinsic to the thinking of civil engineers is 'infrastructure is what you build for your grandchildren', because it is always something that is intended to last centuries and be a foundation for the continuation of civilisation itself. Civil engineers build for a future that they will personally never see and it is absolutely not an ego trip. The *real* question that this chapter poses to mankind is 'do you *really* love your grandchildren?' The answer is that *real adults* stand up and do whatever is necessary to make sure civilisation continues. But the chapter shows that *real adults* are in short supply.

15

Scaling Clean Energy for Data Centres: Trends, Problems, Solutions

Atif Ansar, Dan Madrigal and Seth Collins

15.1 INTRODUCTION

In a world of big data, widespread sharing of content on social media, data-intensive applications enabled by artificial intelligence, the Internet of things (IoT) and Blockchain, the need for data centres is becoming insatiable. Here we argue that a binding constraint to the scaling of data centres is the availability of low-carbon energy. The technology revolution in the making will choke without a satisfactory clean energy solution for scaling data centres. Here we argue that achieving energy optimisation via on-site production and location siting are the key drivers to overcome the clean energy barrier to scaling data centres.

Global data use is estimated to have grown over 1,000 times between 2,000 and 2020 (ITU 2016). As data needs have become ubiquitous, so have data centres: the facilitators of the data's transformational impact upon our society. The tech giants propelling the global economy share a common dependence on a constellation of these interconnected, energy-intensive centres to store and transmit information, and are quickly being joined by telecoms, banking and beyond, making data centres mission-critical computing infrastructure needing physical and digital security and reliability, making them a top priority for managers.

A key driver of the digital transformation has been the growth of cloud services. Cloud computing is the practice of using a network of remote servers hosted on the Internet to store, manage and process data, rather than a local server or a personal computer. Cloud services take advantage of the benefits of aggregating data demands (virtualisation) to better scale computing to maximise the operational capacity of a server (utilisation), ultimately reducing total server need. They are increasingly built by companies who have total ownership of facilities. Moving to cloud-based data centres increases utilisation rates from 12–18 per cent to 65 per cent (NRDC 2014). Virtualisation has allowed higher server utilisation and higher server refreshing, driving efficiencies that have kept data centre energy usage in the United

States almost flat over the past five years, despite the significant growth in demand for computing power (Shehabi et al. 2016).

The aggregation of a once distributed group of servers has brought attention to the energy required to power the modern economy. Controlling electricity costs is essential for competitiveness and financial sustainability. US data centre electricity consumption cost American businesses $13 billion in 2014 (NRDC 2014) and the energy costs of powering a data centre have doubled every five years (Dayarathna et al. 2016). With the growing importance of data centres to business operations, and the growing impact of data centre costs on corporate IT budgets, energy efficiency and the use of renewable energy are in the forefront of data centre managers' minds (Reddy et al. 2017, Bouton et al. 2010). The disruption caused by the interface between power grids and data centres becomes a question of policy as well.

The literature varies as to the overall footprint – Koomey et al. (2011) found data centre electricity use grew at a CAGR of 16.6 per cent from 2000 to 2005, and 9.1 per cent from 2005 to 2010. Estimates of data centre consumption vary between 8 per cent and 13 per cent of worldwide electricity supply in 2020 (Greenberg et al. 2008, Andrae and Elder 2015). This has a clear impact on emissions. When Google consumes as much energy as the city of San Francisco, the industry cannot ignore its impact on the environment, particularly when many of the leading IT and computing companies in the US use outdated information to underestimate their data centre's carbon footprint by as much as 25 per cent (Hardy 2016, Zik and Shapiro 2016). Some estimates suggest data centre emissions will surpass the airline industry by 2020 (EPA 2007, The Climate Group 2008). Focus on data centre sustainability has grown significantly. In 2016, 70 per cent of enterprise IT organisations surveyed by the Uptime Institute reported active participation in corporate sustainability efforts – a significant change from 2014, when under 10 per cent of enterprise IT stakeholders believed sustainability could affect IT efficiency and costs; now less than 10 per cent believe that corporate sustainability efforts pose a risk to performance and availability (Stansberry 2017).

We ultimately argue for the merits of data centres. Data centres are far less power hungry than distributed computing, and have centralised many distributed energy-intensive activities. When this happens, the lens of criticism unsurprisingly intensifies. A key step is to have transparent information provided by accountable managers to truly show the data energy challenge. The growth of the data centre industry, essential and highly energy intensive, echoes other chapters of this book, including Jim Platts' socio-technical presentation on the wind industry. Data centres have experienced both technical innovation – driven by energy efficiency; and policy innovation – driven by political interactions and corporate initiatives on renewable energy use. We see these two elements – the political and technical – align in data centre site selection of localised low-carbon power generation. Both must carefully consider security, affordability and sustainability, a common triad of energy policy normally faced by governments. As we will show in this chapter, these challenges are now embedded in data centre management.

15.2 ENERGY USE IN DATA CENTRES

Energy consumed in a data centre is often categorised into (1) energy use by IT equipment and (2) energy usage by infrastructure facilities, for example, cooling and power conditioning systems. (Dayarathna et al. 2016). Power consumption goes far beyond the servers with increasing dominance of chipsets in modern commodity servers. This section first considers the main topics of innovation in data centre energy minimisation, including utilisation and virtualisation. It will then give a brief survey of the energy-use consequences of different data management arrangements depending on the physical type of data centre (corporate, multi-tenant and hyperscale) and will end with a discussion on the most common measurements and dominant metrics for data centre energy use.

15.2.1 *Utilisation*

The first major driver of energy efficiency is increased utilisation rates. Utilisation is the percentage of data centre servers in use. Research has historically found very low utilisation rates, between 6 per cent and 12 per cent (Forrest et al. 2008, Glanz 2012, Bouton et al. 2010). Even these numbers are at best educated guesses, argue Zik and Shapiro (2017), as most centres 'can't even tell you how many servers they have, let alone their utilization'.

Drivers of low utilisation rates are multi-fold. One is general overprovisioning of resources by IT departments unwilling to not have available server capacity for changing data demands; another is operator concern opposing any quality of service (QoS) violations (Jin et al. 2016). Underutilisation has compounding effects, as energy is not only wasted to power servers but also from additional provisioning of cooling, power distribution and other supporting infrastructure, ultimately wasting both energy and capital (ibid., Bouton et al. 2010). Servers in cloud centres can be activated and released on demand to maximise the number of tasks a server can provide, or to minimise the number of servers to provide a submitted task (Buyya et al. 2008).

The two main techniques to increase utilisation are dynamic speed scaling (DSS, also known as dynamic voltage and frequency scaling), which focuses on lowering the frequency (speed) of devices to save energy, and the use of a power-down mechanism (PDM), where devices move to idle in a low-power standby or sleep mode to save energy. A comprehensive assessment of different applications of both DSS and PDM can be found in Jin et al. (2016). The use of these techniques and more have led to recent reports of significantly high utilisation rates, such as recent reports by Google of 20–40 per cent utilisation.

15.2.2 *Virtualisation*

A second major driver of energy efficiency has been increased virtualisation, which directly works to increase utilisation. Virtualisation optimises server use regardless of physical location. Many servers in different physical locations can perform numerous applications instead of localised applications assigned to each individual server. For example, an email client can be hosted across different servers depending on availability. Moving one step further to cloud computing services significantly increases economies of scale as servers on virtual platforms have different ownership incentives, and cloud system managers incentivised to maximise utilisation and driven by energy costs will use techniques such as scheduling of job queueing to ensure that servers are as close to maximised as possible (Glanz 2012). Common virtualisation techniques include (1) virtual machine assignment, where virtual machines are mapped to servers based on resource matching and performance metrics and (2) network traffic engineering, which use server traffic patterns and network architectures to optimise utilisation (Jin et al. 2016). Virtualisation has been shown to reduce energy use by up to 95 per cent (Masanet et al. 2013, Cook et al. 2017).

15.3 FACILITY TYPES AND ENERGY CONSEQUENCES

Energy efficiency is also determined by the type of data centre. Data centres owned internally overinvest in servers to guarantee capacity at all times and to accommodate any future contingencies regarding expanding data needs (Bouton et al. 2010). While in-house data centres do give organisations more control, these data centres are generally the least energy efficient (Lisica 2016). Multi-tenant data centres have various ownership structures and service-level thresholds: tenant resources may or may not be controlled by data centre operators in a centralised manner, with distributed ownership and aversion to consolidating space (NRDC 2014). There is little research on the energy efficiency of multi-tenant data centres, but it suggests that overhead costs are high and energy-aware resource management can be difficult (Jin et al. 2016). They are designed to accommodate a multitude of users with different redundancy requirements, often resulting in the overprovisioning of a facility. Nearly all server shipment growth in the past decade was directed towards hyperscale data centres: large-scale centres designed for a homogeneous scale-out greenfield application portfolio with increasingly disaggregated, high-density and power-optimised infrastructures (Shehabi et al. 2016, Callan et al. 2017). They are optimised for maximum productivity and operate at high utilisation rates.

15.4 METRICS AND MEASUREMENT

High-quality metrics allow for accurate measurements of resource efficiencies and provide a guide to evaluate progress and relative effectiveness of technological change and ultimately reduce costs. Some of the most common metrics used are described below, while Jin et al. (2016) provide a comprehensive taxonomy.

The Power Utilisation Effectiveness (PUE) is a ratio to measure the electricity consumed directly for computing versus data centre overhead consumption. PUE seeks to measure how much energy going into a data centre is being effectively committed to IT services, or the fraction of the total data centre power used for IT work. The metric was initially introduced by the non-profit industry consortium Green Grid in 2008. As defined by Belady et al. (2008):

Power Utilisation Effectivenss (PUE) = Total Facility Power/IT Equipment Power

The IT equipment power is the power consumed by the servers, network, storage and supplemental equipment (such as computers used for monitoring). Total facility power includes this power plus auxiliary consumption in the data centre. A PUE of 1 would suggest that every kilowatt of power used by the data centre is being 100 per cent used for IT services. A common PUE in 2006 was 2.0 (Sverdilk 2016). In 2013, Barroso et al. suggested that the average value of the PUE is 1.83. The newest data centres for Microsoft's Azure network and Facebook's own data centres have dropped to 1.1, which is significantly less than the average PUE of 1.5 for multi-tenant data centres. PUE is the most widespread, accepted and measured metric for data centres. A survey of 1,000 data centre operators and IT practitioners found that 72 per cent of the companies surveyed measured PUE (Stansberry 2017). PUE has also been the leading metric for the largest technology firms, though it has its limitations: (1) it does not account for environmental conditions of a data centre site and (2) it does not measure the IT equipment itself (Covas et al. 2015). These limitations have led to a proliferation of other metrics (for a comprehensive list, see Jin et al. 2016 and Reddy et al. 2017).

Cloud services take advantage of the benefits of aggregating data demands (virtualisation) to better scale computing to maximise the operational capacity of a server (utilisation), ultimately reducing total server need. They are increasingly built by companies that have total ownership of facilities, leading to a focus on minimising energy costs and power utilisation effectiveness (PUE) values. Moving to cloud-based data centres reduces energy use by up to 95 per cent (Masanet et al. 2013, Cook 2017), increasing utilisation rates from 12–18 per cent to 65 per cent (NRDC 2014). Virtualisation has allowed higher server utilisation and higher server refreshing, driving efficiencies that have kept data centre energy usage in the United States almost flat over the past five years, despite the significant growth in demand for computing power (Shehabi et al. 2016).

15.5 TWIN SOLUTIONS: ENERGY EFFICIENCY AND RENEWABLE GENERATION

15.5.1 *The Case for Efficiency*

'For data centers, as for all uses of energy, efficiency is always the first thing to do—it's cheapest and allows you to get more mileage out of your equipment.'

This quote, by Northwestern Professor of Engineering Eric Masanet, captures the core argument for a focus on energy efficiency in data centres: the greenest data centre is the one not built, made unnecessary by improving the efficiency of IT technology (Koomey et al. 2013). Evidence supports this as well: Shehabi et al. (2016) found that data centre energy consumption growth has decreased from a compound annual growth rate (CAGR) of 90 per cent in 2000–05 to 24 percent (2005–10) to 4 per cent (2014–15), and there is a similar story in the decreasing growth rate of server shipments: 15 per cent (2000–05) to 5 per cent (2005–10) to 3 per cent (2010–15). Efficiency growth in storage devices means that the growth in storage capacity may outpace data storage demand by 2020 (ibid.). US data centres are projected to consume 73 billion kWh in 2020, a number that could be reduced by up to 33 billion kWh via additional efficiency strategies and would have been 110 bill kWh in 2014 without the efficiency improvements of the past decade (DOE 2016). About three and a half times as much computing power today can be delivered for the same amount of electrical power from 2011.

Efficiency is ultimately a management challenge. Companies could double the energy efficiency of their data centres simply through better management and improved forecasting of business demand, and commonly available techniques and technology to both reduce costs – capital and operating – and emissions (Bouton et al. 2010). Pressures are mounting from many fronts for data centre operators to seek energy efficiency, including from (1) REIT managers and investors demanding lower operating costs, (2) governments demanding efficiency and minimal impacts on power grid infrastructure and (3) public demand for environmental and property impact assessments.

15.5.2 *Efficiency Gains in Cooling Technologies*

Electricity consumed by IT equipment is converted to heat, and the ability to maintain a fixed range of temperature for operating the equipment is often the limiting factor in a data centre's capacity. While advances in servers have led to many benefits around utilisation, advances in processing speeds have led to higher heat densities, increasing cooling needs. Cooling systems remove heat via air or water – liquid-based cooling has a higher capacity than air to remove and transfer heat. The increased heat removal allows servers to run at more efficient operating temperatures and presents opportunities to utilise waste heat (Ashenfelter et al.

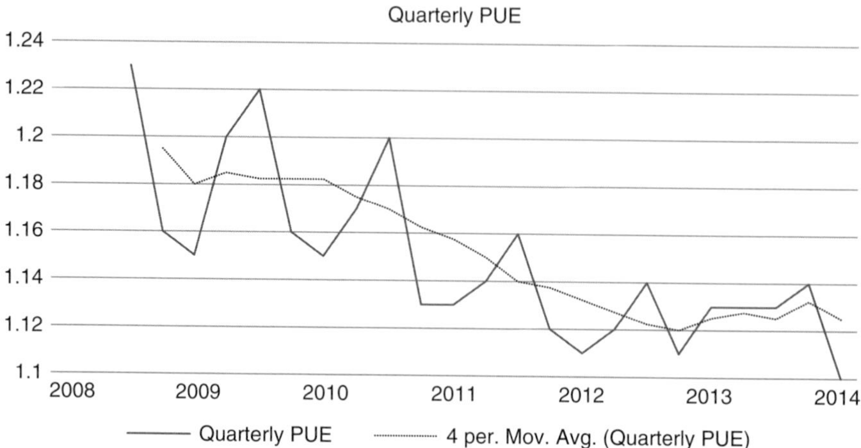

FIGURE 15.1 Historical PUE values at Google
Source: Gao 2016

2014). Similarly, isolating hot and cold airflows to avoid mixing and other design elements, such as day lighting and insulation with bidirectional flow can also improve a data centre's efficiency. Cooling systems have historically been one of the primary energy consumers in data centres, claiming 30–50 per cent of demand and costs (Covas et al. 2015, Belady et al. 2008).

While cooling solutions have driven PUE reduction, limitations to existing cooling technologies correspond to a slowing in the pace of PUE reduction, as most best practices in the industry are now relatively ubiquitous (Gao and Jamidar 2014). The asymptotic nature of approaching a PUE limit of 1 can be seen in Google's historical annualised fleet-wide PUE performance as its progresses along a learning curve.

15.5.3 *PUE Innovation*

Innovations that have brought PUE improvements are many and outside the scope of this chapter. However, the *processes* by which the groups have achieved the innovations, all of which managers and policymakers should be aware of, include machine learning-driven design optimisations, open computing collaborations, in-house server manufacturing (Sverdlik 2016) and in-rack fuel cells (Microsoft 2015). Google and DeepMind's neural network research learned from operations data to reduce energy use for cooling by 40 per cent reduction and overall PUE by 15 per cent to 1.1, the lowest ever on their sites (Jin et al. 2016, Holzle 2016). The neural network minimised PUE by predicting future temperatures and pressures of the data centre to simulate actions within operating constraints informed by data points generated through thousands of sensors daily.

Similarly, Facebook achieved PUE ratios lower than 1.1 at its data centre in Prineville, Oregon, which was 38 per cent more energy efficient and cost 24 per cent less to build and run than a traditional data centre. Facebook's infrastructure team engineered these efficiencies by rethinking every aspect of the data centre, from how each technology component is designed and networked together to the design and construction of the buildings themselves. The company shared these designs via the Open Compute Project. The future of sub-1.1 PUEs is promising. Integration of efficiency metrics will drive improvements in material sustainability, as long as the metrics are transparent, shared and can track the actionable parameters to directly assist operators; are consistent, easy and cost effective to implement and report on for management; and are similarly feasible, simple and inexpensive to monitor (Jin et al. 2016).

Despite the progress in data centre energy efficiency, two caveats apply. First, even with PUE ratios near 1.0, the total absolute energy consumption by data centres will continue to grow – that absolute number has to be brought down. Second, a data centre with a PUE of 1 can still be powered by a dirty grid. Data centres need to consciously move towards cleaner sources.

15.5.4 *The Case for Renewable Power in Data Centres*

A truly sustainable data centre must be powered with renewable energy. The growth of concentrated, large energy efficient data centres emphasises the need to ensure that they are powered by low-carbon sources. Renewable strategies have not been a first choice for emissions reduction, as energy efficiency is selected as a more cost-effective option for marginal emissions reduction (Zik and Schapiro 2016).

Significant progress has been made in some regions and by some companies towards decarbonisation of power from data centres. Large technology companies are already leading in using, and indeed producing, renewable energy. Apple, Google, Facebook, Microsoft and Rackspace are all members of RE100 – an industry consortium of companies that have committed to using 100 per cent renewable energy. Similar commitments have come from Amazon and IBM. Direct corporate procurement of renewable energy reached 3.25 GW in 2015 and over two thirds of that was signed by IT companies (Cook et al. 2017).

Companies have chosen different pathways towards their commitment goals, including embedding the use of renewable power into the data centre (renewable co-location), using local renewable power purchase agreements (PPAs) to decarbonise a local grid or using PPAs on other grids and carbon credits to offset energy demand. However, clean energy innovations are not yet scaling quickly enough to meet low-carbon transition targets. Wind and solar collectively account for 3–4 per cent of global production, and other distributed renewable power solutions are not diffusing beyond small-scale successes. Similarly, less than 20 per cent of electricity used by cloud computing services globally is powered by renewable sources (Lisica 2016).

A potential solution on the path to a low-carbon transition is to use on-site combined cooling heating and power (CCHP) plants. Such plants combust natural gas to supply uninterrupted power and use heat exchange units to provide cooling. A case in point is Citi Group's CCHP plant for its Riverdale Data Centre in London. The project entailed upfront capital expenditure of just under £4.0 M to install two natural gas-fired engines of 1.45 MWe for combined chilling, heating and power for the data centre. The net present value of the investment over fifteen years was approximately £2 M arising from energy cost savings and reduced volatility in prices. Moreover, the investment reduced CO_2 emissions by approximately one fifth (a savings of about 4,000 tonnes of CO_2). These modules can be 'daisy chained' to deliver as much or as little power as a customer needs.

Data centres need uninterruptable power supplies (UPS) that can store energy to reduce power budget violations from the grid and provide energy during peak demand times, or when co-located renewable power is not generating sufficiently (Jin et al. 2016). Battery-based solutions have been shown to effectively cope with short-duration emergencies (see, e.g., Govindan et al. 2011). Aksanli et al. (2013) and Kontorinis et al. (2012) have found that UPS batteries could reduce peak power costs without performance issues; however, they are still an expensive source of power with significant room for technological improvement. Though not always zero-carbon, self-generation like CCHP shows the potential for independent power and the ability even now to significantly reduce emissions from data centres in a modular and scalable fashion. Where complications arise with IT workload fluctuations in short time intervals, workload shaping can adapt the IT workload to fit deviations in available energy (Kirby and Hirst 2000). On-site solutions can provide faster speed to market, higher security of supply, lower cost, faster scalability, lower carbon intensities and lower input price volatilities than traditional grid procurement.

15.6 DATA CENTRE SITING

Optimising and decarbonising energy has very few overarching solutions. Power consumption models tend to not be portable across energy management systems in data centres, and the diversity of workload deployments across data centres and overall poor monitoring environment means there are significant accuracy issues, and it is difficult to apply solutions across data centres due to static, case specific assumptions, (Dayaranthna et al. 2016, Cook et al. 2017). Cooling, renewable power generation and energy efficiency interact and can lead to both trade-offs and complementarities, neither of which are static. For example, initial solutions for cooling challenges led to data centre investments in higher latitudes where data centres could take advantage of lower-temperature climates by drawing upon external air; however, such sites often have geographical risks and higher costs of development, and recent advances in technology have expanded the tolerance of IT hardware to ambient temperatures in the UK, allowing other benefits such as power access and connectivity to take precedence (Covas et al. 2015). These interactions show the need for holistic management of data centre siting.

15.6.1 *The Opportunity of Site Selection*

Siting of data centres is essential for both efficiency and renewable power generation. A geographically diverse portfolio of renewable-powered co-located data centres linked together over a dedicated communication network with a software framework that migrates workloads depending on power availability could significantly decrease the emissions intensity of data centres, though there are outstanding concerns regarding inefficiencies of capital stock and redundant load-matching that could lead to performance loss (Jin et al. 2016). Virtualisation and the introduction of high-density servers that have reduced physical space limitations on information storage, but have increased power needs, have allowed data centres to move away from physical location restrictions requiring data centres to be close to the user and allowed them to be sited almost anywhere (Steenburgh and Okike 2009). This has allowed a much broader range of opportunities for data centre developers to meet the three core requirements: power, space and cooling. Given these engineering constraints, there are myriad factors for a company to consider when building a data centre for sustainability, and the siting of a data centre becomes a strategic corporate choice and thus falls into the realm of management and policy.

One of the core limitations to data centre siting was network latency, or the time required for a packet of data travel between network nodes, quantified in time and viewed as a form of delay. With technological progress, latency has been reduced, while many executives also have learned that many applications do not require the near-zero-latency of high-frequency trading, and could perform many tasks that did not require short time windows in off-hours (Steenburgh and Okike 2009). This has brought latency from an absolute requirement to another variable to consider in a portfolio looking to optimise savings, emissions and performance.

The following table lists many of the considerations (and recommendations) for the development of an IBM data centre, as presented by Intel in Mena et al. (2014). Microsoft considers the environmental conditions, WAN availability and power to be the three critical criteria to meet, though they evaluate many others as well. This list shows the scale of the complexity in selecting, developing and managing a data centre.

Siting decisions can compare the availability and reliability of power plants, the fuels used, local fuel costs, transmission, and electricity pricing regulations – for

TABLE 15.1 *IBM Data centre development considerations*

Metric	Description
Need for Cooling	Areas that have the lowest number of cooling degree days.
Geology	Minimise risk of rockslides or mudslides.
Wind Speeds	Wind speeds greater than 32 kilometers per hour (20 miles per hour) can be disruptive, especially if the data centre design includes free cooling. The wind influences air flows inside the data centre through exhaust venting.
Natural Disaster Risk	Seismic events, floods, tornadoes, hurricanes, areas that experience severe snowstorms and ice storms, and volcanoes can all place the data centre as well as suppliers of power and other services at risk. Volcanoes are particularly problematic. An initial volcanic eruption poses a local risk, and the resulting ash that is distributed according to the prevailing wind patterns poses a prolonged risk.
Pollution	In high-pollution areas with fine particulates, such as those resulting from diesel fumes, dust storms or heavy pollen, the data centre's supply-air system requires more expensive carbon-type filters and more frequent filter changes – adding to initial and operational costs. Smoke can harm equipment and employee health, so avoid heavily wooded areas of near sources of airborne pollution.
Water Availability	Consider two water sources sufficient not only for the cooling towers but also for other industrial needs and fire suppression systems. Sources could be external to the site, or, if the site is over an aquifer, drilling an on-site well is considered.
Water Cost	The direct cost of water, the cost of drilling a well, and the cost and logistics of managing water waste.
Corrosives	High sulfates and natural corrosives (salts) can damage circuit boards, so avoid locating sites near oceans.
Wider Area Network (WAN)	The availability and cost of fiber and communications infrastructure. Any site for a data centre must have adequate WAN fiber capacity for current as well as future needs – or at least the ability to add more fiber as demand grows. Other requirements include hardened WAN access points, below-ground WAN infrastructure and installed fiber/copper inside concrete or PVC instead of direct burial.
Redundancy	Have multiple service providers that use diverse paths and separate main points of entry (the physical location where the service provider's circuits are handed off at the facility).
Power Provision	The data centre's power grid should be powered by two utility providers with good power quality to enable redundancy and reduce risk. The use of two diverse utility providers (not on the same local grid) can negate the need for an uninterruptible power supply (UPS), thus lowering construction costs significantly. Two substations servicing different sides of the facility is preferred. Power cost depends on reliability – inexpensive power may be unreliable.
Power Distribution	Underground power reduces risks from events such as lightning and bird strikes, tree falls and theft of copper or other valuable materials.

TABLE 15.1 *(continued)*

Metric	Description
Other Site-Based Criteria	Includes land acquisition, the construction environment, proximity to resources and proximity to threats, such as natural hazards and workforce disruption.
Socioeconomic	Social and economic stability of the region. Locate data centres in regions that are characterised by moderate economic conditions.
Construction Workforce	Skilled workers, such as framers, concrete workers, electricians and plumbers, contribute to a successful construction project.
IT Workforce	IT personnel, such as network staff, system administrators and data centre architects.
Facility Workforce	Facility technicians and other maintenance staff able to maintain chillers, UPS, power distribution equipment and more throughout the life of the data centre.
Emergency Response Accessibility	Sites that can support business continuity if accidents or disasters occur, such as how quickly emergency responders can reach the site; however, major highways are avoided due to fuel truck accident risk.
Supplier Accessibility	Proximity to a major airport or other transportation venues, such as railroads, trucking routes and distribution warehouses, to improve logistics and reduce the costs associated with shipping supplies (during construction and over the lifetime of the centre).
Real Estate Terms	Sites with an appropriate cost per square metre (acre) and with single owners: multiple owners can slow negotiations and purchasing activities. Avoid parcels with easements because they represent potential legal issues and loss of property due to eminent domain.
Parcel Size and Flexibility	Parcels large enough to accommodate the data centre building(s) and auxiliary equipment (cooling towers, generators). Parcel may need to accommodate storm water-runoff ponds and support ability to expand if necessary.
Zoning Restrictions	Building height restrictions, restrictions of certain power options (solar, smart grid, micro-grid and natural gas power generation fuel cells), permitting required for clean energy, restrictions on data centre capacity and the number of centres, and zoning requirements for communications technologies (satellite, infrared, and microwave)
Reliability Proxies	In many countries, the presence of a military base is associated with a stable area and most likely has a solid utility and communications infrastructure.
Corruption Levels	Avoid constructing data centres or other projects in areas where local business practices are not conducive to the construction that follows site selection
Taxes	The lower the taxation rate, the lower the data centre cost. It is notable whether data centre equipment is taxed as property and whether a sales tax is applied to construction materials, data centre equipment and ongoing data centre supplies.
Tax Incentives	Whether tax incentives already exist or can be negotiated.

Source: Mena et al. (2014)

example, Yao et al. (2012) have shown through simulations of geographic distribution portfolios of data centres that energy consumption can be decreased by 18 per cent. Other locational factors can include: type of utility contract and access to grid and fiber-optic cables; real estate factors including location, land value, construction costs, maintenance costs and climate; strategic factors such as site security, distance between data centre and market served; and environmental factors such as energy-efficient building design, lifecycle pollutants, impact on local community and job creation.

15.6.2 *Limitations to Siting*

Virtualisation has not wholly led to lower-carbon data centres. For example, there has been significant growth in new construction by cloud and co-location companies in Virginia, North Carolina and the US Midwest, where there is abundant and cheap high-emission power and low renewable penetration (Cook et al. 2017). Many of these have been driven by local tax incentives, which have included the following (Cook and van Horne 2011):

- **Apple:** North Carolina's legislature approved $46 m in tax breaks, and local governments slashed both real estate (50 per cent) and personal property (85 per cent) taxes.
- **Google:** North Carolina put together a package of tax breaks, infrastructure upgrades and other incentives, valued at $212 m over thirty years.
- **Facebook:** Facebook is reported to have received $17 m in local subsidies and tax breaks over ten years and exemption from state taxes on all equipment, electricity and construction materials for the data centres.

Location will ultimately determine the carbon intensity of a data centre and the effort needed post hoc to decarbonise it. Cloud companies may extol the benefits of IT products and services but fail to seriously address the significant power demands of this energy aggregation, both in absolute level and emissions intensity (Cook and van Horne 2011). As any company reliant on data centres scales up operations, it will need effective tools to minimise carbon lock-in as it optimises site selection.

15.6.3 *Conflict and Change: Grid Interface and Policy Influence*

Globalisation, virtualisation and co-location have allowed cloud providers to choose any location in the world to install their servers and even their energy load. While previous behaviour has been for technology giants simply to determine the best location for their new data centre and install it, the energy demand of large data centres can create stresses on the power grid that significantly impact grids and can require new power plants or grid infrastructure. Apple's Irish data centre is projected to use between 2 per cent and 8.5 per cent of Ireland's total electricity generation by 2021, spooking the Irish Electricity Supply Board (ABP 2017). Zoning and weak points in the electrical distribution grid can thus cause significant technology company interactions with local utilities. In many regions data centres are perhaps the main driver of power grid upgrades.

Data centre companies such as Apple, Facebook and Microsoft are actively lobbying governments to ensure a more stable and secure energy supply in order to continue building data centres, and thus add jobs to local economies. Apple and Facebook have chosen Denmark and Ireland as locations for their newest data centres due to their stable and secure power grids. Apple has directly lobbied and publicly confronted utilities regarding renewable energy standards and plans. For example, in a recent spat between Apple, Ireland's Galway County Council, EirGrid and a consulting engineer, Apple's newest $850 m data centre faces delays due to concerns over impacts to the national electricity grid.

Some companies have worked effectively with policymakers. When eBay built its first data centre in 2010 in South Jordan, Utah, the site did not meet its renewable energy targets. Utah law restricted non-utility companies from buying and transmitting power directly from renewable energy developers, and so eBay worked with Utah's state senators, data centre associations, large energy end users, a utility, renewable energy producers and consumer groups to draft legislation that was ultimately passed by the state legislature to allow them to purchase renewables energy (Gallo 2012). Additionally, eBay invested heavily in on-site generation opportunities to take the facility off-grid with six on-site fuel cells to complement on-site renewable generation (see Green Grid 2012 for further details).

15.7 ACHIEVING SCALE

As the data centre industry continues to rapidly expand, designing solutions that are not bespoke but are replicable and able to meet the demands of scale will be essential to decarbonise growing energy demands and limit impacts on stressed power grids, particularly in developing countries. Large infrastructure is not the solution. Big infrastructures have long time horizons and often have significant delays. Planning takes even longer once we include the arrangement of financing, benefits do not come online quickly enough and there is often a significant temporal mismatch between when users want services and when they actually become available.

Unmet demand for electricity means that there is unmet growth, opportunity and essential services for some countries to thrive – many of which are now driven by data. From a climate perspective, the world needs to scale up to between US$3.3 and 5.4 trillion per year in core low-carbon power supply and energy efficiency infrastructure investments by 2030 (Mirabile et al. 2017). Unmet electricity demand will be driven primarily in emerging economies (Dobbs et al. 2011). The ultimate size of

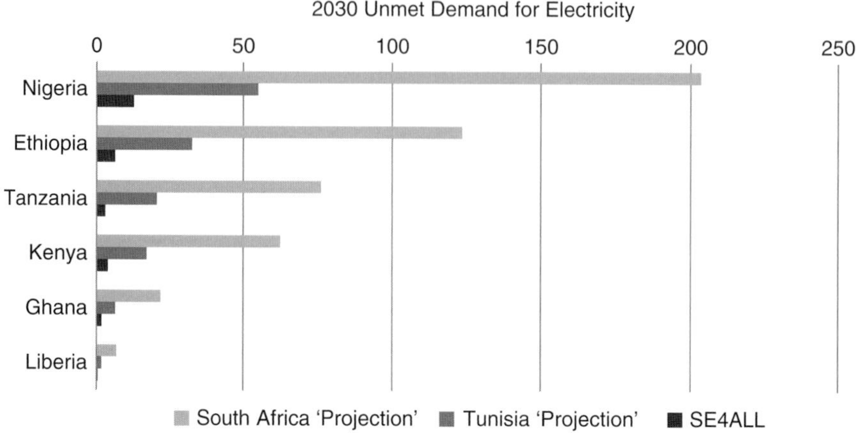

FIGURE 15.2 2030 Unmet demand for electricity
Source: Moss and Gleave (2013)

the gap is clear; the rise of large data centres will likely only increase the stress on this gap.

IBM, Sun Microsystems, Google (now Alphabet), Cisco and Microsoft have experimented with containerising data centres as a solution to scalability problems. The US military has used containerised data centres in war zones for several years (Miller 2012). Google holds a US patent on containerised data centres (Whitted and Ainger 2003). These units were termed IT pre-assembled components (ITPAC) and the very idea was kept secret by Microsoft and Google until 2016 – already four years into their design and use. Although Microsoft decided that containerisation was less efficient than co-location for scalability, it then turned around and demonstrated a simple design for extending the uninterruptible power supply (UPS) to actually store enough power to run the data centre itself (Sverdlik 2016). Virtualisation and co-location techniques – partially using different data centres around the world for different tasks – have shown much more success than physically trying to meet demand with rapid deployment of containerised solutions. An exception has been when deploying in remote regions or areas with very little existing infrastructure (Miller 2009).

Some optimism can be derived from previous infrastructure 'leapfrogs'. The solutions to data centre energy needs may come through renewable energy advancements, smart grid information sharing and autonomous regulation, or energy storage technology in a future form that circumvents the energy infrastructure of today. Alternative investments that can bridge needs quickly, without tremendous time lags, are preferable to investments with a long lead time and hence duration risk (Ansar et al. 2014).

The degree to which a company can maintain modularity in its network of data centres will be valuable. CCHP systems can produce attractive paybacks and are well suited to the steady power and cooling loads of data centres. Distributed generation has the environmental benefits of reduced criteria pollutants and greenhouse gas emissions. Fuel cell-distributed generation systems also offer many attractive qualities, such as DC power output – however, costs, for example, for hydrogen fuel cells, remain prohibitive.

Progress will also continue on the efficiency front. Open-source technology and computing project data centres such as Facebook's Open Compute will rapidly reduce opacity and allow for better systemic decisions and strategy where grids are transparent on strategy and governments are responsive and not burdened by slow planning methods and long timelines for approval, decisions and reviews (OCP 2013) . Such developments may ultimately direct us towards the benefits of neural network algorithms to better adapt to internal or external changes across a data centre's unique architecture and environment – a general intelligence framework as opposed to a custom-tuned model (DeepMind 2016).

The energy scalability challenge for data centres is exacerbated by high total expenditure on electricity by data centre operators; high volatility in electricity prices; suboptimal hedging options; and the pressure to lower the carbon footprint. Thus, there is pressure to maintain security of supply, lower the cost of supply and buy clean energy. We argue that the power grid and cooling sources are the most pressing constraints in scaling data centres. Without deeper innovation, data centres may face intractable limits to growth. Energy is a limiting factor for data centres – and thus for a significant portion of the Internet. Constraints will intensify as Asia Pacific, Africa and the Middle East see more data centre investment, as these data centres pose significant hot climate and power grid challenges (for information on the Asian market, see PWC 2017).

The energy constraints on data centre scaling are not insurmountable. Technical innovation has continued to find efficiencies, and key innovations in predictive intelligence technologies make a world of commonplace PUE ratios near 1 likely. However, absolute power draw will continue to be a limit to scale as the footprint of data centres on local power networks grows. As this chapter has shown, new innovations in on-site power generation and intelligent siting and management can reduce constraints to scale. Further, as other resource constraints grow, particularly regarding carbon emissions, the same solutions will apply. Similar solutions align with the leapfrogging of digital technologies in emerging markets, where grids are less reliable than those being tested by the data centres of today. As the modular backbone of the technological revolution, data centres are essential: as the infrastructure of the twenty-first century, data centres must be built in alignment with the challenges of twenty-first century infrastructure. For humanity to thrive in the digital age, data centre infrastructure much be efficient, decarbonised and resource neutral at scale.

15.8 REFERENCES

Aksanli, B., Pettis, E., & Rosing, T. (2013). Architecting efficient peak power shaving using batteries in data centers. In *Modeling, Analysis & Simulation of Computer and Telecommunication Systems (MASCOTS), 2013 IEEE 21st International Symposium on* (pp. 242–253). IEEE.

An Bord Paeleala (ABP). (2016). Inspectors Report. 07.VA0020. www.pleanala.ie/news/245518-VA0020/RVA0020.pdf

Andrae, A. S. G. & Elder, T. (2015). On global electricity usage of communication technology: trends to 2030. *Challenges*, 6(1): 117–157.

Ansar, A., Flyvbjerg, B., Budzier, A., & Lunn, D. (2014). Should we build more large dams? The actual costs of hydropower megaproject development. *Energy Policy*, 69 (June): 43–56.

Ashenfelter, R., Hodges, K., Luna, A., & Sterman, J. (2014). Final Report for S-Lab Project with Facebook, Inc. MIT Sloan School of Management. 15.915 S-Lab Draft Final Report.

Barroso, L. A., Clidaras, J., & Hölzle, U. (2013). The datacenter as a computer: An introduction to the design of warehouse-scale machines. *Synthesis Lectures on Computer Architecture*, 8(3): 1–154.

Belady, C., Rawson, A., Pfleuger, J., & Cader, T. (2008). Green grid data center power efficiency metrics: PUE and DCIE. Technical report, Green Grid.

Bouton, S., Creyts, J., Kiely, T., Livingston, J., & Nauclér, T. (2010). Energy efficiency: A compelling global resource. McKinsey Sustainability & Resource Productivity.

Buyya, R., Yeo, C. S., & Venugopal, S. (2008). Market-oriented cloud computing: Vision, hype, and reality for delivering it services as computing utilities. In *High Performance Computing and Communications, 2008. HPCC'08. 10th IEEE International Conference* (pp. 5–13), IEEE.

Callan, M., Gourinovich, A., & Lynn, T. (2017). The global data center market. RECAP, cloud lightning, and the Irish Centre for Cloud Computing and Commerce.

The Climate Group (2008). SMART 2020: Enabling the low carbon economy in the information age, June 2008.

Cook, G. (2017). Clicking clean: who is winning the race to build a green Internet? Greenpeace International.

Cook, G. & Van Horn, J. (2011). How dirty is your data? A look at the energy choices that power cloud computing. *Greenpeace (April)*.

Copeland, T. & Tufano, P. (2004). A real-world way to manage real options. *Harvard Business Review*, 82 (3): 90–99.

Covas, M. T., Silva, C. A., & Dias, L. C. (2015). Multi-Criteria Assessment of Data Centers Environmental Sustainability. In *Evaluation and Decision Models with Multiple Criteria* (pp. 283–309). Springer.

Dayarathna, M., Wen, Y., & Fan, R. (2016). Data center energy consumption modeling: A survey. *IEEE Communications Surveys & Tutorials*, 18(1): 732–794.

DeepMind. (2016). DeepMind AI reduces Google data centre cooling bill by 40%. Retrieved January 18, 2018, from https://deepmind.com/blog/deepmind-ai-reduces-google-data-centre-cooling-bill-40/

Dobbs, R., Oppenheim, J., Thompson, F., Brinkman, M., & Zornes, M. (2011). Resource revolution: Meeting the world's energy, materials, food, and water needs. McKinsey Global Institute (MGI). www.mckinsey.com/~/media/McKinsey/Business%

20Functions/Sustainability%20and%20Resource%20Productivity/Our%20Insights/Resource%20revolution/MGI_Resource_revolution_executive_summary.ashx

Economist Intelligence Unit. (2016). The Impact of Cloud. The Economist. Retrieved from http://perspectives.eiu.com/technology-innovation/impact-cloud/white-paper/impact-cloud

Energy Technologies Area, https://eta.lbl.gov/publications/united-states-data-centerenergy/

Forrest, W., Kaplan, J. M., & Kindler, N. (2008). Data centers: How to cut carbon emissions and costs. *McKinsey on Business Technology*, 14(6): 4–13.

Gallo, A. (2012). How eBay and Facebook are cleaning up data centers. Harvard Business Review Online. https://hbr.org/2012/07/how-ebay-and-facebook-are-clea

Gao, J. & Jamidar, R. (2014). Machine learning applications for data center optimization. Google White Paper.

Glanz, J. (2012). Power, pollution and the internet. *New York Times*, September 22.

Govindan, S., Sivasubramaniam, A., & Urgaonkar, B. (2011). Benefits and limitations of tapping into stored energy for datacenters. *ACM SIGARCH Computer Architecture News*, 39: 341–352.

Greenberg, A., Hamilton, J., Maltz, D. A., & Patel, P. (2008). The cost of a cloud: research problems in data center networks. *ACM SIGCOMM Computer Communication Review*, 39(1): 68–73.

The Green Grid. (2012). Breaking New Ground on Data Center Efficiency: How eBay's 'Project Mercury' Used PUE, TCO and DCMM Best Practices to Drive the End-to-End Data Center Ecosystem. Case Study.

Guitart, J. (2017). Toward sustainable data centers: a comprehensive energy management strategy. *Computing*, 99(6): 597–615.

Hardy, Q. (2016). Google says it will run entirely on renewable energy in 2017. *New York Times*, December 6.

International Telecommunications Union (ITC). (2016). Measuring the Information Society Report. www.itu.int/en/ITU-D/Statistics/Documents/publications/misr2016/MISR2016-w4.pdf

Jin, X., Zhang, F., Vasilakos, A. V., & Liu, Z. (2016). Green data centers: A survey, perspectives, and future directions. *ArXiv Preprint:1608.00687*.

Kirby, B. & Hirst, E. (2000). Customer-specific metrics for the regulation and load-following ancillary services. ORNL/CON-474, Oak Ridge National Laboratory, Oak Ridge, TN, January.

Kontorinis, V., Zhang, L. E., Aksanli, B., Sampson, J., Homayoun, H., Pettis, E., … Rosing, T. S. (2012). Managing distributed ups energy for effective power capping in data centers. In *Computer Architecture (ISCA), 2012 39th Annual International Symposium on* (pp. 488–499). IEEE.

Koomey, J. G., Masanet, E. R., Brown, R. E., Shehabi, A., & Nordman, B. (2011). Estimating the energy use and efficiency potential of US data centers. *Proceedings of the IEEE*, 99 (8): 1440–1453.

Koomey, J., Masanet, E., & Shehabi, A. (2013). Characteristics of low-carbon data centres. *Nature Climate Change*, 3(7): 627. https://doi.org/10.1038/nclimate1786

Li, C., Qouneh, A., & Li, T. (2012). iSwitch: coordinating and optimizing renewable energy powered server clusters. In *Computer Architecture (ISCA), 2012 39th Annual International Symposium* (pp. 512–523). IEEE.

Lisica, E. (2016). Data center sustainability: the next dimension. Evoswitch White Paper. https://evoswitch.com/wp-content/uploads/2016/12/Whitepaper_DataCenterSustainability.pdf

Masanet, E., Shehabi, A., Liang, J., Ramakrishnan, L., Ma, X., Hendrix, V., & Mantha, P. (2013). The energy efficiency potential of cloud-based software: A US case study. Ernest Orlando Lawrence Berkeley National Laboratory, Berkeley, CA (US).

Mena, M., Musilli, J., Austin, E., Lee, J., & Vaccaro, P. (2014). Selecting a Data Center Site: Intel's Approach. IT@Intel White Paper. http://media14.connectedsocialmedia.com/intel/02/11447/IT_Best_Practices_Data_Center_Site_Selection.pdf

Microsoft. (2015). Datacenter Sustainability. (Available from microsoft.com.)

Miller, J., Bird, L., Heeter, J., & Gorham, B. (2015). *Renewable electricity use by the US information and communication technology (ICT) industry*. National Renewable Energy Laboratory (NREL), Golden, CO (United States).

Miller, R. (2012). U.S. Army to Deploy Clouds, Modular Data Centers. *DataCenter Knowledge*. 4 April 2012: www.datacenterknowledge.com/archives/2012/04/04/u-s-army-to-deploys-clouds-modular-data-centers

Mirabile, M., Marchal, V., & Baron, R. (2017). Technical note on estimates of infrastructure investment needs: background document to the report Investing in Climate, Investing in Growth. OECD. www.oecd.org/env/cc/g20-climate/Technical-note-estimates-of-infrastructure-investment-needs.pdf

Moss, T. & Gelave, M. (2013). How much power does power Africa really need? Center for Global Development. www.cgdev.org/blog/how-much-power-does-power-africa-really-need

Natural Resource Defense Council (NRDC). (2014). Data center efficiency assessment: scaling up energy efficiency across the data center industry: evaluating key drivers and barriers. Issue Paper August 2014. www.nrdc.org/sites/default/files/data-center-efficiency-assessment-IP.pdf

PWC. (2017). Surfing the data wave: The surge in Asia Pacific's data centre market. PWC. Retrieved from www.pwc.com/sg/en/publications/assets/surfing-the-data-wave.pdf

Reddy, V. D., Setz, B., Rao, G. S. V., Gangadharan, G. R., & Aiello, M. (2017). Metrics for Sustainable Data Centers. *IEEE Transactions on Sustainable Computing*, 2(3): 290–303.

Ristic, B., Madani, K., & Makuch, Z. (2015). The water footprint of data centers. *Sustainability*, 7(8): 11260–11284.

Shehabi, A., Brown, R. E., Brown, R., Masanet, E., Nordman, B., Tschudi, B., Shehabi, A., & Chan, P. (2007). Report to congress on server and data center energy efficiency: Public law 109–431. Ernest Orlando Lawrence Berkeley National Laboratory, Berkeley, CA (US).

Shehabi, A., Smith, S., Sartor, D., Brown, R., Herrlin, M., Koomey, J., & Lintner, W. (2016). United States Data Center Energy Usage Report. Ernest Orlando Lawrence Berkeley National Laboratory, Berkeley, CA (US).

Stansberry, M. (2017). 2016 Data center industry survey results. Uptime Institute.

Steenburgh, T. J. & Okike, N. D. (2009). Verne Global: Building a green data center in Iceland.

US Department of Energy (DOE) (2016). United States Data Center Energy Usage Report.

US Environmental Protection Agency (EPA) (2007). Report to Congress on server and data center energy efficiency Public Law 109–431.

Whitted, W. H. & Ainger, G. (2003). US 7278273B1: Modular Data Center. Google. https://patents.google.com/patent/US7278273B1/en

Yao, Y., Huang, L., Sharma, A., Golubchik, L., & Neely, M. (2012). Data centers power reduction: A two time scale approach for delay tolerant workloads. In *INFOCOM, 2012 Proceedings IEEE* (pp. 1431–1439). IEEE.

Zik, O. & Schapiro. A. (2016). Coal Computing: How Companies Misunderstand Their Dirty Data Centers. Lux Research, Inc White Paper. http://web.luxresearchinc.com/hubfs/White_Papers/Coal_Computing-_How_Companies_Misunderstand_Their_Dirty_Data_Centers_-_Lux_Research_White_Paper_-_February_2016.pdf

Zuckerman, J., Frejova, J., Granoff, I., & Nelson, D. (2016). Investing at Least a Trillion Dollars a Year in Clean Energy. Contributing paper for *Seizing the Global Opportunity: Partnerships for Better Growth and a Better Climate*. New Climate Economy, London and Washington, DC. Available at: http://newclimateeconomy.report/misc/working-papers.

15.9 RESPONSE TO 'SCALING CLEAN ENERGY FOR DATA CENTRES' – A HISTORY AND POLICY PERSPECTIVE

By Tae Hoon Kim

With the increasing datafication of society and the rise of technology companies, data centres have become indispensable in the modern economy. Meeting the energy requirements of the ever-increasing number of data centres while constraining their carbon emissions has become a pressing concern. In this lucidly written paper, Madrigal, Ansar and Collins offer two solutions to meeting this challenge. The first is to improve the efficiency of data centres and the second is to power them with renewable energy.

The greenest data centre, to paraphrase a quote that the authors have used, is the one that is not built, thanks to increasing efficiency. Trying to achieve economies of scale by pushing forward with large infrastructure projects is not the solution, given the timescale and capital involved. This is a sensible suggestion that has been corroborated by a number of infrastructure projects in the past, such as the UK's power station commissioning programme of the 1960s.[1] Data centres can become more efficient by greater virtualisation, more expansive use of cloud computing and increased utilisation by using technologies such as dynamic speed scaling and power-down mechanism.

The paper points to the increasing efficiency of data centres in recent years. For example, the growth of energy consumption of data centres has decreased from a compound annual growth rate of 90 per cent in 2000–05 to 24 per cent in 2005–10. In 2014–15, it fell to 4 per cent. Historically, however, increasing efficiencies in energy have led to increased overall energy consumption, thanks to the economy and ease with which energy can be consumed.[2] In turn, the rise in consumption has been accompanied by rising CO_2 emissions. The authors explain that data centres

[1] Pryke, R., *The Nationalised Industries: Policies and Performance Since 1968* (Oxford: Blackwell, 1981).

[2] See, e.g., Jevons, W., *The Coal Question: An Inquiry Concerning the Progress of the Nation, and the Probable Exhaustion of Our Coal Mines* (London: Macmillan and Co., 1865); Khazzoom, J. D. (1980), 'Economic Implications of Mandated Efficiency in Standards for Household Appliances', *Energy Journal* 1: 21–40. For a historical overview of the trends in energy consumption and efficiency in

are no exception, highlighting the fact that carbon emissions from data centres could surpass the airline industry by 2020. Efficiency alone, therefore, cannot be the greenest solution.

This leads to the second solution that the authors put forward, to power data centres by renewable energy. This can be done either by co-locating data centres near renewable energy generators or by installing low-carbon self-generators. The authors cite Citi Group's Riverdale Data Centre in London to highlight the economic feasibility of installing low-carbon self-generators. The generator in question, however, is a combined cooling heating and power (CCHP) plant that burns natural gas, which still emits CO_2 and has different costs to renewables. A case study of a data centre that is powered by renewable energy would have given a clearer picture of the costs involved.

A common requirement for both increasing efficiency and renewable energy generation is the importance of finding the right location. The authors put considerable analytical weight on explaining the criteria for sites that help save energy costs and use renewable generation. Power, space and cooling are described as the three most important considerations, along with a host of other factors as shown in the metrics chart for a data centre owned by IBM. In fact, the authors go as far as to assert that siting 'will ultimately determine the carbon intensity of a data centre and the effort needed post hoc to decarbonise it', considering it to be more important than virtualisation.

On the whole, Ansar, Madrigal and Collins have provided a succinct and detailed technical account of the challenges involved in scaling clean energy to data centres. There are areas, however, that could have been given more attention.

First, the role of governments and government policy is dealt with in a somewhat perfunctory fashion, in contrast to the activities of private companies. Private companies can take the lead when it comes to increasing efficiency of their data centres and identifying favourable locations. But regarding the use of renewable energy or actually locating the data centres, governments inevitably come into play. Both involve a combination of various policy concerns in energy, technology, economy and the environment. The emphasis put on increasing network security, especially in the wake of recent cyberattacks on numerous governments, should also be factored in. As such, the role of the relevant government departments, as well as that of the different levels of government, should have received more weight.

Second, which is related to the first, a look into the complex decision-making process on scaling clean energy for data centres would have given the analyses a more holistic outlook. The paper does mention a number of cases where technology companies interacted with governments. Unfortunately, this is examined mostly

Western Europe, see Kander, A., Malanima P., and Warde, P., *Power to the People: Energy in Europe over the Last Five Centuries* (Princeton, NJ: Princeton University Press, 2015).

from the standpoint of companies in the narrow context of lobbying decision makers. Making decisions on the provision of clean energy for data centres involves more than just industry lobbying. It could also involve public hearings and debates or discussions in private settings between the parties involved. By drilling down on the fluid interactions between various stakeholders, one could get a better sense of the diverse interests, viewpoints and even tensions involved in an area of such interconnectedness.

Last but not least, extending the analytical perspective to other countries might also help, especially in the emerging economies. What works for Google and eBay in California might not work for Baidu in China. But instead of highlighting differences and similarities between different countries, it might be worth examining the possibility of cross-border linkages or cooperation between relevant stakeholders in the area of data centre infrastructure.[3] This is particularly germane to the suggestion that the authors have offered, but not expounded on, regarding the development of an overarching and repeatable solution to scale clean energy for data centres. Such an approach might also be relevant within the economic and political context of the European Union.

These comments, however, do not weaken the case that the authors have put forward. Instead, they point to the need to take the topic further in a multidisciplinary setting. Scholars of energy policy from different backgrounds should build on the contribution of Ansar, Madrigal and Collins and widen the scope of the debate, as befits the objective of *In Search of Good Energy Policy*.

[3] See Högselius, P., Hommels, A., Kaijser, A., Vleuten, E. eds. *The Making of Europe's Critical Infrastructure Common Connections and Shared Vulnerabilities* (London: Palgrave Macmillan, 2013).

16

Public Participation in the Context of Energy Activities: The Role of the Aarhus Convention Compliance Committee

Leslie-Anne Duvic-Paoli[*]

16.1 INTRODUCTION

In the context of our search for 'good' energy policy, this chapter proposes public participation as a principle of energy governance that brings legitimacy to energy decisions and fosters their social acceptance. Admittedly, doing so risks opening Pandora's box of fundamentally difficult policy questions regarding who should be included, for which purposes and following which methods.[1] This piece concentrates on a multilateral treaty that provides guidance on these questions – the Convention on Access to Information, Public Participation in Decision-Making and Access to Justice in Environmental Matters (Aarhus Convention).[2] The Aarhus Convention was adopted in 1998 under the auspices of the United Nations Economic Commission for Europe (UNECE) and entered into force in 2001. It currently brings together forty-seven parties[3] and is open for membership to states outside of the UNECE region.[4] It requires that states implement the three pillars of 'environmental democracy' consecrated in the 1992 Rio Declaration on Environment and Development[5] – access to information, public participation in decision making and access to justice.

By looking at the role of international law in the field of energy through the spectrum of a multilateral environmental treaty, the chapter puts into evidence three trends in energy governance: (i) energy policies that traditionally have been the

* Lecturer, The Dickson Poon School of Law, King's College London. The research for this piece was undertaken while the author was Philomathia Post-doctoral Research Associate at the University of Cambridge.

1 David Bidwell, 'Thinking through Participation in Renewable Energy Decisions' (2016) 1 *Nature Energy* 1–4.

2 Convention on Access to Information, Public Participation and Decision-Making and Access to Justice in Environmental Matters, Aarhus, 25 June 1998, in force 30 October 2001, (1999) 38 ILM 517.

3 As of 5 March 2018: www.unece.org/env/pp/ratification.html (last accessed 5 March 2018).

4 A possibility that remains until now largely theoretical, as no non-UNECE members have yet joined.

5 Rio de Janeiro Declaration on Environment and Development (Rio de Janeiro, 3–14 June 1992), (1992) 31 ILM 876, Principle 10.

domaine réservé of the state are opening up to public scrutiny; (ii) this process is in part driven by international constraints; and (iii) it falls under the scope of a hybrid treaty at the intersection between environmental law and human rights. In other words, energy governance is becoming increasingly democratic, is influenced by international standards and regulations and is more open to environmental and social sustainability objectives.

A word of caution should be said about the fact that, given its restricted regional scope, the Aarhus Convention does not influence global energy governance in its entirety. Yet, it is widely considered to be an instrument of global significance[6] that represents best practices in the field of environmental democracy.[7] The recent adoption of an international treaty of a similar nature in the Latin American region is indicative of the crystallisation of the principle of public participation beyond the Western hemisphere.[8] Hence, the convention represents international practice pertaining to public participation in its most comprehensive and advanced form and can be used to guide the design of 'better' energy policies.

The chapter starts by explaining how the Aarhus Convention contributes to energy governance (16.2). One of its strengths lies in the existence of a committee charged with reviewing state compliance with the convention's obligations: it gives direct insights into how the instrument affects the design and operation of projects that might impact the environment. Two cases in which the committee found a situation of non-compliance in the context of energy projects are analysed (16.3). The chapter ends by reflecting on the increasingly important role that international law plays in energy governance, and, more specifically, in democratising decision-making processes (16.4).

16.2 THE AARHUS CONVENTION, AN INSTRUMENT OF ENERGY GOVERNANCE

The Aarhus Convention is a hybrid treaty, at the intersection between environmental and human rights law.[9] In addition, it can be depicted as an instrument of energy governance in as much as its obligations constrain energy activities. Of particular interest here is the duty to guarantee public participation in decision-making

6 UNECE, *The Aarhus Convention: An Implementation Guide* (2nd ed, 2014), where Kofi Annan observed that 'Although regional in scope, the significance of the Aarhus Convention is global … [I]t is the most ambitious venture in the area of "environmental democracy" so far undertaken under the auspices of the United Nations.'

7 'Report of the Special Rapporteur on the issue of human rights obligations relating to the enjoyment of a safe, clean, healthy and sustainable environment' (2015) UN Doc. A/HRC/31/53, para 50.

8 'Latin America and the Caribbean Adopts its First Binding Regional Agreement to Protect Rights of Access in Environmental Matters', 5 March 2018, available: https://negociacionp10.cepal.org/9/en/news/latin-america-and-caribbean-adopts-its-first-binding-regional-agreement-protect-rights-access (last accessed 7 March 2018).

9 Alan Boyle, 'Human Rights and the Environment: Where Next?' (2012) 23(3) *European Journal of International Law* 613, at 622.

processes, which extends to energy activities pursuant to Article 6 and energy policies pursuant to Article 7. The application of Articles 6 and 7 to the energy sector is briefly discussed in turn. First, activities falling under the scope of Article 6 are listed in an annex to the convention. The annex categorises activities based on different sectors: strikingly, it starts by referencing activities in the 'energy sector' – hence, presenting the regulation of energy activities as the primary concern of the convention. The category includes nuclear power stations, oil and gas refineries and thermal power plants.[10] A number of uncategorised activities are also listed at the end of the annex, and includes activities relevant to the energy sector such as the extraction of oil and gas,[11] and the construction of dams,[12] pipelines[13] and electrical power lines.[14] In addition, other activities not explicitly covered by the annex, such as wind farm developments, can fall under the convention provided that domestic legislation on environmental impact assessments (EIA) includes requirements to involve the public.[15] Second, Article 7 applies to 'plans and programmes relating to' the environment. Although the terms 'plans' and 'programmes' are not explicitly defined in the convention,[16] they have been considered to include sectoral plans and programmes relative to energy policy, including decarbonisation policies.[17]

The relevance of the Aarhus Convention to the regulation of energy activities and policies highlights the fragmented state of energy governance.[18] Moreover, it provides a new perspective on energy governance that moves beyond interstate forms of energy cooperation to focus on multilevel interactions (local, national and international).[19] The oversight provided by the Aarhus Convention illustrates the role that international governance can play in guiding and constraining domestic energy policies.[20] The energy sector has traditionally been a *domaine réservé* of the state, with governmental authorities making decisions regarding the exploitation of natural resources and the construction of energy infrastructures. However, as a consequence, energy policies have historically been criticised for lacking transparency and energy activities have commonly faced corruption and human rights violation scandals.[21] The Aarhus Convention ensures that energy activities are

10 Aarhus Convention, Annex I, para 1.

11 Aarhus Convention, Annex I, para 12.

12 Aarhus Convention, Annex I, para 13.

13 Aarhus Convention, Annex I, para 14.

14 Aarhus Convention, Annex I, para 17.

15 Aarhus Convention, Annex I, para 20.

16 UNECE, *The Aarhus Convention: An Implementation Guide* (2nd ed, 2014) 175.

17 UNECE, *The Aarhus Convention: An Implementation Guide* 175.

18 Rafael Leal-Arcas, Andrew Fillis, Ehab Abu Gosh, *International Energy Governance: Selected Legal Issues* (Edward Elgar 2014) 15–89.

19 Thijs Van de Graaf and Jeff Colgan, 'Global Energy Governance: a Review and Research Agenda' (2016) 2 *Palgrave Communications* 1, at 9.

20 Van de Graaf and Colgan, 'Global Energy Governance', at 1.

21 See, e.g., Constantino Grasso, 'The Dark Side of Power: Corruption and Bribery within the Energy Industry' in Rafael Leal-Arcas and Jan Wouters (eds), *Research Handbook on EU Energy Law and*

designed with the public interest in mind[22] and contributes to their legitimacy.[23] This role is increasingly important in light of the ongoing shift to more decentralised energy systems.[24] As states transition to new sources of energy to meet their decarbonisation objectives,[25] broad political and community support is needed. Accountability of decision makers and transparency of their decisions are necessary to ensure that the transition to a low-carbon economy is inclusive and fair, taking into account the different interests at play and finding a balance between values that often clash. Additionally, empowering people to participate in policy formulation ensures that new energy projects and policies are accepted socially and also that communities actively participate in their implementation (by self-generating their energy and changing their consumption and transportation habits). In other words, citizens now take direct, and local, initiatives to reduce carbon emissions and find alternative sources of energy, and also claim a right to be consulted in decision-making processes pertaining to energy choices.

The role of the Aarhus Convention in energy governance illustrates how the fields of energy and environmental governance, which have tended to operate as two separate epistemic fields, are becoming increasingly close.[26] Admittedly, the regulation of energy activities operated by international environmental treaties is not a new activity: international treaties on the regulation of oil exploitation and transportation and nuclear power to avoid their negative environmental impacts have significantly contributed to the development of international environmental law.[27] Yet, energy governance and environmental regulation are coming closer in the context of the low-carbon transition, which requires states to review the climate impacts of their energy policies.[28] Energy policies face increasing domestic and international scrutiny as the international community seeks to meet the decarbonisation objectives set by the Paris Agreement to the United Nations Framework Convention on Climate Change.[29] As states make significant changes to their energy policies by diversifying their sources of energy and turning towards new types of energy, international

Policy (Edward Elgar 2017) 237–256; Benjamin Sovacool, *Energy and Ethics: Justice and the Global Energy Challenge* (Palgrave Macmillan 2013) 90–110.

22 Henry Steiner, 'Political Participation as a Human Right' (1998) *Harvard Human Rights Yearbook* 77.

23 Jonas Ebbesson, 'The Notion of Public Participation in International Environmental Law' (1998) 8(1) *Yearbook of International Environmental Law* 51, at 62.

24 Power for All, *Decentralized Renewables: From Promise to Progress* (2017), on how SDG 7 will only be achieved by investing in decentralised renewable energy.

25 David Bidwell, 'Thinking through Participation in Renewable Energy Decisions' (2016) 1 *Nature Energy* 1–4.

26 Van de Graaf and Colgan, 'Global Energy Governance', at 1.

27 Clarence Wilfred Jenks, 'Liability for Ultra-hazardous Activities in International Law' (1966) 117 *Collected Courses of the Hague Academy of International Law* 99–200, at 195.

28 Darren McCauley, *Energy Justice: Re-balancing the Trilemma of Security, Poverty and Climate Change* (Palgrave Macmillan 2018).

29 Paris Agreement to the United Nations Framework Convention on Climate Change, Paris, 12 December 2015, in force 4 November 2016, Doc. FCCC/CP/2015/10/Add.1 190, art 2(1) and 4(1).

environmental law is called upon to regulate the externalities of activities that give rise to new and diverse types of risks.

16.3 THE AARHUS COMPLIANCE COMMITTEE AND ITS CASE LAW ON ENERGY

This chapter started by presenting how energy activities and policies fall under the scope of the convention. It now looks at how the treaty applies in practice by analysing the case law of the committee that reviews compliance with the provisions of the convention. The committee is a 'non-confrontational, non-judicial and consultative' body.[30] Its objective is not to sanction non-compliance but rather to facilitate the return of the party back to compliance. A compliance procedure can be triggered by different entities, including the party itself (self-trigger), another party or the secretariat of the convention. The most common type of trigger is, however, submissions made by members of the public. Communications from the public reached an impressive number of 150 in December 2017: energy activities and policies represent around one fourth of the total communications.[31]

The following section analyses two sets of conclusions and recommendations made by the compliance committee in relation to the energy sector: the first one relates to the decision taken by the United Kingdom to build a nuclear power station in Hinkley Point; the second one pertains to the design and adoption of a renewable energy policy in Scotland. The section ends with a general assessment regarding the role of the committee in overseeing public participation practices in the energy sector.

16.3.1 *Case Study 1 – Construction of a Nuclear Power Station*

A variety of energy activities has been scrutinised by the compliance committee, including projects relevant to oil and gas, hydropower and renewable energies. However, the largest number of communications contest state practices in relation to nuclear activities.[32] One submission of particular interest pertains to the United Kingdom's decision to build a third nuclear station with two European pressurised reactors (EPRs) at Hinkley Point, also known as Hinkley Point C. It will be the first nuclear power plant built in the country in over twenty years and is estimated to cover the electricity needs of 7 per cent of the population.[33] Nuclear power plants fall under the scope of Aarhus Article 6 by virtue of their inclusion in Annex I of the convention. In this case, the communicant, a German member of parliament,

30 Aarhus Convention, art 15.

31 Thirty-three out of the 150 communications are related to energy activities or policies.

32 Around 40 per cent of the overall total of submissions relative to energy.

33 UNECE, Espoo Convention, 'Report of the Implementation Committee on its thirty-fifth session' (2016) UN Doc. ECE/MP.EIA/IC/2016/2, para 18.

alleged a breach of Article 6 in view of the fact that the German public was not given the opportunity to participate in the transboundary EIA.

At the heart of the case was whether the German public is part of the 'concerned public' referenced in Article 6 that is granted a right to participate in decision-making processes.[34] The Convention defines the 'concerned public' as 'the public affected or likely to be affected by, or having an interest in, the environmental decision-making'.[35] In effect, whether the German public falls under that definition in the context of the Hinkley Point C decision depends on how nuclear risks are conceived. The compliance committee took a broad view of this question: it considered that the convention covers risks arising from the possible impacts of the routine operation of an activity but also its effects in case of an accident or exceptional incident.[36] As a result, members of the public may be affected by, or have an interest in, environmental decision making, even if the risk of an accident is very small.[37] The committee noted that given the ultra-hazardous nature of the proposed activity, the possible adverse impacts of the Hinkley nuclear power plant can 'reach far beyond state borders and over vast areas and regions'.[38] In addition, the committee considered that the impacts did not only include measurable impacts (on property or health for instance) but could also include 'less measurable aspects', such as quality of life.[39] Hence, risk assessments should also take into consideration the 'perceptions and worries of persons living within the possible range of the adverse effects'.[40] On that basis, the committee found that the United Kingdom was in non-compliance with Aarhus Article 6.[41]

16.3.2 *Case Study 2 – Design of a Renewable Energy Policy*

The Aarhus committee also evaluates the conformity of energy policies pursuant to Article 7 that provides for public participation in the preparation, modification or review of plans, programmes and policies relating to the environment. In recent years, an increasing number of communications has contested the compliance of renewable energy policies with Aarhus provisions.

Such is the case of the submission made to the committee in 2012 by Ms Metcalfe on behalf of the Avich and Kilchrenan Community Council regarding the implementation of the renewable energy programme in Scotland, which inter alia

34 UNECE, Aarhus Convention, 'Findings and recommendations with regard to communication ACCC/C/2013/91 concerning compliance by the United Kingdom. Adopted by the Compliance Committee on 19 June 2017' (2017) UN Doc. ECE/MP.PP/C.1/2017/14.
35 Aarhus Convention, art 5(2).
36 'Findings and recommendations with regard to communication ACCC/C/2013/91', para 73.
37 'Findings and recommendations with regard to communication ACCC/C/2013/91', para 75.
38 'Findings and recommendations with regard to communication ACCC/C/2013/91', para 75.
39 'Findings and recommendations with regard to communication ACCC/C/2013/91', para 73.
40 'Findings and recommendations with regard to communication ACCC/C/2013/91', para 75; para 90(b).
41 'Findings and recommendations with regard to communication ACCC/C/2013/91', para 89(a)–(b).

required the construction of individual wind energy projects.[42] She alleged that European Union, United Kingdom and Scottish authorities were in breach of their Aarhus obligations. The communicant insisted this was particularly so as to the 'uncontrolled expansion of wind energy farms in Scotland and throughout the European Union space' in light of decarbonisation objectives.[43]

Although the committee rejected a number of allegations of non-compliance,[44] it held that the United Kingdom was in breach of Aarhus Article 7 because the United Kingdom's National Renewable Energy Plan (NREAP), adopted in the context of European Union Directive 2009/28/EC on the promotion of the use of energy from renewable sources, had not been subject to public participation.[45] It recommended that in the future the United Kingdom submit plans and programmes of a similar nature as the NREAP to public participation pursuant to Article 7.[46]

16.3.3 *Assessment*

The case law of the Aarhus committee relative to energy activities and policies is relatively extensive and varied. However, the extent to which the committee's conclusions and recommendations regulate energy governance remains limited for three interrelated reasons: (i) their formal status; (ii) their content; and (iii) their consequences.

Firstly, given the non-adversarial character of the committee, the findings are non-binding and indicative.[47] The normative weight of the committee's conclusions cannot be underestimated, and they are regularly referenced using the common judicial term 'case law'.[48] Nevertheless, while the committee enjoys widespread credibility among states, international tribunals and civil society, its status and role remain distinct from that of a traditional international adjudicatory body.

Secondly, the Aarhus Convention protects procedural rights and, as a result, the committee is not mandated to assess the content of energy decisions as such – it thus does not take a position on very political (and controversial) choices. However, this means that the committee has been reluctant to engage at all with the substance of the case. It has so far paid no attention to the context within which the decisions have been taken, and in particular to the broader decarbonisation objectives that communicants sometimes mention. While it can rightly be argued that the mandate of

42 UNECE, Aarhus Convention, 'Findings and recommendations with regard to communication ACCC/C/2012/68 concerning compliance by the United Kingdom and the European Union. Adopted by the Compliance Committee on 24 September 2013' (2014) UN Doc. ECE/MP.PP/C.1/2014/5.

43 'Findings and recommendations with regard to communication ACCC/C/2012/68', para 48.

44 'Findings and recommendations with regard to communication ACCC/C/2012/68', para 48.

45 'Findings and recommendations with regard to communication ACCC/C/2012/68', para 48.

46 'Findings and recommendations with regard to communication ACCC/C/2012/68', para 108.

47 Aarhus Convention, art 15.

48 Andriy Andrusevych, Summer Kern (eds), *Case Law of the Aarhus Convention Compliance Committee (2004–2014)* (3rd ed.) (Resource and Analysis Center/Society and Environment 2016).

the committee prevents it from making substantive assessments, the absence of such assessments can, nevertheless, have significant consequences on the committee's conclusions. In the case presented above on the United Kingdom's renewable energy policy, the committee was unable to find that the obligation to access information had been violated[49] because it was unable to assess the quantitative data regarding the merits of wind energy projects communicated by the party. The communicant had alleged that the right to access information under Aarhus Article 5 had been violated because the available environmental information relating to the energy policy (such as the greenhouse gas emissions and fossil fuel savings) was not transparent, up to date, accurate and comparable.[50] The committee acknowledged that the information on CO_2 reductions was based on contested modelling methods[51] but it considered that it was beyond its mandate and capacity to 'assess the environmental information in question as to its accuracy or adequacy'.[52] The committee's approach raises an important question, that is, whether the principle of information sharing does not risk becoming an empty shell if the committee concentrates only on the process of information sharing and not on the quality of the information provided. Can information sharing and public participation be ends in themselves and can these principles give decisions full legitimacy without any considerations as to their substance?

Thirdly, the findings of the committee remain rather soft in the sense that they are anticipatory: the committee encourages the party to take its recommendations into account for future practice but does not seek to remedy the situation of non-compliance. For instance, in the context of the Hinkley nuclear power plant case, the Aarhus committee recommended that in the future the United Kingdom notify the concerned public outside its own territory.[53] These conclusions can be contrasted with those of another compliance committee, that of the Convention on Environmental Impact Assessment in a Transboundary Context (Espoo Convention), a UNECE convention that creates an obligation to undertake an EIA in the context of activities likely to create significant transboundary harm.[54] The Espoo implementation committee reviewed the same case on Hinkley Point C in light of the United Kingdom's obligations to undertake an EIA. It also found that the United Kingdom was in non-compliance with its obligations to notify parties potentially affected by the activity.[55] As a result, in a similar conclusion as that made by the Aarhus committee, the Espoo committee recommended that if the United

49 'Findings and recommendations with regard to communication ACCC/C/2012/68', para 87.

50 'Findings and recommendations with regard to communication ACCC/C/2012/68', para 51.

51 'Findings and recommendations with regard to communication ACCC/C/2012/68', para 85.

52 'Findings and recommendations with regard to communication ACCC/C/2012/68', para 86 and 89.

53 'Findings and recommendations with regard to communication ACCC/C/2013/91', para 90.

54 Convention on Environmental Impact Assessment in a Transboundary Context, Espoo, 25 February 1991, in force 10 September 1997, (1991) 30 ILM 802.

55 UNECE, Espoo Convention, 'Report of the Implementation Committee on its thirty-fifth session' (2016) UN Doc. ECE/MP.EIA/IC/2016/2, para 67(a), on the non-compliance with art 2(4) and 3(1).

Kingdom were to plan the construction of other nuclear power plants, it should notify potentially affected parties.[56] However, the Espoo committee also sought to remedy the situation of non-compliance and invited the United Kingdom to reach out to possibly affected parties to decide whether notification might be useful at the current stage for this proposed activity.[57] In addition, after issuing its recommendations, the committee subsequently became concerned that the continuation of construction works at Hinkley Point C might render the discussions with possibly affected parties regarding notification irrelevant. As a result, its chair asked the United Kingdom to 'consider refraining from carrying out works at the proposed activity until it established whether notification was useful'.[58] The committee also recommended to the Meeting of the Parties that if a potentially affected party were to request notification, the United Kingdom would have to 'suspend works related to the proposed activity until the transboundary EIA procedure is finalized'.[59] This recommendation could have significant economic (and political) impact if the construction of the nuclear power plant was to be suspended. In other words, the Espoo committee took a stronger position on the situation of non-compliance compared to the Aarhus committee, which was not concerned with remedying the situation of non-compliance. In light of this, it can be concluded that the role of the Aarhus committee is significant because it contributes to reviewing the legality of energy projects with public participation obligations but its role remains limited by its non-confrontational character.

16.4 INTERNATIONAL LAW AND THE DEMOCRATISATION OF ENERGY POLICIES

This chapter ends with a few comments on the role that international law plays in the democratisation of energy policies in light of Aarhus case law. It might be unexpected that international law puts energy policies under democratic scrutiny, given that international law is often criticised for its democratic deficit.[60] But the practice of the Aarhus committee can be read as realising Franck's prediction, made in 1992, that citizens would soon 'look to international law to guarantee their democratic entitlement'.[61] Although made in a very different context, the comment underpins in essence the rationale driving the work of the compliance committee: to

56 'Report of the Implementation Committee on its thirty-fifth session', para 67(d).

57 'Report of the Implementation Committee on its thirty-fifth session', para 67(b).

58 UNECE, Espoo Convention, 'Report of the Implementation Committee on its thirty-eighth session' (2017) UN Doc. ECE/MP.EIA/IC/2017/2, para 61.

59 'Report of the Implementation Committee on its thirty-eighth session', para 61.

60 Steven Wheatley, 'A Democratic Rule of International Law' (2011) 22(2) *European Journal of International Law* 525, at 527–532.

61 Thomas Franck, 'The Emerging Right to Democratic Governance' (1992) 86(1) *American Journal of International Law* 46–91.

give citizens a forum that protects their right to democratic decision-making processes.

The example of the Aarhus committee puts into light some of the complexities of the democratic exercise. It is widely used to contest activities relative to energy, which raises an important question about the use of law as a strategic advocacy tool: are the communications made to the Aarhus committee manifestations of the infamous 'not in my backyard' syndrome, which describes the common opposition of residents to new developments in their vicinity despite the recognition that these changes are necessary for the broader societal well-being? The selfishness of the motivations driving the public to seize the committee is often evident, especially in light of the fact that the majority of energy cases brought to the committee relate to the most controversial source of energy, nuclear power. The efforts needed to submit a communication to the committee are rather minimal, which means that the communicants can easily use the mechanism to express their discontent with specific energy decisions. Contrary to traditional judicial procedures, the submission does not require in-depth technical or legal knowledge, but only consists of putting together a few pages on the facts regarding the situation of the alleged instance of non-compliance. Admittedly, the law is used strategically to resist changes; however, it does not weaken public participation as a 'good' principle of energy governance. It only means that the committee should be careful of the interests and motivations of a communicant as it analyses the information presented to it.[62] Arguably, the mere democratic process contributes to making – even selfish – individuals more interested in promoting public interests.[63] As it turns out, the cases submitted to the committee often reveal that the state party has not complied with its environmental obligations in the context of decisions pertaining to energy activities and policies. In effect, by bringing a case to the attention of the committee, the communicant is working for the greater good of the international community.

The processual nature of the compliance committee facilitates the democratisation of energy decisions. Its recommendations guide the behaviour of states in the context of their decisions relative to the energy sector and, eventually, constrain parties to be more democratic and inclusive. In addition, the committee, in its non-confrontational role, acts as a mediator between the state and the public by encouraging a dialogue which might have broken down at the local level. The compliance committee goes back and forth between the communicant and the party, playing the role of an intermediary, to gather information and receive comments from both sides. When the compliance committee finds that the state party has met its international obligations, its intervention gives an international stamp of approval to these decisions and contributes to building their social acceptability.

62 UNECE, *Guidance Document on the Aarhus Convention Compliance Mechanism* (2010) 24.

63 Mark Warren, 'Democratic Theory and Self-Transformation' (1992) 86(1) *American Political Science Review* 8.

16.5 CONCLUSIONS

The Aarhus Convention plays an instrumental, sometimes overlooked, role in the international architecture of energy governance by making public participation a core principle of 'good' energy policy. Thanks to the procedural nature of the obligations that the convention protects, it ensures that decision-making processes respect certain minimum standards relative to public involvement without having to engage with the (often controversial) substance of the decision. The Aarhus Convention hence contributes to making decisions involving risky technologies (such as nuclear power) or new types of energies (such as wind farms) more socially acceptable.

The work of the Aarhus compliance committee highlights the role that international obligations at the intersection between environmental and human rights law play in constraining the design and operation of energy projects and policies. It is notable that, in a similar vein, human rights treaty bodies are increasingly assessing whether energy projects and policies might violate existing human rights obligations.[64] This trend reveals that despite the fragmentation of global energy governance, a multiplicity of existing legal instruments can be used to verify that energy decisions comply with international obligations, hence putting energy decisions under increasing international scrutiny.

16.6 RESPONSE TO 'PUBLIC PARTICIPATION IN THE CONTEXT OF ENERGY ACTIVITIES: THE ROLE OF THE AARHUS CONVENTION COMPLIANCE COMMITTEE'

By David Newbery

Public participation in policy development based on access to and confidence in the reliability and completeness of the evidence base can give legitimacy to energy policy, but risks providing a platform for partisan opposition. The Aarhus Convention, which came into force in 2001 and has forty-seven European parties, creates obligations to facilitate access to information and guidelines for public participation. Its emphasis on the *process* of sharing information without attention to the adequacy of that information, nor on the inevitable trade-offs with other environmental and economic objectives, illustrates the Janus-faced nature of this approach to democratic accountability. While the convention offers easy access to complaints (thirty-three in the case of energy) that appear to be normally upheld as non-compliant with the convention by the committee, it does not seek to remedy

64 See, e.g., Committee on Economic, Social and Cultural Rights, 'Concluding observations on the fifth periodic report of Australia' (E/C.12/AUS/CO/5, July 2017), para 11–12; Committee on the Elimination of Discrimination against Women, 'Concluding observations on the ninth periodic report of Norway' (CEDAW/C/NOR/CO/9, 17 November 2017), para 14–15.

non-compliance but only to indicate good practice for future decisions, via an expanding body of case law. The two case studies illustrate the advantages and downsides of its approach.

The construction of the new nuclear power station Hinkley Point C in England was subject to a compliance review at the behest of a German member of parliament, on the grounds that a nuclear accident could have transboundary impacts reaching as far as Germany. A cynic might observe that as with the previous case of acid rain,[65] after Germany had decided to rule out nuclear power in its *Energiewende*, it wanted others to follow suit to make sure that its industry was not undermined by cheaper electricity from other European countries.[66] Hirth (2017) shows that while Germany's massive (and costly) support for renewable energy depressed wholesale electricity prices, the nuclear phase-out under the *Energiewende* almost exactly counterbalanced this price fall. Encouraging other countries to phase out nuclear power might be expected to have a similar impact in raising wholesale prices and reducing the competitive threat to energy-intensive German industry from countries enjoying lower wholesale prices.

A more substantial problem with the complaint and its acceptance by the committee is that the committee was unwilling to balance any risks of harm against global environmental benefits, in this case from mitigating CO_2 emissions from displaced fossil generation. This is relevant given that the German *Energiewende* has failed to reduce the CO_2 emissions from generation by allowing coal and lignite to maintain their output levels (at around 280 TWh), despite a rise in renewable power from 5.6 per cent of the total generation in 1999 to 32.6 per cent in 2015.[67] In 2015 German electricity emitted 345 Mt of CO_{2e} compared to 344 Mt in 2009 and 344 Mt in 1999 as the rise in renewables was offset by a decline in nuclear power.

The second case study of a complaint against the Scottish renewable energy programme for allowing an 'uncontrolled expansion of wind energy farms in Scotland' is a good example of the NIMBYism that led the Conservative Party to promise to stop supporting onshore wind in its Manifesto (rather than allowing each local authority to make that decision). Perhaps the opportunity to protest under the convention may encourage wider debate about the content of energy policy and encourage more attention to be paid to mobilising local support, perhaps following Continental examples of local cooperative ownership of wind farms (British Academy, 2016).

The upside is that the Convention argues for minimum standards of public involvement by international naming and shaming, while its international

65 The EU Large Combustion Plant Directive was promoted by Germany and modelled on the German GFAVo. See Boemer-Christiansen and Skea (1993).

66 The contract signed with Hinkley Point C is likely to lead to substantially higher prices than prices from other electricity sources, but it could be inconsistent to argue for a nuclear phase-out without objecting to a new nuclear power plant.

67 See 'Mapped: How Germany Generates Its Electricity', www.carbonbrief.org/how-germany-generates-its-electricity

dimension appears to offer the prospect of putting more pressure on reducing global harmful impacts of energy policies. It is a useful example of international environmental cooperation, more recently and more impressively illustrated by the COP21 Paris Climate Agreement, which entered into force on 4 November 2016, and which has more parties than the Aarhus Convention (172 at December 2017)[68] with a wider global coverage.

16.6.1 *References*

Boehmer-Christiansen, S. and J. Skea, 1993. *Acid Politics: Environmental and Energy Policies in Britain and Germany*, John Wiley & Sons Ltd.

British Academy, 2016. Cultures of Community Energy: International Case Studies, by Neil Simcock, Rebecca Willis and Peter Capener, at https://www.britac.ac.uk/sites/default/files/CoCE_International%20Case%20Studies_online.pdf

Hirth, L., 2017. What caused the drop in European electricity prices? A factor decomposition analysis. *The Energy Journal*, 39(1), 143–157.

[68] United Nations Climate Change, 'The Paris Agreeement', http://unfccc.int/paris_agreement/items/9485.php

17

Biofuel Energy, Ancestral Time and the Destruction of Borneo: An Ethical Perspective

Michael S. Northcott

In August 1987, while teaching in a theological seminary in Kuala Lumpur, I visited with two of my students on the upper reaches of the Rajang River in the East Malaysian State of Sarawak, basing myself for some days at the logging town of Belaga. While there I saw evidence of extensive destruction of tropical forests at first hand. I also encountered native peoples whose homes and livelihoods had been destroyed by the destruction and pillaging of their ancestral lands. Many native peoples had been forced to move from the forest interior to longhouses situated on the rivers since only a small fringe of forest and garden land on riverbanks was left unmolested by the logging companies. In the longhouses we visited we saw that the people were slowly being drawn into settled and town-based living with televisions, posters of Michael Jackson and other Western cultural paraphernalia in evidence. Nonetheless, in the longhouses many traditional practices were continued including cooking and eating communally, and swidden farming – growing foods, such as wild rice and other plants, in small temporary forest clearings that native peoples have domesticated as a way of supplementing wild food from hunting and gathering (Hong 1987).

I interviewed a flying doctor working for a Christian missionary organisation who told me that she was visiting tribal communities in the highland interior, many miles from riverbanks, and was finding children who were suffering from malnutrition because the fish, mammals and plants they used to live off were no longer available to their parents to hunt and gather. The fish in the rivers had died as the quantity of soil displaced by logging activities had filled the rivers with silt, depriving the fish of oxygen. The mammals and plants the communities had once hunted and gathered, as had their ancestors for thousands of years, were either killed or destroyed by the clear-cutting practices of the logging companies. It is possible to remove the largest trees from tropical forests without destroying forest ecosystems and in such a way as to permit the forest to regenerate. However, in Sarawak and Sabah, and in Kalimantan, which is the Indonesian part of Borneo, the forest is cleared not only to remove tropical timber for sale but to convert the land into oil palm plantations.

Often when the largest and most valuable trees have been extracted the remaining forest is burned as this is a more economical way of clearing the land than removing the remaining trees and undergrowth before draining the land, and terracing it in preparation for oil palm plantation. So extensive is the burning of forests that the cities of Sumatra, West Malaysia, Borneo and Java – including Medan, Padang, Singapore, Malacca, Kuala Lumpur, Penang and Jakarta – are shrouded for days or even weeks at the height of the dry season in August and September by harmful smoke and smog. In the worst year on record for smog – 1997 – most of Southeast Asia was shrouded in smoke and this large-scale pollution incident occasioned a sudden downturn in regional stock markets which precipitated a financial crash throughout Southeast and East Asia that impacted Korea and the Philippines as well as Myanmar, Cambodia, Vietnam, Laos, Thailand and the Malay Archipelago (Swinbanks 1997).

Much tropical forest in Borneo and in Sumatra – the other large area currently being cleared for oil palm – grows on top of very deep peat and in some places the surface fires have led to subterranean peat fires which are impossible to extinguish. When the peat is not burned, it is dried out by drainage channels which are a common feature of oil palm plantations since the oil palm is not a native plant and needs drier soils than those left behind by tropical rainforests. The burning of the forest, together with the drying out of the methane-rich peat, produces vast regional greenhouse gas emissions. In just one quarter of the year 2015 – August to September – the quantity of greenhouse gas emissions from Indonesian forest fires exceeded the total greenhouse gas emissions of the economy of the United States (Anderson et al 2016).

Oil palm is widely used in industrial products including cooking oil, vegetable shortening, detergent, tea lights and candles. It is also used to make liquid fuels – otherwise known as biofuels – for vehicular engines in the form of 'biodiesel'. The 2009 Renewable Energy Directive claims that biofuels are 'renewable' and mandates that petroleum and diesel fuels sold in all European Union nations contain 10 per cent biofuel by 2020. The EU Directive (2009/30/EC) mandates the use of biofuels in order to help the European Community 'meet its greenhouse gas reduction goals through the decarbonisation of transport fuel' and to reduce 'life-cycle greenhouse gas emissions' from the fuel and energy supply of European vehicles. It acknowledges that 'the incentives provided for in this Directive will encourage increased production of biofuels worldwide', but it argues that 'increasing worldwide demand for biofuels, and the incentives for their use provided for in this Directive should not have the effect of encouraging the destruction of biodiverse lands'. This means that biofuel provision must be subject to 'sustainability criteria' which in turn means that biofuels must 'not originate in biodiverse areas' or 'threatened or endangered ecosystems or species' and this means that a 'primary forest' should not be used to grow biofuels.

Biofuels are derived from monocultural production of plants including sugar beet, wheat, sugar cane and oil-rich plants such as oil palm, soya, rape and corn. Other plant sources are possible, including biomass waste from agriculture and forestry, but the main food crops have been used for biofuel, and oil palm is the largest single plant source for biodiesel in the EU. Within and beyond Europe the extent of land now devoted to such plants, together with the widespread use of full-spectrum pesticides and herbicides on the crops, is a major cause of habitat loss for species, and hence of biodiversity decline (Hallman, Sorg et al. 2017). The directive therefore provided a strong market incentive – since it is aimed at 10 per cent of the large EU vehicular fuels market – for companies and national agencies to grow more of such crops, and to continue to convert land areas, including forests and grasslands, to more production of crops with the potential to feed demand for biofuels. The European Commission argues that since primary forests are gazetted worldwide by government agencies it will be possible to prevent the marketing of biofuels from land converted from primary forests. However, the Commission failed to provide a mechanism or a certification scheme to ensure that biofuels, which are liquids refined mostly in the country of origin and shipped thousands of miles to European ports in oil tankers, do not originate from lands that were formerly primary forests and the 2009 directive led to a *fivefold* increase in the marketing of palm oil as biodiesel according to trade data (Transport and the Environment, 2016).

In recognition that there is an ongoing problem with the sustainability criteria in the 2009 directive, the European Commission published a revision in 2015 requiring companies wanting their biofuels to become part of the EU liquid fuels mix to sign up to 'legal or voluntary schemes' to ensure their products are not from recently cleared forests (EC 2015). In the case of oil palm the only internationally recognised scheme for ensuring palm oil is not produced from land converted from primary forests is the Roundtable on Sustainable Palm Oil (RSPO). Begun at a meeting of oil palm company officers in Kuala Lumpur in the 1990s, RSPO was an attempt to underwrite the sustainability of palm oil given the strong scientific evidence that oil palm plantations are appearing on lands that were until recently gazetted as primary forests in Borneo and Sumatra, and, as the industry extends its footprint, in other parts of Southeast Asia. The sustainability production criterion that RSPO introduced was that palm oil carrying the RSPO certification would be guaranteed not to be from lands converted from primary forests for this purpose (Schouten and Glasbergen 2011). But the code has proven difficult to enforce. This is in part because of the nature of the product: it is not possible to certify the liquid itself so it is not easy to enforce certification (Ruysschaerrt and Salles 2014). But there is also good evidence that companies that have claimed RSPO status for their palm oil have been involved in setting fires and clearing primary forest: in the summer of 2013 satellite data revealed that a large number of forest fires in Sumatra were set in areas adjacent to oil palm plantations which have received RSPO certification, and it was evident they were begun purposefully to enlarge those plantations into new forest areas (Greenpeace International 2013)

There is growing recognition that the 2009 (and even the 2015) Renewable Energy Directives, far from reducing greenhouse gas emissions in Europe's vehicular fleet, have increased them because it has promoted tropical forest clearing and replacement with oil palm plantations. Advocacy from NGOs such as Oxfam and Greenpeace, and related scientific studies (Pesqueira and Glasbergen 2013), led the European Commission to publish a revised framework – known as RED II – which lowers the targets for biofuels by 2030 and would phase out the use of palm oil by the same date. However, in the European Parliament MEPs passed motions in 2017, and again in 2018, calling on the European Commission to act more urgently to remove palm oil from European biofuels by 2020 (EU Parliament 2017). Malaysia and Indonesia, the principal producers of palm oil, have said that they will raise a trade dispute with the European Union under World Trade Organisation rules if the European Commission bans the import of biodiesel made from vegetable oils. The plantation companies are closely connected with the governments of Malaysia and Indonesia, and in Malaysia the party that governed continuously since independence in 1957 until 2018 – the United Malay National Organisation – has extensive holdings of shares in plantation companies, and a national Malaysian plantation agency – FELDA – is also a major producer of palm oil. This helps explain why when Malaysian cities including Penang, Ipoh, Kuala Lumpur, Malacca and Johor Bahru are shrouded in extremely unhealthy levels of particulates from forest fires in Sumatra and Borneo – such as in 2013 which saw a peak of burning in Borneo and Sumatra – the government makes very little fuss since the fires are set in many cases by subcontractors acting for Malaysian-owned companies. A significant proportion of shareholder value on the Malaysian and Singaporean Stock Exchanges is therefore directly connected with oil palm plantations, including future projections of ongoing growth in conversion of forest lands.

The conversion of so much of Borneo from primary forest to oil palm has occasioned an ecological disaster on an unprecedented scale. And behind this disaster there is systemic political corruption, extensive criminal activity and destruction of the habitats of native peoples and wildlife. In Sarawak, the people most affected by the destruction of their forests are the nomadic Penan people. Though under Malaysian customary law, known as *adat*, they ought to be considered as the owners of the forests of Sarawak since they have lived in them for generations, this customary ownership has not been recognised by the Sarawakian government. Instead the Sarawak State Government, under its Chief Minister Abdul Taib Muhamad, appointed itself the 'trustee' of the forests of native peoples for sixty years, after which in principle they could hand them back to native peoples, but by then it is unlikely there will be many left since they have been forced out of their longhouses and nomadic dwellings into urban shanties in the growing cities of Sarawak and Sabah while most of the tropical forest outside of the 6 per cent of protected areas has been destroyed.

The chief beneficiary of the exported timber from Sarawak was one man – Abdul Taib Muhamad who was the Chief Minister of Sarawak from 1983 to 2014, and remains titular Head of State. Taib dominated the forest trade in Sarawak and amassed a vast personal and family fortune, much of it held by a company – Sakti International – registered in the State of California which owns and rents offices and residential buildings throughout the world, with significant concentrations in the cities of Adelaide, London, Ottawa and Seattle (Straumann, 2014). The devices for amassing this fortune were various. They included granting licenses to log forests to companies owned by family members; receiving bribes from other logging companies for logging concessions; and the receipt of export 'fees' to a Taib-family company called Regent Star registered in Hong Kong to whose port most of Sarawak's timber was shipped, for onward shipping to timber-importing nations in the region and most notably Japan, Taiwan, Korea and China. Finally in the wealth chain, much of the land, once logged, was turned into oil palm plantations that in many cases also became assets for members of the Taib family, whose product ends up in European biodiesel (Straumann 2014, 108–9). A few other ministers in Taib's government also benefited. James Wong was the Minister for the Environment in Sarawak from 1987 to 2001 and a company he controlled – Limbang Trading – logged 124,000 hectares in Limbang in northern Sarawak (Straumann 2014 111).

The destruction of the forests led to extensive protests and resistance by the Penan and other native groups, including logging blockades, and to claims launched in Malaysian courts to recognise native land rights based upon extensive mapping projects undertaken by the Iban and Penan with help from the Swiss Art for Rainforests Foundation and the Bruno Manser Fund. Bruno Manser was a Swiss adventurer who lived extensively with the Penan in the 1990s and campaigned on their behalf internationally. The Sarawakian government then outlawed land surveying and mapping other than by government surveyors (Straumann 2014 167). Manser was also declared an illegal immigrant by the Malaysian government and eventually disappeared in Sarawak in 2000 on land belonging to Samling, the largest Sarawakian timber and logging company, though he had extensive knowledge of the forests and superb survival skills that he learned from the Penan. His remains have never been found, but it has long been supposed that he was murdered. Individuals from Penan who have led legal actions and non-violent protests against the logging companies also have been killed. These include Headman Kelesau Na'an of the Penan village of Long Kerong, who was a plaintiff in a legal land claim that the Penan had raised in the Sarawak court in 2007. Kelesau met a violent death by persons unknown. Before his death he had been coerced and threatened by an officer of Samling in efforts to persuade him to give up the land claim (Straumann 2014, 174). A pastor from another village met a similar violent death in 1994 after encounters with Samling employees.

Penan women, and mainly young girls, were also regularly raped by Samling employees at the remote village of Middle Baram. Reports of sexual violence against women by logging company employees were investigated by West Malaysian journalist Hilary Chiew and published by *The Star* newspaper – at the time the largest-selling English language newspaper in Malaysia – in 2008.

The interaction between criminality and corruption, primary forest exploitation and wealth accumulation is facilitated through international financial agencies and technologies (Tsing 2005). Deutsche Bank, Goldman Sachs and other international agencies provide Taib and his family enterprises with international investment capital to grow their businesses further, and the financial means to move funds around. Deutsche Bank raised over $700 million in investment capital in the form of bond issues and loans to fund the continued expansion of the Taib family and crony, tropical logging and land conversion activities (Straumann 2014 192–3). International capital also provides the means to launder the ill-gotten gains of crony capitalism into internationally recognised wealth and especially property in North America, Australia and the UK.

In addition to international finance's part in funding and legitimating these activities, there is the role of international science to consider. Science is on both sides of the story of the destruction of Borneo. On the one hand climate science has been used by American and European legislators to promote biofuels as a response to climate change, and this has provided capital opportunities for primary forest conversion to biofuel production. On the other hand climate scientists and conservationists have used satellite imagery and local oral testimony to chart the growing climate impacts of tropical forest conversion and to challenge the claims that biofuels are more 'climate friendly' than fossil fuels.

First and foremost in the saga of the destruction of Borneo is climate science. Under the auspices of the United Nations Framework Convention on Climate Change, nations agreed to monitor and publish inventories of national greenhouse gas emissions from their territories. But of course these inventories are in themselves sites of mediation and manoeuvering by national governments in pursuit of their national interests. So the Malaysian government in its inventory considers oil palm plantations as 'forest', thus discounting the amount of emissions attributable to the drying out of soils that the drainage of tropical forest land requires for the production of palm oil. In Sarawak, official statistics in 2010 indicated that 64 per cent of the land area was forest but this is a significant overestimate (Hon and Shibata 2013). Treating oil palm plantations as forest cover also reduces the public visibility of the gradual conversion of the forests both of East and West Malaysia from tropical rainforest to oil palm, though it is evident to anyone who flies over these lands or drives through them, since oil palm plantations now stretch as far as the eye can see in lowland and parts of upland Sabah and Sarawak, and in large parts of West Malaysia. But the European Commission also uses the UNFCCC as legitimation for its promotion of biofuels arguing in RED that the Kyoto Protocol mandated the commission to reduce greenhouse gas emissions from Europe's vehicle fleet and that this made the aim of 10 per cent of fuels in Europe being derived from plants desirable and even necessary if the EC is to enable its constituent nations to meet their obligations under the Kyoto Protocol. As with the Malaysian government, the European Commission uses greenhouse gas-accounting mechanisms to make the claim that it can foster the continuing growth of European economies and their still growing global ecological footprint, while 'decarbonising' their impact on the atmosphere.

The conventional account of climate change and its causes focuses on greenhouse gas emissions from coal, gas and oil consumption as both the driving force of the tremendous development and financial wealth which characterises modern capitalism and as the driving force behind 'climate forcing'. The European Commission uses greenhouse gas-accounting modes of representation which make it seem as though the 'youthful' biofuel resulting from photosynthesis on present-day plants has a lower climate impact than the 'old' product of photosynthesis on ancient plants and shellfish whose long compaction in the earth's crust creates fossil fuels. But these modes of representation make assumptions which are not based on real-world practices. So, for example, they assume that national inventories of primary forests are diligently kept by governments to prevent their destruction whereas in fact such inventories in the case of the government of Sarawak are viewed as a license to exploit. Science is also used on the other side of the debate to claim that biofuels are more 'climate friendly' than fossil fuels and an environmentally 'efficient' way to use tropical forest lands productively. Hence the governments of Malaysia and Indonesia, and the plantation companies which they in part own, use science in their modes of representation of the greenhouse gas emissions embedded in the biodiesel they produce which, like the European Commission's modes of representation, leave out the vast greenhouse gas emissions from land-use change associated with expanding oil palm plantations. In both cases the modes of representation of greenhouse gas emissions in biofuels use science in their accounting but they both significantly underestimate the climate-forcing impact of biofuels because they leave out greenhouse gas emissions from land-use change, forest fires and peat fires. Because it has acted as a major international driver for tropical forest destruction, and conversion to oil palm plantations, far from reducing Europe's greenhouse gas emissions, RED has increased them. But when the customer buys diesel at the gas station, she is assured the product, because it contains plants, is more climate friendly, because it is partly 'renewable', than a purely fossil fuel-based liquid, and so her conscience is assuaged as she fills up the tank. The European Commission is 'managing' the consumer's impact on the climate and by implication she should carry on driving and without the worry of managing her own 'carbon karma'. It is being taken care of 'upstream' as the energy industry would say.

Science is an ambiguous handmaiden in the biofuels saga. Science and technology facilitate the turning of primary forests and food crops into a substitute for fossil fuels. Science and technology facilitate the extraction of fossil fuels. Science and technology measure the climate forcing, and the impacts on creatures, ecosystems and human habitats of climate forcing from fossil fuels and biofuels. The common culture of science and technology in all these activities facilitates an exchange of ideas and practices between them which helps explain how the European Commission legitimised its turn to biofuels by reference to global climate agreements, such as the Kyoto Protocol. Malaysian and Indonesian governments, and their oil palm companies, also weigh in to this same exchange when they argue that their production of, and trade in, biofuels are appropriate responses to climate change as well as economic development opportunities for tropical economies. But it is only when environmental activists and affected communities protest the environmental injustice, and related corruption and crime, of the conversion of primary forest into biofuel plantations that the paradoxical role of science and technology in promoting biofuels as a replacement for fossil fuels is exposed. Hence the activists realised early on that it was not enough to protest in the forests, or even in the capitals and media of Malaysia and Indonesia. They had to take their case to Europe, to the European Parliament and to European capitals, and one of the key figures in helping to internationalise that case was himself a Swiss environmental activist – Bruno Manser – whom the Penan adopted as one of their own.

Also juxtaposed against cronyism, international finance capital and science-informed accounts of greenhouse gas emissions from biofuels production, are the traditions, customs and beliefs of scientifically uninformed native peoples whose ancestral forests are being destroyed to grow the young plants needed for increased global production of biofuels. The shared assumption among Malaysian politicians and scientific foresters is that indigenous people are not good guardians or managers of forests. However, this is contradicted by what has happened in Sarawak in the last thirty years. The only areas that have been saved from destruction outside of the gazetted boundaries of National Parks, which constitute only 6.6 per cent of the forested area of Sarawak (Hon and Shibato 2013), are areas protected from deforestation by the non-violent actions of native peoples, and in particular the Penan. Using logging-road blockades of persons, posters and bamboo structures, while at the same time registering land claims in Sarawak courts, the Penan successfully saved 163,000 hectares of upland rainforest in the Baram District. Penan villages in this area have collaborated together to form the 'Penan Peace Park'. The ancestral lands and their ecosystem and living creatures are intact and now designated by the Penan as a self-governing nature reserve though it is not included on official maps of nature reserves in Sarawak. As a result the Penan are able to continue to hunt and fish there and plant small gardens and fruit trees (Straumann 2014, 270).

The example of the Penan highlights a broader problem with what Agrawal calls 'environmentality', which is the tendency of environmental, atmospheric and species conservation science and agreements to be used to impose governance regimes on peoples, creatures and habitats in which agency is denied to the ancestral dwellers of such habitats, both human and non-human (Agrawal 2005). The limited success of the Penan in resisting their ancestral forests being logged and then turned into biofuel plantations is an example of what Courtney Jung calls the 'moral force of indigenous politics' (Jung 2008). By resisting the post-colonial regime of a corrupt government and crony capitalists and forcibly blocking logging roads, the Penan became subjects against the consensus in West and East Malaysia that indigenous peoples only acquire recognition as citizens when they come out of the forests and live like 'moderns' in permanent houses. Jung argues that through contestation and resistance to such a consensus indigenous people become agents, subjects, in the public sphere and hence contestation – and not only democratic governance and the law courts – is an essential source of justice in societies where there are groups who are excluded from full participation in normal legal and political processes (Jung 2008, 264–265).

There is another significant element in the Sarawakian case and this is that the post-colonial governance of East Malaysia by West Malaysia has a strong Islamisation as well as financialisation tenor. Taib is a Muslim and so are his family. By acquiring wealth for Muslims they strengthen the larger agenda of the Malay-dominated Barisan Nasional coalition, which is to impose Malay rights on the other constituent groups in Malaysia, and to grow the proportion of wealth, land and businesses owned by Malays who constitutionally are required to be Muslim. Native peoples are encouraged to convert to Islam as part of this Islamisation strategy but even when they do convert their ancestral rights to land and to a fairer share of the wealth of East Malaysia are not recognised.

Bruno Latour argues that modern environmental science lacks sufficient purchase on the public sphere because it has not found ways to include non-human voices in public assemblies and courts (Latour 2004). But the Penan case indicates that the situation is more complex. The Penan are not traditional 'environmentalists', and they are neither students nor agents of environmental science. They resist environmental science because powerful interests invoke environmental science to collude with crony capitalism in the theft and destruction of their forest homes, and at the same time Europeans use the growing of biofuels on their land to alleviate the climate debts of European car drivers. The Penan's environmentalism is an example of what Joan Martinez-Alier calls the 'environmentalism of the poor' (Martinez-Alier 2003). The Penan are not first and foremost protesting the destruction of the rainforests because they are a 'sublime wilderness', or the impacts of this destruction on endangered species such as orangutan or pygmy elephants. They resist logging and the spread of biofuel plantations because the forests are their home, their livelihood and their indigenous capital, and the modern turn of their habitat into liquid fuel, and hence capital, leads to them becoming homeless and excluded from the lands of their ancestors.

In his groundbreaking study of the Tsembaga people of Papua New Guinea, Roy Rappaport was among the first to argue that indigenous peoples, their customs and religious rituals are the best guardians and keepers of ecosystems, forests, savannah and water catchments (Rappaport 1968). Rappaport gathered data from his field study of an annual pig sacrificial ceremony in which he found that the annual ritual sacrifice functioned in such a way as to limit the number of pigs kept by the group of 200 people whom he studied within the carrying capacity of their local ecosystem. Rappaport later developed a fuller theoretical account of the significance of this finding for understanding the role of culture and religion in both the making of humanity and in the governance of ecosystems by pre-modern peoples. Humans dwell both in the midst of linguistic and symbols systems of their own making, and in the midst of natural laws which they do not and have not made and which they never fully understand. The role of religion, Rappaport argues, is to mediate between what is made and what is not made so as to facilitate adaptation of human making, including the making of meaning, to natural laws and the 'unmade' (Rappaport 1999). When religion fails, or becomes pathological, and where ecosystems collapse because of overuse or misuse, this is because of a failure of adaptation. In Rappaport's terms the adoption of biofuels as a response to climate change is post-religious. But this saga can be understood as part of the larger tendency of science and technologies in late modernity to fashion meanings and symbol systems which come to displace the prehistoric and historic role of religions in mediating between the known and the unknown, the made and the mysterious (Noble 1999).

Alfred Russell Wallace formulated what has become known as 'the Sarawak Law' since it was his first published formulation of a theory of the long evolution of life on earth and of the means of variation and distribution, which drew a great deal from his observations in Sarawak. He summarises his theory as follows: 'Every species has come into existence coincident both in space and time with a pre–existing closely allied species' (Wallace 1855). Wallace's law, however, left out the influence of *Homo sapiens* on the process of the evolution and distribution of species. Like John Muir when he went to Yosemite or the Amazon, Wallace preferred explanations of what he saw in the field that did not include persons, particularly when those other persons were non-Europeans lacking scientific education. But *Homo sapiens* had dwelt in Borneo at least 14,000 years before Wallace got there and the shape of the rainforest and the distribution of species within it was in part due to human influence. Analogously, when the indigenous peoples who have shaped and sustained the distribution of species in Borneo over 14,000 years lose influence over its forests and ecosystems, it is unsurprising that their loss of influence coincides with the threat of extinction of many of Borneo's species and their replacement with one alien species – *Elaeis guineensis* from the forests of West Africa.

Robin Hanbury-Tenison led the 1977–78 Royal Geographical Society Expedition into Mulu in North Sarawak and was the first European to find the cathedral-like cave, and cave system, in the Mulu upland forest. That discovery, along with the many endemic species the expedition identified, led to the gazetting of the area as Gunung Mulu National Park. Hanbury-Tenison early on in the expedition was befriended by a Penan – Nyapun – and his family who took him into many places he would never have found on his own and taught him the arts of living in the rainforest with little more than a blowpipe, a machete, a cooking pot and a few musical instruments. Hanbury-Tenison found that the Penan, including their older children, knew the names and medicinal and other uses of hundreds of plants in the rainforest and that they used this knowledge to live long and healthy and free lives in self-built structures which, when they are abandoned, are soon retaken by the forest since they were made from forest materials. He came to realise on his expedition, and through his deep engagement with the Penan, that the native peoples' long trusteeship of the forests is 'the key reason there is so much biodiversity' in Sarawak, and what

> makes the forests so valuable and worth turning into a park is that there have been people looking after it in a symbiotic relationship for ages. And what is more, as we were increasingly to learn on our expedition, their knowledge and understanding of it far exceeded our own superficial scientific analysis (Hanbury-Tenison 2017, 64).

The role of indigenous peoples as guardians of biodiversity is only now being recognised and in so many places, including Borneo, it is mostly too late. Until now the global governance of the climate fostered by the UNFCCC and its treaty negotiations has assumed governments are the best guardians of forests. The agreement concluded at the Conference of the Parties 13 in Bali covering tropical forests resulted in the United Nations Programme on Reducing Emissions from Deforestation and Forest Degradation (or REDD). Like RED, REDD is premised on the assumption that national governments are responsible for managing the carbon cycle in their territories, including emissions from forests. The agreement has enabled developing countries with tropical forests to access development funds under REDD – previously such funds were available under the UNFCCC's Clean Development Mechanism – for development projects in tropical regions that produce biofuel or that use biofuels in development projects (Northcott 2013, 128, 140). But far from slowing tropical deforestation, these development funds are being used for economic development projects which continue to displace the original guardians of the forests, and the myriad creatures whom they have guarded and sustained over many millennia before the modern arrival of colonial regimes, and post-colonial regimes such as REDD. The connection between the European use of biofuels grown on drained tropical forest soils and producing more greenhouse gas emission per kilojoule of net energy than conventional fossil fuels as ways to claim they are meeting their obligations under UNFCCC treaties rests upon an intertemporal calculation, or an 'energy temporality'.

According to the scientific narrative of fuel production and use, burning fossil fuels extracted from the earth's crust results in a real-time increase in carbon dioxide in the atmosphere and the earth system because fossil fuels are the result of ancient photosynthesis. Biofuels are said not to result in net increases in emissions to the atmosphere in present time since the energy comes from plants which photosynthesise solar energy, and it is this newly produced energy which is subsequently burned. However, the use of soils to grow fossil fuels on a planet with seven billion people needing food, and a similar number of domesticated birds and animals fed for human meat consumption, requires the displacement of other activities. Energy supply chains and markets are fungible: they facilitate the transformation of subterranean and surface-derived liquid and electric energy from place to place, region to region, continent to continent and financial account to financial account. Biofuels arrive in EU ports in giant ocean tankers registered in nations with few regulations, such as Liberia, and employing non-unionised non-European workers who are not able to step onto European land while the biofuels are unloaded. But there is no immigration test available which can determine whether the biofuels in the tankers come from lands recently cleared of tropical forests, or lands whose methane has leached into the atmosphere, cancelling out any putative net-present carbon gains of biofuels over fossil fuels.

RED reveals an ontological misunderstanding of persons and other beings in time which puts short-term accumulation of economic value above longer-term values such as ecosystem resilience, biodiversity and long-evolved human traditions including the ancestral guardianship of creatures and ecosystems. The short- and medium-term temporalities of global climate governance, combined with the short-term utilitarian cost–benefit calculus of financialised capitalism, have – in the recent past and currently – come to supplant longer-term temporalities which have evolved over thousands of years, and which traditionally governed the viability of tropical ecosystems and the ways of life that humans and other animals have developed to dwell in them sustainably. The Penan and other indigenous peoples live by a temporality that I call 'ancestral time'. They govern their lands and raise their children and guard their fellow creatures as their ancestors have done for millennia. And they do this from present-day photosynthesis since the materials they use to build their homes and to clothe, entertain and nourish themselves are derived from their local forests. Hence, paradoxically, their ancestral time also promotes a 'presentist temporality' in relation to energy production and use. By presentism I mean that they are able to live off the real-time and renewable energies and biomass production of the ecosystems they inhabit, whereas 'moderns' in the fossil-fuel era have become accustomed to living off energy from sunlight long stored in the crust of the earth, and biomass from regions far distant from their own homes and workplaces.

At the heart of the climate change conundrum is the way in which science and technology have enabled coal, gas and oil engineers to take the earth's carbon cycle to a state of parts per million of CO_2 in the atmosphere that has not occurred in the 200,000-year history of *Homo sapiens*, by burning buried sunlight in the present-day atmosphere. But attempts to fix this error with biofuels reveal a misunderstanding of the temporal nature of the climate problem and of energy production, marketing and use, and a disconnection between present uses of energy and future planetary states (Shirani, Butler et al. 2013). That misunderstanding is resulting in the ongoing destruction of tropical forests to fit UNFCCC-mandated national terrain-based net-present greenhouse gas emission–accounting mechanisms. Governments which turn to biofuels as a means to reduce their net-greenhouse gas emissions need urgently to end the biofuels error and instead invest in ways to reduce per capita *energy* use in the present and near future while at the same time investing in present-day energy from the sun, wind, water flow and hot rocks generated justly and ethically (Northcott 2007). They also need to make amends for the extent to which colonial and post-colonial global economic regimes have extracted natural energies and creatures from places in ways that have reduced the beauty, flourishing and natural wealth of those places for their native inhabitants. This is why it is not possible, despite the protests of rich-world economists, to separate the resolution of global climate damages, and broader ecological damages, from the global distribution of wealth (Nordhaus 2008, Posner and Sunstein 2010).

17.1 BIBLIOGRAPHY

Agrawal, Arun (2005) *Environmentality: Technologies of Government and the Making of Subjects*, Durham NC, Duke University Press.

Colchester, Marcus, Wee Aik Pang, Wong Meng Chuo and Thomas Julong (2006), *Land is Life: Land Rights and Oil Palm Development in Malaysia*, Bogor, West Java and Moreton-in-Marsh, Perkumpulan Sawit Watch and Forest Peoples Programme.

European Commission (2009) Directive (EU) 2009/30/EC of the European Parliament and of the Council of 23 April 2009.

European Commission (2015) Directive (EU) 2015/1513 of the European Parliament and of the Council of 9 September 2015 amending Directive 98/70/EC relating to the quality of petrol and diesel fuels and amending Directive 2009/28/EC on the promotion of the use of energy from renewable sources, *Official Journal of the European Union* L 239/1–29.

European Commission Fuel Quality Directive (2015) http://eur-lex.europa.eu/legal-content/EN/TXT/?uri=CELEX:32009L0030

European Union Parliament (2017) Report 20 March 2017 on palm oil and deforestation of rainforests 2016/2222(INI).

Greenpeace International (2013) *Certifying Destruction: Why Consumer Companies Need to go Beyond the RSPO to Stop Forest Destruction*, Amsterdam, Greenpeace International.

Hallmann, Caspar A., Martin Sorg et al. (2017) More than 75 percent decline over 27 years in total flying insect biomass in protected areas. *PLOS One*, Article e0185809.

Hanbury-Tenison, Robin (2017) *Finding Eden: A Journey into the Heart of Borneo*, London, I B Tauris.

Hon, Jason and Shozo Shibata (2013), A Review on Land Use in the Malaysian State of Sarawak, Borneo and Recommendations for Wildlife Conservation Inside Production Forest Environment, *Borneo Journal of Resource Science and Technology*, 3, 22–35.

Hong, Evelyn (1987) *Natives of Sarawak: Survival in Borneo's Vanishing Forests*, Pinang, Institut Masyarakat.

Jung, Courtney (2008) *The Moral Force of Indigenous Politics: Critical Liberalism and the Zapatistas*, Cambridge, Cambridge University Press.

Latour, Bruno (2004) *The Politics of Nature: How to Bring the Sciences into Democracy*, Cambridge MA, Harvard University Press.

Martinez-Alier, Joan (2003) *The Environmentalism of the Poor: A Study of Ecological Conflicts and Valuation*, Cheltenham, Edward Elgar.

Noble, David F (1999) *The Religion of Technology: The Divinity of Man and the Spirit of Invention*, Harmondsworth, Penguin.

Nordhaus, William (2008) *A Question of Balance: Weighing the Options on Global Warming Politics*. New Haven, Yale University Press.

Northcott, Michael (2007) *A Moral Climate: The Ethics of Global Warming* London, Darton, Longman and Todd.

Northcott, Michael (2013) *A Political Theology of Climate Change* Grand Rapids, MI, Eerdmans.

Pesqueira L and Glasbergen P (2013) Playing the politics of scale: Oxfam's intervention in the Roundtable on Sustainable Palm Oil, *Geoforum* 45, 296–304.

Posner, Eric A. and Cass R Sunstein (2010) 'Justice and climate change: the unpersuasive case for per capita allocations of emissions rights' in Joseph E. Aldy and Robert N. Stavins (eds.) *Post-Kyoto International Climate Policy: International Architectures for Agreement* Cambridge, Cambridge University Press, 343–371.

Rappaport, Roy (1967) *Pigs for the Ancestors: Ritual in the Ecology of a New Guinea People*, New Haven, Yale University Press.

Ruysschaert, Denis and Denis Salles (2014), Towards global voluntary standards: Questioning the effectiveness in attaining conservation goals: The case of the Roundtable on Sustainable Palm Oil (RSPO), *Ecological Economics* 107, 438–467.

Schouten, G and Glasbergen, P (2011), Creating legitimacy in global private governance: The case of the Roundtable on Sustainable Palm Oil, *Ecological Economics*, 70, 1891–1899.

Shirani, Fiona, Catherine Butler, Karen Henwood, Karen Parkhill & Nick Pidgeon (2013), Disconnected futures: exploring notions of ethical responsibility in energy practices, *Local Environment* 18, 455–468.

Straumann, Lukas (2014) *Money Logging: On the Trail of the Asian Timber Mafia*, Zurich, Bergli Books.

Swinbanks David (1997), Forest fires cause pollution crisis in Asia, *Nature* 389: 321.

Transport and the Environment (2016) 'Cars and trucks burn almost half of palm oil used in Europe', *Briefing by Transport and the Environment*, www.transportenvironment.org/sites/te/files/publications/2016_05_TE_EU_vegetable_oil_biodiesel_market_FINAL_0_0.pdf

Valin, H., Peters, D., van den Berg, M., Frank, S., Havlík, P., Forsell, N., & Hamelinck, C. (2015). *The land use change impact of biofuels consumed in the EU Quantification of area and greenhouse gas impacts*. Study commissioned by the European Commission. 261. Utrecht, Netherlands: ECOFYS Netherlands B.V. Retrieved from https://ec.europa. eu/energy/sites/ener/ les/documents/ Final%20Report_GLOBIOM_publication.pdf

Wallace, Alfred Russell (1855) On the law which has regulated the introduction of new species. *Annals and Magazine of Natural History*, 2nd Series, 16, 184–196.

Zachary R. Andnerson et al. (2016) 'Green growth rhetoric versus reality: Insights. from Indonesia.' *Global Environmental Change* 38: 36–40.

17.2 WORKS CITED

Aksanli, B., Pettis, E., & Rosing, T. (2013). Architecting efficient peak power shaving using batteries in data centers. In *Modeling, Analysis & Simulation of Computer and Telecommunication Systems (MASCOTS), 2013 IEEE 21st International Symposium on* (pp. 242–253). IEEE.

An Bord Paeleala (ABP). (2016). Inspectors Report. 07.VA0020, www.pleanala.ie/news/245518-VA0020/RVA0020.pdf

Andrae, A. S. G., & Elder, T. (2015). On Global Electricity Usage of Communication Technology: Trends to 2030. In *Challenges*, 6(1), 117–157.

Ansar, A., Flyvbjerg, B., Budzier, A, & Lunn, D. (2014). Should We Build More Large Dams? The Actual Costs of Hydropower Megaproject Development. *Energy Policy*, March, pp. 1–14, DOI:10.1016/j.enpol.2013.10.069.http://bit.ly/1ekyL7Q.

Ashenfelter, R., Hodges, K., Luna, A., & Sterman, J. (2014). MIT Sloan School of Management.

Barroso, L. A., Clidaras, J., & Hölzle, U. (2013). The datacenter as a computer: An introduction to the design of warehouse-scale machines. *Synthesis Lectures on Computer Architecture*, 8(3), 1–154.

Belady, C., Rawson, A., Pfleuger, J., & Cader, T. (2008). *Green grid data center power efficiency metrics: PUE and DCIE*. Technical report, Green Grid.

Bouton, S., Creyts, J., Kiely, T., Livingston, J., & Nauclér, T. (2010). Energy efficiency: A compelling global resource. *McKinsey Sustainability & Resource Productivity*.

Buyya, R., Yeo, C. S., & Venugopal, S. (2008). Market-oriented cloud computing: Vision, hype, and reality for delivering it services as computing utilities. In *HPCC'08. 10th IEEE International Conference on High Performance Computing and Communications* (pp. 5–13). IEEE.

Callan, M., Gourinovich, A., & Lynn, T. (2017). The Global Data Center Market. RECAP, Cloud Lightning, and The Irish Centre for Cloud Computing and Commerce.

The Climate Group (2008). *SMART 2020: Enabling the low carbon economy in the information age*, June 2008.

Cook, G. (2017). Clicking Clean: Who Is Winning The Race To Build A Green Internet? *Greenpeace International*.

Cook, G. & Van Horn, J. (2011). How dirty is your data? A look at the energy choices that power cloud computing. *Greenpeace* (April 2011).

Copeland, T. & Tufano, P. (2004). A real-world way to manage real options. *Harvard Business Review*. 82 (3), 90–9.

Covas, M. T., Silva, C. A., & Dias, L. C. (2015). Multi-Criteria Assessment of Data Centers Environmental Sustainability. In *Evaluation and Decision Models with Multiple Criteria* (pp. 283–309). Springer.

Dayarathna, M., Wen, Y., & Fan, R. (2016). Data center energy consumption modeling: A survey. *IEEE Communications Surveys & Tutorials*, 18 (1), 732–794.

DeepMind. (2016). DeepMind AI Reduces Google Data Centre Cooling Bill by 40%. (n.d.). Retrieved January 18, 2018, from https://deepmind.com/blog/deepmind-ai-reduces-google-data-centre-cooling-bill-40/

Dobbs, R., Oppenheim, J., Thompson, F., Brinkman, M., & Zornes, M. (2011). Resource Revolution: Meeting the world's energy, materials, food, and water needs. McKinsey Global Institute (MGI). www.mckinsey.com/~/media/McKinsey/Business%20Functions/Sustainability%20and%20Resource%20Productivity/Our%20Insights/Resource%20revolution/MGI_Resource_revolution_executive_summary.ashx

Economist Intelligence Unit. (2016). The Impact of Cloud. *The Economist*. Retrieved from http://perspectives.eiu.com/technology-innovation/impact-cloud/white-paper/impact-cloud

Final Report for S-Lab Project with Facebook, Inc. MIT Sloan School of Management. 15.915 S-Lab Draft Final Report.

Forrest, W., Kaplan, J. M., & Kindler, N. (2008). Data centers: How to cut carbon emissions and costs. *McKinsey on Business Technology*, 14(6), 4–13.

Gallo, A. (2012). How eBay and Facebook are Cleaning Up Data Centers. Harvard Business Review Online. https://hbr.org/2012/07/how-ebay-and-facebook-are-clea

Gao, J. & Jamidar, R. (2014). Machine learning applications for data center optimization. *Google White Paper*.

Glanz, J. (2012). Power, pollution and the internet. *New York Times*, 22 September.

Govindan, S., Sivasubramaniam, A., & Urgaonkar, B. (2011). Benefits and limitations of tapping into stored energy for datacenters. In *ACM SIGARCH Computer Architecture News* (Vol.39, pp. 341–352). ACM.

Greenberg, A., Hamilton, J., Maltz, D. A., & Patel, P. (2008). The cost of a cloud: research problems in data center networks. *ACM SIGCOMM Computer Communication Review*, 39(1), 68–73.

The Green Grid. (2012). Breaking New Ground on Data Center Efficiency: How eBay's 'Project Mercury' Used PUE, TCO and DCMM Best Practices to Drive the End-to-End Data Center Ecosystem. Case Study. www.poweranalytics.com/pa_articles/pdf/Case_Study_1-Breaking_New_Ground_on_Data_Center_Efficiency.pdf

Guitart, J. (2017). Toward sustainable data centers: a comprehensive energy management strategy. *Computing*, 99(6), 597–615.

Hardy, Q. (2016). Google says it will run entirely on renewable energy in 2017. *New York Times*. 6 December 2016.

International Telecommunications Union (ITC). (2016). Measuring the Information Society Report. www.itu.int/en/ITU-D/Statistics/Documents/publications/misr2016/MISR2016-w4.pdf

Jin, X., Zhang, F., Vasilakos, A. V., & Liu, Z. (2016). Green data centers: A survey, perspectives, and future directions. *ArXiv Preprint ArXiv:1608.00687*.

Kirby, B. & Hirst, E. (2000). Customer-specific metrics for the regulation and load-following ancillary services. *ORNL/CON-474, Oak Ridge National Laboratory, Oak Ridge, TN, January*.

Kontorinis, V., Zhang, L. E., Aksanli, B., Sampson, J., Homayoun, H., Pettis, E., … Rosing, T. S. (2012). Managing distributed ups energy for effective power capping in data centers. In *Computer Architecture (ISCA), 2012 39th Annual International Symposium on* (pp. 488–499). IEEE.

Koomey, J. G., Masanet, E. R., Brown, R. E., Shehabi, A., & Nordman, B. (2011). Estimating the energy use and efficiency potential of US data centers. *Proceedings of the IEEE*, 99 (8), 1440–1453.

Koomey, J., Masanet, E., & Shehabi, A. (2013). Characteristics of low-carbon data centres. *Nature Climate Change*, 3(7), 627. https://doi.org/10.1038/nclimate1786

Li, C., Qouneh, A., & Li, T. (2012). iSwitch: coordinating and optimizing renewable energy powered server clusters. In *2012 39th Annual International Symposium on Computer Architecture (ISCA)* (pp. 512–523). IEEE.

Lisica, E. 2016. Data Center Sustainability: The Next Dimension. Evoswitch White Paper. https://evoswitch.com/wp-content/uploads/2016/12/Whitepaper_DataCenterSustainability.pdf

Masanet, E., Shehabi, A., Liang, J., Ramakrishnan, L., Ma, X., Hendrix, V., & Mantha, P. (2013). *The energy efficiency potential of cloud-based software: A us case study*. Ernest Orlando Lawrence Berkeley National Laboratory (LBNL), Berkeley, CA (United States).

Mena, M., Musilli, J., Austin, E., Lee, J., & Vaccaro, P. (2014). Selecting a Data Center Site: Intel's Approach. IT@Intel White Paper. http://media14.connectedsocialmedia.com/intel/02/11447/IT_Best_Practices_Data_Center_Site_Selection.pdf

Microsoft. (2015). Datacenter Sustainability. download.microsoft.com/download/ … /Datacenter_Sustainability_Strategy_Brief.pdf

Miller, J., Bird, L., Heeter, J., & Gorham, B. (2015). *Renewable electricity use by the US information and communication technology (ICT) industry*. National Renewable Energy Laboratory (NREL), Golden, CO (United States).

Miller, R. (2012). U.S. Army to Deploy Clouds, Modular Data Centers. *DataCenter Knowledge*. 4 April 2012: www.datacenterknowledge.com/archives/2012/04/04/u-s-army-to-deploys-clouds-modular-data-centers

Mirabile, M., Marchal, V., & Baron, R. (2017). Technical note on estimates of infrastructure investment needs: Background document to the report Investing in Climate, Investing in Growth. OECD. www.oecd.org/env/cc/g20-climate/Technical-note-estimates-of-infrastructure-investment-needs.pdf

Moss, T. & Gelave, M. (2013). How Much Power Does Power Africa Really Need? Center for Global Development. www.cgdev.org/blog/how-much-power-does-power-africa-really-need

Natural Resource Defense Council (NRDC). (2014). Data Center Efficiency Assessment: Scaling Up Energy Efficiency Across the Data Center Industry: Evaluating Key Drivers and Barrier. Issue Paper August 2014. www.nrdc.org/sites/default/files/data-center-efficiency-assessment-IP.pdf

Open Compute Project (OCP). (2013). Open Compute Project: Overview. AMD White Paper: AMD Open 3.0. http://contentz.mkt6303.com/lp/17305/85018/OpenComputeOverview-WP-FINAL-051713.pdf

PWC. (2017). Surfing the data wave: The surge in Asia Pacific's data centre market. PWC. Retrieved from www.pwc.com/sg/en/publications/assets/surfing-the-data-wave.pdf

Reddy, V. D., Setz, B., Rao, G. S. V., Gangadharan, G. R., & Aiello, M. (2017). Metrics for Sustainable Data Centers. *IEEE Transactions on Sustainable Computing*.

Ristic, B., Madani, K., & Makuch, Z. (2015). The water footprint of data centers. *Sustainability*, 7(8), 11260–11284.

Shehabi, A., Brown, R. E., Brown, R., Masanet, E., Nordman, B., Tschudi, B., Shehabi, A., & Chan, P. (2007). *Report to congress on server and data center energy efficiency: Public law 109–431*. Ernest Orlando Lawrence Berkeley National Laboratory, Berkeley, CA (US).

Shehabi, A., Smith, S., Sartor, D., Brown, R., Herrlin, M., Koomey, J., & Lintner, W. (2016). United States data center energy usage report.

Stansberry, M. (2017). 2016 Data Center Industry Survey Results. *Uptime Institute*.

Steenburgh, T. J. & Okike, N. D. (2009). Verne Global: Building a Green Data Center in Iceland.

US Department of Energy (DOE). (2016). United States Data Center Energy Usage Report. https://eta.lbl.gov/publications/united-states-data-centerenergy/

US Environmental Protection Agency (EPA). (2007). Report to Congress on Server and Data Center Energy Efficiency Public Law 109–431.

Whitted, W. H. & Ainger, G. 2003. US 7278273B1: Modular Data Center. Google. https://patents.google.com/patent/US7278273B1/en

Yao, Y., Huang, L., Sharma, A., Golubchik, L., & Neely, M. (2012). Data centers power reduction: A two time scale approach for delay tolerant workloads. In *INFOCOM, 2012 Proceedings IEEE* (pp. 1431–1439). IEEE.

Zik, O. & Schapiro. A. (2016). Coal Computing: How Companies Misunderstand Their Dirty Data Centers. Lux Research, Inc White Paper. http://web.luxresearchinc.com/hubfs/White_Papers/Coal_Computing-_How_Companies_Misunderstand_Their_Dirty_Data_Centers_-_Lux_Research_White_Paper_-_February_2016.pdf

Zuckerman, J., Frejova, J., Granoff, I., & Nelson, D. (2016). Investing at Least a Trillion Dollars a Year in Clean Energy. Contributing paper for *Seizing the Global Opportunity: Partnerships for Better Growth and a Better Climate*. New Climate Economy, London and Washington, DC. http://newclimateeconomy.report/workingpapers/wp-content/uploads/sites/5/2016/05/NCE_CleanEnergy_financing_final_web-Copy.pdf

17.3 RESPONSE TO 'BIOFUEL ENERGY, ANCESTRAL TIME AND THE DESTRUCTION OF BORNEO: AN ETHICAL PERSPECTIVE'

By David Reiner

Michael Northcott offers a clarion call on the ethical problems associated with developing biofuels to meet Western (especially European) countries' commitment to address climate change. He focuses in particular on the impact that palm oil cultivation has had on indigenous populations in Malaysia and provides vivid examples of the human effects of kleptocracy and trampling on the rights of native groups.

By contrast, relying more on statistical analyses or studies of the path dependence of national polities or of institutional actors, political scientists have sought to explore many of these same questions associated with the challenges of development in the face not of scarcity but of abundance, especially an abundance of natural resources.

Over the last fifteen to twenty years, there have been literally hundreds of articles written on the broader subject of the political economy of the 'resource curse' (Ross, 1999). Robinson et al. (2006) highlight how resource abundance leads to over-extraction and discourages a focus on other aspects of the economy. The rents from exploiting resources offers a stronger rationale for politicians to stay in office and provides more resources to influence the outcome of elections. They note how countries without institutions that 'promote accountability and state competence' will find it difficult to resist the 'perverse political that such booms create'. Summarising the existing scholarship (primarily conducted on the subject of oil), Ross (2015) describes how a resource endowment: 'tends to make authoritarian regimes more durable; [. . .], leads to heightened corruption; and [. . .] helps trigger violent conflict in low- and middle-income countries, particularly when it is located in the territory of marginalised ethnic groups'. The existing literature on forest governance is much smaller, but many of the more general findings of the resource curse resonate in the forest sector (Harwell, Farah & Blundell, 2011).

Political science would also point to the need for institutional responses, while acknowledging potential failings, notably at the implementation stage. Northcott describes the flawed RSPO process because of the lack of enforcement, but there has been some recent evidence of RSPO acting more aggressively and punishing bad actors since certification is becoming increasingly valuable. For example, in 2016, IOI Group based in Sarawak was suspended from RSPO as a result of complaints from several NGOs. Although its certification was reinstated a few months later, many multinationals removed IOI from their list of approved suppliers (Cuff, 2016).

There are also other international initiatives designed to foster greater transparency and hence accountability in natural-resources sectors. The Extractive Industries Transparency Initiative (EITI) is not focused on forest resources, but rather on assessing how nations are doing measured against a standard for good governance of oil, gas and minerals (Sovacool et al., 2016). Even though Malaysia has a large oil and gas sector and is a relatively advanced country with a nominally democratic political system, it is striking that it is not a member of EITI even though most sub-Saharan African countries participate, as do many of Malaysia's regional neighbours including Indonesia, Timor-Leste, Philippines, Papua New Guinea and Myanmar. Although this highlights the current governance problems across the board in Malaysia, this may create a dynamic whereby international peers, donors and neighbours exert pressure for reforms over time.

Crucially in all this is the question of the expropriation of rents, which directly relates to political power. Nominally, Malaysia is a multi-ethnic society where the constitution explicitly enshrines fair treatment of all groups, but ethnic tension is a long-standing thread in Malaysian politics. Although the long-ruling Barisan Nasional Party is designed as a coalition made up of Malays, Chinese, Indians and other indigenous groups, effectively the Malays dominate most aspects of national politics and patronage plays a key role in domestic politics and keeping the other groups placated (Gomez & Jomo, 1999). Overall, Muslim Malays make up some 55 per cent of the Malaysian population compared to 23 per cent Chinese and 7 per cent Indian, in addition to the 11 per cent of indigenous non-Malay ('bumiputera') groups. On Sarawak, however, the demographic mix is more finely balanced with the largest group being the native Iban (30 per cent) followed by Malays (23 per cent), Chinese (23 per cent) and other indigenous groups including the Bidayuh, Orang Ulu and Melanau (21 per cent in total).

The long-time Chief Minister Taib actually comes from the Melanau, but he is a Muslim and a supporter of the larger national coalition. By contrast, a tribe like the Penan, as hunter-gatherers and small in absolute numbers (less than 20,000), lies completely outside of all existing power and influence structures. Indeed, as Northcott highlights, it took Bruno Manser, a Swiss activist, to help internationalise the local concerns and bring the issues of deforestation and impacts on local communities to the European stage. The Penan are a marginalised people in Sarawak, which has long been treated as a backwater or fiefdom both in colonial and modern times. Until remarkably recently Sarawak was dominated for over a century (from 1841 to 1946) by 'white rajah' from the dynastic Brookes family in a very paternalistic fashion (Runciman, 1960) and it is not accidental that the Taib is known as the 'white-haired' rajah (Asia Sentinel, 2010).

Finally, Northcott does not use the word 'Anthropocene', but he does clearly highlight the importance of impacts not just on the natural surroundings but on wider society. He contrasts his approach and those of others such as Rappaport with that of Alfred Russell Wallace and John Muir, who focus on nature absent human intervention. This compartmentalisation is often the case for much of the field of environmental politics where the emphasis has long been on damage to the natural world. In recent years, a politics of the Anthropocene (Purdy 2015; Haraway 2015) has emerged which seeks to understand environmental politics and politics more generally as the product of an era where such a separation is no longer viable and as a result our analysis of typical 'environmental' problems needs to change to reflect the reality of the human role in the system.

17.3.1 References

Asia Sentinel (2010). Sarawak's White-Haired Rajah, *Asia Sentinel*, 10 August. https://www.asiasentinel.com/society/sarawaks-white-haired-rajah/

Cuff, M. (2016). Palm oil giant IOI Group regains RSPO sustainability certification, *The Guardian*, 8 August. https://www.theguardian.com/environment/2016/aug/08/palm-oil-giant-ioi-group-regains-rspo-sustainability-certification

Gomez, E. T., & Jomo, K. S. (1999). *Malaysia's Political Economy: Politics, Patronage and Profits*. Cambridge University Press.

Haraway, D. (2015). Anthropocene, Capitalocene, Plantationocene, Chthulucene: Making Kin. *Environmental Humanities*, 6(1): 159–165

Harwell E., Farah D., & Blundell A. (2011). *Forests, Fragility, and Conflict: Overview and Case Studies*. Washington, DC: World Bank

Purdy, J. (2015). *After Nature: A Politics for the Anthropocene*. Harvard University Press.

Robinson, J. A., Torvik, R., & Verdier, T. (2006). Political foundations of the resource curse. *Journal of Development Economics*, 79(2): 447–468.

Ross, M. L. (1999). The political economy of the resource curse. *World Politics*, 51(2): 297–322.

Ross, M. L. (2015). What have we learned about the resource curse? *Annual Review of Political Science*, 18, 239–259.

Runciman, S. *The White Rajah: A History of Sarawak from 1841 to 1946*. Cambridge University Press, 1960.

Sovacool, B. K., Walter, G., Van de Graaf, T., & Andrews, N. (2016). Energy governance, transnational rules, and the resource curse: exploring the effectiveness of the Extractive Industries Transparency Initiative (EITI). *World Development*, 83, 179–192.

18

From Inspiration to Implementation: *Laudato Si'*, Public Theology and the Demands of Energy Policy

Jonathan Chaplin[1]

18.1 INTRODUCTION

The papal encyclical *Laudato Si': On Care for our Common Home* (Pope Francis 2015) is of considerable significance in the evolution of public theology as the first encyclical devoted exclusively to environmental issues. Timed to influence the Paris summit on climate change in December 2015 (COP21), it is already set to become the most widely discussed magisterial document since Pope John Paul II's *Centesimus Annus* (Pope John Paul II 1991), occasioned by the collapse of communism.[2] Compared to many other such documents, the tenor of the 246-paragraph *Laudato Si'* is radical and passionate, deploying the full weight of magisterial authority behind an urgent summons to a far-reaching 'ecological conversion'[3] that should involve every person and every institution and potentially every aspect of human life. It has received widespread endorsement from many in the environmental movement (see, e.g., McKibben 2015).

In Chapter 5, I noted that one of the benefits for public theology of an interaction with the specific demands of a policy sector such as energy, is the challenge to come up with 'steps that are concretely available to the diverse individual and institutional energy actors which alone can effect change'. In this chapter, I offer a critical assessment of *Laudato Si'*, appreciating its capacity to inspire reflection and action towards 'good' energy policy, while also highlighting the institutional and policy

[1] This is a revised and abridged version of a two-part article published in *Comment*, a publication of the Canadian think tank Cardus (Chaplin 2015a, 2015b). It appears by permission of the editors of *Comment*.

[2] A 'magisterial' document is one propounded on the authority of the papal 'magisterium' or teaching authority. An 'encyclical' letter is one type of such document. It is not claimed to be 'infallible' although its positive moral teachings are held to be 'binding on the consciences' of Catholics, who are then granted a wide degree of autonomy in deciding how to put it into practice. Often, encyclicals are addressed more generally to 'all people of good will', as is this one.

[3] Pope Francis 2015, §216ff. Subsequent references in the text are to paragraph numbers of the encyclical. The term 'ecological conversion' was coined by John Paul II in 1991 (John Paul II 1991).

work it does not itself do but leaves those engaged in the construction and implementation of feasible energy policy to take up.

This is not, however, to suggest that it has so far proved impotent to generate concrete responses. For example, on the second anniversary of the encyclical, the Global Catholic Climate Movement (GCCM 2017) launched the 'Laudato Si' Pledge' aiming to mobilise one million Catholics to take action on climate change. Closer to the policy arena, it has also inspired two venture capitalists to launch the 'Laudato Si' Startup Challenge',[4] a 'tech accelerator' programme channelling private equity into initiatives to combat climate change. Energy is listed as the first of the seven designated areas open to bids. The goal is to 'take inspiration from the pope's encyclical, and make an investment in for-profit companies whose technology will make the world a better place' (Ungerleider 2017). Francis himself appealed for just such initiatives in an influential TED talk to technology firms in April 2017 (Wamsley 2017).

Yet such initiatives could still benefit from an elaboration of the inspiring content of *Laudato Si'* into more specific strategic environmental and energy policy guidelines. Further, gaining purchase on the strengths and limitations of one globally influential work of religious environmental thought – a rather specific type of 'case study' – may be instructive on how to bridge the often evident gap between the aspirations of normative environmental theory generally and the concrete requirements of implementation in what is, as the Introduction admits, one of the 'messier' areas of public policy.

18.2 *LAUDATO SI'* ON THE ECOLOGICAL CRISIS

Laudato Si' cannot be charged with settling for the platitudinous fence-sitting that sometimes vitiates ecclesial declarations on matters of public concern. It sides decisively with those who argue that we face not merely a series of discreet environmental 'issues', each supposedly solvable on its own terms by yet more technical fixes (§111), but rather a global 'ecological crisis' (§15) of unprecedented scale, complexity and severity, one mandating urgent and far-reaching responses. It gives no comfort to those who claim that concerns about environmental degradation are being exaggerated or are somehow generated by a global conspiracy of leftist megalomaniacal bureaucrats carrying most of the world's climate scientists in their pockets.[5]

The document is replete with forceful observations on many dimensions of the crisis and its impact on human life. It opens with familiar disturbing reminders of the multiple symptoms of the global environmental crisis, such as pollution, loss of biodiversity, global warming, depletion of non-renewable resources, deforestation and decline of fish stocks. Equally, it catalogues many of the damaging impacts of

4 www.laudatosichallenge.org/

5 It draws on the work of influential climate scientist John Stellenburger.

this crisis on human well-being, such as widening inequality, rising sea levels, corrosive consumerism and threats to local (especially indigenous) cultural communities powerless before larger economic forces (§145). We are caught, Francis holds, in 'a spiral of self-destruction' (§163).

> Doomsday predictions can no longer be met with irony or disdain ... The pace of consumption, waste and environmental change has so stretched the planet's capacity that our contemporary lifestyle, unsustainable as it is, can only precipitate catastrophes, such as those which even now periodically occur in different areas of the world. The effects of the present imbalance can only be reduced by our decisive action, here and now (§161).

Laudato Si' can thus also be read as an example, within public theology, of the genre of 'lament', which in Jewish and Christian theology is the necessary prelude to effective 'prophecy' – the summons to 'conversion'. Yet Francis avoids the bleak 'catastrophism' of voices such as the Dark Mountain project which asserts that 'ecocide' is already upon us.[6] For the 'prophecy' that follows 'lament', while it may warn of present 'judgment', is, in Francis' Christian theology, oriented to 'eschatological renewal': 'hope would have us recognise that there is always a way out, that we can always redirect our steps' (§61), that 'gestures of generosity, solidarity and care cannot but well up within us, since we are made for love' (§58). Ultimately, this is because the 'God who created the universe out of nothing can also intervene in this world and overcome every form of evil. Injustice is not invincible' (§74).

18.3 A THEOLOGY OF INTERCONNECTEDNESS

The spirit of the theology of *Laudato Si'* is metaphorically captured in the classic 'Franciscan' notion that 'our common home is like a sister with whom we share our life and a beautiful mother who opens her arms to embrace us' (§2), and that 'soil, water, mountains: everything is, as it were a caress of God' (§84). Its substantive content (not itself new) straddles a wide range of themes: cosmological, anthropological, sacramental, Trinitarian, Christological, contemplative, Marian and others. These echo several of the converging themes in wider religious ecological thought I identified in Chapter 5. They are presented as cohering around a notion of the 'interconnectedness' of all creatures, human and nonhuman – among themselves and with God (§66). 'Creation is of the order of love. God's love is the fundamental moving force in all created things ... Even the fleeting life of the least of beings is the object of his love, and in its few seconds of existence, God enfolds it with his affection' (§77).

Thus, in what is a challenge to a persisting Christian anthropocentrism, Francis asserts that organisms and ecosystems 'have an intrinsic value independent of their usefulness [to humans]' (§140). The current precipitous collapse of biodiversity of

6 http://dark-mountain.net/about/manifesto/

plants and animals, for example, is therefore at bottom a spiritual issue: 'Because of us, thousands of species will no longer give glory to God by their very existence, nor convey their message to us' (§33).[7]

This theology of a creational web of reciprocal interdependency is deployed to undergird a forceful denunciation of the secular modernist ideology of human 'mastery' over the nonhuman creation. The 'tyrannical anthropocentrism' (§68) this entails – the assertion of 'an unlimited right to trample [God's] creation underfoot' (§75) – is a repudiation of the proper posture of human creatures as those 'called to lead all creatures back to their Creator' (§83). Francis affirms this 'priestly' role of humans alongside their 'kingly' role as 'responsible steward' (§87) requiring them to 'till and keep' the earth – to cultivate and preserve it rather than ravage it for their own self-gratification (§§67, 82). *Pace* philosophies of eco-centrism, these roles are bestowed uniquely on humans as those 'made in the image of God' (§§60, 65, 78, 81).

The result of the human ravaging of creation is that 'the earth, our home, is beginning to look more and more like an immense pile of filth' (§21). We will only be fitted to take up our unique vocation of stewardship again if we are prepared to undergo an 'ecological conversion', the ramifications of which range from campaigning for political change at local, national and global levels – practising an 'ecological citizenship' (§211) – to refashioning our lifestyles by embodying an 'ecology of everyday life' (§147ff.) – for example, reducing our dependence on 'harmful habits of consumption', such as excessive air conditioning (§55).

18.4 ECOLOGICAL CRISIS AND SOCIETAL STRUCTURE: 'INTEGRAL ECOLOGY'

Building on these foundations, the diagnostic and constructive proposals of *Laudato Si'* are organised around the document's leitmotif, the notion of an 'integral ecology'. An integral ecology searches out the deep interconnections between environmental degradation and the social and economic forces that drive it. The 'environment' is not just an external physical reality, so often experienced at worst as a constraint or at best as a mere resource. Rather it is 'a relationship existing between nature and the society which lives in it … We are part of nature' (§139). The human and the natural environments sink or swim together, so that 'we cannot adequately combat environmental degradation unless we attend to causes related to human and social degradation' (§48). For 'one cannot prescind from humanity. There can be no renewal of our relationship with nature without a renewal of humanity itself. There can be no ecology without an adequate anthropology' (§118).

[7] This important nuance is missed in Weigel's technically correct statement that the encyclical is 'primarily about us, and not primarily about trees, plankton, and the Tennessee snail darter' (Weigel 2015).

This claim could, perhaps, be rendered more precise by utilising Karl Polanyi's notion of 'embeddedness'. Human society, we might say, is marked by a 'double embeddedness': as Polanyi argued, the economy does not, as neoclassical theory originally suggested, operate according to self-sustaining autonomous laws but is completely 'embedded' in a network of dependencies on myriad social practices and relationships (Polanyi 2001). Developing Polanyi, we can add that the whole of society, including the economy, is embedded in the enveloping and sustaining biophysical womb of non-human nature. An 'integral ecology' would not regard such double embeddedness as a constraint to be surmounted – as if the relationship between human ambition and creation's plenitude is one of competition or conflict – but receive it as a gift to be celebrated and honoured.

What, then, are the dominant social and economic forces wreaking such havoc with the environment, and on ourselves? Here Francis paints in arresting macro-level brush strokes illustrated by a series of evocative concrete micro-examples. I shall argue that, notwithstanding his often insightful large-scale diagnoses, what is missing is something in between: an adequate meso-level analysis, focused on specific institutional sectors, capable of linking the macro to the micro. Some might suggest that one should not look for such an analysis in an encyclical; indeed, such documents typically disavow the objective of offering 'technical' solutions. But it is precisely the force field between the macro and the micro generated in the document itself that actually mandates it. I briefly explore three institutional sectors where more work is evidently needed to bridge this gap: technology, states and markets.

18.5 MINDING THE GAP: TECHNOLOGY, THE MARKET AND THE STATE

18.5.1 *Technology*

The largest macro-stroke on Francis' canvas is the proposal that the ecological crisis reflects the cultural pathologies of a globalised 'dominant technocratic paradigm' (§101ff.). On the one hand, Francis praises the extraordinary advances brought to human life by modern science and technology as manifestations of a 'God-given creativity'. Yet, on the other, he argues that while formerly, the human use of nature was disciplined by receptivity, humility and partnership, today's awesome techno-scientific power has placed in human hands a 'dominance over the whole of humanity and the entire world' (§104). Our 'undifferentiated and one-dimensional' conception of technology (§106) reflects a radical shift in the human stance towards nature. We now treat it as a formless, wholly manipulable object containing infinitely extractable resources for the satisfaction of human desire (§106). The result is that 'technology tends to absorb everything into its ironclad logic' (§108) – even our relationship to our own bodies (§155). Our Promethean lust for unbounded human freedom thus entraps us in a new kind of subordination.

Francis' stark theological reading of modern technology is not entirely novel (and finds many parallels in secular critiques). It recalls, for example, the penetrating but bleak analysis already proposed in 1954 by French Christian sociologist Jacques Ellul in *The Technological Society*.[8] Francis' own source, however, is the austere Catholic modernity critic Romano Guardini, whose *The End of the Modern World* (1950) is cited several times. Francis seems to struggle here between determinism and hope: while today it is 'inconceivable' that we could promote the idea of technology as a mere instrument (§111), yet we still retain the freedom to put technology 'at the service of another type of progress, one which is ... more human, more social, more integral'. Citing the example of small, non-consumerist producer cooperatives using less polluting technologies, he yet holds out the hope that an 'authentic humanity ... seems to dwell in the midst of our technological culture, almost unnoticed, like a mist seeping gently beneath a closed door' (§§112).

Such small-scale initiatives are indeed urgently necessary, and not only in poorer countries. Yet what is also required is wider structural analysis of the nature of interdependencies – some of them constructive, others dangerously corrupting – between the various institutional players in the technocratic drama: science, corporations, capital markets, universities, the defence industry, governments and so forth. Only with the aid of such a middle-level institutional analysis are we able to provide meaningful guidance for those working within these demanding institutional settings on how to nudge an often domineering technology incrementally towards the alternative, 'integral' model of progress Francis calls for. The same point emerges when we examine the market and the state.

18.5.2 *The Market*

Francis' critique of the technological paradigm grounds a forceful critique of the pathologies and injustices of the contemporary global market economy. He argues that the conception of nature as an infinite storehouse of resources to meet human desires feeds the illusion of the possibility of unlimited economic growth, which in turn is the chief driver of the environmental and social degradations making up the ecological crisis (§106). Such a claim will be widely seen as plausible (even if in need of closer specification). It is illustrated by what appears to be our deep structural dependency on fossil fuels. For example, in his 2006 State of the Union address, President George W. Bush admitted as much in conceding frankly that 'we are addicted to oil' – while promptly adding that 'the best way to break this addiction is through technology'. Francis' call to wean ourselves off such fossil fuel dependency

[8] For a more constructive Christian critique, see Schuurman 1980.

'without delay' (§165) is increasingly accepted, even within sectors of the industry itself.

Yet the steps in this argument from technology to economy to ecology, however, need to be spelled out more carefully, as do the *specific* pathologies of the *particular* corporations, markets, consumption patterns and governmental actions which are converting 'illusion' into 'crisis'. Again, we need to do this if actors in the economy, many of whom genuinely intend to act responsibly, are to be given concrete guidance when faced with complex decisions under tight constraints. For example, Francis boldly asserts that 'the economy accepts every advance in technology with a view to profit, without concern for its potentially negative impact on human beings' (§109).

On the one hand, he is right to point out that, too often, new technologies are hastily introduced in order to maximise profits, even though they destroy the jobs of many who have no alternative sources of livelihood (§128). To respond by claiming that introducing such technology is *mandated* by the imperatives of global market competition would indeed amount to a form of what Francis calls 'idolatry'. But his assertion about the use of technology cannot be admitted without qualification. Many entrepreneurs are already motivated not first by profit maximisation but by a genuine concern for human welfare and seek to deploy technology to that end. Many businesses, especially small and medium-sized enterprises (SMEs), strive to protect the jobs of their employees even as they introduce new technologies. And even if intense market pressures mean that they do not (or cannot), government regulations increasingly require them at least to meet demanding, and costly, conditions protecting other dimensions of human and environmental well-being. The implied contrast between heroic small-scale cooperatives and the malign forces of the 'global technological paradigm' is an oversimplification. Thus, the technology required to develop renewable energy supplies (wind and wave turbines, photovoltaic panels, etc.) depends on advanced science, significant venture capital, market opportunities, government licensing and (sometimes) subsidy.

Three of Francis' other critiques of markets would be widely endorsed. One is that markets of themselves tend to 'externalise' many of the social and environmental costs of economic activity, either imposing them on the public at large or forcing governments to regulate or socialise them, often inadequately (§195). Another is that markets are inherently incapable of supplying certain categories of human need. Here Francis reiterates John Paul II and Benedict XVI's claim that markets alone cannot guarantee environmental common goods, integral human development or social justice (§§109, 190). This is a challenge to those who would seek to marketise as many public goods or services (health care, prisons) or natural resources (land, water, tropical forests) as possible. But while this is true, it must also be acknowledged that none of the above goods could be secured without *some* role, sometimes a prominent one, for markets.

A third claim, is that, left to themselves, market forces are unable to generate internal limits to economic growth or nurture new definitions of growth that would reflect a more integral view of 'progress' (§§191–194). Swimming against the tide, Francis ventures that 'the time has come to accept decreased growth in some parts of the world in order to provide resources for other places to experience healthy growth' (§193). That goal may be defensible (indeed some economists argue that it has already been forced upon us by our own economic mistakes). Again, however, a closer analysis is required of what is meant by 'growth' – Francis probably means *slower rates of* growth rather than negative growth; how Western nations can be brought to such a point through the proper 'statecraft' he calls for; and how, given that growth is not a global zero-sum game, that might translate into benefits for non-Western economies.

Here, Francis' colourful attacks on a 'magical conception of the market' (§190) or 'deified markets' need to be supplemented, to say the least, by more discriminating analyses of the variety of markets that actually exist. Some are relatively open and healthily dynamic, others deeply distorted by oligopolies (the UK energy market excessively dominated by the 'big six'), or dangerously volatile (financial markets prior to 2008) (§189).

Francis' passionate criticisms of economic inequality – both between developed and less developed nations, and within both – and his championing of the rights of the poor, are exemplary. He urges that the voice of the poorest of the world be heard much more loudly in environmental debates than they usually are (§48). They, after all, are the ones set to bear the brunt of the environmental fecklessness of Western nations. They are owed an enormous 'ecological debt' (§51), yet in such debates 'they frequently remain at the bottom of the pile' (§49). Yet while he does acknowledge, in passing, that 'business is a noble vocation' (§129), his analyses would carry greater weight if he also acknowledged that those countries with dynamic market economies – those where the rule of law facilitates entrepreneurial initiative and enforceable contracts, where markets are not excessively constrained by governments, which are open to international trade and which are weaning themselves off corporatism, clientelism and corruption – have contributed greatly to lifting millions out of poverty over the last thirty years, albeit not without heavy costs to some.

In fleshing out what model of political economy might incorporate these varying concerns, Francis might in the first instance simply have seized on the promising insights contained in his predecessor Benedict XVI's landmark 2009 encyclical *Caritas in Veritate*.[9] One of its key sources is the distinctive stream of economic thought emerging from the Italian 'civil economy' school associated with economists such as Luigino Bruni and Stefano Zamagni (Bruni and Zamagni 2007), which has in turn inspired the work of, inter alia, British 'Blue Labour' thinkers such as Maurice Glasman and Adrian Pabst (Geary and Pabst 2015) and 'Red Tory'

[9] Geary and Pabst 2015.

initiatives such as the think tank *ResPublica*.[10] Such work at least makes possible a conversation about the kind of strategic policy objectives at issue in the quest for 'good energy policy'.

18.5.3 *The State*

Francis urges the need for a 'new politics' that will be marked by three things: first, resistance to the distorting imperatives of 'an efficiency-driven paradigm of technocracy' and the power of large corporate interests; second, far-sightedness and integral thinking; third, freedom from corruption, more transparency and a positive seeking out of the voices of those most affected by political decisions, especially the poor (§§183, 189, 197) – the latter concern occasioning the specific injunction that 'environmental impact assessments' (EIAs), in which local voices are heard, should be carried out before and not after an environmentally risky development or policy is adopted (§183).

The encyclical does not, however, include a dedicated discussion of the environmental role of the state as such. Yet it does, explicitly or implicitly, call upon states and other tiers of political authority to implement a wide range of environmental policies, pursuant to the common good. Government, he says, has a 'proper and inalienable responsibility to preserve its country's environment and natural resources, without capitulating to spurious local or international interests' (§38).

That general claim will be widely endorsed. One telling example he cites of where it is likely that public authorities will need to play a leading role is in guaranteeing clean water supplies (§30) – one of the most basic of human 'common good[s]'. Another is the claim that political authorities 'have the right and duty to adopt clear and firm measures in support of small producers and differentiated production'. These, he claims, are easily threatened by the predatory designs of large corporations who, taking advantage of economies of scale, force smallholders to sell their land and abandon traditional production methods which are not only vital sources of employment but also more ecologically responsible (§129).

But even in these relatively clear cases, and much more so on more complex ones, difficult questions arise regarding what threshold of environmental risk or damage, or what degree of distortion by vested interests, is required to trigger a political intervention. For political authorities cannot oversee or respond to every possible environmental transgression. Once such a threshold (however defined) is reached, the next question is which among the many available policy instruments – proscription, prescription or permission; regulation or citizen empowerment; taxation, incentive or subsidy, etc. – should be deployed to address the problem in view.

While, as noted, encyclicals typically disavow competence to offer detailed answers to such questions (§188), they are more helpful when the overall direction

10 www.respublica.org.uk/

of travel they want to commend is clearly signposted. For example, Francis quite specifically criticises carbon trading schemes (§171), and he is not alone in doing so. But then one looks for clear criteria as to why some specifics like this, or EIAs, are singled out for blame or praise while other, equally important ones (such as tax perks for fossil fuel energy providers), are not, and why, on yet others (such as GM crops) the document remains agnostic (§134). Again, Francis is good at citing telling examples of desirable concrete outcomes of policy but less assured when it comes to sketching the institutional routes by which those outcomes can be secured. Consider three further examples.

First, he is eloquent on the acute deprivations and indignities experienced by many people living in the world's exploding 'mega-cities' (§148). He generously praises those poor urban communities which practice solidarity even while living in a 'hell on earth' (§148–9). Many would support his call to give priority to public over private transport (§153), since crowded urban spaces are evidently common goods that mandate governmental oversight. But apart from a passing mention of 'urban planning', he offers no analysis of how the many other agencies within cities might work in complementary ways to improve urban conditions.

Second, he rightly alerts us to the chronic lack of adequate and sanitary housing in many nations. But the implication is that this is first of all a matter for governments: 'Lack of housing is a grave problem . . . *since state budgets* usually cover only a small portion of the demand' (§152; my emphasis). He offers no commentary on the indispensable roles of commercial property developers and non-profit housing associations, nor on a theme we might have expected a pope to notice, namely the fact that the reduction in the size of households, due, for example, to declining marriage rates or rising divorce rates, is a key factor in putting pressure on housing markets, especially in the West.

Third, Francis powerfully endorses the need for binding international environmental agreements. He rightly praises successful treaties on hazardous wastes, trade in endangered species and the ozone layer (§168), while lamenting the lack of progress on biodiversity, desertification, deterioration of oceans and climate change. His key concerns here are efficacy (better integration and implementation of agreements), persistence (in the face of stubborn national and corporate self-interest), and, most of all, global equity. The burdens of addressing climate change should fall most heavily on those most responsible for it and not further penalise poorer nations by, for example, expecting them to pay the full costs of a transition from fossils fuels to renewable energy (§165, 170–172).

All of these seem convincing examples of those 'global commons' for which adequate protection will require (among many other initiatives) binding and enforceable global political agreements (§173). Francis is right that these are achievable only through determined and patient diplomacy and through 'stronger and more efficiently organised international institutions'.

But we may hesitate, however, at his more expansive calls for 'one world with a common plan' and, reiterating Benedict XVI and John XXIII, for 'a true world political authority' (§175). The *singular* article in these assertions will be troubling to many charged with designing global environmental and energy policies. On the one hand, if the emerging international order is to be better equipped to address pressing threats to global common goods, it will certainly need an increasingly well-coordinated array of more powerful political agencies and authorities. On the other, only by maintaining a *plurality* of such entities will the risk of a slide into some unwieldly and/or authoritarian world state be forestalled. The way forward can surely only be through dogged, long-term incremental negotiated reforms to the existing sluggish, underperforming and sometimes badly dysfunctional institutions of the United Nations.

The other lacuna in the document's treatment of political authorities is that it does not sufficiently spell out how many of the eminently desirable goals on which it urges international political consensus – sustainable and diversified agriculture, renewable energy, better management of marine and forest resources, access to drinking water (§164), the elimination of poverty (§175) and more – are already being advanced, and could only ever be further realised, through the primary initiatives of non-governmental entities: enterprises (commercial and social), universities and research institutes, trade unions, households and many more. Precisely how political authorities might collaborate with, support, regulate, constrain – or just leave alone – these entities is the central challenge for any area of public policy. Laudably, Francis praises and endorses, more than any other pope, the campaigning and oppositional efforts of grass-roots community organisations towards such goals (§§179–181, 206). He might also have given greater prominence to the indispensable role of those other organisations which will usually be the ones actually delivering the desired results.

18.5.4 *Challenges Ahead*

The absence of adequate meso-level structural analyses of technology, markets, states (and other institutional sectors) in *Laudato Si'* is somewhat puzzling, not least because Francis could have begun to remedy the deficit merely by making better use of the existing battery of Catholic social principles.

Some of these principles are invoked effectively, notably the 'common good'. Thus, the natural environment is cited as 'a collective good, the patrimony of all humanity and the responsibility of everyone' (§95). Three further implications of the common good are also cited. One is the need to respect the 'dignity of the person', from which flow, for example, the right to life (§120) and the right to work (§§94, 124ff.). Another is concern for the 'overall welfare of society', including its intermediate groups (notably the family) pursuant to the principle of 'subsidiarity'. A third is the need for a 'social peace', including 'distributive justice' (which also implies a duty of justice to future generations (§159)). Given current global injustices, 'the principle of the common good immediately becomes ... a summons to solidarity and a preferential option for the poorest ... ' (§157). For God calls humanity to a 'universal communion' (§89ff.), and thus to the principle of the 'subordination of private property to the universal destination of goods and ... the right of everyone to their use' (§93).

Yet there is no sustained demonstration of how these foundational Catholic social principles might explicitly inform a structural analysis of the causes of the ecological crisis or point us to the institutional remedies to it. Reno may exaggerate when he claims that the document contains 'no clearly articulated principles guiding analysis of the ecological and social crises precipitated by global capitalism', but he is right to complain that it 'begs for analysis in terms of the classical notions of solidarity and subsidiarity' (Reno 2015).

Subsidiarity gets only half a paragraph. The principle, we are reminded, 'grants freedom to develop the capabilities present at every level of society' (§196). Readers might miss that this, in fact, is the reason for the strong preference in Catholic social thought for an open (if 'social') market economy over a state-dominated one. Francis then immediately warns, rightly, that the principle also demands 'a greater sense of responsibility for the common good from those who wield greater power'. But what subsidiarity might further imply for a normative framework of state–business relationships in a globalising market economy is left unaddressed.

There are also occasional references to 'solidarity', but the structural implications of this evocative term are left unexplored – even though much of the document's diagnosis of society is in effect an extended lament on the destruction of human solidarity. Francis cites Benedict XVI's striking statement that 'every violation of solidarity ... harms the environment'. He then rightly adds that 'social ecology is necessarily institutional [gradually extending] from the primary social group, the family, to the wider local, national and international communities' (§142). But he passes by the opportunity to draw on the Catholic tradition's extensive body of reflection on plural intermediate communities as distinctive sites of solidarity, each oriented to a particular dimension of human flourishing. Had he done so, he might have been able to outline how failures of solidarity both within and between these communities generate specific manifestations of environmental irresponsibility – agribusiness using polluting fertilisers, unions clinging on to fossil fuel employment, etc. – and how they might offer distinctive forms of ecological renewal, including suitable energy policies pursuant to that goal, where, as so often, multiple actors with very diverse responsibilities are involved. Some of the ingredients of such renewal are mentioned here and there, for example, the educative role of the family and religious communities towards an 'ecological spirituality' (§§213–214, 216ff.), and the environmentally friendly practices of small cooperatives. But they are not integrated into a larger account based on a coherent set of social principles.

For those engaged in energy policy who might find genuine inspiration in Francis' stirring summons to 'ecological conversion', then, there remains much work to do in moving from inspiration to implementation. The task is to elaborate, in much greater depth and detail, the concrete implications of this summons for the complex social, economic, political and technological factors that generate and sustain bad energy policies and for the fitting and feasible policy responses that will promote better ones.

18.6 REFERENCES

Bruni, Luigino and Zamagni, Stefano (2007). *Civil Economy: Efficiency, Equity, Public Happiness*. Bern: Peter Lang.

Bush, President George W. (2006). 'State of the Union' address, 31 January 2006, https://georgewbush-whitehouse.archives.gov/stateoftheunion/2006/, accessed 9 October 2017.

Chaplin, Jonathan (2015). '*Laudato Si'*: Structural Causes of the Ecological Crisis', *Comment* (24 September and 1 October), www.cardus.ca/comment/article/4697/laudato-si-structural-causes-of-the-ecological-crisis/ and www.cardus.ca/comment/article/4715/laudato-si-structural-causes-of-the-ecological-crisis-part-ii/, accessed 9 October 2017.

GCCM (Global Catholic Climate Movement) (2017). 'Laudato Si' Pledge Launched to Mobilize 1 Million Catholics on Climate Change', https://catholicclimatemovement.global/pr-laudato-si-pledge/, accessed 9 October 2017.

Geary, Ian and Pabst, Adrian (2015). *Blue Labour: Forging a New Politics*. London: I. B. Tauris.

Guardini, Romano (2001 [1956]). *The End of the Modern World*. Wilmington, Delaware: ISI Books.

McKibben, Bill (2015). 'The Pope and the Planet'. *New York Review of Books*, 13 August, www.nybooks.com/articles/2015/08/13/pope-and-planet/, accessed 9 October 2017.

Pentin, Edward (2015). 'Full Text and Guidance Map for Pope Francis' Encyclical '*Laudato Si'*'', *National Catholic Register*, 17 June, www.ncregister.com/blog/edward-pentin/full-text-of-laudato-si-and-guidance-notes, accessed 9 October 2017.

Polanyi, Karl (2001 [1944]). *The Great Transformation: The Political and Economic Origins of Our Times*. Boston: Beacon Press.

Pope Benedict XVI (2009). *Caritas in Veritate*, http://w2.vatican.va/content/benedict-xvi/en/encyclicals/documents/hf_ben-xvi_enc_20090629_caritas-in-veritate.html, accessed 9 October 2017.

Pope Francis (2015). *Laudato Si': On Care for our Common Home*, http://w2.vatican.va/content/francesco/en/encyclicals/documents/papa-francesco_20150524_enciclica-laudato-si.html, accessed 15 April 2016.

Pope John Paull II (2001). General Audience 17 January, http://w2.vatican.va/content/john-paul-ii/en/audiences/2001/documents/hf_jp-ii_aud_20010117.html, accessed 9 October 2017.

Reno, R.R. (2015). 'The Weakness of *Laudato Si'*. *First Things*, 1 July, www.firstthings.com/web-exclusives/2015/07/the-weakness-of-laudato-si, accessed 9 October 2017.

Schuurman, Egbert (1980), *Technology and the Future: A Philosophical Challenge*. Toronto: Wedge.

Ungerleider, Neal (2017). 'Inside the Vatican-Blessed Tech Accelerator Tackling Climate Change', *Fast Company*, 6 June, www.fastcompany.com/40424655/inside-the-vaticans-tech-accelerator-thats-targeting-climate-change, accessed 9 October 2017.

Wamsley, Laurel (2017). 'In Surprise TED Talk, Pope Francis Asks the Powerful for "Revolution of Tenderness"', *NPR* 17 April, www.npr.org/sections/thetwo-way/2017/04/26/525699847/in-surprise-ted-talk-pope-francis-asks-the-powerful-for-revolution-of-tenderness, accessed 9 October 2017.
Weigel, George (2015). 'The Pope's Encyclical, At Heart, Is about *Us*, Not Trees and Snail Darters'. *National Review*, 18 June, www.nationalreview.com/article/419933/popes-encyclical-heart-about-us-not-trees-and-snail-darters-george-weigel, accessed 9 October 2017.

18.7 RESPONSE TO 'FROM INSPIRATION TO IMPLEMENTATION: *LAUDATO SI'*, PUBLIC THEOLOGY AND THE DEMANDS OF ENERGY POLICY'

By Vladimir Kmec

This chapter by Jonathan Chaplin discusses the papal encyclical *Laudato Si'* while highlighting its capacity to inspire for action, including on the side of decision and policy makers, towards 'good' energy policy. Chaplin praises the significance of the encyclical for public theology. This acclamation unequivocally extends to the field of politics and international relations. The encyclical was published in the wake of the Paris summit in 2015 which adopted the Paris Agreement on climate change committing states to undertake efforts to combat climate change. While the purpose of the encyclical was to influence the decision makers at the Paris summit, its value appears to be more momentous in the post-summit times of turbulent political changes with the Trump administration denouncing global warming and even dropping it from the list of global threats in the US national security strategy.

According to Chaplin, Francis' reflection on the global ecological crisis with its multiple dimensions and the damaging impacts of this crisis caused by human activity on society, humans and the world can be read as a form of a lament, a prophecy and hope at the same time. Chaplin summarises the main ideas of the encyclical, starting with the theological understanding of the interconnectedness of the ecological world. This perspective extends to the idea of an integral ecology which highlights the interlinkage between environmental degradation and the social and economic forces that drive it. Chaplin discusses the main arguments of the encyclical on technology, the global economy, the state and ecology. The author emphasises Francis' reflections on the advantages and disadvantages of technology with regard to ecology and his call towards an 'integral' model of technological progress. The reflection provides a ground for Francis' critique of the injustices of the contemporary global market economy. Francis' arguments shed light on what kind of economic models and technologies can make 'good' energy policy possible.

However, Chaplin disapproves of Francis' one-sided view that the economy uses advances in technology to generate economic profit without any concern for its potentially negative impact. He notes that advances in technology and science as well as market opportunities, government licensing and capital are often necessary to develop renewable energy systems. Chaplin criticises Francis for being good at highlighting impressive examples of desirable policy outcomes but not offering solutions on institutional changes for the realisation of such outcomes. He also argues that the encyclical could benefit from more references to advancements in efforts to combat climate change. Chaplin correctly observes that the notion of the interconnectedness between technology, the economy and ecology is not new. From a theological perspective, the encyclical builds on the ideas of theologians such as Pierre Teilhard de Chardin, Jürgen Moltmann, Paul Tillich and others, especially those from the field of eco-theology.

Despite the criticism, it is perhaps too ambitious to expect a theological document to be rigorously scientific and grounded in political economy. Neither is the aim of such a document to provide concrete policy solutions, which Chaplin agrees with. Although Chaplin wishes the Pope was more vocal about the environmental role of the state, though acknowledging that the encyclical calls upon political authorities to implement environmental policies, it is important to note that the document is not a political manifesto. An encyclical is a statement by a pope outlining the position and doctrine of the Catholic Church. *Laudato Si'* presents the theological, ethical and philosophical doctrine of the Church on climate change issues. It is different from statements by intergovernmental organisations and governments, which are expected to have direct policy implications. From the perspective of international relations, the encyclical simply adds to the catalogue of similar documents which discuss climate change and emphasise the necessity to fight it.

Nevertheless, this does not diminish its value, as clearly emphasised by Chaplin. As a document open to the international audience, the encyclical contributes to the international debate on climate change and environmental issues. It does not stay at the level of the theoretical reflection; it moves to actively calling upon society, individuals and leaders to engage in efforts to combat climate change and ecological injustice. As Chaplin notes, the core message of the document is the notion of an 'ecological conversion' that should involve every person, every institution and every aspect of human life. The value of this document lies with the capacity of the Church to advocate the message of combating climate change to the world. As a transnational community, the Catholic Church has important social and advocacy functions. It impacts on political systems and political decisions in many countries. As a charismatic religious leader enjoying high respect worldwide, the Pope can influence political decisions on the world stage.

The encyclical is mainly directed towards the members of the Catholic Church. With its almost 1.3 billion members, this community of people adhering to the same faith is endowed with a powerful voice to influence the opinion of its believers, which can impact on ethical standards and state policies. The purpose of this document lies in its ability to inspire for a religiously and ethically motivated mobilisation concerning climate change. The implementation of this doctrine is dependent on the agency and responsibility of individuals and religious communities. In a religiously pluralistic world, a united voice of religious leaders, which requires a strengthened ecumenical and interreligious cooperation, to appeal to their followers could enhance the effectiveness of such a call. Religious communities possess a wide range of modalities for the realisation of the call to combat climate change and ecological injustice. With a view that every change starts at the local level, they can, for example, take civic actions, implement their own good energy policies in their parishes, provide training to their members on good practices and engage in constructive dialogue with local and state authorities. By inspiring such a grass-roots engagement, the encyclical can find its added value in supporting national and international efforts to implement good energy policies.

PART III

Multidisciplinary Cases

19

Introduction to Multidisciplinary Approaches

Marc Ozawa and Michael Pollitt

Up to this point, the information and cases presented have been bi-disciplinary, so to speak. We have endeavoured to draw out insights on energy policy topics by introducing them from the perspectives of a variety of disciplines. Additionally, these cases received comments from respondents coming from different disciplines. This approach is a first step towards a multidisciplinary approach. In Part III, the editors and some of the authors aim to push this forward towards a multidisciplinary analysis. This is a natural development in the approach we have taken by first identifying cases that would benefit from an analysis of multiple disciplines. Next, we identified authors that were willing to make a conceptual jump in opening their analyses to scrutiny and investigation from colleagues in other departments and universities. A blind peer review is the standard approach to academic critique, but extending this to other disciplines is less common, and we wish to thank the contributing authors for agreeing to participate in this added level of critical analysis.

The aim of this chapter is two-fold. First, we present a practical application of multidisciplinary research as we, the editors, experienced when preparing this book and the two cases that comprise this section. There are many theoretical accounts of how one may approach multidisciplinary research, but here we offer a practical account of how the theoretical goal of multidisciplinary research can play out in the 'real world'. Throughout this book, we have presented cases and perspectives with the aim of identifying common points in each case that may be approached from two or more disciplines from the social sciences and humanities. This is a step towards bridging disciplines that are not inherently 'bridging disciplines'. As Youngblood notes, there are some disciplines that share traits of interdisciplinarity.

> It should be recognized that all disciplines have not followed parallel pathways. Some are, by nature, bridging disciplines. Bridging disciplines involve domains so broad as to encompass the physical and social sciences as well as the humanities. Two such disciplines are geography and anthropology.[1]

[1] Dawn Youngblood, 'Multidisciplinarity, Interdisciplinarity, and Bridging Disciplines: A Matter of Process', *Journal of Research Practice* 3, no. 2 (5 December 2007): 2.

Within the academic discussions, the terms multidisciplinary and interdisciplinary are often interchangeable. In a recent study by Choi and Pak,[2] they acknowledge that the terms, and how they are used, have depended on the context of the literature. Choi and Pak group them into three categories, as 'dictionary definitions', 'definitions in online literature' and 'definitions in peer-reviewed publications'. Considering the context of this book and the fact that the contributing authors are all academic writers, we ascribe to the 'peer-reviewed publications' distinction between multidisciplinary and interdisciplinary according to Flinterman et al., which is a common starting point in the academic literature.

> In multidisciplinary research, a variety of disciplines collaborate in one research program without integration of concepts, epistemologies, or methodologies. The degree of integration between disciplines is restricted to the linking of research results.[3]
>
> Interdisciplinary research is a collaboration of several disciplines, but in this case concepts, methodologies, or epistemologies are explicitly exchanged and integrated, resulting in a mutual enrichment.[4]

We also recognise that there are different processes of putting together a multidisciplinary research project. As Youngblood notes:

> No discipline is an island entire in itself. That is to say, disciplines are by no means discrete entities–they necessarily overlap, borrow, and encroach upon one another. Within each discipline are sub-disciplines that may behave with as great a sense of separation as exists between separately defined disciplines.[5]

To this end, the two cases comprising this section also had varying degrees of face-to-face communication, and the direction and leadership style of the lead authors were also different. For example, the first case on air pollution trends had a lead author who coordinated the research and defined the structure of the chapter at the beginning of the process. The second case on the Eurasian pipeline, Power of Siberia, had more of a lead coordinating author who guided discussions among the authors and integrated different pieces of the chapter rather than defining a structure at the outset. In the case of the latter, the process was one of discovery, and a structure emerged over the course of time. Based on the definitions of multidisciplinary versus interdisciplinary research, we recognise that Chapter 20 may resemble more interdisciplinary work whereas the latter is more of a 'collaboration of different disciplines' where there is not one dominant discipline or perspective. But the process teaches us that the distinction between interdisciplinarity and

[2] Bernard C K Choi and Anita W P Pak, 'Multidisciplinarity, Interdisciplinarity and Transdis-Ciplinarity in Health Research, Services, Education and Policy: 1. Definitions, Objectives, and Evidence of Effectiveness', *Clin Invest Med* 29, no. 6 (2006): 354.

[3] Choi and Pak *op cit.*

[4] Choi and Pak *op cit.*

[5] Youngblood *op cit.*

multidisciplinarity is not black or white, but rather resembles a spectrum with projects oftentimes falling somewhere between these two poles. The experience has also taught us the importance of communication and the value of face-to-face communication above all. As Klein explained, 'Expert praxis does not lie in generic formulas. It emerges from communicative actions in an iterative process that requires collaborative readiness, robust platforms, negotiation of differences, management of conflict, collective communication competence (CCC), mutual learning, interactions in trading zones of language communities, and construction of common ground.'[6] This may explain why Cummings and Kiesler found that multidisciplinary articles that were conducted within a university had a greater success rate in academic publishing than multi-university studies because the context of collaborating and communicating within one university, however solid or porous the wall barriers between departments, was still easier to coordinate than between universities.[7] It should be noted that Chapter 20 by Lam et al. was a collaboration between faculty from two universities, the University of Cambridge and the University of Hong Kong. Because of the favourable circumstances unique to this case, namely the deeper collaboration between the two universities and the significant time spent by authors in the partners' institutions, the editors do not believe that inter-university collaboration posed an obstacle to effective communication.

In the next sections of this chapter, we discuss the process by which the authors organised their research project and conducted their research. We will focus on four dimensions of this process that will hopefully be instructive to other researchers who wish to conduct multidisciplinary research. These include the process of selecting the topic, how the team was organised, what each author contributed to the project through her or his individual discipline, and finally, the communication process.

19.1 TWO TEAMS, TWO UNIVERSITIES AND TWO COUNTRIES

The topic for Chapter 20 is 'A Comparative Study of Air Quality in London (1950–1966) and Beijing (2000–2016)'. This topic arose from two sets of conversations. The first was the foundational set of conversations around the 'In Search of "Good" Energy Policy' grand challenge. Two of the editors, economist Michael Pollitt and historian Paul Warde, had an initial conversation in January 2015 in which the 1956 UK Clean Air Act emerged as an excellent historical case study in 'good' energy policy. The case study had the richness to stand scrutiny from a large number of disciplines, was recent enough to be reasonably well documented, but

[6] Julie Thompson Klein, 'Communication and Collaboration in Interdisciplinary Research', in *Enhancing Communication and Collaboration in Interdisciplinary Research* (London: Sage, 2014), 11, https://msu.edu/~orourk51/800-Phil/Handouts/Readings/ID/02-Orourke.pdf.

[7] Jonathon N. Cummings and Sara Kiesler, 'Collaborative Research across Disciplinary and Organizational Boundaries', in *Scientific Collaboration on the Internet*, ed. Gary M. Olson, Ann Zimmerman, and Nathan Bos (The MIT Press, 2008), 98, https://doi.org/10.7551/mitpress/9780262151207.003.0006.

yet under-researched from a multidisciplinary perspective. In the course of the first year of our seminar series hosted at the Centre for Research in the Arts, Social Sciences and Humanities (CRASSH), we had a talk about the case (in November 2015) and ended up writing our first multidisciplinary study on this.[8] The second set of conversations took place in the context of our emerging collaboration with the University of Hong Kong (HKU), Department of Electrical and Electronic Engineering. In the course of 2015, Jacqueline Lam (a social scientist) from HKU, was a visiting scholar at the University of Cambridge at the same time as we were thinking about the In 'Search' of Good Energy Policy grand challenge. Jacqueline was working with her colleague Victor Li (an electrical engineer) on air pollution in China. Severe air pollution in Beijing since 2000 serves as a case study where policy makers have struggled, in spite of extensive legislative effort, to have the same impressive effect on air quality that was observed in London following 1956. This collaboration between HKU and the University of Cambridge has now blossomed with the formation of the HKU-Cambridge Clean Energy and Environment Research Platform (CEERP) in November 2015 and a number of exchanges both ways between the two universities. CEERP adopted the subject of this chapter as one of its research projects, within a wider project looking at clean air policy in China. This project involved an economist (Michael Pollitt) and an historian (Paul Warde) from Cambridge and a social scientist (Jacqueline Lam) and an engineer (Victor Li) from HKU. When the editors of this volume were looking for a multidisciplinary chapter this was an obvious chapter to commission under the circumstances.

In terms of writing the paper, the HKU team, one of whom was spending a significant amount of time as a visiting scholar at Cambridge, took the lead on drafting both the London and Beijing sections. The HKU team also recruited a Cambridge MPhil student, Shanshan Wang, as a research assistant and co-author to undertake archival work in the UK, and an HKU PhD student and co-author, Han Yang, to assist with the air-pollution data analysis. The HKU focus was on the challenge of the measurement of air quality in two different cities over two different time periods. With advice from the historian on the team they led archival research on the London data and spent significant amounts of time trying to organise and format the air pollution data from Beijing with advice from the team's economist. We had a significant number of iterations of the paper where we tried to balance up the historical discussion with the discussion of contemporary Beijing. This involved a lot of editorial input from the economist and the historian. The historian provided detailed input on the historical literature and exactly what could be said and could not be said about the London experience. The economist concentrated on comparability issues.

8 Chaplin, J., Lewins, T., Newbery, N., Ozawa, M., Pollitt, M. G., Reiner, D. M., Vinuales, J. E., Warde, P. and de Wouters, I. (2016), In Search of 'Good' Energy Policy: Multi-disciplinary approaches to the UK's 1956 Clean Air Act, mimeo.

The HKU team was very attuned to the international attention to air quality in China and to issues regarding the representativeness of the air quality data the team obtained, and the central–local relationship between the extensive legislation on clean air and the difficulty of enforcement.

The paper followed a well-trodden process for a multi-authored paper in science and engineering: that is one or two of the authors doing most of the 'heavy lifting'. However, what was perhaps more unusual was that the original idea for the paper was the result of a deep multidisciplinary engagement within the University of Cambridge and between two universities, HKU and Cambridge. There was also a long-running process of editing the draft paper, which resulted in substantial changes, involving all four of the disciplinary specialists. The process was enjoyable but challenging and illustrates the importance of picking a good topic for a multidisciplinary engagement, one that is rich enough to be worth exploring from multiple perspectives.

19.2 FIVE DISCIPLINES ACROSS ONE UNIVERSITY

The topic for Chapter 21 is 'The Power of Siberia: A Eurasian Pipeline Policy "Good" for Whom?' The authors arrived at this topic over the course of a variety of academic activities that began with conversations that one of the editors, Michael Pollitt, joined by the head of Energy@Cambridge, Isabelle de Wouters, conducted with faculty across the University of Cambridge along with industry and government stakeholders prior to the establishment of the In Search of 'Good' Energy programme at the University of Cambridge. These conversations aimed to solicit suggestions from a variety of groups on which topics would be of interest to both academics and practitioners from a multidisciplinary perspective. These initial conversations took place in 2015 and 2016, shortly after the Ukraine crisis and the Russian government's announcement that it had concluded a price negotiation with Chinese partners and intended to begin construction of an interlinking pipeline network between the Russian Far East region and China. At the time, the global price of oil, to which the natural gas price negotiations were indexed, was lower than the above $100 per barrel mark but still well above the $60–65 per barrel range at the time of this book's publication. These factors all contributed to the interest in what was going on in Eurasia then, and continuing to this day as infrastructure is still under construction.

After the first round of conversations, Energy@Cambridge, a university-wide Interdisciplinary Research Centre that supports multidisciplinary research activities, adopted In Search of 'Good' Energy Policy as a research theme and initiated a series of multidisciplinary seminars hosted at CRASSH. The speaker who presented the topic of Eurasian pipelines, Jonathan Stern from the Oxford Institute for Energy Studies, framed the discussion in terms of geopolitics, and four out of the six co-authors of this chapter took part in this seminar.

Shortly after the seminar, the lead author, Marc Ozawa, engaged in a series of individual conversations with the other co-authors who had attended this seminar. Over the course of several face-to-face discussions, the lead author then organised a workshop with the goal of devising a structure for a joint research paper on the topic of Eurasian pipelines broadly. Each of the co-authors had, in a sense, self-selected to participate in the workshop because of their interest in the topic as demonstrated by their participation in the seminar. These individuals included two political scientists (Kun-Chin Lin and Marc Ozawa), one economist (Chi Kong Chyong) and one regional studies expert on energy and the Arctic from the Scott Polar Institute (Tim Reilly). In preparation for the workshop, two of these individuals invited two other researchers to participate, given their known interest in the topic. They included one anthropologist (Caroline Humphrey) and one researcher from the geography department (Corine Wood-Donnelly). All of the co-authors were faculty and researchers from the University of Cambridge.

The structure of the workshop was an open discussion with two goals. The first was to identify a research question that would be worthwhile exploring in a multidisciplinary context. The second was to devise a structure for the paper and to the degree it would be possible, assign sections to the individuals. Considering that the lead author had repeated communications with most of the others, this allowed for the discussion to begin at a more advanced point. The workshop lasted over the course of one day, and four out of six authors stayed for the entire day. At the conclusion of the workshop, the group agreed to a research question, focusing on whether new pipeline infrastructure was good for the region, and 'good' defined by the most common criteria in each of the five disciplines represented. It should be noted that the research question and scope of the paper subsequently evolved after follow-up face-to-face discussions and email exchanges. The workshop was the only time that the entire group met. The rest of the communication took place face-to-face between the lead author and one or two co-authors. Email exchanges were among the entire group.

The evolution of the topic began with Eurasian pipelines for the region and then shifted to a narrower scope, examining infrastructure between Russia and China. Finally, the topic and scope narrowed again to the form that the chapter addresses, focusing on the case of one pipeline, Power of Siberia, from the perspective of Russia primarily, and China secondarily. This evolution was due in large part to the expertise of the co-authors who had more expertise on Russia than China. The second factor was simple tractability. Examining the pipeline on both sides of the border from multiple disciplinary perspectives was simply not possible given the word limit of a single chapter. The constraints of the topic and scope gradually and naturally became apparent in the course of communication and also in the process of putting drafts together. This reinforces the notion that 'expert praxis does not lie in generic formulas'.[9] As Klein explains, '[expert praxis] emerges from communicative

9 Klein *op cit*: 11.

actions in an iterative process that requires collaborative readiness . . . "[10] The process for writing the chapter resembled this iterative process. Each author submitted a draft of her/his individual section. The lead author then integrated the sections, offered suggestions and did minor editing. Next, the lead author circulated the completed draft among the authors, who responded to suggestions, revised their sections and offered their own suggestions for how to improve the paper. The chapter went through five iterations of this process in total.

[10] Klein *op cit*: 11.

20

A Comparative Study of Air Pollution Trends in Historical London and Contemporary Beijing

Jacqueline CK Lam[*], *Yang Han, Shanshan Wang, Victor OK Li, Michael Pollitt and Paul Warde*[#]

20.1 INTRODUCTION

In this chapter, we compare the air pollution trends in historical London and contemporary Beijing due to two characteristics they shared. First, air pollution was a serious problem in London during the 1950s and in Beijing during the 2000s, marked by very frequent pollution episodes, especially during the winter. In both London and Beijing, coal was the main source of air pollution, due to coal-fired electricity generation and coal burning activities to provide heating. Second, decreasing trends of smoke/PM_{10} equivalent concentrations were observed after strong air pollution control regulations and policies were introduced in the respective cities. It is thus valuable to compare and contrast the air qualities in these two cities and determine if their respective air pollution control regulations/policies were effective, and how the results of air pollution control differed in each case.

For London, the period 1950–1966 was selected. This covers the years during which the Great Smog of London occurred in 1952, followed by a peak in black smoke concentration/PM_{10} equivalent in 1956 and the enactment of the Clean Air Act that same year. For Beijing, 2000–2016 was selected. This was a period marked by extremely high economic growth rates, coupled with extremely high energy consumption intensities and fluctuating PM_{10} pollution levels, and repeated government policy and regulatory interventions, including stringent Air Pollution Control Laws and action plans introduced at the national and the municipal levels.

This chapter is structured as follows. In Section 20.2, we highlight the air pollution trend (represented by the black smoke and PM_{10} equivalent concentration) in London during 1950–1966. We outline the socio-economic and energy landscape, and the regulatory/policy landscape. In Section 20.3, we highlight the air pollution trend (represented by the PM_{10} concentration) in Beijing during 2000–2016, and characterise

* Corresponding Author

This research is supported in part by the Theme-based Research Scheme of the Research Grants Council of Hong Kong, Grant No. T41-709/17-N.

the socio-economic, energy and transport landscape, and the regulatory/policy landscape. In Section 20.4, we compare the air pollution trends in both London and Beijing, and identify the difference in patterns of pollution through the lens of various landscapes. The chapter concludes with policy implications targeting specifically Beijing and more generally China.

20.2 LONDON 1950–1966

20.2.1 *Air Pollution Trends 1950–1966*

Air pollution was a very serious problem during this period. Severe pollution episodes were recorded during the winter seasons, creating serious health consequences. Based on the publicly available historical air quality data, the mean monthly concentration of black smoke equivalent PM_{10}[1] was 184 μg/m³ in 1950 and 63 μg/m³ in 1966, with the maximum monthly concentration of 510 μg/m³ recorded in January 1956 (Department for Environment, Food and Rural Affairs, 2017; Department of Scientific and Industrial Research, 1955, 1957, 1958, 1959, 1960, 1967). Seasonal patterns were observed, with black smoke equivalent PM_{10} concentration peaking during the winter seasons and dropping during the summer. This can mainly be attributed to heavy coal burning by the Londoners during the winter seasons in the 1950s and in the early 1960s (Greater London Authority, 2002, p. 21; Committee on Air Pollution, 1954, p. 20.). Overall, the city's air quality saw a substantial improvement during the period. Mean monthly black smoke equivalent PM_{10} concentration dropped steadily (see Figure 20.1).

Starting from the early 1950s, there was little dispute that air pollution in London was an extremely serious problem requiring immediate attention. The smoky, dusty fumes from London's million or more coal stoves and local factories imposed a heavy societal cost. Extremely high episodes of black smoke were recorded in 1952, with the city-level daily black smoke concentration achieving an average record of 925 μg/m³ from 2 December to 10 December during the year (Wilkins, 1954). During a five-day period in December 1952, 4,000 excess deaths were recorded, with the daily black smoke concentration achieving a five-day maximum of 4460 μg/m³ (Brimblecombe, 1987, p. 124). Davis et al. (2002) reported that 'hospital admissions, pneumonia reports, applications for emergency bed service, and mortality followed the peak of air pollution. Mortality remained elevated for a couple of months after the fog' (p. 1). Twelve thousand unexplained and additional deaths were reported during the episode (Davis, 2002, cited in Davis et al., 2002) and such deaths were observed in the next two months

[1] For black smoke (BS) equivalent PM_{10}, we use the conversion BS/PM_{10} = 1:1, based on the following justifications: 1) coal was dominant source of energy consumption in the UK during the 1950s and 1960s, 2) empirical studies showed that BS/TSP ratio was ~ 0.5 on average based on measurements of a monitoring site in London in 1955–62 (Commins and Waller, 1967), and 3) PM_{10}/TSP ratio is about 0.5, as reported by Dockery and Pope (1994).

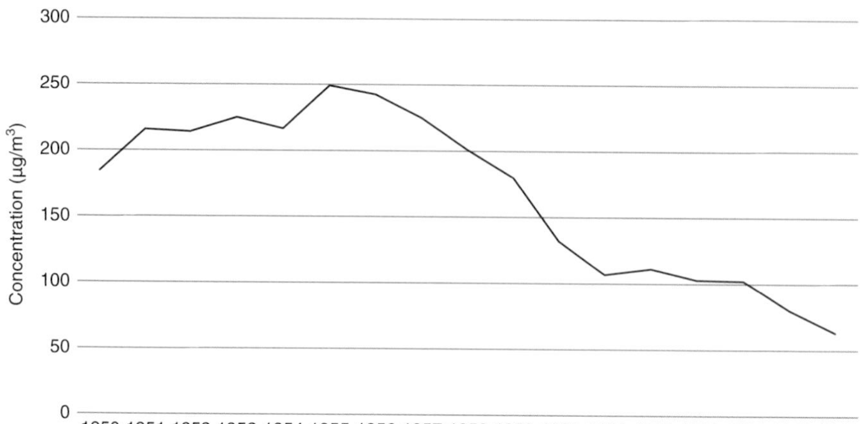

FIGURE 20.1 Annual concentration of black smoke/PM_{10} equivalent in London, 1950–1966
(Source: Department for Environment, Food and Rural Affairs, 2017; Department of Scientific and Industrial Research, 1955, 1957, 1958, 1959, 1960, 1967)

after the peak London fog had faded (Bell and Davis, 2001, cited in Davis et al., 2002). Attempts to attribute such a large number of deaths directly to air pollution attracted criticism, with some arguing that influenza contributed to the high death rates. However, evidence showed that air pollution was a likely culprit contributing to a substantial fraction of the 12,000 unexplained and additional deaths recorded during the two-month period following the high episode in London (Bell et al., 2004).

20.2.2 *Socio-economic and Energy Landscape*

London was a sizeable metropolis in the 1950s and 1960s. There were 8.2 million people in London in the 1950s (Office for National Statistics, 2015). Per capita GDP in constant prices (2000) in London[2] increased from approximately GBP 6,509 (USD 9,842) in 1950 to approximately GBP 10,028 (USD 15,163) in 1966, with an average annual growth rate of 2.6 per cent recorded over the seventeen-year period (Office for National Statistics, 2016; Thomas & Williamson, 2017).

By the 1950s, the smog of London had become part of the character of the city, even viewed nostalgically and affectionately, even though it posed serious health problems (Corton, 2015, p. 272). As a palliative response to air pollution, the National Health Service allowed doctors to prescribe masks for those who were potentially

[2] Per capita GDP in constant prices (2000) in UK was about GBP 5,424 (USD 8,201) in 1950 and GBP 8,357 (USD 12,636) in 1966 (Thomas & Williamson, 2017). Based on the earliest available data from Office for National Statistics, UK, the average ratio of per capita GDP in Greater London to per capita GDP in UK is about 1.2 during a seventeen-year period (1971–87), with a small standard deviation equal to 0.03 (Office for National Statistics, 2016). We use this ratio to estimate per capita GDP in London during 1950–1966.

exposed to the high risks of air pollution (Corton, 2015, p. 299). In a memorandum, Harold MacMillan, the then Housing Minister, acknowledged that such measures were simply a means of 'meeting people's evident need to see something being done' (Corton, 2015, p. 300).

The cause of the Great Smog of 1952 was believed to be 'a mixture of industrial pollution and domestic coal burning' (Committee on Air Pollution, 1953; Greater London Authority, 2002, p. 1). In fact, the heavy reliance on coal was closely linked to the economic restructuring that occurred during this period. In the 1950s, the coal industry represented a substantial fraction of UK's economy, with 699,000 people employed by the coal industry by 1958. This accounted for more than 1 per cent of the nation's total population (The World Bank, 2017). Towards the end of the 1960s, the number decreased steadily to 331,000 (Department of Energy and Climate Change, 2009, p. 10). Despite the increasing demand for oil during this period, coal remained popular due to its relatively lower costs, its dominance in complementary infrastructures and persistent consumer preference (Trentmann and Carlsson-Hyslop, 2017). In London, a high percentage of coal was consumed by the households. Sir Hugh Beaver's Committee on Air Pollution described the household use of coal as 'the biggest single smoke producer'. In 1952, coal supplied 61 per cent of London's energy needs, and 28 per cent of it was channelled for household use. At the time, domestic use was estimated to have caused 60 per cent of the pollution during the Great Smog. The consumption of coal started to decline from the late 1950s onwards and was increasingly replaced by oil, as it was relatively less polluting and labour intensive (Greater London Authority, 2002, p. 21; Committee on Air Pollution, 1953, p. 6). Advertisements during that period helped stimulate a change in consumer preference. A government committee on housing standards reported in 1961 that higher standards of heating had triggered new household demands for oil (Scarrow, 1972). In 1965, natural gas was discovered in large volume in the North Sea. This discovery incentivised a national shift towards boilers and other gas-burning equipment fuelled by natural gas instead of town gas during the 1970s. As town gas is generated via coal combustion, replacement of town gas by natural gas further decreased coal consumption (Greater London Authority, 2002, p. 22).

20.2.3 *Regulatory and Policy Landscape*

Even though the London smog may be remembered for prompting an effective regulatory response to air pollution, the UK government did not directly confront the issue at the beginning. Immediately after the Great Smog of London, the government responded coldly towards this issue. Such non-responsive attitude was heavily criticised by the media (Bates, 2002; Thorsheim, 2004). The government's initial response was to 'deny that it had any responsibility in the matter or that there was any need for further legislation' (Greater London Authority, 2002, pp. 13–14). It was only after tremendous pressure from the

Members of Parliament (MPs) and the London County Council (LCC) that a committee of inquiry was finally set up by the government, chaired by Sir Hugh Beaver. The Beaver Committee produced an interim report, titled 'Report of the Beaver Committee on air pollution: comments from outside bodies' (Committee on Air Pollution, 1953) in 1953 and a final report in 1954 (Committee on Air Pollution, 1954).

In the interim report, the prevailing statutory provisions for smoke control were reviewed. The key provisions were included in the section titled 'smoke nuisance' under the Public Health Act 1936, whose deficiencies were noted, which included the following (Committee on Air Pollution, 1953, p. 21):

1) It required only the use of 'best practicable mean' for preventing black smoke from industries.
2) It prioritised industrial production over abatement of pollution, as there were saving clauses, specifying that the provisions of the Acts may not be applicable to certain industrial processes so as to obstruct or interfere with the working of mines or with a number of operations in iron and steel works.
3) The Public Health Act was not applicable to private houses.

Even though reports from the Beaver Committee had pointed out the limitations and provided recommendations for improvement, it was not until 1956 that the new Clean Air Act (CAA, 1956) was enacted, after ongoing pressures from the MPs (Greater London Authority, 2002, p. 15; Thorsheim, 2004).

The Clean Air Act is a milestone in the history of air pollution abatement in the UK. It is considered to be much improved over the Public Health Act 1936, even though it did not completely address the deficiencies identified by the Beaver Committee. The Act made it an explicit aim to 'make provision for abating the pollution of the air', which was proof of the UK government's remarkable new commitment to air pollution control and management. The Clean Air Act 'constituted the primary legislation limiting pollution by smoke, grit and dust from domestic fires as well as commercial and industrial processes not covered by other pollution control legislations' and was not supplanted until 1993 (Greater London Authority, 2002, p. 15; Brimblecombe, 2007). Other innovations of CAA 1956, which constituted the recipe for success, included the following:

1) Regulations were extended to cover dark smoke, smoke from furnaces, and grit and dust from furnaces in addition to smoke nuisances. The extension of regulatory objects reflected a shift towards *ex ante* prevention from *ex post* nuisance abatements.
2) The concept of 'Smoke Control Areas' was introduced. Within a Smoke Control Area, it is an offence to emit smoke from a chimney unless it is the result of burning an authorised fuel. Such fuels are specified in regulations and include solid smokeless fuels (Greater London Authority, 2002, p. 15).

3) Domestic sources of smoke, such as household heating and cooking, were also brought under regulation. Some compensation was allowed to facilitate the transition towards smokeless installations for private occupiers meeting certain criteria.
4) Local authorities (municipal governments) were granted greater powers in order to implement CAA 1956, the most prominent of which was the right to declare smoke control areas within their jurisdiction. The term 'local authority' was mentioned sixty-eight times in thirty-seven clauses of CAA 1956.
5) Penalties for offence were specified in Section 27 of CAA 1956, with local authorities and county courts authorised to enforce the law as specified in Clauses 28 and 29.

The support of local authorities significantly contributed to successful implementation of CAA 1956. Longhurst et al. noted that CAA 1956 is one of 'the few examples of local control in the UK's otherwise centralised history of air pollution control' (Longhurst et al., 2009, p. 66). This arrangement was perhaps not surprising, as municipal authorities such as Manchester and Coventry had pioneered policies designed in the 1930s and implemented around 1950 that were later adopted in the CAA 1956 (Thorsheim, 2006, p.175). Some local authorities were notable in their enthusiasm for ensuring successful implementation of CAA 1956. The Metropolitan Borough of Holborn in London was the first local authority in the country to complete its designation of Smoke Control Areas in 1962. By 1969, when the Greater London Council undertook a review on the effectiveness of smoke control for the London Boroughs Association, over 60 per cent of premises and over 50 per cent of the areas in Greater London already had been designated as Smoke Control areas (Greater London Authority, 2002, p. 16).

The UK government also provided financial support and conducted the necessary monitoring to ensure smooth implementation of the legislation. In smoke control areas where households inevitably needed to upgrade their facilities, the UK government provided 40 per cent of the reimbursement and the local authorities were expected to contribute at least another 30 per cent of the total costs incurred by the homeowners (McMillan and Murphy, 2017). Industries were able to petition for exemptions for specified periods once a smoke control zone was established, and a period of up to seven years was permitted for conformity to the new requirements. While domestic households were granted financial support to enable this tradition, industry had to make a choice between relocation and/or adopting cleaner technology under market conditions (CAA 1956). To monitor the effectiveness of the Act, in 1961 the UK government established the world's first coordinated national air pollution monitoring network, the National Survey (Department for Environment, Food and Rural Affairs, 2011; Mosley, 2009). The survey selected the statistically representative communities to provide reliable data for evaluating the cost-effectiveness of remedial measures, including the health effects of black smoke (Clifton, 1964). The release of monitoring data improved the transparency of policy impacts, and held the local authorities responsible for performing their tasks. These efforts brought together local authorities, the central government and NGOs (Longhurst et al., 2009, p. 66). For example, the Standing Conference of Co-operating Bodies (renamed the Investigation of Air Pollution Standing Conference after 1986) started to facilitate the capacity building of local authorities in air quality monitoring and management, starting in the 1960s (Ricardo Energy and Environment on behalf of the Investigation of Air Pollution Standing Conference, 2015). Longhurst et al. thought that such a 'supportive and developmental' approach ensured that the UK's fight against the Great London Smog would be a great success (Longhurst et al., 2009, p. 66).

20.3 BEIJING 2000–2016

Beijing is located in northern China, surrounded by mountains to the north and the west, and plains in the south and the east, occupying an area of 16,000 km^2. The city is located in the warm temperate region and enjoys a continental monsoon climate with well-defined seasons. Dust blowing from the northwestern desert during the spring and high temperatures, as well as the relatively high humidity during the summer, have turned Beijing into a city of low visibility and low air quality (Chan and Yao, 2008). Further, prevailing winds from the south and mountains from the north exacerbate the local air pollution, resulting in poorer air qualities in the south than in the north (Chen et al., 2015). Daily, weekly and seasonal variations in PM concentration have been noted in Beijing. Air quality is generally the worst during early mornings and late nights, weekdays, and winters, and improves during afternoons, weekends, and summers (Chen et al., 2015).

20.3.1 *Air Pollution Trends 2000–2016*

Over the last three decades, rapid socio-economic development plus urbanisation and transportation have resulted in serious air pollution consequences. In June 2000, based on the National Ambient Air Quality Standard (NAAQS) established in 1996, Beijing started publishing a daily city-average air pollution index (API).[3] Starting in 2008, the US Embassy in Beijing began reporting hourly $PM_{2.5}$ ambient concentration, based on its own monitor mounted on the building's rooftop. Starting in 2013, apart from PM_{10}, NO_2 and SO_2, three additional pollutants, including $PM_{2.5}$, CO and O_3 ambient concentrations, have been included in the new air quality index (AQI). Air pollution readings, including PM_{10} and $PM_{2.5}$ ambient concentrations, have been

[3] API had been used to indicate the level of air quality in China before 2013. PM_{10}, NO_2 and SO_2 ambient concentrations are included in the calculation of API. API is the maximum value of the three individual APIs. The pollutant with the highest value of API is denoted as the primary pollutant. Primary pollutant is reported if API is greater than 50.

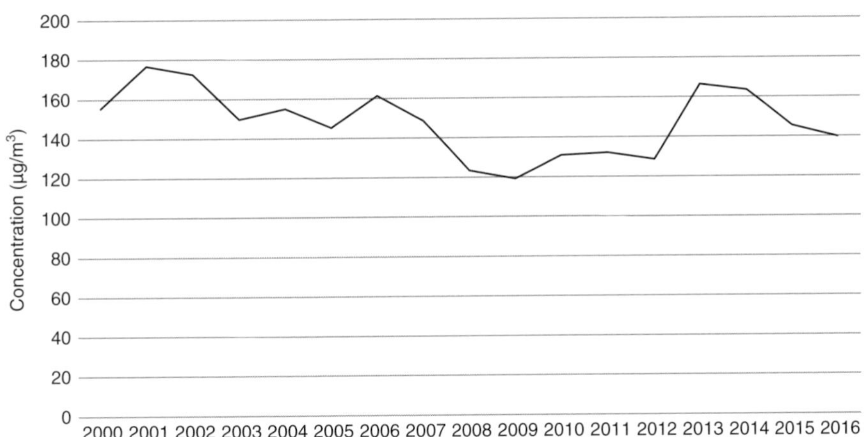

FIGURE 20.2 Annual concentration of PM_{10} in Beijing, 2000–2016
(Source: Beijing Municipal Environmental Monitoring Center, 2017; Ministry of Environmental Protection of China, 2017)

reported hourly to the public online by the Beijing Municipal Environmental Monitoring Center. The hourly report can better inform the public of the near real-time level of pollution to which they are exposed as they travel around the city.

Based on the publicly available API and AQI data[4] collected during 2000–2016 (Beijing Municipal Environmental Monitoring Center, 2017; Ministry of Environmental Protection of China, 2017), the mean monthly PM_{10} concentration was 155 μg/m³ in 2000 and 140 μg/m³ in 2016 (see Figure 20.2). There was no clearly identifiable trend across the seventeen-year period. It fluctuated, bouncing up in 2001, then dropping in 2005, bouncing up again in 2006, then dropping again in 2008 after the Olympic Games, bouncing up again in 2013 and dropping again afterwards.

The fluctuating trend in annual PM_{10} concentration expressed in Figure 20.2 shows that China has achieved only a sporadic, rather than persistent, downward trend in PM_{10} concentration/air pollution levels. In 2016, the number of days with daily city-average $PM_{2.5}$ exceeding national and international WHO standards ranged from 137 to 287 (see Table 20.1, Beijing Municipal Environmental Monitoring Center, 2017). Furthermore, high pollution episodes in Beijing were common during the observed period. For instance, the six-hour concentration of

4 Air pollutants in Beijing are measured by air pollution monitors installed at different official municipal monitoring stations, scattered across different parts of the city. The number of monitoring stations has been increased from twelve in 2000 to thirty-five starting from 2012. Daily city-level API data and AQI data are available from 5 June 2000 to 14 Jan 2013 and 1 Jan 2014 to 31 Dec 2016, respectively, from Ministry of Environmental Protection, China. For missing values of daily city-level AQI from 15 Jan 2013 to 31 Dec 2013, we use station-level AQI data available from Beijing Municipal Environmental Monitoring Center, assuming the city-level air pollution concentration is the average of the values reported in all monitoring stations.

PM_{10} could reach a maximum of 600 μg/m³ in December 2004 (Sun et al., 2006), and the twenty-four-hour concentration of $PM_{2.5}$ could reach a maximum of 500 μg/m³ in January 2013 (Yang et al., 2015).

This has led to significant environmental and public health challenges. Increased $PM_{2.5}$ and PM_{10} concentrations were considered to be associated with the increased years of life lost and respiratory diseases in Beijing (Guo et al., 2013; Xu et al., 2016), while serious pollution episodes have contributed to poor health and economic losses. The number of deaths and economic losses due to increasing levels of $PM_{2.5}$ and PM_{10} pollution concentration were estimated to be 690 premature deaths and USD 253.8 millions, respectively, in just one single month in January 2013 (Gao et al., 2015). There is an urgent need to reduce citizens' exposure to poor air and improve environmental sustainability of the city in the long term.

20.3.2 *Socio-economic, Energy and Transport Landscape*

Beijing has experienced rapid economic development over the last few decades. The average growth rate of per capita GDP was approximately 6.3 per cent per annum during the period of 2000–2016. Per capita GDP in constant (2000) prices and total energy consumption in Beijing increased from CNY 24,127 (USD 2,915) and 41.4 million tons of standard coal equivalent (SCE) in 2000 to CNY 63,868 (USD 7,716) and 68.5 million tons of SCE in 2015 (Beijing Statistical Yearbook, 2001, 2016). The residential population of Beijing increased from 16.6 million in 2000 to 21.7 million in 2015 (Beijing Transport Institute, 2001, 2016).

However, such rapid economic development has been achieved at a high price. Coal burning, vehicular emissions, industrial production and construction generated very serious air pollution (UNEP, 2016). While annual coal consumption decreased substantially from 27 million tonnes in 2000 to 10 million tonnes in 2016, the number of registered vehicles increased about three and a half-fold from 1.6 million in 2000 to 5.6 million in 2015 (Beijing Environmental Bulletin, 2000, 2016; Beijing Transport Institute, 2001, 2016). Regional transport emissions accounted for 28 to 36 per cent of $PM_{2.5}$ pollution in Beijing from 2012 to 2013, respectively (Beijing Municipal Environmental Monitoring Center, 2014). The city's air pollution landscape gradually shifted from coal-fired emissions to mixed coal-fired and vehicular-based emissions. Not all pollutants detected in Beijing were generated locally. It was estimated that one third of the $PM_{2.5}$ pollution in Beijing was transported from the neighbouring regions (Zhu et al., 2015).

Traditionally, coal was the fuel used for power generation and heating in Beijing. To create a cleaner environment, Beijing replaced coal-fired power generation with natural gas-fired generation, renovated coal-fired heating boilers and replaced old residential heating systems with new units (UNEP, 2016). Coal-fired power plants were gradually replaced with natural gas counterparts beginning in 2005. During 1996–2015, emission-control systems were upgraded and installed in power plants in different phases. Since 1998, coal-free zones also have been established, and new development of coal-based facilities has been forbidden. During 1998–2016, coal boilers for industrial and residential heating in the urban areas were phased out and replaced by cleaner alternatives (i.e., natural gas), while centralised heating was introduced to suburban areas. Starting in late 2017, 'coal-free zones' were established in Hebei, a province neighbouring Beijing, targeting the phasing out of coal heating from all households and factories in the region. The proportion of coal in total energy consumption decreased dramatically from 67.8 per cent in 2000 to 13.7 per cent in 2015. Energy consumption per CNY10,000 (USD 1,208) of GDP in constant (2000) prices decreased dramatically from 1.311 tonnes of SCE to 0.496 tonnes of SCE (Beijing Statistical Yearbook, 2001, 2016). This has reduced subsequent particulate emissions from the energy sector and total energy consumption in Beijing.

While the total energy consumption is moving in a dramatic, downward trend, the road transport volume is moving in an increasingly upward trend, with a two and a half-fold increase in registered vehicles recorded over a sixteen-year period (2000–2015). This presents a new environmental challenge to Beijing. Many efforts have been attempted to improve the city's air quality, including improving fuel qualities and emissions standards, subsidising the phasing out of outdated vehicles, reducing vehicle usages during the peak hours, imposing quotas on newly registered vehicles and developing public transportation networks (Beijing Transport Institute, 2016; UNEP, 2016). Since 1998, diesel fuel and the level of sulphur content in gasoline have been reduced significantly. A year later, emission standards set for both newly registered and in-use vehicles were tightened. Stricter examination of emission control technologies is required before vehicles are allowed to enter the market. Since 2003, registration of light-duty diesel vehicles has been banned. For operating vehicles, an annual inspection with improved testing techniques for emissions is now required. Filtering devices and financial incentives are provided to improve and replace outdated vehicles, and low-emission zones are introduced to avoid high-traffic emitters. Recently, a number of transportation polices have been introduced to the city[5] to limit transport growth. Meanwhile, the city has relied upon public transportation to reduce the volume of private cars. The number of subway lines in Beijing increased substantially from two in 2000 to seventeen in 2015. By late 2015, the number of public electric buses had been increased to 23,287, which covered bus routes with a total length of 20,186 kilometers; public commutes represented one half of all passenger miles (Beijing Transport Institute, 2016). However, given the continuous growth in the number of registered vehicles in Beijing, current measures to control fuels and

5 Since 2011, the city has started limiting the quota of vehicle registrations via new license plate lotteries. Following the traffic control exercise during the 2008 Olympic Games and the 2014 Asia-Pacific Economic Cooperation (APEC), restricting vehicles from operating in certain areas during the workdays based on the odd/even number of license plates, has been introduced.

pipelines and private car growth may not produce much positive effect on urban air quality over the short term, as any immediate improvement attributable to the environmental measures can be easily counterbalanced by the substantial increase in traffic volume.

20.3.3 *Regulatory and Policy Landscape*

Many air pollution control policies have been proposed and implemented in phases during the observed period, focusing on optimisation of energy structures and control of vehicle emissions. This has led to a decrease in the concentration of air pollutants despite an increase in population, vehicles, buildings and energy consumption. Even though these pollution control measures have led to a substantial reduction in air emissions, the city's air remains a grave condition. By 2016, the annual concentrations of major pollutants were far exceeding the national annual limits. In addition, the daily concentration of PM continues to exceed the WHO guidelines and the national standards most of the time. There is an urgent need to improve air quality and improve sustainability and healthy city living in Beijing (see Table 20.1).

In response to the serious concerns over the deterioration of air quality in Beijing raised by the central government and the local public, a number of key air pollution control regulations and policies have been proposed and implemented during the period, characterised by increasingly stringent regulatory standards, reflecting the central government's determination to reduce air pollution in Beijing. A list of major air pollution control regulations and policies at different administrative levels is summarised in Table 20.2.

These regulations and policies have covered the emissions control of coal-fired power generation, as well as industry and vehicular emissions, dust prevention and control, energy structure and traffic system optimisation, clean technology innovation, emergency response to episodic air pollution events, and legal responsibility. It should be noted that while the air pollution level may be generally high across all seasons in the city, such problem is not exclusive to Beijing. National and provincial regulations and policies introduced during this period, therefore, have served as guidelines to spearhead municipal air pollution control.

At the national level, the Air Pollution Control Law has been updated twice. The first update took place in 2000, basically rewriting the 1995 version, which lacked teeth in pollution control. Its major goal was to stabilise total pollution emissions at the 1995 level by the year 2010. The tenth Five-Year Plan and the eleventh Five-Year Plan (2000–2010) aimed to reduce total emissions by 10 to 20 per cent in each five-year period. Yang (2017, p. 5) noted that 'the 2000 amendment reflects a shift in the prevention strategy by providing measures for monitoring the total volume of pollutants entering an air shed'. When it was again updated in 2015/16, new elements were introduced, including 'an explicit emphasis on the link between public health and air pollution, a call for more decentralised emissions governance, and the introduction of

TABLE 20.1 *China national ambient air quality standards and WHO air quality guidelines*

China National Ambient Air Quality Standards				
Air Pollutant	Averaging Periods	Concentration Limit		Unit
		Grade I	Grade II	
SO_2	Annual average	20	60	µg/m^3
	24h average	50	150	
	1h average	150	500	
NO_2	Annual average	40	40	
	24h average	80	80	
	1h average	200	200	
CO	24h average	4000	4000	
	1h average	10000	10000	
O_3	Daily maximum 8h average	100	160	
	1h average	160	200	
PM_{10}	Annual average	40	70	
	24h average	50	150	
$PM_{2.5}$	Annual average	15	35	
	24h average	35	75	

WHO Air Quality Guidelines			
Air Pollutant	Averaging Periods	Concentration Limit	Unit
SO_2	24h average	20	µg/m^3
	10-minute average	500	
NO_2	Annual average	40	
	1h average	200	
O_3	8h average	100	
PM_{10}	Annual average	20	
	24h average	50	
$PM_{2.5}$	Annual average	10	
	24h average	25	

Source: Ministry of Environmental Protection of China (2012), WHO (2016)

new mechanisms for controlling sources of air pollution' (Yang, 2017, p. 6). The new legal mechanism includes an expanded centralised list of pollutants used to be governed in a more decentralised fashion by various authorities, and a pollutant discharge permit system.

Air quality objectives were set out in the action plans. According to the Action Plan for Clean Air in Beijing introduced in June 2013, targets were set for the 2013–17 period, requiring the city's PM_{10} and $PM_{2.5}$ concentration to be reduced by 10 per cent and 25 per cent, respectively, and the annual concentration of $PM_{2.5}$ to not exceed the threshold of 60 µg/m^3 by the end of 2017.

TABLE 20.2 *Major air pollution control policies from 2000 to 2016*

Policy	Date Passed/Issued	Coverage	Description
Air Pollution Control Law in China	Passed on 29 April 2000, effective from 1 September 2000 onwards	National level	National air pollution control regulation, with restrictions on emissions from coal-fired power plants and vehicles, dust prevention and control and legal responsibilities.
Action Plan for Air Pollution Prevention and Control in China	Issued on 10 September 2013	National level with specific indicators applicable to Beijing	National action plan, consisting of ten measures for air pollution control, with specific targets set for Beijing by 2017: 25% $PM_{2.5}$ reduction and annual $PM_{2.5}$ concentration not exceeding 60 μg/m^3.
China Environmental Protection Law	Passed on 24 April 2014, effective from 1 January 2015 onwards	National level	Revised version of the national China Environmental Protection Law, covering prevention and control of air pollution.
Air Pollution Control Law in China	Passed on 20 August 2015, effective from 1 January 2016 onwards	National level	Revised version of the Air Pollution Control Law in China (2000), specifying plans and deadlines for air quality objectives, emissions control for industrial and agricultural pollution, regional collaboration and emergency response to pollution episodes.
Implementation Details of Action Plan for Air Pollution Prevention and Control in Beijing-Tianjin-Hebei Region	Issued on 17 September 2013, with goals set for the period 2013–2017.	Regional level	Complementary to the national Action Plan, covering implementation details on emissions control, traffic management, industry structure optimisation, technological innovation, regional collaboration and emergency response.

Guidelines on Vertical Integration and Reform for Monitoring of Law Enforcement of Environmental Protection Units under Provincial Governance	Issued in September 2016	Regional level	Delegates the full responsibility of overseeing air pollution monitoring, environmental performance evaluation and environmental fund distribution to the provincial governments, taking it away from municipal governments.
Action Plan for Clean Air in Beijing during 2013–2017	Issued on 11 September 2013	City level	Developed from the national Action Plan, providing details on emissions reduction, protective measures and public participation.
Air Pollution Control in Beijing	Passed on 22 January 2014, effective from 1 March 2014	City level	City level air pollution control regulation, providing restrictions on major air pollution emissions, prevention and control of air pollutants from fixed sources, vehicles and dust, and legal responsibilities.

In September 2016, a new administrative guideline was introduced to transfer responsibility for pollution monitoring and control to provincial governments, and granting provincial authorities the full power to directly access municipal air pollution monitoring data, assess the city governments' performance in air pollution control, and discharge environmental funds to their governed municipalities based on their environmental performance. The transfer of monitoring, performance assessment and financing from the city government back to the provincial government provides the means for the provincial and the central governments to exercise more effective administrative control of air pollution at the city level. Given that the release of environmental funds is now coupled with their environmental performance, there is a much greater incentive for municipalities to reduce air pollution. However, the positive regulatory effect may not be evidenced until the longer term.

Air pollution control regulations and policies introduced at various levels of government may facilitate air quality improvement in Beijing over the longer term, though the current regulatory thresholds still exceed the national and international thresholds, especially for particulate matters (UNEP, 2016). Despite the potential positive regulatory and policy effects, there are potential obstacles preventing China from fully implementing these stringent air pollution control measures. First, there is a gap between the enactment and implementation of air pollution control polices in China (Zhang et al., 2014). Second, these legal/policy measures often adopt a top-down and command-and-control approach. These challenges mean that even with the introduction of stringent air pollution control regulations with high air quality objectives, decision making on air pollution control could still be constrained by potential conflicts of interest, given the lack of proper monitoring and enforcement mechanisms, until very recently. For a long time, air quality has been taken as a performance evaluation criterion by the local officials. As the central government often relies upon the self-reported data from the local governments, it was argued that local officials could have exploited such a system (Ghanem and Zhang, 2014).

Starting in 2012, some regulatory measures were introduced to close the implementation gap. For example, the new NAAQS released in 2012 introduced stricter standards to ensure validity and disclosure of air-pollution monitoring data. Implementation details for strengthening environmental supervision and law enforcement were included in the Action Plan for Clean Air in Beijing effective during the period of 2013–2017. Public participation in air pollution control was covered in the Action Plan in 2013. The new administrative guideline on vertical integration released in September 2016, the coupling of municipal environmental performance with environmental fund release and the delegation of the full power of air pollution monitoring back to the provincial government have made it possible for an emerging regulatory system supported by better monitoring and enforcement. This will likely strengthen the accountability of the Beijing city government to the central and the provincial governments.

20.4 COMPARING THE AIR POLLUTION TRENDS AND THE SOCIO-ECONOMIC AND REGULATORY LANDSCAPE IN HISTORICAL LONDON AND CONTEMPORARY BEIJING

In London during the 1950s, the major sources of black smoke, and hence PM_{10}, were coal-fired power generation and household heating. In Beijing, however, particulates such as PM_{10}, are emitted from coal-fired power generation and heating, from the exhausts of more than 5 million fossil-fuel vehicles in the city, and from the steel and construction industries. Emissions also have been sourced from neighbouring regions, including Hebei Province. While air pollution sources in London were concentrated within the city, air pollution in Beijing is much more distributed. In fact, non-local air pollution contributed about 28 to 36 per cent of the city's air pollution in 2013, in terms of $PM_{2.5}$, based on the latest figures released by the Environmental Monitoring Center of Beijing municipality (Beijing Municipal Environmental Monitoring Center, 2014). Given the decentralisation of air pollution in Beijing, tackling the city's air pollution is a much more challenging task as it involves multiple sources and stakeholders, with the expected associated stakeholder interests and political hurdles.

The UK relies on local authorities to implement air pollution control regulations and policies. In the case of London, economic growth is not always the primary concern of the local authorities. Equally, the 1950s and 1960s were not a period of population expansion and economic growth was relatively much slower than in modern Beijing. In Section 20.2 we illustrated the important role played by the metropolitan boroughs in managing the Smoke Control Areas. These metropolitan boroughs and their governing councils were established under the London Government Act, 1899. This act (in Section 2.2) specified that the 'council of each borough shall consist of a mayor, aldermen and councillors' and they shall be elected to serve in terms by the local electorate, which from the 1920s included the entire adult population from the age of eighteen (Terry and Morle, 1899). At the time that air pollution became the focus of the public, such representative democracy provided an important means of communication with, and influence on, the public and those who implemented pollution controls, and created a strong motivation for the local authorities to tackle this problem. However, given that both pollution and some forms of limited electoral franchise could be dated back to the nineteenth century, democratic pressure was clearly insufficient in itself to generate effective action. If business interests had powerful representation on the councils, they might even create an opposite effect (Mosley, 2001; Thorsheim, 2006). However, once effective legislation was passed by parliament, the combination of public pressure, NGO and central government monitoring, and motivated local authorities meant that implementation could be achieved over a period of years, although some areas of the UK had to wait until the early 1980s for complete success (Mosley, 2009). London has, like Beijing, followed national policies towards restricting vehicle emissions and imposing driving restrictions on high-emission vehicles, but not during the period with which we are concerned in this study. During the 1950s and 1960s, the regulatory emphasis was much more on penalising infringements of pollution controls than directly incentivising technological shifts. This was enabled by minimising conflicts of interest among actors and ensuring accountability through a variety of institutions, trusted legal systems and an observant and empowered public.

In the case of Beijing, however, local authorities, including Beijing and its neighbouring municipal governments – from whose cities much pollution originates – do not have enough motivation to tackle air pollution, as most of the pollution is generated from coal-fired electricity power plants and heavy industries, apart from fossil-fuel vehicles, and reducing the pollution would have to be conducted at the expense of their own cities' economic growth. Traditionally, local environmental protection bureaus played a very weak role in the national air pollution control system. Most are subject to being overruled by other local offices, whose primary foci are economic growth, employment and social stability. Meanwhile, central government policies in reducing air pollution appeared to be inconsistent, likely due to economic realities. For instance, after almost two years of continuous decrease in $PM_{2.5}$ level, the level in the Beijing-Tianjin-Hebei area witnessed an increasing trend in April 2016, after the central government had introduced incentive measures to stimulate steel production (Gan, 2017). If Beijing is juggling between air quality improvement and economic growth, it is not surprising that the neighbouring municipalities (which are poorer and less affected by their own air pollution) might face even more intensive struggles. As such, neither Beijing nor the neighbouring municipalities are properly incentivised to improve air quality in Beijing. The recent shifting of power of environmental monitoring and control back to the provincial governments should in theory provide Beijing and the neighbouring municipalities with more incentives to implement more effective local air pollution control policies and clean up their own backyards. Unfortunately, given that such administrative guideline on vertical integration of responsibility for monitoring of pollution has just been in place for less than a year, positive effects of the new measures, if any, are yet to be envisaged.

Finally, it must be noted that the successful phase-out of dirty coal use in London must also be examined in the context of intensive global energy transition from coal to oil and the availability of cleaner coal-based fuels and electrification. Starting from the end of World War II, oil has emerged as the key energy commodity in global transportation, electricity generation and heating, thanks to the mass production of oil-fired ships, vehicles and aircraft during the wars (Podobnik, 1999, pp. 156, 160; Kander et al., 2013). Coal consumption in domestic households and industry almost halved between its peak in 1954 and 1970. Use on the railways almost disappeared altogether. It is likely that these trends were even more accelerated in London. In industry this was achieved by a major substitution by heavy fuel oils, which accounted for the bulk of the growth in oil use during the post-war decades. The domestic picture is harder to interpret, as we lack a detailed breakdown of household use. Electricity use in households and commercial premises rose from 35 TWh in 1956 to 83 TWh by 1966 (Dept. for Business, Energy and Industrial Strategy, 2016). With new services provided such as the more widespread use of domestic appliances encouraging electricity's use, the price of electricity relative to coal persistently fell over the period, not so much from a decline in the retail price of electricity as a doubling in the retail price of coal between 1954 and 1966 (see price series assembled for Gentvilaite et al., 2015). These invisible hands lent their power to London in battles against bad air. However, while some recent work has stressed wider economic and technological change as the primary driver of improved air quality since 1956 (Brimblecombe, 2007), there was no break in price trends in the late 1950s when more polluting coal use peaked and began to decline rapidly. It seems very plausible that much of the credit for the large gains in air quality achieved in London by the mid-1960s can still be attributed to the passing of the CCA 1956.

The wider forces of economic and technological change are increasing in Beijing, as they did during the period from 2000 to 2016. China has become the country with the largest electric car stock, with about a third of the global total in 2016, which offers a potential solution to combat vehicular pollution, though the market share of electric cars reached only 1.1 per cent globally in 2016 (International Energy Agency, 2017). By the end of 2016, Beijing had the highest EV penetration, with 109,000 EVs registered, representing the highest number of EVs among all Chinese provinces (General Office of the People's Government of Beijing Municipality, 2017). This still represents, however, only a small share of the cars in Beijing.

20.5 CONCLUSIONS AND POLICY IMPLICATIONS

Although the Great London Smog in 1952 was unfortunately a great catastrophe (Bates, 2002), air pollution mitigation, fortunately, was helped by an eventual response in the form of a strong national anti-pollution act, CAA 1956.

Various policy implications can be derived from our examination of the causes of air pollution in London over the period 1950–1966 and in Beijing over the period 2000–2016. First, air pollutants in London originated from coal alone, but in the case of Beijing, it is more complex. The different sources in Beijing include both locally and non-locally generated pollutants, thus making it harder to regulate air pollution in Beijing.

Second, the UK relied substantially on the local authorities for successful policy implementation. London was subject to the UK Parliament and the government was shamed into action by bringing forward a bill in the parliament. However, in Beijing, this approach might not work effectively, given that local authorities in China tend to prioritise economic growth, and a third of the air pollution in Beijing is non-locally generated. The municipalities generating these pollutants are unwilling to sacrifice their own economic growth to improve Beijing's air quality. Furthermore, the possible solution of greater provincial control proposed by the central government in China is yet to be proven. In view of the more complicated air pollution landscape in Beijing, given that different interests of multiple stakeholders competing with each other, regulatory implementation at the local level will be a more daunting task.

For effective implementation of air pollution policies at the local level, China has to move beyond simply introducing strong policies and regulations at the central or the provincial level. More resources have to be redirected to resolving the competing interests of stakeholders across different levels of jurisdictions. Apart from introducing high thresholds for compliance at the local level and making the local authorities accountable for their air pollution control performance via vertical integration, more schemes based on voluntary action and incentives can be adopted in parallel to encourage the local authorities and industries to comply with the standards and increase their capacity and competence for change (Jaffe et al., 2002). It is also time to introduce more information-based and health-centric measures that address one's personal needs, such as the use of environmental reporting to educate the public regarding the health consequences and costs of air pollution, thus creating the pressure for social change and increasing the reputation costs borne by polluting industries and companies which are not yet ready to comply with the regulations.

20.6 REFERENCES

Bates, D. (2002), 'A Half Century Later: Recollections of the London Fog It', *Environmental Health Perspectives* 110(12): A735.

Beijing Environmental Bulletin. (2000), Beijing Municipal Environmental Protection Bureau. Retrieved July 15, 2017, from www.bjepb.gov.cn/bjhrb/xxgk/ywdt/hjzlzk/hjzkgb65/bsndhjzkgb/507205/index.html

Beijing Environmental Bulletin. (2016), Beijing Municipal Environmental Protection Bureau. Retrieved July 15, 2017, from www.bjepb.gov.cn/2016zt_jsxl/index.htm

Beijing Municipal Environmental Monitoring Center. (2014), Beijing PM2.5 source appointment. Retrieved July 15, 2017, from www.bjmemc.com.cn/g327/s921/t1971.aspx

Beijing Municipal Environmental Monitoring Center. (2017), Database of historical AQI in Beijing. Retrieved March 17, 2017, from www.bjmemc.com.cn/g372.aspx

Beijing Statistical Yearbook. (2001), Beijing Municipal Bureau of Statistics. Retrieved July 15, 2017, from www.bjstats.gov.cn/nj/main/2011-en/index.htm

Beijing Statistical Yearbook. (2016), Beijing Municipal Bureau of Statistics. Retrieved July 15, 2017, from www.bjstats.gov.cn/nj/main/2016-tjnj/zk/indexeh.htm

Beijing Transport Institute. (2001), *Annual Report of Transportation Development in Beijing*. Retrieved July 15, 2017, from www.bjtrc.org.cn/JGJS.aspx?id=5.2&Menu=GZCG

Beijing Transport Institute. (2016), *Annual Report of Transportation Development in Beijing*. Retrieved July 15, 2017, from www.bjtrc.org.cn/JGJS.aspx?id=5.2&Menu=GZCG

Bell, M. L., Davis, D. L., & Fletcher, T. (2004), 'A Retrospective Assessment of Mortality from the London Smog Episode of 1952: The Role of Influenza and Pollution', *Environmental Health Perspectives* 112(1): 6–8.

Brimblecombe, P. (1987), *The Big Smoke: A History of Air Pollution in London since Medieval Times*. London: Routledge.
Brimblecombe, P. (2007), 'The Clean Air Act after 50 Years', *Weather* 61: 311–314.
Chan, C. K. & Yao, X. (2008), 'Air Pollution in Mega Cities in China', *Atmospheric Environment* 42(1): 1–42.
Chen, W., Tang, H., & Zhao, H. (2015), 'Diurnal, Weekly and Monthly Spatial Variations of Air Pollutants and Air Quality of Beijing', *Atmospheric Environment* 119: 21–34.
Clifton, M. (1964), 'The National Survey of Air Pollution', *Proceedings of the Royal Society of Medicine* 57(10 Pt 2): 1013–1015.
Commins, B. T. & Waller, R. E. (1967), 'Observations from a Ten-Year Study of Pollution at a Site in the City of London', *Atmospheric Environment* 1(1): 49–68.
Committee on Air Pollution. (1953), *Interim Report*. London: Her Majesty's Stationery Office.
Committee on Air Pollution (1954), *Report*. London: Her Majesty's Stationery Office.
Corton, C. L. (2015), *London Fog: the Biography*. Cambridge, MA: The Belknap Press of Harvard University Press.
Davis, D. L., Bell, M. L., & Fletcher, T. (2002), 'A Look Back at the London Smog of 1952 and the Half Century Since', *Environmental Health Perspectives* 110(12): A734–A735.
Department for Business, Energy and Industrial Strategy (2016), *Historical coal data: Coal production, availability and consumption 1853 to 2016*. Retrieved February 27 2018, from www.gov.uk/government/statistical-data-sets/historical-coal-data-coal-production-availability-and-consumption-1853-to-2011
Department for Business, Energy and Industrial Strategy (2016), *Historical electricity data, 1920–2017*. Retrieved February 27 2018, from www.gov.uk/government/statistical-data-sets/historical-electricity-data-1920-to-2011
Department for Environment Food and Rural Affairs (2011), *Monitoring Networks – Brief history*. Retrieved December 13, 2017, from https://uk-air.defra.gov.uk/networks/brief-history
Department for Environment Food & Rural Affairs (2017), UK-AIR database. Retrieved March 12, 2017, from https://uk-air.defra.gov.uk/data/data_selector
Department of Energy and Climate Change (2009), *Digest of UK Energy Statistics (DUKES): 60th Anniversary*. London: Her Majesty's Stationery Office. Retrieved December 13, 2017 from www.gov.uk/government/publications/digest-of-uk-energy-statistics-dukes-60th-anniversary
Department of Scientific and Industrial Research (1955), *The Investigation of Atmospheric Pollution – A Report on Observations in the 10 Years Ended 31st March, 1954 (27th Report)*. London: Her Majesty's Stationery Office.
Department of Scientific and Industrial Research (1957), *The Investigation of Atmospheric Pollution – A Report on Observations in the Year Ended 31st March, 1955 (28th Report)*. London: Her Majesty's Stationery Office.
Department of Scientific and Industrial Research (1958), *The Investigation of Atmospheric Pollution – A Report on Observations in the Year Ended 31st March, 1956 (29th Report)*. London: Her Majesty's Stationery Office.
Department of Scientific and Industrial Research (1959), *The Investigation of Atmospheric Pollution – A Report on Observations in the Year Ended 31st March, 1957 (30th Report)*. London: Her Majesty's Stationery Office.
Department of Scientific and Industrial Research (1960), *The Investigation of Atmospheric Pollution – A Report on Observations in the Year Ended 31st March, 1958 (31st Report)*. London: Her Majesty's Stationery Office.
Department of Scientific and Industrial Research (1967), *The Investigation of Atmospheric Pollution 1958–1966 (32nd Report)*. London: Her Majesty's Stationery Office.

Dockery, D. W. & Pope, C. A. (1994), 'Acute Respiratory Effects of Particulate Air Pollution', *Annual Review of Public Health* 15(1): 107–132.

Gan, N. (2017, February 2), 'China Firing Blanks in "War on pollution" as smog worsens'. Retrieved August 9, 2017, from *South China Morning Post*, at www.scmp.com/news/china/policies-politics/article/2066503/china-firing-blanks-war-pollution-smog-worsens

Gao, M., Guttikunda, S. K., Carmichael, G. R., Wang, Y., Liu, Z., Stanier, C. O., . . ., & Yu, M. (2015), 'Health Impacts and Economic Losses Assessment of the 2013 Severe Haze Event in Beijing Area', *Science of the Total Environment* 511: 553–561.

General Office of the People's Government of Beijing Municipality (2017). *Beijing Government Work Report*. Retrieved February 3, 2018, from http://zhengwu.beijing.gov.cn/zwzt/hb/nr/t1465690.htm

Gentvilaite, R., Warde, P., & Kander, A. (2015), 'The Role of Energy Quality in Shaping Long-Term Energy Intensity in Europe', *Energies* 8: 133–153.

Ghanem, D. & Zhang, J. (2014), '"Effortless Perfection": Do Chinese Cities Manipulate Air Pollution Data?', *Journal of Environmental Economics and Management* 68(2): 203–225.

Greater London Authority (2002), 50 *Years On: The Struggle for Air Quality in London since the Great Smog of December* 1952. London: Greater London Authority.

Guo, Y., Li, S., Tian, Z., Pan, X., Zhang, J., & Williams, G. (2013), 'The Burden of Air Pollution on Years of Life Lost in Beijing, China, 2004–08: Retrospective Regression Analysis of Daily Deaths', *BMJ* 347: f7139.

He, K., Yang, F., Ma, Y., Zhang, Q., Yao, X., Chan, C. K., . . ., & Mulawa, P. (2001), 'The Characteristics of PM 2.5 in Beijing, China', *Atmospheric Environment* 35(29): 4959–4970.

Heidorn, K. C. (1978), 'A Chronology of Important Events in the History of Air Pollution Meteorology to 1970', *Bulletin of the American Meteorological Society* 59(12): 1589–1597.

International Energy Agency. (2017). *Global EV Outlook 2017*. Retrieved December 13, 2017, from www.iea.org/publications/freepublications/publication/global-ev-outlook-2017.html

Jaffe, A. B., Newell, R. G., & Stavins, R. N. (2002), 'Environmental Policy and Technological Change', *Environmental and Resource Economics* 22(1–2): 41–70.

Kander, A., Malanima, P., & Warde, P. (2013), *Power to the People. Energy in Europe over the Last Five Centuries*. Princeton, NJ: Princeton University Press.

Longhurst, J., Irwin, J., Chatterton, T., Hayes, E., Leksmono, N., & Symons, J. (2009), 'The Development of Effects-Based Air Quality Management Regimes', *Atmospheric Environment* 43: 64–78.

McMillan, R. & Murphy, J. (2017), 'Measuring the Effects of Severe Air Pollution: Evidence from the UK Clean Air Act', Center for Urban Economics and Real Estate, University of Toronto, www.sauder.ubc.ca/Faculty/Research_Centres/Centre_for_Urban_Economics_and_Real_Estate/News_and_Events/~/media/Files/Faculty%20Research/Urban%20Economics/Summer%20Symposia/2017-June%2023-24/3-Rob%20McMillan-UKCAA_UBC.ashx.

Ministry of Environmental Protection of China (2012, February 29), 'Ambient Air Quality Standards'. Retrieved July 13, 2017, from http://kjs.mep.gov.cn/hjbhbz/bzwb/dqhjbh/dqhjzlbz/201203/t20120302_224165.htm

Ministry of Environmental Protection of China (2017), 'Daily Air Quality Reports in Major Cities in China'. Retrieved March 17, 2017, from http://datacenter.mep.gov.cn/index!MenuAction.action?name=402880fb24e695b60124e6973db30011

Mosley, S. (2001), *The Chimney of the World: A History of Smoke Pollution in Victorian and Edwardian Manchester*. Cambridge: White Horse Press.

Mosley, S. (2009), '"A Network of Trust": Measuring and Monitoring Air Pollution in British Cities, 1912–1960', *Environment and History* 15: 273–302.

Office for National Statistics (2015, September 7), *Historical Census Population*. Retrieved October 14, 2017, from https://data.london.gov.uk/dataset/historic-census-population

Office for National Statistics (2016, March 10), *Historical Regional GDP 1968 to 1970 and 1971 to 1996*. Retrieved December 6, 2017, from www.ons.gov.uk/economy/grossvalueaddedgva/adhocs/005458historicalregionalgdp1968to1970and1971to1996

Podobnik, B. (1999), 'Toward a Sustainable Energy Regime: A Long-Wave Interpretation of Global Energy Shifts', *Technological Forecasting and Social Change* 62: 155–172.

Ricardo Energy & Environment on behalf of the Investigation of Air Pollution Standing Conference (2015, September 18), *Rules and Standing Orders of the Investigation of Air Pollution Standing Conference (IAPSC)*. Retrieved July 25, 2017, from www.iapsc.org.uk/assets/documents/RULES-SO-Sep2015.pdf

Scarrow, H. A. (1972), 'The Impact of British Domestic Air Pollution Legislation', *British Journal of Political Science*, 2(3): 261–282.

Stoerk, T. (2016), 'Statistical Corruption in Beijing's Air Quality Data has Likely Ended in 2012', *Atmospheric Environment* 127: 365–371.

Sun, Y., Zhuang, G., Tang, A., Wang, Y., & An, Z. (2006), 'Chemical Characteristics of PM2.5 and PM10 in Haze–Fog Episodes in Beijing', *Environmental Science & Technology* 40 (10): 3148–3155.

Terry, G. & Morle, P. (1899), *The London Government Act 1899: with Explanatory Notes*. London: Law Publishers.

Thomas, R. & Williamson, S. (2017), *What Was the U.K. GDP Then?*, MeasuringWorth. Retrieved December 6, 2017, from www.measuringworth.com/ukgdp/

Thorsheim, P. (2004), 'Interpreting the London Smog Disaster of 1952', in DuPuis, E. M., ed., *Smoke and Mirrors. The Politics and Culture of Air Pollution*. New York: New York University Press.

Thorsheim, P. (2006), *Inventing Pollution. Coal, Smoke, and Culture in Britain since 1800*. Athens: Ohio University Press.

Trentmann, F. & Carlsson-Hyslop, A. (2017), 'The Evolution of Energy Demand in Britain: Politics, Daily Life, and Public Housing, 1920s–1970s', *Historical Journal*. Available at https://doi.org/10.1017/S0018246X17000255

UNEP (2016, May), *A Review of Air Pollution Control in Beijing: 1998–2013*.), Nairobi: United Nations Environment Programme (UNEP).

WHO (2016, September), 'Ambient (Outdoor) Air Health'. Retrieved July 15, 2017, from www.who.int/mediacentre/factsheets/fs313/en/

Wilkins, E. T. (1954), 'Air Pollution and the London Fog of December, 1952', *Journal of the Royal Sanitary Institute* 74(1): 1–21.

The World Bank (2017). *United Kingdom's Population from 1960–2016*. Retrieved October 25, 2017, from https://data.worldbank.org/indicator/SP.POP.TOTL?end=2016&locations=GB&start=1960&view=chart

Xu, Q., Li, X., Wang, S., Wang, C., Huang, F., Gao, Q., Wu, L., Tao, L., Guo, J., Wang, W. & Guo, X. (2016), 'Fine Particulate Air Pollution and Hospital Emergency Room Visits for Respiratory Disease in Urban Areas in Beijing, China, in 2013', *PLoS One* 11(4): e0153099.

Yang, C. H. (2017), 'Atmospheric Pollution', in *Oxford Handbook of Comparative Environmental Law*. Oxford: Oxford University Press.

Yang, Y., Liu, X., Qu, Y., Wang, J., An, J., Zhang, Y., & Zhang, F. (2015), 'Formation Mechanism of Continuous Extreme Haze Episodes in the Megacity Beijing, China, in January 2013', *Atmospheric Research* 155: 192–203.

Zhang, D., Liu, J., & Li, B. (2014), 'Tackling Air Pollution in China – What Do We Learn from the Great Smog of 1950s in London', *Sustainability* 6(8): 5322–5338.

Zhu, J., Yan, Y., He, C., & Wang, C. (2015, July 13), *China's Environment – Big Issues, Accelerating Effort, Ample Opportunities*. Goldman Sachs. Retrieved December 13, 2017, from www.goldmansachs.com/our-thinking/pages/chinas-environment.html

21

The Power of Siberia: A Eurasian Pipeline Policy 'Good' for Whom?

Marc Ozawa, Chi Kong Chyong, Kun-Chin Lin, Tim Reilly, Caroline Humphrey and Corine Wood-Donnelly

21.1 INTRODUCTION

The Euromaidan protests of 2014 have had ripple effects instigating transitions throughout Eurasia, not only political but also in the energy sector. The Ukraine crisis sparked a debate which drew Russia, Europe's largest natural gas supplier, into a geopolitical conflict between Russia and its main market, Europe. Responding to the subsequent Russian annexation of Crimea, the European Union, the United States and most NATO member states instituted economic sanctions against Russia that indirectly targeted Russia's main industrial sector, energy. In what appeared to be a tit-for-tat response, President Putin followed with an announcement for renewed interest in turning Russia to the East away from Europe as its primary trading partner. Pipelines were at the heart of Russia's previous economic rapprochement with Western Europe during the Cold War, and it appears that they are again playing a central role in Russia's 'eastern pivot' with the construction of the new showcase pipeline, *Sila Siberii* (Power of Siberia).

In light of recent events the time is right to ask whether Russia's planned pipelines in Eurasia are, in fact, good for the country and its neighbours. Whom do they benefit and what lessons may stakeholders on the Asian side of Russia draw from the European experience? In order to address these questions, a multidisciplinary group of researchers from the University of Cambridge came together to discuss how one might approach these questions given the complexity of issues that Eurasian natural gas pipelines present. Proceeding from these discussions, the first area of enquiry that we identify is, what constitutes 'good' and 'good for whom?' Subjective terms such as 'good' or 'trust' imply positive effects across disciplines, but what qualifies as positive may vary according to disciplinary context.[1] For example, positive political results may be measured in stability of institutions. Economic gains may be measured in the efficient distribution of resources whereas social effects could be

[1] Denise M. Rousseau et al., 'Not so Different after All: A Cross-Discipline View of Trust', *Academy of Management. The Academy of Management Review* 23, no. 3, (July 1998): 393.

examined through social welfare or disruption of indigenous community practices. Some social scientists may not make value claims of 'good' or 'bad', aiming rather to describe and explain what takes place.[2] This value-neutral approach is in line with the natural sciences, but it is also not necessarily mutually exclusive from normative, value-based investigations. The discussions of our multidisciplinary group attest to common analytical ground between descriptive and normative approaches.

The main findings of this chapter are the following. It is still too early to tell what the geopolitical outcomes will be, but typically a major pipeline such as the Power of Siberia (PoS) that will bind two economies together, one of which is the second largest economy in the world, is bound to have regional and global ripple effects in energy prices, first in gas and then oil, and on energy transportation routes to and from Asia. We present conditions of a most likely scenario based on information available today. This points to a growing competition between Russia and the United States to play a dominant role in supplying and ensuring security of supply in the Asia Pacific Region (APR).

Next, the economics of the project have changed since the signing of the thirty-year long gas agreement between Russia and China. Considering oil price fluctuations, the current price environment, which has a lower oil price than in 2014 when the pipeline agreement was finalised, PoS looks to be more beneficial to Russia. This could put pressure to renegotiate the terms of the project should the price of oil remain low relative to 2014 levels.

Much like what happened between Russia and Europe when the first oil and gas pipelines were constructed in the 1970s, PoS has the potential to link the Russian and Chinese economies creating deep interlinkages.[3] However, it remains to be seen if the incentives for this are sufficient for the PRC to allow itself to become dependent on Russia in the same way as Europe. Although the pipeline is already under construction, China may still withdraw from the project if cost-effective substitutions are found either in Central Asia or through LNG. This scenario is less likely in the current environment considering Turkmen supply is now back under Russian control. It is important to note, however, that Chinese long-term interest is not purely market based and also hinges on geopolitical gains, domestic industrial reforms and Beijing's expectations of Russia, which are based on the experience of often having to wait on Russia.[4]

Concerning the environment and the impact on local indigenous communities, the pipeline's effects have posed problems. Owing partly to opaque legal and institutional conditions that are characteristic of authoritarian countries, the commercial and government stakeholders have neglected important steps in the design,

[2] Simon Caney, 'Just Emissions', *Philosophy & Public Affairs* 40, no. 4 (1 September 2012): 255–300.

[3] Angela E. Stent, *From Embargo to Ostpolitik: The Political Economy of West German-Soviet Relations, 1955–1980* (Cambridge: Cambridge University Press, 2003), 7.

[4] Gaye Christoffersen, 'China's Intentions for Russian and Central Asian Oil and Gas', *National Bureau of Asian Research* 9, no. 2 (1998): 19.

assessment and enforcement of environmental precautions. Likewise, the project has neither generated the expected number of new jobs for local employment nor benefited indigenous communities as Gazprom had initially extolled.

The approach that we take draws on multiple disciplines to investigate this pipeline and its effects. We make no claims of producing interdisciplinary work; however, our group consists of four disciplines that are inherently interdisciplinary, what Youngblood refers to as 'bridging disciplines'.[5] These include social anthropology, geography, area studies and international relations. We also draw on economics. In accordance with analyses of multidisciplinary studies, we focused on process of cooperative exchange rather than showcasing the methods or findings of any single discipline.[6] This cooperative process, which began with a working group, and continued through the drafting of this chapter, is what Dillon, Norwell and Repko describe as standard multidisciplinary work where '[m]ultidisciplinarity is what happens when members of two or more disciplines cooperate, using tools and knowledge of their disciplines in new ways to consider multifaceted problems that have at least one tentacle in another area of study'.[7]

Our multidisciplinary group identified four features that will form the structure of our approach including: 1) type of pipeline, 2) perspectives of 'good policies', 3) geographic scope and 4) comparative dimensions. With respect to the type of pipeline, this refers to the distinction between natural gas and oil. We have chosen to focus on natural gas because the market dynamics of gas are bound to a region as opposed to oil, which tends to be more global. The physical constraints are the pipelines themselves. Whereas oil may be transported through multiple means, i.e. lorry, rail, ship and pipeline, natural gas typically depends on pipelines for transportation, and pipelines are notoriously unmovable. The exception to this is natural gas that is transported in its liquefied state (Liquefied Natural Gas or LNG), but this represents only 32 per cent of the total natural gas market in 2017.[8] As such, pipelines, which bind natural gas to regional markets, impact the political and social dimensions more profoundly than oil.[9]

As regards perspectives of 'good' policies, these will qualify what is meant by 'good' in the context of geopolitics, economic measurements of welfare, impact on the environment and social structures of populations.

Next, the difference between national versus regional levels refers to the question, 'good policy for whom?' Although examining policies at the regional level may seem like a worthwhile exercise, the reality is that there are different perspectives on what

5 Dawn Youngblood, 'Multidisciplinarity, Interdisciplinarity, and Bridging Disciplines: A Matter of Process', *Journal of Research Practice* 3, no. 2 (5 December 2007): 18.

6 Youngblood: 2.

7 Youngblood: 2.

8 BP, 'BP Energy Outlook 2017 Edition', Energy Outlooks (London, 2017), www.bp.com/content/dam/bp/pdf/energy-economics/energy-outlook-2017/bp-energy-outlook-2017.pdf.

9 Jonathan P. Stern and Howard Rogers, 'The Pricing of Internationally Traded Gas' (IEEJ, Tokyo, 6 March 2013).

constitutes a good energy policy at the national versus regional level. Pipeline policies are usually made at the national level, with the exception of the EU, so it is not possible to speak of a regional pipeline policy for Eurasia. Notwithstanding the existence of the Eurasian Economic Union (EAEU), natural gas contracts within the EAEU are still negotiated bilaterally, and the signatories of this treaty organisation, Russia, Belarus, Kazakhstan, Kyrgyzstan and Armenia, do not include Russia's primary market, the EU, or its main target market to the east, China.[10] Thus, the structure of this analysis focuses on the most important Eurasian supplier state, Russia, with an emphasis on the most recent pipeline project, Power of Siberia. Because pipelines bind states and have geopolitical ripple effects, we will also examine some demand-side factors for PoS in the pipeline's primary market, China, first at the interstate level, and then secondary effects in Europe and the United States with respect to geopolitics. We will also comment on events in Russia's Artic Region as they relate to developments in Russian pipeline projects, geopolitics and non-state actors such as energy companies and their role as pipeline developers.

To sum up, the analysis includes three levels, Russia, China as a demand market and regional ripple effects beyond, which introduces a variety of new players, both state and non-state actors. Each bilateral relationship is, of course, grounded in a mini-regional context, and likewise impacts security of supply and demand. It is worth mentioning that other neighbouring countries figure into geopolitical dynamics. The fact that PoS links Russia to China testifies to China's primacy of place for Russia, but there are still incentives for Russia to play China's neighbours off of one another in Russia's negotiations with China, namely Japan and the Republic of Korea. And Russia has a history of doing this since the early 1990s.[11]

With respect to the literature, we draw on studies from multiple disciplines. The multidisciplinary nature of this chapter makes a comprehensive overview of the relevant scholarship untenable. However, the contribution to extant scholarship that we offer is by way of introducing a multidisciplinary perspective to the analysis of pipeline policies, and specifically in the region of Eurasia. Another aspect that makes this analysis relevant to current scholarship is the recent timing of the primary pipeline case, Power of Siberia, whose agreement between Russian and Chinese partners was only finalised in 2014. Thus far, journalists and industry commentators have provided most of the analysis on PoS; however, there is a burgeoning body of work from academics such as Stern and Paik.[12] This chapter will contribute not only

10 'The Eurasian Economic Union: Power, Politics and Trade', Crisis Group, 20 July 2016, www.crisisgroup.org/europe-central-asia/central-asia/eurasian-economic-union-power-politics-and-trade.

11 Christoffersen, 'China's Intentions for Russian and Central Asian Oil and Gas'.

12 Jonathan P. Stern (ed.), *The Pricing of Internationally Traded Gas* (Oxford: Oxford University Press for the Oxford Institute for Energy Studies, 2012); Keun-Wook Paik, *Sino-Russian Oil and Gas Cooperation: The Reality and Implications* (Oxford: Oxford University Press for the Oxford Institute for Energy Studies, 2012).

to the growing multidisciplinary scholarship on energy policy but also to the subject-specific work on new pipeline projects in east Eurasia.

The chapter examines the project from multiple perspectives. In the beginning we address the geopolitics of the region before examining the economic impacts in the east of Russia and China. Next, we will explore some of the geographic and environmental dimensions in addition to potential impacts on local communities. And lastly, we include a discussion of the implications of this study, general conclusions and directions for further research.

21.2 GEOPOLITICAL CONSIDERATIONS

Russia's geographical position spanning Eurasia, from the EU in the west, to China in the Asia Pacific Region (APR), means that the construction, ownership and destination of gas pipelines, and increasingly LNG facilities too, plays a strategic role in delineating both Russian and Eurasian territory and underpinning its sovereignty.

Geopolitically, it is at its borders and frontiers that Russia most perceives its strategic vulnerability. In the melting Arctic for instance, China now owns equity in the Yamal LNG project.[13] This is the location of the Russia-dominated Northern Sea Route (NSR), a critical maritime energy conduit between the Russian Arctic and the APR. It is still unclear if this economic access to the Arctic, via the NSR, represents a moat or a bridge, in relation to Russo-Chinese energy relations.

Nonetheless, the singular unintended consequence of Western sanctions against Russia is the deepening and broadening of Russia's relations with China, nowhere more so than in energy collaboration, infrastructure and investment in Russia. The perceived danger of this geographical energy alliance by Russia's European neighbours, coupled with waning US leadership in Europe, has made Russian energy policy in Eurasia the latest geopolitical chessboard, upon which Chinese and US interests appear to be converging.

In short, Russia will now have to factor in US political positioning and commercial competition, in their own energy policy formulation for and with China, across the APR region. Competition is fierce in the fight for capture of EU and APR gas markets in Eurasia, both of which are key to these regions' emerging economic development and continued sustainability. United States LNG suppliers are already making inroads into replacing Russian pipeline gas in Europe with LNG deliveries, on the back of recently tightened sanctions.[14]

President Putin's response has been swift; his aim is for Russia to become the world's largest LNG producer, competing directly with the United States to supply

[13] Henry Foy, 'Russia Ships First Gas from $27bn Arctic Project', *Financial Times*, 8 December 2017, www.ft.com/content/515d451c-dc11-11e7-a039-c64b1c09b482.

[14] Nicole Gaouette, 'Latest US Sanctions against Russia a Work in Progress', *CNN*, accessed 9 January 2018, www.cnn.com/2017/12/14/politics/trump-russia-sanctions-explainer/index.html.

the growing APR LNG market. The Arctic's Yamal LNG and Arctic LNG (II) projects, both with Chinese ownership, are critical to this aim. Accordingly, China announced in July 2017 that Russia's Arctic will be part of its Belt and Road Initiative (BRI) alongside its associated Silk Road Fund's investment in Yamal LNG.[15] Most recently Russia has gone on to designate the NSR as one of its three 'Blue Economic Corridors'.[16] Russia's message to the United States is clear; the Russo-Chinese energy alliance in Eurasia is funded, increasingly commercial and strategic.

Besides the numerous geopolitical implications of PoS's thirty-year commitment to Russia's trade with China, the project is intended be one of the pillars of the Russia's economy, providing thousands of jobs, improved infrastructure and new facilities. The route runs through some of the country's poorest regions, especially at its southern end in Zabaikalsky Krai and Amurskii Oblast. In this area high prices for electricity and industrial supplies, as well as a low and decreasing population, have held up economic development. It would be expected that the urban population would welcome the project with open arms, yet some obstacles have emerged. Construction staff is difficult to recruit in these extreme environmental conditions. Rather than providing for jobs for the local population, the pipeline construction draws on workers from other regions. Furthermore, protests against Gazprom are emerging in the region because of a lack of local energy supplies. It is shameful, said Prime Minister Medvedev in 2016, that a country producing more gas than any other in the world does not supply gas to a greater proportion of its citizens.[17] At the end of 2016, on average, 67.2 per cent of dwellings in Russia were supplied with gas, but with huge disparities according to region and level of urbanisation. Many remote small towns and villages have no gas at all. Gazprom was accused of providing funding for the gasification of Kyrgyzstan, where the level is 22 per cent, while giving considerably less towards the Novosibirsk *Oblast*, or district, where only 10 per cent of homes have access to gas. The issue has become so politically charged that it was raised in a public discussion between Putin and Alexei Miller, the head of Gazprom.[18] The company responded that it provided gas as far as town borders, but it was up to the municipal authorities to supply it to dwellings within those borders. However, local township district budgets are rarely sufficient to fund expensive infrastructure undertakings that would be required for residential gas distribution. Furthermore, there is the problem that residential consumers in

[15] 'China, Russia Jointly Launch Yamal LNG Project in the Arctic', Belt and Road Portal, accessed 30 March 2018, https://eng.yidaiyilu.gov.cn/home/rolling/39155.htm.

[16] 'Railway and Arctic Routes Enhance China–Europe Trade', Belt and Road Portal, accessed 30 March 2018, https://eng.yidaiyilu.gov.cn/info/iList.jsp?tm_id=139&cat_id=10058&info_id=26102.

[17] Nikolai Makeev, 'Rossiya bez gaza: pochemu tret' straniy im postydno ne obespechena', accessed 31 March 2018, www.mk.ru/economics/2017/04/11/rossiya-bez-gaza-pochemu-tret-strany-im-postydno-ne-obespechena.html.

[18] 'Alexey Miller Briefs Vladimir Putin on Gasification of Russian Regions', accessed 31 March 2018, www.gazprom.com/press/news/2017/july/article340619/.

Siberia and the Russian Far East are used to subsidised energy prices and may not be able to pay for gas with infrastructure costs that are passed through to consumers.[19]

This has deeper geopolitical implications too for both Russia and its neighbours in Eurasia. Pipeline gas delineates de facto territorial borders, physically facilitates economic integration between regions and countries, and thus requires and encourages partnership and mutual trust between governments. The economics and associated geopolitics of LNG are different from pipeline gas, however. There is an enormous and growing LNG market in the APR, which will impact Gazprom's pipeline-based business, both domestically and abroad. Gazprom's recent announcement of gas volumes to be carried by the PoS pipeline, and resumed talks concerning the much-delayed development of Sakhalin II (LNG), suggest that it has yet to implement a clear strategy on how to manage competing interests between these two markets.

This has strategic implications for future control of energy markets in Asia, something that Russian politicians are well aware of. The Russian gas industry, aligned with China's enormous and growing economic power demand is, arguably, fundamental to northeast Asia's growth and stability, and could provide the economic underpinning of, albeit partial, Eurasian integration.

21.3 REGIONAL GEOPOLITICAL CONSIDERATIONS, RUSSIA AND EUROPE

Russia's energy relations with Europe, as with China, are not binary. United States interests in Europe create an inevitable triangular energy discourse in the EU. Any binary energy relationship is therefore always informed, tempered, and often altered, by the excluded party's anticipated, or actual, reaction to it.

The public emergence of this triangular energy relationship is largely because energy security in Europe and, similarly in the APR, is a strategic and economically vital issue. However, the US involvement in Russia's current relations with Europe, also reflects wider US geopolitical reservations about Russia's conduct in Europe. The two issues are related. On the one hand, the challenge for the EU is that the battlefield between the United States and Russia is in Europe, and Europe has been here before as the proverbial meat in the Cold War sandwich.

By way of example, the latest 2017 US sanctions against Russia's energy industry, which now includes Gazprom, are instructive in understanding the complexity of the geopolitics determining the Russian–EU energy relationship. Brussels is concerned that replacing Gazprom pipeline gas with US shale gas, in the form of LNG, is not necessarily in Europe's interest, especially as US LNG is more expensive than Russian pipeline gas, and Europe will have to foot the bill for

19 Evgenia Vanadzina, *Capacity Market in Russia: Addressing the Energy Trilemma* (Lappeenranta University of Technology, 2016), 25, https://ieeexplore.ieee.org/document/7521191.

expensive LNG re-gasification import facilities as well. On the other hand, the sub-Baltic Sea Nord Stream pipeline route connecting Russia to the EU gives Europe further pause for thought, as does declining gas production within Europe.[20]

For the United States the real prize deriving from sanctions is not so much gaining dominance as a supplier in the EU gas market at the cost of Russia's economy, but rather the steady unification of the European and US markets in the Transatlantic Partnership. For the EU there is temptation to use this US LNG threat to Russian gas supply as a lever for pushing Gazprom for greater volume discounts, alternative pricing arrangements and an end to 'take or pay' long-term contracts.[21] This EU negotiation strategy appears to be effective from an economic point of view. However, this last point about long-term contracts carries substantial regional dangers.

One of the critical mechanisms for Russo-European relations and semi-European integration for the last fifty years has been mutual energy interdependence.[22] This has taken the form of Russia's need for security of gas demand, and the EU's need for security of supply. Thus, pushing Gazprom too hard on contract terms and likewise placing too much trust in US LNG as an alternative to Gazprom supply is a highly nuanced, multifactorial and risk-laden act of European statecraft. How this triangular relation transpires will have profound strategic implications for Russia, Europe and the United States beyond the issue of just energy.

As global political alliances shift, Europe may not remain confident in alternative gas supplies from other states in the Middle East and Central Asia. This has happened before as the result of the oil price shock of 1972 and political instability in the Middle East. Suppliers in these regions are being courted for loyalties and energy alliances by either Russia or China, or in combination, working together across Eurasia. The interconnectedness of energy with its supporting financial initiatives such as China's BRI, alongside Russia's less potent EAEU, will be a critical part of future shifting geopolitical forces.

As part of the $450 billion Russian gas deal with China, Russia will, in time, commission its Siberian pipeline gas project, known as Altai, to feed western China.[23] Turkmen gas is the prime competition to Altai, but Turkmenistan is reluctant to sell equity in the designated pipeline to China. In a stroke, with Altai operational, Russia may well become the 'swing' provider of gas to Europe. This combination of alternative gas supplies, alongside potential BRI infrastructure

20 'The Outlook for Natural Gas Demand in Europe', *Oxford Institute for Energy Studies* (blog), 10 June 2014, www.oxfordenergy.org/publications/the-outlook-for-natural-gas-demand-in-europe/.

21 'LNG Isn't Freeing Europe from Gazprom Yet', *The American Interest* (blog), 10 January 2017, www.the-american-interest.com/2017/01/10/lng-isnt-freeing-europe-from-gazprom-yet/.

22 Øistein Harsem and Dag Harald Claes, 'The Interdependence of European–Russian Energy Relations', *Energy Policy* 59 (1 August 2013): 784–91, https://doi.org/10.1016/j.enpol.2013.04.035.

23 'The Commercial and Political Logic for the Altai Pipeline', *Oxford Institute for Energy Studies* (blog), 5 December 2014, www.oxfordenergy.org/publications/the-commercial-and-political-logic-for-the-altai-pipeline/.

financing, altering energy alliances across Eurasia and the inexorable movement of Chinese energy interests into places such as Greece (port of Piraeus) and Ukraine (Yalta), will not be lost on EU energy negotiators.

Seismic change in the international order today is such that to suppose the EU can continue to achieve security of energy supply in a regional cocoon, unrelated to altering global energy developments, is unlikely given current developments. Similarly Russia's faith in European security of demand, for primarily similar reasons, presents risks of its own.

21.3.1 *Regional Geopolitical Considerations for China*

The vision of a network of Eurasian pipelines supplying oil and gas to China started around 1996 when a group of Chinese oil analysts wrote about the 'Pan-Asian continental oil bridge' extending oil and gas pipelines from eastern China across western China, through Central Asia, Russia and into the greater Middle East and Caucuses.[24] The basic security argument was that land-based pipelines diversified risks of supply disruption away from sea lanes controlled by the US navy.[25] There was, however, a far more complex and sophisticated geopolitical imagination at work. Gaye Christoffersen argued that China's initial conception was to leverage its burgeoning refining capacities to link Middle Eastern and Central Asian crude supplies to Asian consumer markets, but over time China's strategic thinking became more global with separate regional subplots including its own relationship with Central Asia.[26] China exploited the prospect of its role as a plausible counterweight to Russia, helping energy producers such as Kazakhstan alleviate energy dependency on Russia.[27] Beijing also counted on strengthened intergovernmental ties in the region to keep ethnic unrests in the region from spilling over to inflame the already highly charged Han–Uyghur relations in Xinjiang.[28] Hence underlying China's regional economic diplomacy via the Shanghai Cooperative Organization (SCO) was an effort to secure member states' agreement on, and policy support for, suppression of the 'three evils' of terrorism, religious extremism and secessionism in Central Asia.[29]

24 Radtke, Kurt W. et al. (eds.), *Dynamics in Pacific Asia* (Routledge, 2014), 80.

25 Chen Shaofeng 2010, China's Malacca Dilemma; Meidan pp. 185–8. Erickson Collins DTIC 2010 called China's overland oil supply plans a 'pipe dream': p. 91.

26 Gaye Christoffersen, 'The Dilemmas of China's Energy Governance: Recentralization and Regional Cooperation', *The China and Eurasia Quarterly Forum*, Energy and Security, 3, no. 3 (November 2005): 55.

27 Christoffersen, 'China's Intentions for Russian and Central Asian Oil and Gas'.

28 James P. Dorian, Brett H. Wigdortz, and Dru C. Gladney, 'China and Central Asia's Volatile Mix: Energy, Trade, and Ethnic Relations', 1997, 1–2, http://scholarspace.manoa.hawaii.edu/handle/10125/3791.

29 Roland Dannreuther, 'China and Global Oil: Vulnerability and Opportunity', *International Affairs* 87, no. 6 (November 2011): 1345–64; Radtke, *Dynamics in Pacific Asia*.

Also in the second half of the 1990s China actively promoted energy regionalism centred on Northeast Asia, with the hope that the Republic of Korea – South Korea (ROK) – and Japan would be willing to invest in the infrastructure and upstream projects in the Russian Far East (RFE), and Russia would be willing to offer assets to China in return for the promise of access to the potentially biggest market in the Northeast Asia region (NEA). China was very disappointed with one project that was stalled in Tyumen, for example. With respect to NEA cooperation, Christoffersen described it concisely: 'China, Japan and Russia, in what could be called a two-level bargaining game, each took a path towards regional cooperation that involved reconciling conflicting domestic interests into a national consensus, necessary before there could be regional consensus'.[30] In the early 2000s, China invested heavy political capital on the Angarsk–Daqing oil pipeline, but came out on the losing end as President Putin relegated the supply to China as a spur from the main pipeline to the Pacific.[31] China took away lessons in this disappointment and political shock to focus on domestic solutions, global acquisitions and long-term ties with other energy-producing countries. Christoffersen observed that the 'lessons from the struggle for Angarsk were added to the lessons from the Iraq War. Both contributed to the securitisation of Chinese energy issues'.[32] In the end, the first concept of a Northeast Asian regional energy regime was reduced to a minimal result of shared supplies, and no NEA regional architecture emerged from the effort.[33]

Nevertheless, all parties in the NEA recognised the fundamentals of the geo-economics of oil and gas in the region, which make it a matter of time for regionalism to develop in the RFE and the Pacific Arctic with Japan, South Korea and China. Gulick stated strongly that 'the gradual integration of the RFE's raw materials and transport networks into a regional division of labour has been punctuated by much more geopolitical friction than anticipated' by market-oriented industry analysts.[34] Gulick further argues that Russian tactics of playing off Japan against China for short-term economic gains or strategic leeway would eventually give way to the overwhelming synergy in Sino-Russian energy cooperation, which

30 Gaye Christoffersen, 'Angarsk as a Challenge for the East Asian Energy Community', *Mongolian Journal of International Affairs* 0, no. 11 (15 September 2013), 107.

31 Joseph Yu-shek Cheng, 'Chinese Perceptions of Russian Foreign Policy During the Putin Administration: U.S.-Russia Relations and "Strategic Triangle" Considerations', *Journal of Current Chinese Affairs* 38, no. 2 (28 July 2009): 145–68; Kun-Chin Lin and Brad Williams, 'Pipeline Politics: Comparative Bargaining Capacity', Working Paper, CRP Working Paper Series (Cambridge: U. of Cambridge, October 2012).

32 Christoffersen, 'The Dilemmas of China's Energy Governance: Recentralization and Regional Cooperation', 67.

33 John Gulick, 'Russo-Chinese Energy Cooperation: Stepping Stone from Strategic Partnership to Geo-Economic Integration?', *International Journal of Comparative Sociology – INT J COMP SOCIOL* 48 (1 April 2007): 203–33.

34 Gulick, 204.

would push for a more a profound strategic partnership.[35] One could argue that this partnership is unfolding before us in the form of mega-oil and gas and pipeline deals such as PoS, underpinned by the merger of the EAEU and BRI as respective conceptions of Eurasia for Moscow and Beijing.[36] Both Moscow and Beijing could agree on putting transport infrastructure in place for future exploitation of the whole industrial value chain for oil and gas, and for establishing the economic viability of the Eurasian markets.

21.4 ECONOMIC CONSIDERATIONS AND THE VALUATION OF THE POWER OF SIBERIA GAS PIPELINE – GAZPROM AND RUSSIAN PERSPECTIVES

From an economics perspective, the valuation of natural gas pipelines as a policy and the question of whether a pipeline policy is good, and for whom, involves several rather complex analytical exercises. First, one must evaluate whether the project will bring economic benefits to its developers – Gazprom, and in this case China National Petroleum Company (CNPC) as well. And secondly, one must evaluate how the project may impact governments on both sides of the deal – Russia and China. Lastly, related to the second point, is the question of how the project would impact consumers.

21.4.1 *Benefits to Gazprom as a Supplier to China through Power of Siberia*

The evaluation of a gas pipeline project depends on several factors: (i) the outlook for the gas price in the destination market for the entire economic lifetime of the pipeline, which is usually assumed to be from twenty-five to thirty-five years, (ii) off-take volume, delivery and ramp-up schedules agreed under the contract between Gazprom and CNPC and (iii) the overall cost of the project – in other words, the price the customer is willing to pay, the amount of gas the customer is estimated to buy and the total cost of constructing, operating and maintaining the pipeline. We discuss these items in turn now.[37]

The Power of Siberia deal was announced in May of 2014 at a time when crude oil prices traded in a range of $110 per bbl while spot gas prices in Asia Pacific (EAX index assessed by pricing agency ICIS, Figure 21.1, left panel) were being traded in

35 Gulick, 205.

36 Michael Clarke, 'Beijing's March West: Opportunities and Challenges for China's Eurasian Pivot', *Orbis* 60, no. 2 (1 January 2016): 296–313, https://doi.org/10.1016/j.orbis.2016.01.001; Dmitri Trenin, 'From Greater Europe to Greater Asia?', Carnegie Moscow Center (Moscow: Carnegie Endowment, April 2015).

37 Chi Kong Chyong, Pierre Noël, and David Reiner, 'The Economics of the Nord Stream Pipeline', Working Paper, EPRG Working Paper Series (Cambridge: U. of Cambridge, September 2010); Chi Kong Chyong and Benjamin F. Hobbs, 'Strategic Eurasian Natural Gas Market Model for Energy Security and Policy Analysis: Formulation and Application to South Stream', *Energy Economics* 44 (1 July 2014): 198–211.

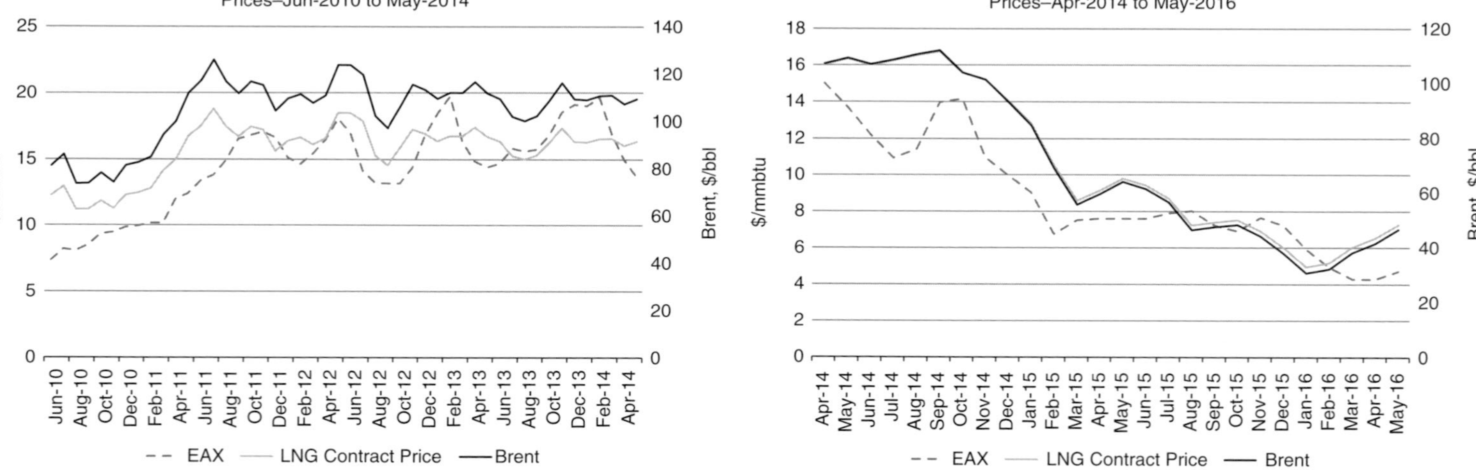

FIGURE 21.1 Gas price dynamics in Asia Pacific region before (left panel) and after (right panel) the deal was announced (May 2014)
Note: EAX is a price index assessed by pricing and information agency ICIS and it covers spot gas trade in Asia; LNG contract price is a proxy which assumes 14.5 per cent slope of Brent plus 0.5 constant.

TABLE 21.1 *NPV of Power of Siberia under various contract price and CAPEX assumptions*

Crude oil price, $/bbl	Implied contract gas price[a], $/tcm	Project CAPEX, $bn				
		50	55	60	65	70
29	100	−33.5	−38.7	−44.0	−49.2	−54.4
59	200	−14.7	−19.9	−25.1	−30.4	−35.6
88	300	4.2	−1.1	−6.3	−11.5	−16.8
103	350	13.6	8.3	3.1	−2.1	−7.4
117	400	23.0	17.8	12.5	7.3	2.1

Note: [a] Implied contract price was calculated assuming indexation to Brent at 9.3 per cent with 'straight line'; we also assume annual OPEX at 3 per cent of total project CAPEX.

the range of $15–20 per mmbtu with LNG contract prices following those same dynamics. The gas supply deal between Russia and China was signed for a period of thirty years and was worth $400 bn at the time when it was announced. This value was based on the period when oil prices were high, ca. $110 per bbl. Under the agreement, CNCP agreed to buy 38 bcm per year, and the project was planned to ramp up from 2019 to 2020, reaching this capacity by the mid 2020s. At the time of the contract signing this translated into an average price of $350 per tcm ($9.5 per mmbtu) or $375 per tcm ($10.2 per mmbtu) with the ramp-up schedule reaching to full capacity by 2026. So, compared to European spot prices (NBP) of $7–8 per mmbtu at that time, the deal was not bad from Gazprom's point of view.

Despite this, a few months after the deal was announced, crude oil prices crashed and stabilised at roughly half the level they were at the time of the deal's signing (Figure 21.1, right panel). The spot and LNG contract gas prices in Asia also followed this trend. Thus, the outlook for whether the project will be worthwhile economically has become questionable. The deal for Gazprom depends much on contract prices, which in turn are determined by crude oil prices from the early 2020s until the end of the contract. To demonstrate this, Table 21.1 below shows results from a sensitivity analysis of various possible contract price levels, associated crude oil prices and total project capital expenditure (CAPEX). For these calculations we assume that the construction of the project started in 2016 and that total CAPEX will be evenly distributed for the five years of construction (2016–20). We also assume a 10 per cent discount rate and thirty years of project lifetime, which corresponds to the length of the supply agreement between Gazprom and CNPC. The deliveries start with 5 bcm per year in 2020 and fully ramp up by 2026 to 38 bcm per year for thirty years until the end of 2049. Given the contract parameters, we found that the net present value (NPV) of the Power of Siberia project ranges from −$54 bn if the crude oil price is as low as $29 per bbl while total CAPEX is $70bn to a positive value of $23bn if crude oil prices trade at $117 per bbl and CAPEX is as low as $50bn. When the deal was signed at a crude price of $110 per bbl the profitability was relatively good for Gazprom but under 2016 crude prices ($50–60 per bbl) the project brings losses to the company irrespective of the actual CAPEX level.

In addition to the pricing issue, the other important factor that could undermine the project's economic viability is the total capital expenditure as well as the required off-take volume agreed with CNPC. This is the minimum amount of natural gas that CNPC is required to purchase as stipulated in the contract. We should note that since the oil price drop in 2014 and the financial sanctions against Russia in the aftermath of the Ukraine crisis, Russia's national currency has greatly devalued against the US dollar. This may help the project's economic viability in the sense that most of project CAPEX is valued in Russian roubles (₽) and hence overall project cost valued against US dollars could be lower relative to the May 2014 date when the agreement was signed. Thus, most current estimates of total CAPEX of the project stand at $50–60 bn, whereas when the deal was announced, it was closer to $70 bn.

The second factor is the agreed export volume of 38 bcm per year. Long-term gas contracts are usually signed with a minimum off-take level (called minimum take-or -pay), which is usually 70–80 per cent of the agreed annual export volume. The buyer can reduce the volume down to that level but also has the right to make up for this reduced volume in later contract years. Gas contracts are usually very stringent and once signed will have limited room for renegotiation both in terms of volume and the pricing formula applied in the contract. However, the recent renegotiations between Gazprom and its European customers suggest that if the downstream market is structurally changing then these contracts can be renegotiated in favour of the customers. Thus, the risk associated with export volumes for CNPC to sell at least 38 bcm of gas per year may not be as high as stipulated in the contract. However, any potential change of contract volumes could undermine the project's economic case for Gazprom.

21.4.2 *Wider Benefits to Russia*

As we have shown, when the deal was signed back in 2014 the economics of the project for Gazprom looked relatively attractive. And the timing was good for the Russian government, too. The signing of the contract showed that Russia could diversify away its gas exports from Europe, albeit the volume that was agreed (38 bcm per year) is rather insignificant compared to its annual export to Europe (150–170 bcm per year). That said, Russian officials stated that the deal is just a first step in fulfilling its energy strategy aim of exporting at least 100 bcm per year to Asia by 2030. Despite this strategic objective of diversifying away from Europe, one that has been around in Russia for as long as Gazprom emerged as a semi-private entity, the timing of the deal obviously had huge political benefits for Russia when the relationship with Western countries deteriorated in the aftermath of the Ukraine crisis. And so, as global oil and gas markets have evolved since 2014, the political benefits of this project for Russia have become more pronounced. Global gas markets are over-supplied while crude oil prices are expected to remain at the current, relatively low, level for the foreseeable future. The other way to look at this is that when the deal for PoS was signed the economics of the project supported the political objective of ensuring any deal with CNPC/China, but as time passes, the only strong rationale left is its political and strategic objectives, to cement its gas relationship with the soon-to-become largest gas market in the region, China.

One can argue that it was also good timing for Gazprom itself. The company has been facing increasingly competitive gas markets in Europe with further prospects of intensive competition from overseas LNG coming from around the world. The dramatic structural changes in European gas markets coupled with an increasingly flexible LNG trade coming from the United States forced Gazprom to change its traditional business model in order to adapt to the new needs of European gas markets, which include increased volumes, flexible destination deliveries and pricing that is effectively tied to spot markets.[38] In light of these developments, Gazprom, which has always been an advocate of long-term, rigid and large gas supply contracts indexed to crude oil – like all its supply contracts with European buyers used to be – happily rushed into the agreement with China seeking similar trading structures that it used to enjoy with European buyers.[39]

Therefore, the timing of this agreement has great political capital for the Russian government because it is a powerful symbol to the outside world that Russia and its national champion, Gazprom, can diversify away from its partners in Europe, if needed, for the first time since the collapse of the Soviet Union. In other words, Russia is no longer dependent on Europe as its main customer. This is probably one of the substantive, and no doubt unintentional, consequences of European sanctions against Russia. The Power of Siberia is an even bigger symbol within Russia itself as the pipeline deal mobilised internal support for President Putin and his administration at a time when the Russian economy was hit hard by falling oil prices and financial sanctions.

Apart from these political considerations, the economic benefits of the project for Russia include budget revenues from export duties as well as local economic benefits such as the 'gasification' of remote regions of Russia where gas has not been available before, the creation of jobs and the procurement of local goods and services as part of the pipeline's construction and operation. One should note that, in principle, the Russian government will receive 30 per cent of contract price times the volume of sales to China under the agreement, which is undeniably 'good' for the state.

38 Chi Kong Chyong, 'Markets and Long-Term Contracts: The Case of Russian Gas Supplies to Europe', Working Paper, EPRG Working Paper Series (Cambridge: U. of Cambridge, December 2015); Chi Kong Chyong and Roman Kazmin, 'The Economics of Global LNG Trade: The Case of Atlantic and Pacific Inter-Basin Arbitrage in 2010–2014', Working Paper, EPRG Working Paper Series (Cambridge: U. of Cambridge, January 2016).

39 Chyong, 'Markets and Long-Term Contracts: The Case of Russian Gas Supplies to Europe'.

The project could of course have economic benefits at the local level, too. Eastern Siberia provinces are relatively less gasified, and it is believed that the project will motivate Gazprom and the Russian government to invest in connecting more households to the gas grid. No doubt these benefits are clearly positive for citizens, but they are somewhat marginal when taking into account the country's total population, the majority of whom reside in the 'European' part of Russia west of the Urals. In the later sections, we explore how these benefits have or have not yet materialised.

All in all, from the Russian perspective the gas pipeline policy has always been based on both economic and geopolitical considerations. The economic and political dimensions of Russia's gas export policy are indistinguishable. For Russia, the pipeline presents clear benefits in both respects.

21.5 CONSIDERATIONS FOR CHINA AS A DEMAND MARKET FOR POWER OF SIBERIA

The past decade has seen a gradual rise in economic interdependence between Russia and China, but on terms not sustainable and satisfactory to either. Overall trade and investment flows have reinforced the asymmetry in favour of China but showed diversification from an initial profile of arms transfers and petty merchandising in the 1990s, with the Russian Far East–Northeast China economic integration playing a key role in an increased Chinese economic stake in Russia.[40] Swanström points out that Russia would rather see itself as an exporter of technology and machinery than just raw materials and energy, and seemed to constantly remind itself that its Asian exchanges are less important than its ties to Europe.[41] The amount of gas that Russia plans to sell to China is still around one quarter of what it supplies to Europe. From Beijing's energy security perspective, given the protracted negotiation and remaining uncertainties in oil and gas and pipeline deals, Russia has not stepped up historically to become a trusted partner for meeting China's rapidly rising natural gas needs. Natural gas made up around 3 per cent of China's total energy consumption until the 2010s, and currently stands at around 6 per cent. The domestic supply growth has been gradual, facing disappointing outputs in coal-bed methane production and water resource barriers to the exploitation of shale gas deposits.[42] Natural gas imports, which did not begin until 2006, grew from 1 bcm

[40] Gulick, 'Russo-Chinese Energy Cooperation'; Nodari Simonia, 'The Energy Dimension in Russian Global Strategy: Russian Energy Policy in East Siberia and the Far East', Report, James A. Baker III Insitute for Public Policy (Houston: Rice University, October 2004).

[41] Niklas Swanström, 'Sino–Russian Relations at the Start of the New Millennium in Central Asia and Beyond', *Journal of Contemporary China* 23, no. 87 (4 May 2014): 483–4.

[42] Raj Rattanavich, 'Unconventional Gas and Lng: The Yin and Yang of Chinese Natural Gas Planning', n.d., 11.

that year to over 58 bcm in 2014.[43] With its imports split almost evenly between pipeline and LNG, China became the fourth largest natural gas importer in the world in 2015. The *IEA Medium-Term Gas Market Report 2014* forecasts demand to reach 315 bcm in 2019, with a 12 per cent year-on-year increase. The twelfth Five Year Plan (FYP) called for gas to comprise 7.5 per cent of China's primary energy mix by 2015, compared to 4.3 per cent in the eleventh FYP.[44]

These domestic non-traditional gas output shortfalls have driven Chinese planners to increasingly turn to imported LNG to meet the south-eastern coastal demand.[45] Three West–East gas pipelines including the WEPP I, operational in 2005; the WEPP II, operational in 2012; and the WEPP III near completion, have been constructed by Chinese National Oil Companies (NOCs) to deliver Xinjiang and Central Asian (Turkmenistan, Uzbekistan and Kazakhstan) gas to the Yangtze River Delta area, Guangdong and Fujian respectively.[46] The fact that China's gas transport infrastructure remains underdeveloped and administered prices are sticky should make LNG an attractive option for these demand hotspots. However, China pays an 'Asian premium' from major suppliers such as Qatar. LNG imports from Australia, Malaysia and Indonesia are significantly cheaper, even lower than the average pipeline gas cost.[47]

While in absolute terms Russia has been a motivated seller of both its RFE regional development opportunities and its natural gas to China, in relative power terms its commitment to China depends a great deal on Russia's strategies to regain its slipping leverage vis-a-vis the West.[48] In 2006 Putin used the 'gas war' with Ukraine to lend credence to competition with Asia for Russian gas, prompting European clients to renegotiate their long-term contracts. Yet Gazprom did not follow up the threat by providing sound deals to China. After 2014, Putin stepped up his offers to China while the United States and the EU shut Russia out of deepening energy and economic relations. Yet Kadri Liik argues that this 'pivot to Asia' reflected more of 'Russia's "disappointment in the West" than the "promise of the East"', indicating Putin's Europe-centric foreign policy mindset, effectively using Asia as an economic counter-weight to the EU.[49] In order to maintain demand flexibility and security, Russia would need to engineer new forms of security of demand in both

43 Michael Ratner, Gabriel M Nelson, and Susan V Lawrence, 'China's Natural Gas: Uncertainty for Markets', n.d., 31.

44 IEA, *Update on Overseas Investments by China's National Oil Companies*, IEA Partner Country Series (IEA, 2015).

45 '2017 World LNG Report', Annual, IGU World LNG Report (International Gas Union, 2017).

46 'West-East Gas Pipeline Project', *Hydrocarbons Technology* (blog), accessed 3 April 2018, www.hydrocarbons-technology.com/projects/west-east/.

47 '2017 World LNG Report'.

48 Kadri Liik and European Council on Foreign Relations, *Russia's 'Pivot' to Eurasia* (London, UK: European Council on Foreign Relations (ECFR), 2014), 1, https://www.ecfr.eu/publications/summary/russias_pivot_to_eurasia310.

49 Liik and European Council on Foreign Relations, 13.

markets; thus there can be no definitive 'leaning to one side' to borrow Mao Zedong's reference.[50] LNG provides an opportunity for a new leverage for Moscow as an alternative market to Europe. As lucrative as global LNG markets may be, if Russia was already a strong LNG supplier, it would be less beholden to its bilateral pipeline markets in a potential dispute as the deteriorating relations between Europe and Russia are demonstrating. From the Chinese perspective, this calls into question the soundness of deep economic relations with Russia.[51]

While both Russia and China operate under state capitalism that privileges political directives over commercial interests, analysts have noted that at times state–business relations have generated tension and delays in implementation.[52] Since their corporatisation and asset restructuring in the late 1990s, Chinese NOCs have steadily become more market-oriented and consider Beijing's demand for energy security in direct relation to the firms' gains in competitiveness and profitability.[53] In contrast, until recently, Gazprom, Rosneft and Transneft have behaved comparatively more as Soviet-style administrative companies, emphasising exclusive control of resources and retention of domestic market monopolies. Having been burnt by the Yukos deal, Chinese decision makers recognise that the betrayal of national interest is an accusation that could be directed at any time against private firms such as Novatek and even state-owned firms such as Rosneft.[54] The key significance of these different corporate forms and culture is in how the firms interact with bureaucracies and international opportunities.

Lastly, China achieves the important commercial and economic statecraft objective of renminbi (RMB) internationalisation in its energy projects with Russia. RMB has been used to settle cross-border trade transactions between the two countries since 2010, and it could be used for direct payment in the $400 billion CNPC–Gazprom gas deal in 2014.[55] In September 2017 China announced a plan to launch a crude oil futures contract denominated in Chinese Yuan and convertible into gold. The most far-reaching scenario would have Saudi Arabia following Iran, Russia and other major oil producers in

50 'Wilson Center Digital Archive', accessed 29 March 2018, http://digitalarchive.wilsoncenter.org/document/119300.

51 David Sheppard, 'US Gas Cargo Turns towards UK as Russia Spat Intensifies', *Financial Times*, 15 March 2018, www.ft.com/content/11fc43bc-2844-11e8-b27e-cc62a39d57a0.

52 Elena Shadrina, 'Russia's Dilemmas about China's Gas Market', *ERINA – Economic Research Institute for Northeast Asia* 2, no. 2 (2014): 51–73.

53 Christoffersen, 'China's Intentions for Russian and Central Asian Oil and Gas'; Erica S. Downs, 'The Chinese Energy Security Debate', *The China Quarterly* 177 (March 2004): 21–41, Kun-Chin Lin, 'Disembedding Socialist Firms as a Statist Project: Restructuring the Chinese Oil Industry, 1997–2002', *Enterprise & Society* 7, no. 1 (March 2006): 59–97.

54 Nina Poussenkova, 'Russia's Eastern Energy Policy: A Chinese Puzzle for Rosneft', Russia/NIS Center (IFRI, 2013).

55 Chris Wright, '$400 Billion Gas Deal Shows Russia Looking To China To Replace Western Money', Forbes, accessed 3 April 2018, www.forbes.com/sites/chriswright/2014/05/22/400-billion-gas-deal-shows-russia-looking-to-china-to-replace-western-money/.

switching to trading oil in Yuan.[56] Currently on the ground, the China-led model of integration in Central Asia, through pipelines and transportation infrastructure facilitating the transit of Chinese goods to other regions, has already built a strong lead over the rival models of Russian EAEU and the American New Silk Road Initiative.[57] A measurable effect is the de-dollarisation of local economies as they move to RMB, especially in Kazakhstan.

In short, Chinese considerations as a demand market include diversification of supply contributing to greater energy security while at the same time creating a degree of economic interdependence with Russia. The Power of Siberia helps to meet growing demand in the Chinese market and is a step towards the internationalisation of the RMB in global oil and gas trade. These factors are certainly not in conflict with Russian goals of diversifying its gas markets away from Europe and positioning itself as an important economic and political actor in Asia. Even the Chinese goal of internationalising the RMB is supported by Russia as a step towards breaking the monopoly of oil trade in USDs.

21.6 LEGAL AND INTERNATIONAL INSTITUTIONAL DIMENSIONS

Whether one is examining the relationship of environmental policy in Europe, Russia or China and the role of gas pipelines in improving national economic or energy security, a clear trend emerges. The assessment of environmental impact, both physical and human, is gradually improving through legislation at both international and national levels. However, there is varied effectiveness due to different levels of domestic enforcement of procedures and regulations in Russia and China. Therefore, progress is needed on this front before the gas pipeline policy can be valued as universally 'good' for stakeholders with respect to fairness.

Despite the importance of the environment to economic and social well-being, most progress and advancement in environmental law and policy is reactionary when the consequences of accidents are realised in the wake of oil spills or gas leaks.[58] Given this, there is a close correlation, and often a negative correlation, between the development of energy resources and the environmental consequences of this development.

Environmental impact assessment policies emerged in policy considerations when first formalised by the United States in the National Environmental Policy Act (NEPA) of 1969 during the rise of the environmental movement. Since then, along with growing realisation of the possible negative consequences of

56 Sam Meredith, 'China Will "Compel" Saudi Arabia to Trade Oil in Yuan – and That's Going to Affect the US Dollar', 11 October 2017, www.cnbc.com/2017/10/11/china-will-compel-saudi-arabia-to-trade-oil-in-yuan–and-thats-going-to-affect-the-us-dollar.html.

57 Nate Schenkkan, 'Impact of the Economic Crisis in Russia on Central Asia', no. 165 (2015): 6.

58 Philippe Sands et al., *Principles of International Environmental Law*, 3rd ed. (Cambridge: Cambridge University Press, 2012).

development on economic and social well-being, many states, including Russia and China, have developed environmental impact policies. European states, in addition to individual national provisions, also have in effect the EU-level Environmental Impact Directive of 1985. At the international level, the Espoo Convention of 1991 establishes guidelines on communication and management of environmental impacts in transboundary development projects. Neither Russia nor China is party to the Espoo Convention, although Russia is a signatory to the treaty.

'Environment' and 'impact' have been broadly defined in the Espoo Convention and in Russian domestic statutes to include many factors that can be affected by alterations to the current conditions, encompassing everything situated between the subsoil and the atmosphere. The convention's comprehensive definition of the environment includes 'human health and safety, flora, fauna, soil, air, water, climate, landscape and historical monuments or other physical structures . . . [and] also includes effects on cultural heritage or socio-economic conditions resulting from alterations to those factors'.[59] Statutes in Russian law include articles to cover protection of the environment and provisions for ecological safety and make some guarantees for the rights of numerically small indigenous peoples 'as well as matters of indigenous participation in decision-making'.[60]

Despite the widespread presence of, and even similarities in, environmental impact legislation in Russia and China, in the actual course of pipeline negotiations and the construction of the PoS, the experiences appear to differ greatly in the assessment, policy dialogue, transparency of the process and the potential environmental and social impact of pipeline projects from Russia to Europe (such as Nord Stream) and from Russia to Asia (such as Power of Siberia). The differences in these experiences highlight some of what could constitute good pipeline policy while revealing the weaknesses of environmental impact regimes in establishing international megaprojects because transborder pipelines are frequently imbedded with greater emphasis on national economic security than considerations for the environment.

In the case of transboundary pipeline construction outside of the parameters of EU states' national regulations and the influence of the Espoo Convention, the effectiveness of environmental impact assessments is not so straightforward, especially considering the combined effects of environmental impacts and possible economic and social consequences for the populations within the zone of pipeline construction, including indigenous populations. Although environmental impact considerations exist *de jure* within the legal frameworks of Russia and China, the

59 UN, 'Convention on Environmental Impact Assessment in a Transboundary Context', in *Convention on Environmental Impact Assessment in a Transboundary Context (As Amended on 27 February 2001 and on 4 June 2004)* (United Nations, 2018), 3–11, https://doi.org/10.18356/cbfd9988-en.

60 Roman Sidortsov, Aytalina Ivanova, and Florian Stammler, 'Localizing Governance of Systemic Risks: A Case Study of the Power of Siberia Pipeline in Russia', *Energy Research & Social Science*, Arctic Energy: Views from the Social Sciences, 16 (1 June 2016): 54–68, https://doi.org/10.1016/j.erss.2016.03.021.

implementation and the de facto application of these regulations is uneven, given disparities in regulatory enforcement between regional and national jurisdictions, considerations of distance from the centre of government in these states with vast territories and the necessity of the project for national security.

Even with the existence of environmental impact assessment provisions in national legislation, in authoritarian regimes such as Russia, the process is structured in such a way as to avoid opposition from economic and political interests of the elites who often are major shareholders or decision makers on the boards of large companies and who are sometimes themselves part of the legislative process of environmental impact reports. As a result, the rigour of the process is 'susceptible to dominant economic interest within the party-state establishment . . . undermining its effectiveness as a tool in environmental protection'.[61] The policies of resource nationalism and the use of resource agreements as a tool of foreign policy are impacted by the fact that 'extractive industries are increasingly state-owned or at least state-controlled'.[62]

The impact of environmental assessment policies is extremely diminished under conditions in which political approval has been obtained and, often, the construction of the project has even begun, before environmental impact assessments (EIA) have been scheduled. It would appear that 'EIAs for large and middle-scale construction projects have had little effect in determining reasonable locations, prevention of pollution and protection of the environment'.[63] This makes the policy of having EIAs, in reality, a mere tick-box exercise for public relations rather than an effective tool of good energy policy, and under these circumstances it is not very surprising that 'the Power of Siberia project as a whole never underwent an environmental review'.[64]

As Russia is a vast country with many administrative layers, there are problems in the effectiveness of the implementation of environmental impact regulations given both the possible distances from the core of central government and the likelihood of overlapping institutional responsibility within the different layers of government at the regional level. These variations introduce the potential for 'misinterpretation, legal circumvention and competition among authorities . . . and developers' and often result in 'perverse decisions' on the implementation of legislation and the approval of projects that are in contravention of the legal provisions of national

61 Shui-Yan Tang, Ching-Ping Tang, and Carlos Wing-Hung Lo, 'Public Participation and Environmental Impact Assessment in Mainland China and Taiwan: Political Foundations of Environmental Management', *Journal of Development Studies* 41, no. 1 (January 2005): 1–32.

62 Florian Stammler and Aitalina Ivanova, 'Resources, Rights and Communities: Extractive Mega-Projects and Local People in the Russian Arctic', *Europe-Asia Studies* 68 (12 September 2016): 1–25.

63 Robert B. Wenger, Wang Huadong, and Ma Xiaoying, 'Environmental Impact Assessment in the People's Republic of China', *Environmental Management* 14, no. 4 (1 July 1990): 429–39.

64 Sidortsov, Ivanova, and Stammler, 'Localizing Governance of Systemic Risks'.

legislation.[65] Therefore, measures to strengthen weak enforcement, transparency and the creation of straightforward institutional structures are necessary in order to improve the policy value of EIAs for countries such as Russia and China.

It is also worth mentioning the work and history of the Shanghai Cooperative Organization (SCO) in the development of regional legal structures, which have translated into working frameworks for bilateral engagement between Russia and China. The SCO has had a fairly successful history of mediating Sino–Russian power rivalry in the region. This framework has focused on regional cooperation in areas of suppression of terrorism, religious extremism and secessionism in the region. It is still too early to tell, but the SCO could broaden its scope of issues at some point to include energy and the environment, which could become a platform for mediating and negotiating the environmental and commercial factors presented by PoS and similar projects.

In sum, good pipeline policy establishes clear regulatory frameworks, consistency and transparency in reporting and effective mechanisms for public participation in EIAs for both environmental and sociocultural concerns, especially for indigenous peoples. 'Energy and the environment are two sides of the same coin and they must be considered by looking at their ramifications on domestic and multinational socioeconomic and political factors and their strategic implications'.[66] In the pursuit of national security, pipeline policy should endeavour to minimise the footprint of the project and minimise disruption to the landscape and the peoples that rely on the land for their livelihood and well-being, both economic and cultural. A sound policy would not only address the benefits of development, but effectively implement environmental impact assessments with agendas that achieve energy justice through improving the processes of 'distribution, recognition, and procedure' of pipeline projects, mitigating the impact on the environment and civil society.[67]

21.7 ENVIRONMENTAL AND SOCIAL FACTORS

Social and environmental problems associated with Russia's energy industries were already becoming evident in the last years of the Soviet Union. Projects for exploitation of large gas deposits in the Yamal peninsula in northwest Siberia in particular aroused vociferous protests from lobbies for the environment and for indigenous peoples.[68] Since that time, four types of stakeholders have emerged in the public

65 Lixin Gu and William R. Sheate, 'Institutional Challenges for EIA Implementation in China: A Case Study of Development versus Environmental Protection', *Environmental Management* 36, no. 1 (July 2005): 125–42.

66 Ellen Karm, 'Environment and Energy: The Baltic Sea Gas Pipeline', *Journal of Baltic Studies* 39 (1 June 2008): 99–121.

67 Kirsten Jenkins et al., 'Energy Justice: A Conceptual Review', *Energy Research & Social Science* 11 (31 January 2016): 174–182.

68 Piers Vitebsky, 'Gas, Environmentalism and Native Anxieties in the Soviet Arctic: The Case of Yamal Peninsula', *Polar Record* 26, no. 156 (January 1990): 19–26.

debate: the Russian president and government, major gas and oil production companies, local administrations, and various groups from amongst the populations affected. Socio-economic and political issues are often inseparable from environmental ones, since the protests are often about ecological damage that affects local populations adversely. Nevertheless, the overlap is not total, and it therefore makes sense to divide this section, first to describe the environmental-geographical risks, then the ways these have been taken up by social lobbies, and finally to discuss the wider political environment inside contemporary Russia with regard to PoS and similar major gas pipeline projects in Siberia and the RFE.

21.7.1 *Responses from Local and Indigenous Communities*

Transneft, the developer of the East Siberia–Pacific Ocean (ESPO) pipeline, ran into trouble in 2006 because it attempted to use approval by the council of the President of Sakha (Yakutia) as a form of 'public discussion'. This was a move that not only aroused protest from local environmental NGOs but also shed an unwelcome light on Russia internationally, when the Association of Event people sent representatives to Alaska to learn about Inupiat methods of protecting their way of life in the face of similar problems.[69] Gazprom, when developing the PoS project, was no doubt aware of the history of vocal opposition to gas and oil pipelines in Russia. This went back to the Yukos Affair in 2002, when academics, religious leaders and shamans joined cattle-breeders, farmers and pensioners in large-scale protests at a route proposed 'from above' through a national park in Buryatia.[70] So Gazprom avoided making the same mistake with PoS. But as noted earlier the public meetings that Gazprom held were woefully inadequate. Meanwhile, a law of the Sakha Republic, 'On Ethnological Review', offered the opportunity for consultation with at least some of the indigenous communities along the route. The problem here has been that these communities have a radically different relationship to the land than the gas company executives. This makes meaningful dialogue very difficult, though not impossible. More holistic, experiential and cosmological, the native perspective involves entities such as sacred grounds and spirits of the land and rivers, indeed a whole ethical 'lifeworld' which the officials have no way to accommodate within their commercial and political outlook. This native and more holistic view of the environment is incompatible with Gazprom executives' world-view. As a result, the pipe itself is viewed differently. For the bureaucrats and gas workers, the pipeline enables movement (natural gas flowing to China) but for the locals it is not only 'like a road block, making part of their forest inaccessible' but also something that

69 Philip Burgess, 'Evenki, Reindeer and the East Siberian Pacific Pipeline', Reindeer Herding (blog), April 15, 2008.

70 Natalia L. Zhukovskaya, 'Heritage versus Big Business: Lessons from The YUKOS Affair', *Inner Asia* 11, no. 1 (1 June 2009): 157–67.

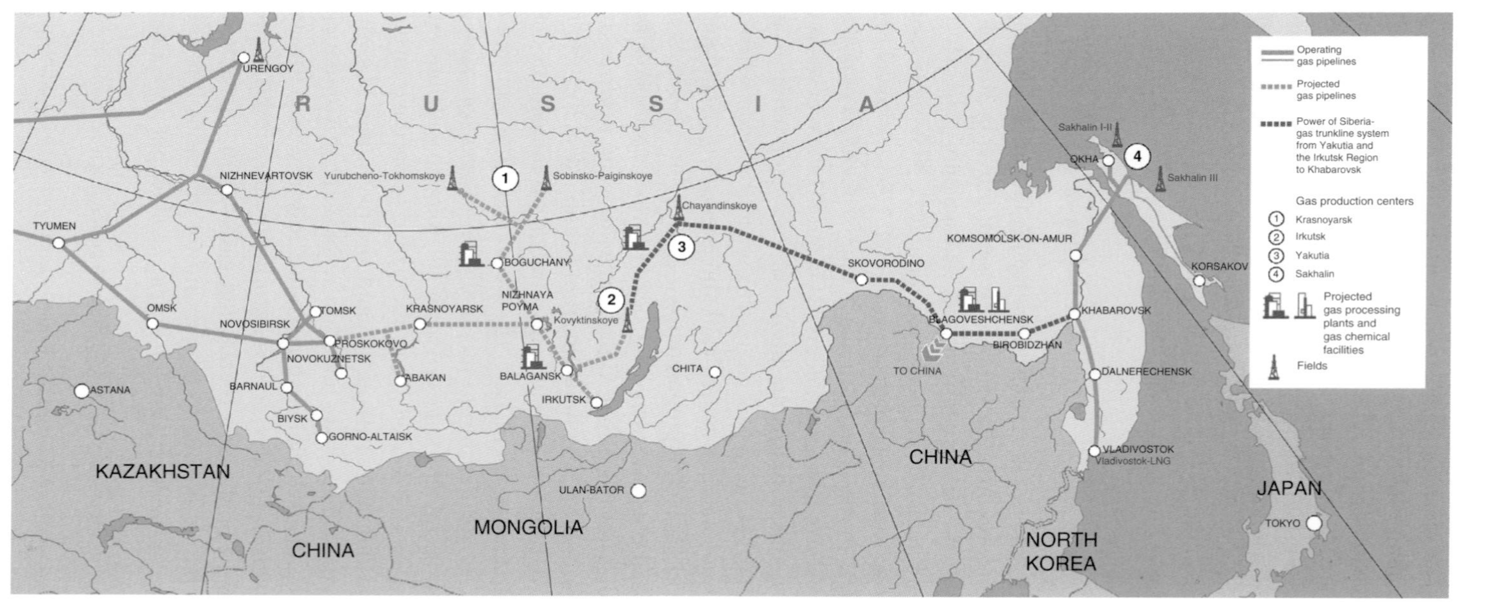

FIGURE 21.2 Map of Russian Far East pipeline projects
Source: http://www.gazprom.com/about/production/projects/pipelines/ykv/

creates a cessation in their temporal understanding of a continuous way of life extending over countless generations.[71]

'On Ethnological Review' offers indigenous peoples the right to participate in the expert commissions supposed to examine any large project proposed to take place in traditional inhabited areas. In theory, it offers real legal power, because no activity subject to such a review can proceed without the commission's approval. However, a provincial law, such as Sakha's 'Ethnological Review', cannot contradict federal laws, and this gives developers a means to overturn regional legal constraints. Moreover, local arguments to compel restraint on developers are difficult to muster, since many 'traditional areas' have not been formally designated as such. For these reasons, although the PoS crosses indigenous lands, no ethnological assessment was carried out (as of 2016), even though construction work commenced in 2014. Instead, local governments attempted to persuade subcontractors to carry out the assessments of isolated individual sections. The response of the widely scattered herders and hunters has been equally piecemeal. Some are categorically opposed while others settle for quick economic benefits such as overhunting to profit from the sudden demand for meat. A few, however, attempt to include the pipeline project in careful long-term plans for their future.[72]

21.7.2 *Environment*

Pipeline construction is just one among many sources of environmental degradation in the RFE and the Amur–Heilong River Basin. These include: commercial coal mining; industrial pollution of river waters; uncoordinated construction of hydroelectric stations by Russia and China; uranium mining and waste disposal; logging of forests; conversion of wild lands to farming in China; wind erosion of the humus layer as a result of agriculture and overgrazing; floods caused by draining of marshes that could absorb overflows; unregulated hunting, fishing and collecting; and anthropogenic forest fires.[73] Gas pipelines bring particular threats: accidents, explosions and leakages, disruption of wildlife migration corridors and the impact of the construction of associated infrastructure (quarries, roads, railways and processing plants) that disturbs swathes of fragile land surface. The PoS route passes through swampy, mountainous, seismically active, permafrost and rocky areas with extreme environmental conditions.[74] In this situation thermal damage to pipes, forest and tundra landscape stripped of vegetation, undisposed hazardous materials, abandoned and mishandled equipment and influxes of temporary workers create

71 Sidortsov, Ivanova, and Stammler, 'Localizing Governance of Systemic Risks'.

72 Sidortsov, Ivanova, and Stammler, 63.

73 Dahmer, Thomas D. and Eugene A. Simonov (eds.) *Amur-Heilong River Basin Reader*. 1st edition. Hong Kong: Ecosystems Limited, Hong Kong, 2008.

74 The absolute lowest air temperatures along the Power of Siberia route range from minus 62 degrees Celsius in the Republic of Sakha (Yakutia) to minus 41 degrees Celsius in the Amur Region.

multiple sources of environmental risks. The chief human risk is to indigenous communities of reindeer herders, fishers, hunters and small farmers leading a largely subsistence existence. Left with polluted, divided and insufficient hunting grounds and reindeer pastures, their way of life becomes unsustainable.

Gazprom claims to pursue environmentally sustainable business practices. Its website states, for example, that in order to mitigate environmental impacts, the PoS pipeline was designed so as to run primarily through sparse woods and fire sites, or areas with burned trees. However, Russia lacks the institutional capacity for overall environmental risk governance, in particular for trunk pipeline systems. Public consultation is not required at the policy-making stage. The federal law 'On Environmental Review' underwent a series of amendments between 1995 and 2006, one of which excluded trunk pipelines from the purview of the law.[75] Thus PoS as a whole never underwent an environmental review, and only certain units of the supporting infrastructure, such as some waste disposal sites near compressor stations, remained subject to mandatory assessment. The public meetings were poorly advertised. In one case studied, only one member of the public and no indigenous peoples were present.[76] And in any case, 'On Environmental Review' does not specify the extent to which public preferences need to be taken into account in the decision-making process.

21.8 CONCLUSIONS

This chapter has advanced our understanding of Eurasian pipeline policies in several ways. We began by presenting the most recent developments that have led to the agreement for the first major and dedicated natural gas pipeline, Power of Siberia, connecting Russia's eastern fields in Sakha (Yakutia) to China. Upon exploring the geopolitical implications of this project, we defined 'good policies' through different disciplinary lenses examining the effects of this pipeline on the grounds of political and geostrategic advantage, economic benefits, legal and institutional structures and impacts on the environment and indigenous communities. From a political and geostrategic perspective, regional and international power would be the goal in addition to energy security defined as access to markets for the supplier, in this case Russia. Likewise from an economics perspective, the pipeline policy that provides the greatest return on investment plus the greatest welfare for the state's population would be the optimal policy. On the other hand, geopolitical advantages would add not only power but also stability, as measured both domestically and internationally. With respect to indigenous populations and the environment, a pipeline policy that is the least disruptive to the environment and

75 Sidortsov, Ivanova, and Stammler, 'Localizing Governance of Systemic Risks'.

76 Sidortsov, Ivanova, and Stammler, 'Localizing Governance of Systemic Risks'.

social institutions would be the 'better' policy, particularly one that is transparent and in line with international norms and standards.

Given these criteria, this particular Eurasian pipeline policy has had a mixed track record since its inception. While providing the state with greater access to new markets, the economics are constrained by global oil price fluctuations. When Russia and China first agreed to the PoS pipeline, the price of oil was above $100 per bbl, which made the project cost worthwhile over the long term. The price of oil has since dropped from these original expectations. This makes the pipeline currently more advantageous to Russia than China, which is likely to be an unsustainable scenario if the Russian–European experience is at all instructive.

The Power of Siberia appears to create interdependencies that will benefit Russia as a vehicle to market diversification, moving Russia away from its dependence on Europe. This could have the double positive effect of creating more interstate stability between Russia and China plus greater regional and international power for Russia as the emerging main supplier for the Asia Pacific Region and the same for China. With respect to regional geopolitics, if however one accepts that the United States is a stabilising force in the APR, then the pipeline could work to destabilise the region in the long term by reducing the US's interest, and consequently presence, as an energy supplier in the region. These views are more commonly held in China's neighbouring countries that depend on the United States for their security, such as South Korea and Japan.

The effects of PoS do not appear to bode well for the environment when compared to similar projects between Russia and European partners. Considering that PoS pushes one authoritarian state, Russia, to work with another, China, the likelihood that the governments and operators will disregard international norms is higher than if Russia was working with a more democratic state. The Nord Stream pipeline connecting Russia with the EU, for example, had to undergo far more environmental impact scrutiny under both EU and international law.

More research is needed, however, in order to understand the trade-offs between the dimensions that we identified. For example, is a greater economic return more important than maintaining the environment? Would regional political stability trump social disruptions among a small minority of the population particularly when the majority benefits? And are these trade-offs different in states that lean more towards autarky than democracy? These questions would benefit from further multidisciplinary examination based on our findings.

21.9 REFERENCES

International Gas Union '2017 World LNG Report'. Annual. IGU World LNG Report. International Gas Union, 2017.

'Alexey Miller Briefs Vladimir Putin on Gasification of Russian Regions'. Accessed 31 March 2018. www.gazprom.com/press/news/2017/july/article340619/.

BP. 'BP Energy Outlook 2017 Edition'. Energy Outlooks. London, 2017. www.bp.com/content/dam/bp/pdf/energy-economics/energy-outlook-2017/bp-energy-outlook-2017.pdf.

Burgess, Philip. 'Evenki, Reindeer and the East Siberian Pacific Pipeline', *Reindeer Herding* (blog), April 15, 2008.

Caney, Simon. 'Just Emissions'. *Philosophy & Public Affairs* 40, no. 4 (1 September 2012): 255–300.

Cheng, Joseph Yu-shek. 'Chinese Perceptions of Russian Foreign Policy During the Putin Administration: U.S.-Russia Relations and "Strategic Triangle" Considerations'. *Journal of Current Chinese Affairs* 38, no. 2 (28 July 2009): 145–68.

'China, Russia Jointly Launch Yamal LNG Project in the Arctic', Belt and Road Portal. Accessed 30 March 2018. https://eng.yidaiyilu.gov.cn/home/rolling/39155.htm.

'China's Intentions for Russian and Central Asian Oil and Gas'. *National Burean of Asian Research* 9, no. 2 (1998): 19.

'Angarsk as a Challenge for the East Asian Energy Community'. *Mongolian Journal of International Affairs* 0, no. 11 (15 September 2013).

Christoffersen, Gaye. 'The Dilemmas of China's Energy Governance: Recentralization and Regional Cooperation'. *The China and Eurasia Quarterly Forum*, Energy and Security, 3, no. 3 (November 2005): 55–80.

Chyong, Chi Kong. 'Markets and Long-Term Contracts: The Case of Russian Gas Supplies to Europe'. Working Paper. EPRG Working Paper Series. Cambridge: U. of Cambridge, December 2015.

Chyong, Chi Kong, and Benjamin F. Hobbs. 'Strategic Eurasian Natural Gas Market Model for Energy Security and Policy Analysis: Formulation and Application to South Stream'. *Energy Economics* 44 (1 July 2014): 198–211.

Chyong, Chi Kong, and Roman Kazmin. 'The Economics of Global LNG Trade: The Case of Atlantic and Pacific Inter-Basin Arbitrage in 2010–2014'. Working Paper. EPRG Working Paper Series. Cambridge: U. of Cambridge, January 2016.

Chyong, Chi Kong, Pierre Noël, and David Reiner. 'The Economics of the Nord Stream Pipeline'. Working Paper. EPRG Working Paper Series. Cambridge: U. of Cambridge, September 2010.

Clarke, Michael. 'Beijing's March West: Opportunities and Challenges for China's Eurasian Pivot'. *Orbis* 60, no. 2 (1 January 2016): 296–313. https://doi.org/10.1016/j.orbis.2016.01.001.

'The Commercial and Political Logic for the Altai Pipeline'. *Oxford Institute for Energy Studies* (blog), 5 December 2014. www.oxfordenergy.org/publications/the-commercial-and-political-logic-for-the-altai-pipeline/.

Dahmer, Thomas D. and Eugene A. Simonov (eds.) *Amur-Heilong River Basin Reader*. 1st edition. Hong Kong: Ecosystems Limited, Hong Kong, 2008.

Dannreuther, Roland. 'China and Global Oil: Vulnerability and Opportunity'. *International Affairs* 87, no. 6 (November 2011): 1345–64.

Dorian, James P., Brett H. Wigdortz, and Dru C. Gladney. 'China and Central Asia's Volatile Mix: Energy, Trade, and Ethnic Relations', 1997. http://scholarspace.manoa.hawaii.edu/handle/10125/3791.

Downs, Erica S. 'The Chinese Energy Security Debate'. *The China Quarterly* 177 (March 2004): 21–41.

'The Eurasian Economic Union: Power, Politics and Trade'. Crisis Group, 20 July 2016. www.crisisgroup.org/europe-central-asia/central-asia/eurasian-economic-union-power-politics-and-trade.

Foy, Henry. 'Russia Ships First Gas from $27bn Arctic Project'. *Financial Times*, 8 December 2017. www.ft.com/content/515d451c-dc11-11e7-a039-c64b1c09b482.

Gaouette, Nicole. 'Latest US Sanctions against Russia a Work in Progress'. CNN. Accessed 9 January 2018. www.cnn.com/2017/12/14/politics/trump-russia-sanctions-explainer/index.html.

Gu, Lixin, and William R. Sheate. 'Institutional Challenges for EIA Implementation in China: A Case Study of Development versus Environmental Protection'. *Environmental Management* 36, no. 1 (July 2005): 125–42.

Gulick, John. 'Russo-Chinese Energy Cooperation: Stepping Stone from Strategic Partnership to Geo-Economic Integration?' *International Journal of Comparative Sociology* 48 (1 April 2007): 203–33. https://doi.org/10.1177/0020715207075400.

Harsem, Øistein, and Dag Harald Claes. 'The Interdependence of European–Russian Energy Relations'. *Energy Policy* 59 (1 August 2013): 784–91.

IEA. *Update on Overseas Investments by China's National Oil Companies*. IEA Partner Country Series. IEA, 2015.

Jenkins, Kirsten, Darren McCauley, Raphael Heffron, Hannes Stephan, and Robert Rehner. 'Energy Justice: A Conceptual Review'. *Energy Research & Social Science* 11 (31 January 2016): 174–82.

Karm, Ellen. 'Environment and Energy: The Baltic Sea Gas Pipeline'. *Journal of Baltic Studies* 39 (1 June 2008): 99–121.

Liik, Kadri, and European Council on Foreign Relations. *Russi's 'Pivot' to Eurasia*. London, UK: European Council on Foreign Relations (ECFR), 2014. http://www.ecfr.eu/page/-/ECFR103_RUSSIA_COLLECTION_290514_AW.

Lin, Kun-Chin. 'Disembedding Socialist Firms as a Statist Project: Restructuring the Chinese Oil Industry, 1997–2002'. *Enterprise & Society* 7, no. 1 (March 2006): 59–97.

Lin, Kun-Chin, and Brad Williams. 'Pipeline Politics: Comparative Bargaining Capacity'. Working Paper. CRP Working Paper Series. Cambridge: U. of Cambridge, October 2012.

'LNG Isn't Freeing Europe from Gazprom Yet'. *The American Interest* (blog), 10 January 2017. www.the-american-interest.com/2017/01/10/lng-isnt-freeing-europe-from-gazprom-yet/.

Makeev, Nikolai. 'Rossiya bez gaza: pochemu tret' straniy im postydno ne obespechena'. Accessed 31 March 2018. www.mk.ru/economics/2017/04/11/rossiya-bez-gaza-pochemu-tret-strany-im-postydno-ne-obespechena.html.

Meredith, Sam. 'China Will "Compel" Saudi Arabia to Trade Oil in Yuan – and That's Going to Affect the US Dollar', 11 October 2017. www.cnbc.com/2017/10/11/china-will-compel-saudi-arabia-to-trade-oil-in-yuan--and-thats-going-to-affect-the-us-dollar.html.

'The Outlook for Natural Gas Demand in Europe'. *Oxford Institute for Energy Studies* (blog), 10 June 2014. www.oxfordenergy.org/publications/the-outlook-for-natural-gas-demand-in-europe/.

Paik, Keun-Wook. *Sino-Russian Oil and Gas Cooperation: The Reality and Implications* (Oxford: Oxford University Press for the Oxford Institute for Energy Studies, 2012).

Poussenkova, Nina. 'Russia's Eastern Energy Policy: A Chinese Puzzle for Rosneft'. Russia/NIS Center. IFRI, 2013.

Radtke, Kurt W. et al. (eds.). *Dynamics in Pacific Asia*. Routledge, 2014.

'Railway and Arctic Routes Enhance China–Europe Trade', Belt and Road Portal. Accessed 30 March 2018. https://eng.yidaiyilu.gov.cn/info/iList.jsp?tm_id=139&cat_id=10058&info_id=26102.

Ratner, Michael, Gabriel M Nelson, and Susan V Lawrence. 'China's Natural Gas: Uncertainty for Markets', n.d., 31.

Rattanavich, Raj. 'UNCONVENTIONAL GAS AND LNG: THE YIN AND YANG OF CHINESE NATURAL GAS PLANNING', n.d., 11.

Rousseau, Denise M., Sim B. Sitkin, Ronald S. Burt, and Colin Camerer. 'Not so Different after All: A Cross-Discipline View of Trust'. *Academy of Management. The Academy of Management Review* 23, no. 3 (July 1998): 393–404.

Sands, Philippe, Jacqueline Peel, Adriana Fabra, and Ruth MacKenzie. *Principles of International Environmental Law*. 3rd ed. Cambridge: Cambridge University Press, 2012.

Schenkkan, Nate. 'Impact of the Economic Crisis in Russia on Central Asia', no. 165 (2015): 4.

Shadrina, Elena. 'Russia's Dilemmas about China "China" Fs Gas Market'. *ERINA – Economic Research Institute for Northeast Asia* 2, no. 2 (2014): 51–73.

Sheppard, David. 'US Gas Cargo Turns towards UK as Russia Spat Intensifies'. *Financial Times*, 15 March 2018. www.ft.com/content/11fc43bc-2844-11e8-b27e-cc62a39d57a0.

Sidortsov, Roman, Aytalina Ivanova, and Florian Stammler. 'Localizing Governance of Systemic Risks: A Case Study of the Power of Siberia Pipeline in Russia'. *Energy Research & Social Science*, Arctic Energy: Views from the Social Sciences, 16 (1 June 2016): 54–68.

Simonia, Nodari. 'The Energy Dimension in Russian Global Strategy: Russian Energy Policy in East Siberia and the Far East'. Report. James A. Baker III Institute for Public Policy. Houston: Rice University, October 2004.

Stammler, Florian, and Aitalina Ivanova. 'Resources, Rights and Communities: Extractive Mega-Projects and Local People in the Russian Arctic'. *Europe-Asia Studies* 68 (12 September 2016): 1–25.

Stent, Angela E. *From Embargo to Ostpolitik: The Political Economy of West German-Soviet Relations*, 1955–1980.Cambridge: Cambridge University Press, 2003.

Stern, Jonathan P. (ed.), *The Pricing of Internationally Traded Gas* (Oxford: Oxford University Press for the Oxford Institute for Energy Studies, 2012).

Stern, Jonathan P., and Howard Rogers. 'The Pricing of Internationally Traded Gas'. Presented at the IEEJ, Tokyo, 6 March 2013.

Swanström, Niklas. 'Sino–Russian Relations at the Start of the New Millennium in Central Asia and Beyond'. *Journal of Contemporary China* 23, no. 87 (4 May 2014): 480–97.

Tang, Shui-Yan, Ching-Ping Tang, and Carlos Wing-Hung Lo. 'Public Participation and Environmental Impact Assessment in Mainland China and Taiwan: Political Foundations of Environmental Management'. *Journal of Development Studies* 41, no. 1 (January 2005): 1–32.

Trenin, Dmitri. 'From Greater Europe to Greater Asia?' Carnegie Moscow Center. Moscow: Carnegie Endowment, April 2015.

UN. 'Convention on Environmental Impact Assessment in a Transboundary Context'. In *Convention on Environmental Impact Assessment in a Transboundary Context (As Amended on 27 February 2001 and on 4 June 2004)*, 3–11. United Nations, 2018.

Vanadzina, Evgenia. *Capacity Market in Russia: Addressing the Energy Trilemma*. Lappeenranta University of Technology, 2016.

Vitebsky, Piers. 'Gas, Environmentalism and Native Anxieties in the Soviet Arctic: The Case of Yamal Peninsula'. *Polar Record* 26, no. 156 (January 1990): 19–26.

Wenger, Robert B., Wang Huadong, and Ma Xiaoying. 'Environmental Impact Assessment in the People's Republic of China'. *Environmental Management* 14, no. 4 (1 July 1990): 429–39.

'West-East Gas Pipeline Project'. *Hydrocarbons Technology* (blog). Accessed 3 April 2018. www.hydrocarbons-technology.com/projects/west-east/.
'Wilson Center Digital Archive'. Accessed 29 March 2018. http://digitalarchive.wilsoncenter.org/document/119300.
Wright, Chris. '$400 Billion Gas Deal Shows Russia Looking to China to Replace Western Money'. *Forbes*. Accessed 3 April 2018. www.forbes.com/sites/chriswright/2014/05/22/400-billion-gas-deal-shows-russia-looking-to-china-to-replace-western-money/.
Youngblood, Dawn. 'Multidisciplinarity, Interdisciplinarity, and Bridging Disciplines: A Matter of Process'. *Journal of Research Practice* 3, no. 2 (5 December 2007): 18.
Zhukovskaya, Natalia L. 'Heritage versus Big Business: Lessons from The YUKOS Affair'. *Inner Asia* 11, no. 1 (1 June 2009): 157–67.

22

Responses and Final Thoughts

This final chapter offers a few responses to the subject and aims of this book rather than traditional remarks of conclusion. It aims to do so in the unconventional pattern of the multidisciplinary approaches presented in the book so far. For conventional summaries of each of the previous chapters, please see the introductory chapter.

Because most of the authors of this book have interacted with policy makers and their colleagues in the traditional subject-based departments of their respective universities, the editors decided to engage a small transatlantic sample of 'technologists' and policy makers to ascertain what value they see in a multidisciplinary approach. How could the ideas presented in this book assist departments on the other side of the disciplinary spectrum and ultimately benefit decision makers in their quest to conceive, design and implement better energy policies? In this final chapter, we present the responses of three informed experts including Dr Emily Shuckburgh, Professor John Deutch and Lord Ronald Oxburgh, all of whom kindly accepted our invitation to contribute. They were asked to respond to a draft of the introductory chapter along with the book proposal for our publisher, both of which encompassed the main ideas of the book, and a description of the cases and seminar discussions at the Centre for Research in the Arts, Social Sciences and Humanities (CRASSH) at the University of Cambridge, which were the impetus for this book. Following these, we the editors offer our own comments to the responses along with the main lessons we observe from this book and a few suggestions on further avenues of multidisciplinary research.

22.1 'MULTICULTURAL' POLICY: INTEGRATING EXPERTISE FROM A SPAN OF DISCIPLINES TO INFORM POLICY

By Emily Shuckburgh

My eyes were opened to the complexity of the human decision-making process when I undertook a study of public attitudes to climate change involving a survey of the UK population and a series of focus groups (Shuckburgh et al., 2012). As part of this work we conducted two focus groups with academics – one with those from an arts and humanities domain and another with those from a scientific domain. This clearly demonstrated that the 'two cultures' were still strongly divided, with the division mapping into differing attitudes and approaches to decision making and hence to policy making. Moreover, I have observed that even within each domain, strong silos exist, with for example the science, engineering, technology, economics and social science perspectives on a policy topic generally advanced separately. Clearly 'good' policy, whether related to energy or any other topic, needs to be supported by a 'good' evidence base (in its broadest sense) coupled to a 'good' policy process. Each of these elements must surely draw on and appropriately integrate the relevant knowledge from each of the perspectives listed above. I suggest that what is needed is not just a meeting of the two cultures, but comprehensive and holistic 'multicultural' policy making.

The scale and urgency of the response that is required to address the climate change threat is substantial. At our current rate of carbon dioxide emissions, we are on course to exhaust the budget to stay below Paris Agreement temperature limits within the next twenty to thirty years. Managing and delivering the rapid and dramatic energy transition that is required over the coming few decades to stay within budget will be extremely challenging.

Evidence must surely form the heart of the rationale for, and objectives of, a good policy. It must also be right to inspect carefully the character of that evidence and the way in which it is gathered. The scientific community tends to view the scientific method as providing a means to collate such evidence in a manner that is entirely free from bias. The reality is of course more nuanced. Famously the climate science community was caught by surprise by the inclusion of a 1.5°C goal within the Paris Agreement, resulting in a call for a special report by the IPCC. Can lessons be learnt from this? Encouraging a fuller appreciation among researchers of the wider context and ways in which values and other influences can shape the gathering and interpretation of evidence may be beneficial. Encouraging also a broader understanding of the landscape in which specific expertise resides and providing more incentives for the 'evidence' community to synthesise results across traditional silos may lead to the production of more valuable input to the policy process and to positive feedback in terms of informing research priorities.

Impact assessments usually form a key component of the appraisal of a policy. This typically constitutes scrutiny in which costs and benefits are monetised and aggregated to ensure consistent analysis of trade-offs and other implications. However, for much of energy policy – and indeed many other policies – this alone may not be sufficient. For example, as emphasised by Mark Carney, Governor of the Bank of England (the UK's central bank), the potentially catastrophic impacts of unchecked climate change are likely to be felt beyond the traditional horizons of most actors. The implication is that appropriate consideration of the impact of policy choices taken today needs to account for long-term issues. It is challenging to do this within a cost–benefit analysis, in part because of numerous uncertainties that cascade over time, making monetisation highly subjective. Within the climate sphere this challenge is exemplified by the fact that a wide range of estimates of the social cost of carbon have been proposed, each encompassing a myriad of assumptions. Attempts to provide monetised assessments relevant to energy security are also bedevilled by the need to make subjective assumptions. A broader cross-disciplinary framework is required to account for the longer-term perspective. The UK energy regulator, Ofgem, developed such a framework in response to the intergenerational issues associated with energy policy and in recognition of intragenerational issues such as the distributional impacts of its decisions, most notably on vulnerable customers, and on the regions of the UK (Grubb and Mills, 2014). This type of strategic and sustainability framework could usefully be applied more widely in the policy world.

The monitoring, evaluation and feedback stages of the policy process may also benefit from input from a wider range of disciplines. Assessments of the success of a policy are part of the policy evaluation process and inform whether to maintain, halt or adjust course. Such assessments are highly contextual, will be judged differently by the different actors involved, and are intertwined with the means and purposes of assessment. One example here is the roll-out of smart meters in homes (Robison and Foulds, 2018). Ostensibly, the primary aim of this policy is to promote energy saving, with a core, but questionable, assumption being that more information can lead to positive changes in action. A range of success measures are promoted, however, that extend beyond demand management and suggest the conflation of different policy goals (e.g., energy saving and accurate billing). The numbers do need to add up with regard to energy demand reduction, but recognising the complex behavioural responses at an individual level and the wider context of policy interventions is also important.

The danger of incorporating evidence from a wider range of spheres of expertise is that complexity is increased to the point at which transparency is compromised and the overall policy objective becomes confused. However, with suitable coordination and synthesis, it seems that policy could be enhanced by being grounded in a richer and more comprehensive evidence base.

22.1.1 *References*

Grubb, M. and Mills, J. 2014, Factoring strategic and sustainability considerations into energy sector regulation: A case study of developments in the UK Office of Gas and Electricity Markets (Ofgem), Proceedings of the 37th Int. Ass. for Energy Economics Conference, www.usaee.org/usaee2014/submissions/OnlineProceedings/Grubb%20Ofgem%20SSA%20Paper%20for%20IAEE.pdf

Robison, R. A. V. and Foulds, C. 2018, Constructing policy success for UK energy feedback, J. Building Research & Information, 46, 316–331.

Shuckburgh, E., Robison, R. and Pidgeon, N. 2012, Climate science, the public and the news media. Summary findings of a survey and focus groups conducted in the UK in March 2011, Living with Environmental Change, http://nora.nerc.ac.uk/id/eprint/500544/1/lwec-climate-science.pdf

22.2 CROSSING THE CHASM TO 'GOOD' GLOBAL CLIMATE POLICY

By John Deutch

The poster child for energy policy failure is climate change. A 'good', i.e. more successful, approach to climate change policy requires deeper investigation and understanding of past and current policy failures – for example, the inability of the United States to adopt either a cap and trade or carbon emission charge, the first steps to put OECD countries on a path to significant mitigation of greenhouse gas, GHG, emissions. On a global basis, the causes of the failures are more fundamental but these causes are easy to uncover: sharing responsibilities between large, rich, developed nations who have been responsible for the bulk of greenhouse gas emissions in the past and the emerging, poor, rapidly growing nations that will be responsible for greenhouse gas emissions in the future. Is the 'right' principle to apply a rule on nations that limits emissions per capita or per dollar of GDP? Perhaps historians, anthropologists and social psychologists using their unforgiving tools will identify new paths to follow but it is sure that no progress is now occurring.

I believe progress is unlikely to come from discovery of a brilliant new paradigm for policy formulation; rather it will come from informed insights that may suggest experiments to be tried in tailored circumstances and carefully evaluated, possibly on a regional basis.

The fiducial points on the usual policy map may not be good starting points. Wider consultation with a large set of 'stakeholders' has not resulted in compromise or even tolerance; instead it has encouraged the formation of subgroups with common interests that seek to resist change. Although energy security and climate change are global issues, in hindsight, it was a mistake to rely on a frail and powerless global organisation – the United Nations – to find a global policy solution, as over twenty years of fruitless UNFCCC Conference of the Parties shows. The inquiries of the International Panel on Climate Change, intended to reach a consensus on the science of global warming and consequent impact on climate change has resulted, at least in the United States, in a small and stubborn minority who have successfully resisted policy change. All of this is a consequence of a naïve belief in the United States and in international organisations that ever more elaborate and inclusive processes will result in better and more acceptable outcomes. Perhaps the world needs to wait for a new personality such a Napoleon or Gandhi who will deliver successfully a global message about the devastating future social and economic global consequences if action is not taken.

In my youth (and perhaps still today) I firmly believed that good policy is greatly helped if it is based on quantitative analysis, hopefully supported by valid empirical field data, on the costs and benefits of alternative courses of action. I have become weary of explaining the limitations of such quantitative analysis that records, but does not resolve, the difference between winners and losers, or manage to harmonise multiple objectives, such as reducing carbon emissions, encouraging renewable technologies, creating jobs and protecting national security. The cacophony surrounding the search for good or politically acceptable energy policy that serves multiple, conflicting objectives suggests that having no quantitative analysis to support a policy position is worse than having no guidance for what is socially desirable.

For global climate policy, the most prominent quantitative 'good energy policy' effort is the determination of the 'social cost of carbon', SCOC. The SCOC seeks to set a dollar cost on the discounted present value of the economic damage caused by marginal emission of one kilogram of CO_2, or its equivalent from other greenhouse gases such as methane. This noble effort is impossibly complex and encounters literally hundreds of uncertainties such as future regulatory policies, economic growth, industry performance, different regional impacts, social costs outside the economic metric, and most important, what is the appropriate discount rate between future and present welfare.

I greatly admire the dedication and skill of the several research groups around the world working on the SCOC. It is a necessary benchmark to justify proposed energy efficiency regulation in a country with a market economy. But it is a useless concept to reach global agreement among nations most of whom see a SCOC of say $30 per metric ton of CO_2 emitted as an impossibly high price to pay to avoid a distant climate catastrophe instead of paying for immediate social needs such as better health, education and job creation. There is no greater danger than a policy analyst becoming involved in politics who has an *idée fixe* as a result of imagined inevitable conclusions of quantitative analysis.

In an act of collective hypocrisy, 196 nations at the 2015 twenty-first Conference of the Parties in Paris agreed to reduce their carbon output 'as soon as possible' and to do their best to keep global warming 'to well below 2°C'. It is manifestly impossible to reach this goal and it is wrong to characterise the Paris Agreement as defining a credible path to reducing greenhouse gas emission at a rate that will avoid global average temperature increases above 2°C. Achieving a 'good energy policy' begins with realism: adverse global warming will not be achieved through mitigation alone. It will require adaptation and most likely geoengineering as well. We have little experience with national or international adaptation policies and the governance issues for managing global geoengineering measures are challenging indeed.

22.3 CLIMATE CHANGE – WILL CHINA SAVE THE PLANET?

By Ronald Oxburgh

How many of the world's population have ever heard of the Intergovernmental Panel on Climate Change or even the idea that human activity is driving changes in global climate? At a guess fewer than a half. Rather more might have been concerned that their weather seemed to be changing. In rural areas they perhaps accepted this as part of the natural order of things; that life in land that had hitherto been just about habitable was now becoming impossible; that all they could do was to move, possibly to a city.

Yet another group – perhaps 15 per cent of the world's population – live in the so-called developed and more urbanised world and is more environmentally informed. Even within such communities there is limited understanding and less than universal agreement over the need to take action. Nevertheless, many governments have introduced regulations to limit or reduce the use of fossil fuels. They have walked a fine line between what they judge to be popularly and economically acceptable and the urgency of steering their countries in the direction of long-term sustainability.

Against this background, the Paris Agreement of 2015 committed nearly all the countries of the world to reducing their greenhouse gas emissions, each country setting its own target. But there are two problems. First, the emissions reduction that would be achieved if every country met its own target is almost certainly insufficient to keep global warming within the limits of the Paris aspiration – an average increase in temperature of not more than two degrees and preferably one and a half degrees Celsius. Second, many of the countries seem unlikely to have the political determination, technical capability or financial resources needed to achieve their declared targets. That said, the greatest doubts relate to some of the poorest countries that currently have rather small carbon footprints. Nevertheless their footprints will surely grow as their living standards rise.

What then is the appropriate strategy for the developed world, recognising that continuing to burn fossil fuels as we do today will bring about changes to the global climate that will make human life increasingly difficult? We must also recognise that, although it has been leading the way towards decarbonisation, the developed world is responsible for much of the historical accumulation of greenhouse gases in the atmosphere that lies at the heart of the present problem.

Thus both a moral obligation and self-interest should be moving the developed world beyond targets to reduce their own emissions to assisting developing countries to meet their energy needs without damaging the environment. Otherwise political realities will force developing countries to burn coal, gas and oil regardless.

This is a fine aspiration for the developed world but implementing it is another matter altogether. There are problems of cost and politics. Although some of the routes to lower emissions may not involve significant expense, many do and so cash has to be found. Politically the challenge is that the climate will respond to emissions reductions rather slowly because of the carry-over effect of past emissions. Honest politicians will have to point out that those who pay for decarbonisation today are unlikely to see any substantial benefit during their lifetime, except in city air quality.

This means that even in the developed world decarbonisation can be a politically hard sell.

It can be a hard sell for another reason. Understanding the future of natural systems in detail will always be complicated and although it is beyond reasonable doubt that increasing concentrations of greenhouse gases in the atmosphere will change the climate and indirectly raise sea level, detailed predictions are based on probabilities not certainties. However, the central probability based on the science that we have today, indicates that we should waste no time in taking action. The risks of not doing so are too serious: it would be irresponsibly complacent to assume that our children will simply innovate their way out of the looming difficulties.

Part of the answer is more use of renewable energy. But the most valuable renewable sources are not available everywhere and tend to be intermittent. Technology will certainly improve but it is hard to see a future that does not include nuclear. Although there is wide agreement that fossil fuels should be phased out, this is a long-term policy. In the meantime, carbon capture and storage (CCS) is needed to manage the emissions of existing plants and of the new coal-fired power stations being built in SE Asia with design lives of forty to sixty years. Without CCS, temperature targets that are already difficult appear unattainable.

So what of the future? The accumulation of greenhouse gases in the atmosphere continues to grow. The technology to tackle the problem exists but both resources and a global determination are needed to do so. There is little doubt that if the problem was tackled with sufficient urgency and sufficiently widely the costs could be brought down with CCS as the most urgent priority. At present those countries with the technical capability appear reluctant to incur the costs of urgent action if their competitors are not doing so as well.

A few major emitters of greenhouse gases – North America, China and Europe – account for some two thirds of current global emissions, with Southeast Asia hard on their heels.

Although the United States has indicated that it will withdraw from the Paris Agreement, the policies of individual states and an economically driven shift from coal to gas mean that US emissions are likely to continue to fall. Europe has plans for major emissions reduction by 2050. China is very much an economy in transition that is balancing the need to decarbonise against the need to bring power rapidly to its remotest areas. Its total emissions are the highest in the world but its per capita emissions are low (relative to OECD countries). However, as a growing economic superpower and a country that is likely to be one of the greatest losers from climate change, China could well emerge as the driving force behind global decarbonisation. It would be rational for the country to use its growing economic influence to require any country that wishes to trade with it to take active and possibly painful measures to curb their emissions. If China's major trading partners were obliged to fall into line there is little doubt that the rest of the world would follow.

We therefore have a world that is taking faltering steps towards decarbonisation. The main actors are aware that the more protracted the transition the more difficult it becomes to bring climate change under control but progress is impeded by the near-term economics and politics. For real and timely progress something else is needed to drive climate to the top of the agenda. Could that be action by China?

22.4 RESPONSE FROM THE EDITORS, MARC OZAWA, JONATHAN CHAPLIN, MICHAEL POLLITT, DAVID REINER AND PAUL WARDE

In the spirit of attempting to identify 'good' energy policies rather than resigning to what some policy makers have deemed hopeless, our three contributors to this chapter have each acknowledged challenges, sometimes appearing overwhelming, in conceiving and implementing energy policies that they deem 'good' in their roles as experts and decision makers. This is no easy task, and without having instructed them to provide any solutions or examples, each has offered at least one in their assessments based on their experiences.

Interestingly and perhaps unsurprisingly, all three (unprompted by us) take addressing climate change as their example of where 'good' energy policy is most pressing. While acknowledging the difficulties facing the policy-making process, it is interesting to note that none of the responses have focused on process solutions. On the contrary, two of the three appear to present process as part of the problem. In the case of Professor Deutch, the more inclusive the UN process became, the greater the obstacles. Likewise, Lord Oxburgh was equally critical of recent public statements by governments and international organisations for not being 'realistic' and looks to a non-democratic power, China, to 'lead' the way on 'good' climate policy. And the solutions that both suggest as possibly overcoming political and economic obstacles are based on technologies, geoengineering for Professor Deutch and a combination of CCS and nuclear for Lord Oxburgh. By contrast, Dr Shuckburgh cites the efforts of the Office of Gas and Electricity Markets (Ofgem) in the United Kingdom as a good example of reconciling different types of evidence and evidence-based approaches for informing the policy-making process. All of our contributors acknowledged the value of bringing a broader disciplinary knowledge base to the analysis of policies because no matter how imperfect, policies should be based on evidence of some sort. Shuckburgh and Deutch acknowledge that the type of evidence is likely where a multidisciplinary approach will be most valuable.

Considering the breadth of experience that our contributors have, it is not surprising that their essays reinforce many of the factors identified in the previous chapters. These include the importance of political and economic context. Perhaps assumed as part of the problem when implementing policies in different locations, Deutch and Oxburgh implicitly acknowledge the role of culture and power in their emphasis on regional policies and influential states in the international system. And in this respect, Lord Oxburgh most clearly raised the prospect of China as playing a strong role in reducing global carbon emissions. The cases included in this book certainly reinforce these themes. The emphasis of decentralisation in the context of Denmark or the impact of Fukushima on the political discourse in Germany are examples of policy developments that are unique to those states given the local historical social, political and economic institutions. It is interesting, however, that only one of the contributors to this chapter cited an example of a process solution in the case of Ofgem, whereas many of the cases and responses included in this book point to process making as either the cause of the problem or intrinsic to designing and promulgating 'good' energy policies.

Dr Shuckburgh explicitly takes us back to where we began by reminding us that there are 'two cultures' across the intellectual disciplines which contribute to energy policy making: one that focuses on the governance process and one which generates technical solutions. Our book has taken both seriously but has attempted to illustrate more broadly still how those disciplines that focus on how humans make decisions in society can contribute to better energy policy making. These expand our horizons to areas that are not directly focused on governance or technical problems as such. In contrast to the pessimism of Deutch about the role of governance processes, it is important to point out that 'climate policy' is a tough test for energy governance in terms of the scale of the problem and that it is an energy policy problem whose policy parallels are not in energy but in global development and global security. Most other energy policy issues are much more limited in scope and hence more tractable. Many of the chapters of our book focus on the implementation of 'good' rather than 'bad' policies in nuclear power governance (Chapter 10), Swedish carbon taxes (Chapter 12), Danish heating policies (Chapter 13), energy-efficient data centres (Chapter 15) and local clean air policy in London (Chapter 20); and indeed in international energy governance via the Aarhus Convention (Chapter 16) and Russian gas pipelines (Chapter 21). The use of climate as the paradigmatic case runs the risk of making good energy policy a more intractable issue than it often is, precisely because it draws in so many variant perspectives on what is 'good'.

With the exception of Jonathan Chaplin's chapter on Pope Francis' encyclical letter, *Laudato Si'*, it is also noteworthy that only one of the contributors, and likewise only one of the case study chapters, emphasised the role of leadership rather than the political system, whether it be democracy or a more authoritarian type of political system such as that of Russia or China. Deutch's point about the need for a Napoleon or a Ghandi in the area of climate policy is that leaders may emerge who can mobilise support for policies in a way that an international organisation is unable to do. Whether this was his intention, the argument strongly resembles Max Weber's description of the 'charismatic leader' whose potential to impact social and political institutions, for better or worse, is the proverbial 'wild card' of history. Whether that leadership will be benign and inspirational (like Ghandi) or authoritarian and backed by military and economic might (like

Napoleon) is an intriguing question. Whether such leaders ever actually have a significant and positive influence on issues like energy policy is also an empirical question, that despite the frequency with which it is evoked, is rarely subject to any serious evidence-based testing.

22.4.1 General Lessons From the Editors

In the introductory chapter, we offered an overview of research centres and situated the subject of this book in the academic literature. While discussing the topics comprising this book with the authors and in discussions among the editors at various stages of the book's development, there are lessons we have learned that are either under-represented in previous multidisciplinary studies or completely absent. These are practical points for academic collaboration among disciplines that we hope will benefit future research.

Firstly, it was clear that the issue of scale of analysis is an important one. Some disciplines are predisposed to a limited geographic scope, such as social anthropology, while others have developed research approaches for both limited and broad geographic scope. Other domains, such as history, emphasise the role of multiple simultaneous scales (as discussed in Chapter 7). It is critical to be aware of this at the outset of the project because the scale of analysis can create barriers, or even incompatibility, for multidisciplinary research.

Scale is also important when it comes to the problem being addressed. The narrower the policy issue, the easier it is to address it in a way that can be deemed to be 'good'. If the question is what colour to paint a nuclear power plant to make it blend in with the local environment, it is relatively straightforward to run a public consultation on which colour to choose. However, if the question is how to remove fossil fuels from the energy mix – this is several orders of magnitude more difficult. Indeed, one starts from the position that no country has, as yet, done this. The clearer the energy policy problem to be addressed is, the more urgent the problem and the more readily feasible solutions are at hand, the easier it is to implement a solution in a reasonable time frame. In such circumstances the law, the economics and the politics of the situation are likely to favourably align.

Pollution policy can be at any scale, whether local clean air policy in Beijing (Chapter 20) or European biofuel policy contributing to environmental destruction in Borneo (Chapter 17). Indeed, our examples of policies that lead to excessive environmental degradation are often those where philosophy and theology have profound critiques to make. Thus, the scale of climate policy problem posed by fossil fuels requires a global change of heart as exemplified by the Pope's encyclical (Chapter 18), while domestic European policies towards nuclear energy in Germany (Chapter 11) or on biofuels (Chapter 17) may have negative consequences for neighbouring countries.

Related to the differences in scale among disciplines, we find it is also helpful to identify a lead discipline when setting out to do multidisciplinary research. Just as it is important to have a lead author driving the writing of a collaborative written work, having a lead discipline can help in building a framework that can encompass the various methodologies of the researchers. This is particularly important when there are more than two disciplines comprising the research. The effectiveness and benefits of multidisciplinary research applied to energy policy issues may be applied to other policy areas such as healthcare. Similarly implementation is important both in terms of the policy and the management of the delivery. Many of the examples of good policy implementation take place in sophisticated policy environments with high quality management teams; what remains more challenging is transferring lessons from these environments to less sophisticated regimes.

Perhaps less obvious is the recognition that human interaction and communication are at the heart of multidisciplinary research. The same interpersonal obstacles that may impact academic research may become more pronounced in multidisciplinary interactions because the language and research approach of each discipline is unique. Although academics have recognised this issue in previous scholarship, our experience reinforces this, and researchers endeavouring to conduct multidisciplinary projects will be well advised to be reminded of the importance of this human dimension. As such, if relationships already exist between collaborators, the process of working together is likely to be more fruitful. If the contributors have addressed this point, they have tended to speak in terms of different kinds of evidence when it comes to multidisciplinary research. Perhaps the underlying issue is not the type of evidence, but rather different styles of thinking in cooperation, which would underscore the importance of mixing personnel rather than evidence.

What the previous chapters also made apparent is that some disciplines may have an inherent tendency towards advocacy of issues. The clearest examples from this book were those chapters representing theology and social anthropology. This raises the question of whether academic disciplines should claim advocacy roles as such. In fact, this is an ongoing debate in the study of politics, and it has important methodological and epistemological implications. This characterises the distinction between descriptive and normative approaches in the study of politics, for example.

22.4.2 *Editors – Future Multidisciplinary Research on Energy Policy and Final Thoughts*

The process of selecting the cases comprising this book and the multiple interactions the editors have shared with the authors also identified fruitful areas for future multidisciplinary research. The first concerns the presence or absence of diverse philosophical paradigms at work in disciplinary research on energy. Much like historiography takes a broad perspective on historians' treatment of historical research, each discipline, whether academics recognise it or not, operates in its own philosophical paradigm. An understanding of these paradigms can help inform decision makers on the foundations upon which their evidence is based and thereby address a consistent point raised by our 'technologists' and reinforced by our own interactions with policy makers.

Another area that was a repeated theme among the authors is the distinction between multidisciplinary and interdisciplinary as a conceptual framework for conducting research. Despite the fact that there is burgeoning literature on these subjects, the distinction is not always apparent and the development of a collaborative project will at times shift between the two. Our experience is that it is probably more appropriate to view multidisciplinary and interdisciplinary as concepts along a spectrum of degrees of integration of disciplines. The fact that many of the authors, well versed in the literature, would often revisit this distinction speaks to the fact that the conceptual frameworks are as yet underdeveloped. Further work in this area would be helpful to inform academic collaboration across departments, and it is much needed because funding calls are increasingly requiring this.

It is perhaps worth emphasising that we, as editors, remain committed to disciplinarity itself. We have sought to highlight the contributions that individual and multiple disciplines can bring to the study of energy policy. We have aimed at identifying and celebrating the often unique emphases that individual disciplines can bring to the study of energy policy. This is in contrast to transdisciplinary approaches which work across disciplinary boundaries with non-academics and de-emphasise the academic perspectives that individual disciplines bring to the study of societal problems.[1] Our approach has also focused on the analysis of specific energy policy problems rather than seeking to make use of general models of energy policy making, often focusing on how energy systems change over time.[2] This is because of our desire to take the particular policy context seriously.

Returning to the theme of what has been a rewarding but equally challenging endeavour, the authors of this volume have sought out to build a clearer picture on what constitutes a 'good' energy policy, and implicit to this question, what multiple disciplines can contribute to this pursuit. Most of the cases presented in this book have examined instances of energy policy design and implementation in democratic societies. This is because democracy and transparency in policy making typically go together, and hence 'good' energy policy case studies tend to arise from democratic countries.[3] But a more developed understanding of the social constraints that policies will face when being implemented will give politicians and their constituents a better chance at designing policies that will have 'better' impacts, however construed by the stakeholders.

In the Introduction we listed seven representative questions that arise in attempting to define what 'good', or at least 'better', energy policy might amount to (see

1 See Spreng (2014).
2 See Geels (2004) for a good example of this.
3 See Hollyer et al. (2011).

Section 1.4). While we have not presumed to offer anything like a comprehensive response to these questions, it is worth briefly highlighting a few provisional findings that have emerged.

First, it has become clear how very differently various disciplinary approaches even define the 'problem' that is to be addressed in any energy policy question – and how demanding yet potentially fertile this plurality of approaches can be. We can distinguish two kinds of difference. Some may reflect the divergent philosophical paradigms shaping a discipline (see Chapter 2) or, perhaps, more than one discipline (utilitarianism is at work in both economics and philosophy). We have noted this as a question for future research. For example, while the question of the basis of well-being assessments for those affected by energy policies is raised from a normative perspective in Chapters 4, 5, 17 and 18, it is not addressed at length from an empirical perspective in the social science chapters (but see Chapter 10 on the ethics of nuclear energy). Thus, a definition of 'inefficiency' utilised by mainstream welfare economics (Chapter 3) is likely to differ from one proposed in the much newer field of 'ecological economics' (not represented here) on account of contrasting criteria of 'well-being'.

Our focus has been rather on distinctive and complementary disciplinary subject matters in a specific case. For example, defining what might be the best way to attain a secure and sustainable energy supply from a technological or economic point of view needs to be complemented by asking what domestic, regional and global political conditions – historical and contemporary – are likely to be most conducive to the actual implementation of such a policy, and what trade-offs between the three poles of the 'energy trilemma' might have to be negotiated if they are to be realised (Chapters 7, 9, 10, 11, 12, 20 and 21).

To take another example, asking what is the best 'legal form' of an instrument of, say, environmental democracy such as the Aarhus Convention (Chapters 9 and 16), is very different from asking what are the obstacles to the emergence of a democratically effective coalition of political interests behind a desirable energy policy (such as CCS; see Chapter 14); how the social, cultural, professional or even ethical attitudes and practices required for the success of policies such as decentralised heating or the construction of wind turbines might be construed by academics and harnessed by practitioners (Chapters 3, 5, 6, 8 and 18); or how to assess philosophically the value of democratic 'process' versus policy 'outcome' at all (Chapter 4).

Evidently, questions of environmental democracy and other dimensions of the policy process are closely linked to the question of how to build the necessary degree of public 'trust' in energy policies for them to have any chance of being effective over the long term (Chapters 10, 11, 20). To generate and sustain such trust will depend on a host of diverse conditions, and the desirable package will differ according to sector, regional context, legacy constraints, and so forth. Such conditions might include the existence and successful communication of scientific and academic expertise; popular attitudes to the lead actors in energy policy – businesses, governments, cultural opinion-formers such as environmental NGOs or other civil society groups, community leaders, even religious leaders where they might have some influence on popular attitudes to energy use; energy affordability; the presence of effective channels of popular participation; and so on. Trust will be substantially enhanced where there is a wide public perception of the competence and good faith of those charged with delivering policy and hampered where there is a perception of what we termed 'hubris in delivery'. Divergent cultural and regional expectations of what counts as competence and hubris (see Chapters 9, 10, 11 and 20) will also play a role.

Finally, good energy policy will require a carefully calibrated and contextually sensitive balance between the roles of the lead actors in energy policy. Evidently, no one agent can determine, initiate, deliver, monitor or sustain 'good' policy on its own. Even if we focus on one agent, a wide variety of responses will inevitably be called for across different settings: central governments, for example, can do certain things very well and are sometimes uniquely suited for these tasks – megaprojects such as pipelines, CCS and the construction (or decommissioning) of nuclear power plants, for example (Chapters 10, 11, 14 and 21). But as set out in Chapters 17 and 20, the examples of the Sarawakian regional government in Malaysia or the influence of urban environmental experiences illustrate the pivotal role of regional and city governing entities. Equally, Chapters 8 and 13 show that non-governmental initiatives are frequently decisive in promoting good energy policies, whether in the development of wind turbine technology or smart electricity networks.

As the previous chapters have taught us, in particular those in Part III, multidisciplinary research and collaboration present a unique set of challenges that have sometimes more to do with communication, individual personalities and interpersonal dynamics than those presented by the topic or research. In addition to the importance of selecting the right topic, it is also important to carefully plan how the group communicates and interacts, balancing both the need for clear milestones but also allowing for the creative discovery process that is one of the benefits of multidisciplinary research. Ultimately, only the researcher may answer the question of whether the result of this collaboration is worth the effort. From our perspective, considering the scope and depth that a multidisciplinary group can cover in the examination of complex social dynamics, it goes without question that it is well worth the effort. Even if the process does not yield a written outcome, the relations that working across departmental lines offer can only challenge and broaden the perspective of the researcher. Finally, considering the growing need for multidisciplinary collaboration for funding academic research, the relations that emerge from the process can only benefit the researchers' future projects.

22.4.3 *Editors' response references*

Geels, F. (2004), 'From sectoral systems of innovation to socio-technical systems Insights about dynamics and change from sociology and institutional theory', *Research Policy*, 33: 897–920.

Hollyer, J. R., Rosendorff, B. P., and Vreeland, J. R. (2011), 'Democracy and Transparency', *The Journal of Politics*, 73 (4) (1 October 2011): 1191–1205.

Spreng, D. (2014), 'Transdisciplinary energy research – Reflecting the context', *Energy Research & Social Science*, 1 (March): 65–73.

Index